THE MARK
of the
SCOTS

THE MARK

of the

SCOTS

Their Astonishing Contributions to History, Science, Democracy, Literature, and the Arts

DUNCAN A. BRUCE

"When a nation goes down or a society perishes,
one condition may always be found.
They forgot where they came from."
—*Carl Sandburg*

"Cuimhnich air na daoine o'n d'thainig thu."
(Remember the men from whom you have come.)

ƛ
CITADEL PRESS
Kensington Publishing Corp.
www.kensingtonbooks.com

CITADEL PRESS books are published by

Kensington Publishing Corp.
850 Third Avenue
New York, NY 10022

Copyright © 1996, 1998 Duncan A. Bruce

BOOK DESIGN BY ROBERT FREESE

All Kensington titles, imprints, and distributed lines are available at special quantity discounts for bulk purchases for sales promotions, premiums, fund raising, educational, or institutional use. Special book excerpts or customized printings can also be created to fit specific needs. For details, write or phone the office of the Kensington special sales manager: Kensington Publishing Corp., 850 Third Avenue, New York, NY 10022, attn: Special Sales Department, phone 1-800-221-2647.

Kensington and the K logo Reg. U.S. Pat. & TM Office
Citadel Press is a trademark of Kensington Publishing Corp.

First printing 1998

10 9 8 7 6 5 4 3

Printed in the United States of America

Library of Congress Cataloging-in-Publication Data

Bruce, Duncan A.
    The mark of the Scots : their astonishing contributions to history, science, democracy, literature, and the arts / Duncan A. Bruce.
        p. cm.
    "A Citadel Press book."
    ISBN 0–8065–2060–4 (pbk.)
        1. Civilization, Modern—Scottish influences.   2. National characteristics, Scottish.   3. Scotland—Civilization.   4. Scots.   I. Title.
DA72.B78   1996
941.1—dc20   95–50374
                                                         CIP

For Tamara

Contents

Acknowledgments

I would like to thank my wife, Tamara, and my daughters Jennifer and Elizabeth, for having put up with so much for so long so this book could happen. Special thanks to Lord Elgin for writing the foreword. And for their influence on me and this book, exceptional thanks to my parents, Archibald Duncan Bruce and Marian Colley Bruce, and to my three Scottish grandparents, Archibald Bruce, Mary MacTavish Bruce, and James Grant Colley.

Many others have been of help or have tried to be over the years. Among them I would like to mention the following people: Bernard Adnet, Alan L. Bain, Dave Black, Hillel Black, Robert M. Bowes, Jim Bruce, Donald J. Davidson, Bill Eakins, Ellen Gooch, Charles Haws, Deirdre Livingstone, Duncan MacDonald, William Naylor McDonald III, Charles MacLean, Martha Millard, Ian Ogilvy, Carol Swift, Jack Webster, and Nathaniel Weyl.

And thanks, also, to those who subscribed to the book and waited patiently for its arrival: Sarah Ford, Anne Robertson Kennedy, A. Ranald Mackenzie, Seumas MacNicol, James Harrison Monroe, J. Wallace Reid, and Marilyn Lucas Ross.

Foreword

Duncan Bruce has been an inspiring friend for a quarter of a century. When first we met in New York, his calm appearance, all through a great, if complicated, series of occasions, made an abiding impression. It was a feeling built of many parts—business ability, historic recall, joy of music, and delight in marriage and family—but above all he had curiosity. Many Scots are so obsessed, but seldom had I met one who was so totally enthralled, and as he spoke he was, in turn, enthralling.

Duncan saw with immense clarity the power of the members of a small nation when opportunity offers. He knew that the very compact nature of the diverse regions of Scotland had spawned too many skills and much more enterprise than could be required at home, so he tracked the personalities of those who had left their native land. In succeeding years, every time I met him, this remarkable table of names and deeds grew larger. Perhaps I, like others who will come to read the story, may have put a different emphasis on the achievements of certain people, but their names are there and you can do your own varied research as you will.

Much of the tale which unfolds shows the extraordinary ability of the Scot, when abroad, to be part of their surrounding nation first and use innate strength to reach the highest goal just by knowing the supremacy of their origin. The most illustrious of my Bruce forbears was King Robert I of Scots, whose supreme ability was to forge a most disparate people into one nation. Duncan Bruce has assembled those Scots who then went to other lands and amassed their contributions on a wider scene.

Nevertheless, Mr. Bruce has not forgotten his homeland. Contemporary accounts of King Robert the Bruce described him, in the courtly language of that time, as *"de bon air."* This is indeed the way in which *The Mark of the Scots* has been written. As the present Chief of the Name of Bruce, I salute my kinsman Duncan Bruce and trust his research will long excite, amuse, and enthrall its readers.

Earl of Elgin and Kincardine, KT
Broomhall, Dunfermline   25th August 1995

Author to Reader

Somewhere within the depths of all of us who are of Scottish blood, there is a knowledge that despite our dispersion throughout the continents and our constantly increasing assimilation into other nations, we are still somehow one people, held together by fragments of a common culture and genes inherited of ancient kings. And because of this awareness we perceive with pride that our nation, though one of the smallest and poorest in origin, is nonetheless one of the most successful.

We notice the unusual frequency of minority Scots in a list of British prime ministers. We note the Scottish names of some of the richest families throughout the English-speaking world and of the greatest newspaper publishers of Australia, Canada, England, and the United States. Throughout modern history we observe an endless tide of Scottish scientists and inventors and a constant parade of actors, actresses, soldiers, artists, authors, and statesmen bearing the unique surnames of the grand old families created long ago in the misty little land beyond the River Tweed.

Various aspects of the phenomenon of Scottish achievement have been documented in hundreds of books and articles for more than two centuries, but none before has ever put forth the story on a worldwide historical basis, revealing Scotland's mark in all lands, from the earliest times to the present. This book is an attempt to do that.

A subsidiary purpose of this work is to supplement the one-dimensional peasant image the Scots have chosen to present to the world which thus has been convinced that we are a people who spend most of our time swilling whiskey, eating haggis, throwing tree trunks around and emitting war whoops while listening to bagpipe music. That Scots should take great pride in their rustic past is commendable, of course, but it is time to inform the world of the intellectual might that has surged out from the glens and made such a rich contribution to civilization.

As the achievement of a nation is the sum of the individual attainments of its people, hundreds of men and women are mentioned in this book. Everyone named can be shown to have been born in Scotland or to have had an ancestor born in Scotland. This includes the Presbyterian Ulster Scots, who moved from Scotland to northern Ireland in the seventeenth century, and in the eighteenth and early nineteenth centuries from there to North America, where they are known as the Scotch-Irish. Although it has been shown often that during their sojourn these people rarely intermarried with the Irish because of religious and other differences, there are still many who think of them as ethnically Irish, or partly so. Their background is comparable to the English Puritans who moved to Massachusetts after a short stay in Holland. As one historian has put it, "If the Scotch-Irish be Irish, then the Puritans must be Dutch."[1]

Most of the people mentioned in this book are either entirely or largely descended from the old Scottish national stock, which existed, rather more homogeneously than is usually thought, before the immigrations of the Industrial Revolution.[2] When the occasional person is cited who is only remotely of Scottish ancestry, such as George Washington or Winston Churchill, I have tried to disclose this remote origin. Often I have mentioned people who are less than half Scottish, realizing that some will say that their minority Scottish heritage is irrelevant to this type of study. I can only respond, in advance, that I do not agree.

For example, I believe the fact that Marconi, the Italian inventor of radio, was partly Scottish is highly significant, since such an unusual share of the world's most important inventions have been developed by people with Scottish ancestry.[3] (By the same token, I was not surprised to learn that one of Scotland's greatest instrumental musicians of this century, Ron Gonnella, was one-fourth Italian, as Italians have produced far more eminence in music than Scots have.)

Nor, in my opinion, does the dispersion of the Scots to the far ends of the world make their diluted genes and culture irrelevant. As the Scottish scholar Gordon Donaldson has said, "The history of the Scottish nation has for many centuries now been something more than the history of a small, poor and remote country. A study of the spectacular movement of people from Scotland is part of Scottish history."[4]

However diluted they have become in this emigration, the Scots in their diaspora have had an enormous impact on many countries, as we shall see. And this impact has been masked by the unusual tendency of the Scots to assimilate completely into the general population. Thus, in Toronto, it is usually only immigrant Scots, often poor and humble folk, who are considered by most Canadians to be Scots. The sons and daughters of these immigrants, who may be millionaire businessmen, professionals, authors, and scientists, are thought of as Canadians. It is hoped that this book will help to rectify this unfair perception and expose the hidden contributions of the Scottish nation.

It is their tendency to assimilate that allows these perceptions to develop, and that has allowed the mark of the Scots to go largely unrecognized, even by the Scots themselves, whether in Scotland or in the diaspora. In America we have seen how important group self-esteem, or lack of it, can be to the fortunes of minority groups in a pluralistic society, and for this reason I do not mind being the boastful representative of a normally reticent people. It is time those of us who are Scottish know who we are and what we have done. This book therefore makes no attempt to be "fair" or present all sides of an issue. This book is an advocate's brief for the Scottish nation.

The inspiration, as well as the research for this book, began when I was a child on my immigrant grandmother's knee and continued at my father's table. They were always talking about the Scottishness of prominent people in the news and how, as Scots, we had an obligation to work hard for success and some mandate from heaven to achieve in life. I had often wondered if the Scots were really as good at things as they believed, and in 1969 I was astonished to learn that Nathaniel Weyl, a writer, had actually made an ingenious statistical survey that tended to prove it.[5]

Around the same time I read two other books. One, *Jews, God and History*, by Max Dimont, is an historical review of the achievements of the Jews all over the world. It is a marvelous book, and I wondered why there wasn't one about the Scots. The second is *The Scotch*, by John Kenneth Galbraith, which describes with great humor the rather mediocre Scottish neighborhood in Canada from which he comes. It portrays the Scots as honest and law-abiding but also as unwashed, semiliterate, and slaves to money. It does not mention that out of such Scottish-Canadian ghettoes have come an inordinate number of prominent Canadians, including Professor Galbraith himself. Altogether, Galbraith's somewhat negative book showed me that there was a need for a book on Scottish achievement, Dimont's that there might be a market for it, and Weyl's that an empirical study on Scottish achievement could be backed up statistically.

The long research for this book followed immediately. This included reading the amazing *New York Times* virtually every day, clipping relevant material, and perusing every interesting title in the wondrous catalogue of the New York Public Library as well as the subject index of the Edinburgh Public Library under such subjects as

Scot, Scotch, Scotch-Irish, Scotland, Scots, and Scottish. (Alas, the Scottish National Library has no subject index for books before 1978.)

I have pursued all citations I thought might be pertinent in Donald Whyte's bibliography of *Scots Abroad*, as well as every issue of the *Scottish Historical Review* from 1904 through 1986; *Scottish Studies* from 1957 through 1983; the *Scottish Genealogist* through 1986; the twentieth-century version of *Scots* magazine through 1987, and every issue of the *Highlander* and the *Scottish-American* (later incorporated into the *Scottish Banner*) up to the present. I have turned every page of the *Encyclopaedia Britannica*, fourteenth edition, 1969. I have read, in their entireties, the excellent *Collins Encyclopaedia of Scotland* and *Chambers Scottish Biographical Dictionary*. I have read dozens of books, including several on Scottish history, and have written hundreds of letters to prominent people asking if they were of Scottish descent, and have received many answers.

Although I have tried scrupulously to avoid errors, I must apologize, in advance, for the mistakes in this book, which I am sure will turn out to be more than several. I have tried to check source information, but sometimes there was only one source. At other times, sources contradicted each other. Also, I must apologize that, as time has passed, it has not been possible to keep all of the information up-to-date and, therefore, someone who is described as living may now be dead or some world record mentioned may have been surpassed.

This is a book about people of Scottish ancestry who have had an influence on the world outside Scotland. Thus, artists such as Raeburn are included, while others, who are not well-known outside Scotland, are not. William Wallace is only mentioned as a soldier, while Douglas MacArthur gets some discussion.

There is still much work to be done, but as the number of new facts I learn rapidly decreases each year, I am confident that most of the story, or at least the most important parts of it, are somewhere within these pages and that, in the words of my late friend, Sir Iain Moncreiffe of that Ilk, it is time to "write something now" rather than "everything never." It has been my idea that, for the most part, only the truly great, famous, or unique should be included.

Duncan A. Bruce
New York
February 5, 1996

THE MARK
of the
SCOTS

"No people so few in number have
scored so deep a mark in the
world's history as the Scots have done."
—J. A. Froude (1818–1894), English historian

1

The Mark of the Scots

By any standard, the Scots constitute a tiny minority in the
population of the world, yet their presence has been felt as if they
were a mighty nation. Only about 28 million,[1] or a relatively
insignificant one-half of one percent of the globe's 5.7 billion
inhabitants, are Scottish by either birth or descent. Yet amazingly,
people of entirely or partly Scottish extraction have been recipients
in almost 11 percent of all the Nobel Prizes awarded through 1990.[2]

Scientists of Scottish ancestry are credited with an almost incredible number of major achievements, from the pivotal inventions of
the steam engine, steamboat, and railroad; through the telegraph,
telephone, and television; to the motion picture, phonograph, radar,
computer, transistor, and pocket calculator. Scottish mathematicians
have invented logarithms and calculus, and Scottish physicians have
found the causes of sleeping sickness and malaria, and have developed insulin, the typhoid and smallpox vaccines, and penicillin.

Tiny Scotland has been, perhaps, the source of more beneficial
advances to civilization than any other country; and the positive
impact of its people, representatives of which have been honored on
the postage stamps of some sixty nations, is arguably greater than
that of any other land. Modern Scotland, devastated after World War
II by the loss of her great heavy industry, has made a successful
switch to high technology. Silicon Glen now makes 10 percent of the
world's computers and has more than three hundred electronics

plants. Little Scotland supplies England with most of its semiconductors and even has 11 percent of the huge European market.[3]

But Scotland's greatest wealth has always been the talent and character of her people, which she continues to export too generously. A world survey in 1973, examining secondary students in reading comprehension, literature, and science, placed Scottish students second only to heavily-Scottish New Zealand and ahead of students in England, the United States, Italy, Israel, the Netherlands, Sweden, and Belgium, among others.[4]

The United States of America, the most powerful nation of all time and the model for the foundation of countless countries and governments is, to a great extent, a Scottish creation, born largely of Scottish ideas and efforts: from the governing of the English colonies to the writing of the Declaration of Independence and the Constitution, to the first presidential administration, to the settling of the wild frontier. All of the American territory outside the original thirteen colonies, all the way to Hawaii, was acquired by Scottish-American presidents, diplomats, and soldiers. Many, perhaps the majority, of the greatest generals and admirals who have defended the country since its beginnings have been Scots, and the great wealth and industrial might of America has been disproportionately created and managed by Scottish-Americans. Several times the "richest man in America" has been of Scottish descent, and today in many of the fifty states the richest family is of Scottish origin. In recent years two Scottish-Americans (one by way of Canada), John Kenneth Galbraith and Dwight MacDonald, were chosen by their peers as among the top five intellectuals in the country.[5]

Despite the fact that fewer than 5 percent of the American population claims Scottish ancestry, more than three-quarters of the American presidents have been at least partly of Scottish descent.[6] All of the seven presidents of the United States since Kennedy have had at least some Scottish ancestry, although this is sometimes not noticed. In the 1984 election, for instance, Reagan and Mondale were perceived as "Irish" and "Norwegian," while their Scottish-American mothers went unrecognized.

In 1940, according to one estimate, 45 percent of all the people listed in *Who's Who in America* had either fathers or mothers bearing Scottish surnames.[7] In 1966, Nathaniel Weyl's work used an ingenious name-frequency technique that has supported the empirical evidence of Scottish overachievement in America.[8] And the 1980 U.S. census corroborating all of this, concluded that of all the diverse ethnic groups that make up America, Scottish-Americans were the only ones with no illiteracy. The census also reported that Scottish-Americans had the most education, the highest income, and the lowest unemployment rate of any ancestral group.[9]

So broadly based was the Scottish contribution to the construction of the British Empire that some have suggested it should have been called the Scottish Empire. Indeed, throughout the histories of Canada, Australia, New Zealand, South Africa, and many other lands, the Scots have provided vastly more than their share of the explorers, pioneers, soldiers, governors, businessmen, and politicians who made the empire great.

Canada could not have conquered her vast wilderness without her cadres of Scottish fur traders. She might never have been a cohesive country had it not been for the brilliant humanity of a Scottish governor general who was sincerely just in dealing with the French-speaking minority, or without the herculean efforts of those Scots who financed, engineered, and built the unifying Canadian Pacific Railway across the barren continent. Scottish-Canadian prime ministers have governed more than two-thirds of the time since the confederation of 1867. Recently, for more than a decade and a half, the prime minister was the half-Scottish Pierre Elliott Trudeau. More recently, Kim Campbell became the first woman to hold that office.

Australia was a distressed penal colony until a Highland administrator restored order and promoted education and enterprise, while another Scot founded the country's vital wool industry. The first British settlements in New Zealand, South Africa, and many other outposts were dominated by Scots, and in countless battles all over the globe a "thin red line" of Scottish soldiers made the difference in defending the imperial interests. Today, throughout the commonwealth remnant of the empire, the Scottish minority continues to play a part in politics, education, commerce, and the arts more appropriate to that of a majority.

In Great Britain itself, where only about one-seventh of the people are Scots, about half of the twentieth-century prime ministers have been at least partly of Scottish blood.[10] And the Scottish prominence in British politics continues. In recent years, Highlander John Smith died suddenly while leading the Labour party. He had succeeded Neil Gordon Kinnock, a Welshman of Scottish descent. The current head of Labour bears the Scottish name of Blair. In the past decade or so David Steel has led the Liberals, and Robert Adam Ross Maclellan the Social Democrats. The long-running Prime Minister Margaret

Thatcher is descended from Ulster Stevensons and is therefore quite likely of Scottish descent.

Despite the fact that few Scots are Episcopalians, the head of the Church of England, the archbishop of Canterbury, has been Scottish most of the time for over a century. The very queen of the United Kingdom, without doubt the grandest monarch in the world, is in fact largely of Scottish, rather than English, descent. The symbolic stone upon which she was crowned belongs to Scotland, and its ancient traditions to the Scottish rather than to the English royalty.

The overachievement of the Scots in Britain was noticed as early as 1869 by Sir Francis Galton, a cousin of Darwin, who noted in his *Hereditary Genius* that "... the Scots produced more outstanding minds in proportion to their numbers than any other group. Per million of population, Scotland produced four class I geniuses to England's 1 ... ."[11] Other studies showing Scottish overachievement in Great Britain include those by Sir Arthur Conan Doyle, in 1888, A. H. H. Maclean, in 1900, Havelock Ellis, in 1926, and Ellsworth Huntington, in 1927, the last demonstrating a Scottish overrepresentation in British science almost double that of England and Wales.[12]

The entire world economy has been greatly influenced by Scots. To the extent that it is capitalistic, the world rests upon firm Scottish philosophical foundations, particularly through the work of Adam Smith. To the extent that the world is industrialized, it is indebted to the entrepreneurs, financiers, inventors, artisans, and workers of Glasgow and its environs, where so great a part of the Industrial Revolution began and developed.

Even in countries where almost no Scots or people of Scottish descent live, the Scottish nation has left its mark in such representatives as the "father" of the Russian navy; the founder of the Indian tea industry; an admiral of the fleet of the Queen of Portugal; Norway's most esteemed composer and also her greatest dramatist; mayors of the capital cities of Spain, Sweden, Bolivia, and Poland; commanders in chief of the armies of Persia, Finland, Morocco, Sweden, Russia, Austria, Venezuela, and France; a governor general of Finland; personal physicians to the monarchs of Sweden, France, Russia, Poland, and Denmark; one of Germany's greatest philosophers; a king of Ireland and a queen of Bohemia; a president of France and a prime minister of Holland; the most prominent families of the fortified wine industries of both Spain and Portugal; a president of Nicaragua; the author of the first Chinese dictionary; a hero of the Greek independence movement; a postmaster general of

Japan; a founder of the Argentine beef industry; and one of the principal liberators of Chile, Peru, and Brazil.

The story of the achievement of the Scots is truly remarkable and can serve as a model for other small, poor, and remote countries, for everywhere they have gone their industry has produced benefits to society, in general.

The mark of the Scots is indelible.

"I, who had ambitions not only to
go farther than anyone had done
before, but as far as it was
possible for man to go."

—*Capt. James Cook*

"Resistless seas
Surge round the storm-swept Orcades
Where erst Saint-Clair bore princely sway
O'er isle and islet, strait and bay."

—*Sir Walter Scott*

2

The Exploring Scots

The Scots played a very great part in the Age of Exploration.
Following the ancient tradition of their Celtic ancestors, they wan-
dered over the globe, establishing Scottish place names in its most
remote reaches. There are Aberdeens in Saskatchewan and Africa,
and Perths in Australia and Kansas. The great Clan Campbell has a
cape in New Zealand named after it, an island in Oceana, and a
town in Pakistan. Their redoubtable rivals, the Macdonalds, have an
island in the Indian Ocean, a lake in Australia, and a mountain
range in British Columbia. The Murrays, not to be outdone, have a
cape in Antarctica and a river in Australia. The Mackenzies, one of
the most northern Scottish clans, have appropriately chosen, several
rather cold places as their memorials: a bay, river, and some
mountains in Canada's frigid Northwest Territory, and a bay in
Antarctica.[1]

In subsequent chapters of this book many Scottish explorers are
mentioned where their efforts pertain to a specific country. This
chapter will discuss some of the Scots who have made contributions

to exploration in general. Not all of them were great or famous men. Robert Pitcairn was only a Scottish midshipman in 1767, when he first sighted and discovered Pitcairn Island (of the *Bounty* mutiny) and had it named after him.[2] Alexander Selkirk was the stranded Scottish sailor whose tales of survival on Juan Fernandez Island became the basis for Defoe's *Robinson Crusoe*.[3]

The Scottish Discovery of America
June 2, 1398

Perhaps the greatest, as well as the least-known, Scottish explorer was Prince Henry Sinclair, who was, according to Frederick J. Pohl, a grand sea lord who commanded an expedition that reached North America almost a century before the first voyage of Columbus. Although this may seem a concocted claim, flying in the face of conventional wisdom, much of the story is accepted as standard history. The *Encyclopaedia Britannica* says, "Sir Henry...(d.*c*.1400)... rediscovered Greenland with the Venetian travelers Niccolò and Antonio Zeno."[4]

The scholarly detective work that proves that the voyage went past Greenland to America has been done by Mr. Pohl, who, after years of research, produced the book *Prince Henry Sinclair*, from which the following can be extracted: that Henry Sinclair was born near Edinburgh in 1345 to a noble Scottish family;[5] that through his partly Norwegian mother he inherited the earldom of Orkney (then under Norway) wielding power "near to that of a King";[6] that he built a great fleet in the Orkney Islands;[7] that Niccolò Zeno, brother of the Venetian naval hero Carlo Zeno, was shipwrecked in the Orkneys and was rescued by Sinclair;[8] that Niccolò died but was survived by his son Antonio Zeno, who became admiral of Sinclair's fleet;[9] that Sinclair himself decided to lead an expedition to the "new world" described to him by Orcadian fishermen who had found it by accident;[10] that Sinclair's party made land at what is now Guysborough, Nova Scotia, on June 2, 1398;[11] and later went on to what is now Westford, Massachusetts, where they proceeded to punch into a rock the arms of a member of the Scottish Clan Gunn, which are still visible;[12] and that Antonio Zeno's narrative of the expedition, some of which still survives, makes this transatlantic voyage "the earliest for which we have the written record of a participant."[13]

The Zeno Narrative is also the first document to refer to the Western Hemisphere as a new world (*grandissimo e quasi un nuovo mondo*).[14] Mr. Pohl presents detailed geographical and geological evidence as well as Indian legends which corroborate his case. And visits to the sites in both Nova Scotia and Massachusetts have shown his entire explanation to be eminently plausible and, at least in Nova Scotia, completely convincing. Independent evidence of Henry Sinclair's discovery of America can still be seen near Edinburgh at Roslin Chapel, which was founded in 1446 by Henry's grandson William, the third earl of Orkney. As we know that construction on the chapel stopped in 1484,[15] the carvings of Indian corn (maize) and aloe cactus on the chapel's walls prove that the Sinclair family knew of these American plants before the first voyage of Columbus.[16] Since it is known that Europeans, including Norsemen and Scots, were in North America long before Columbus and as early as A.D. 1010,[17] it is not really surprising to learn of the Sinclair voyage.

The probable reason no one paid immediate attention to the Sinclair discovery was that there was no practical way of informing the world of it. The Zeno manuscript had been consigned to a musty archive fifty years before Gutenberg's invention of movable type, which was around 1447. However, the new technique of printing was widely available throughout Europe by 1492, in time to give the voyages of Columbus great renown. It seems quite possible that had the Zeno manuscript of the Sinclair expedition been printed and distributed immediately (it lay unpublished for a century and a half) Americans might now celebrate Sinclair Day on June 2, instead of Columbus Day on October 12.

The Great Navigator

Captain James Cook (1728–1779), one of the greatest explorers in history, was born in Yorkshire to Scottish parents.[18] Cook was the first of the scientific navigators, and his three long voyages brought back more information on the far reaches of the Southern Hemisphere than all of the explorers before him.[19] Cook was the first to cross the Antarctic Circle and circumnavigate the Antarctic continent, proving the nonexistence of habitable continental land north of the Antarctic Circle. He discovered, named, and charted New South Wales. He circumnavigated New Zealand and was the first to chart it. He was also the first to chart the northwest coast of North America all the way to the Arctic Circle. Captain Cook is regarded as the discoverer of Hawaii, South Georgia, the South Sandwich

Islands, and New Caledonia, which he named, appropriately, in 1774.[20] He also rediscovered and named the New Hebrides.[21]

North America

A fur trader, born on the isle of Lewis in the Outer Hebrides, became Canada's most important explorer. In 1789, at the age of twenty-five, following the great river which is named for him, Alexander Mackenzie trekked almost three thousand miles in four months, discovering the water route from Fort Chippewyan, in what is now Alberta, to the Arctic Ocean. In 1793 he crossed the Rockies to the Pacific shore, where he scrawled on a rock, visible still:

> Alex Mackenzie
> from Canada
> by land
> 22 July 1793

Mackenzie thus became the first person to make an overland crossing of the full width of the North American continent.[22] At the age of thirty, he was paid a quarter of a million dollars for his accomplishment and became the youngest senior partner of the mighty North West Company. He returned to Britain with his fortune, was knighted, and became a member of Parliament. He died on a farm in Scotland in 1820.[23]

William Clark, a redheaded Virginian of Scottish ancestry and brother of frontiersman George Rogers Clark, was comanager of the famous Lewis and Clark expedition of 1804–1806.[24] Launched by President Jefferson, also of Scottish ancestry,[25] the expedition followed the Missouri and Columbia rivers to the Pacific, returning to give the world its first clear picture of the American West. Lewis and Clark were the first to cross the North American continent in what is now the United States.

Russia to the Far East

In the early eighteenth century, a twenty-three-year-old physician named John Bell went to St. Petersburg in search of adventure and joined several Russian embassies traveling to Persia, China, Mongolia, and Siberia. In 1722 Peter the Great asked Bell to accompany him on a trip to the Caspian Gates. Bell's writings of these journeys gave Europeans a vivid picture of the peoples of the East.

Later, the Russian and British governments sent Bell to Constantino-
ple, where he became a merchant, acquiring enough wealth to retire
to his birthplace in Scotland at age fifty-six.[26]

Africa

The participation of Scotland in the exploration of Africa was
perhaps the most significant of any nation, regardless of size. It
began in 1770 when James Bruce (1730–1794), a Stirlingshire wine
merchant, found the source of the Blue Nile river in Abyssinia.[27]

In 1796 Mungo Park (1771–1806), a surgeon from Selkirkshire,
became the first European to see the upper reaches of the Niger
River while exploring the Gambia. Park, who had managed to escape
from a four-month imprisonment at the hands of an Arab, returned
to Scotland, but in 1805 he revisited the Niger and was killed by
natives.[28] He made a great contribution to the knowledge of the area
around what is now Nigeria which, for thousands of square miles,
had been just a blank on the map before his efforts.[29]

The Niger quest was continued by Alexander Gordon Laing
(1793–1826), a soldier from Edinburgh who discovered the source of
the Rokell in 1822 but was prevented from reaching the source of the
Niger by hostile tribesmen. On a later expedition, in 1826, he became
the first European to attain Timbuktu, only to be murdered two days
afterward.[30] A physician, William Balfour Baikie (1825–1864), opened
the Niger to commerce. In 1857 he founded the town of Lokoja, at the
confluence of the Niger and the Benue. Acting as ruler, doctor, and
educator, he established a market, collected words in a dozen
dialects, and translated parts of the Bible into Hausa.[31]

Another Scottish explorer, Hugh Clapperton (1788–1827), became,
along with the Englishman Dixon Denham, the first to cross the
Sahara desert, a feat they performed in 1823.[32] Rev. John Campbell
(1766–1840) discovered the source of the Limpopo River.[33] In 1862
James Grant (1827–1892), a Scot, and John Speke, an Englishman,
discovered and named Lake Victoria and proved it to be the
principal source of the Nile.[34] In 1875 still another Scot, Lovett
Cameron, became the first man to cross equatorial Africa from sea to
sea.[35] Joseph Thomson (1858–1895) explored unknown territory between Lake Nyasa and Lake Tanganyika in 1879, discovering Lake
Rukwa in the process. Thomson, then only twenty-one, did not lose
a single man and did not kill a single African, even when encounter-
ing hostile peoples. On a subsequent trip he discovered Thomson's

Falls, in what is now Kenya.[36]

The greatest of all the African explorers was the Lowland missionary David Livingstone (1813–1873) who discovered Victoria Falls, the Zambesi River, and Lake Nyasa in the 1850s.[37] His travels, covering thirty thousand miles in unknown areas, were so extensive, and his accounts so complete, that he is credited with opening up the entire southern half of the continent.

Livingstone, a largely self-educated physician who had been a poverty-stricken child laborer at age ten, was shocked and disgusted when he encountered the slave trade and became obsessed with ending it. He spent most of his career trying to find trade routes which he hoped would provide profitable alternatives to slavery, and although he never succeeded, his fame and work greatly contributed to the ultimate demise of the horrid traffic. Due to his efforts slavery was ended in Zanzibar in 1873.[38]

Livingstone also forcefully liberated thousands of captives from the slave caravans in the Victorian spirit of "muscular Christianity." He was a Christian in the best sense of the word: hated by the slave traders and beloved by the Africans. By 1869 Livingstone's work had made him world famous, but nothing had been heard from him for several years. It was then that James Gordon Bennett, Jr., the Scottish-American publisher of the *New York Herald*, sent Henry Morton Stanley to "find Livingstone." Stanley relieved Livingstone at Ujiji in 1871, greeting him with the timeless, "Dr. Livingstone, I presume."

In 1973, on the centennial of his demise, a thousand people, led by Kenneth Kaunda, the Presbyterian president of Zambia, made a pilgrimage to the interior to pay homage at the site of Livingstone's death. Blantyre, named after Livingstone's birthplace in Scotland, is the largest city in the republic of Malawi, and the Presbyterian Church of Scotland is still a very significant presence in the country.[39]

The Polar Regions

Scots have been among the leaders in most of the significant explorations of the far north and south. Dr. John Rae (1813–1893), was a native Scot who mapped vast areas of the Arctic, completing the survey of the northern North American coast in 1846. In 1854 Rae won the ten-thousand-pound prize for bringing in the first evidence of the lost Franklin expedition, which had set out to try to find the Northwest Passage in 1845. Sir John Richardson (1787–1865) mapped

550 miles of Arctic coast and worked with Rae in the search for Franklin.[40] Thomas Simpson (1808–1840), born in Dingwall, made accurate maps of the Arctic and probably viewed, and therefore can be said to have "discovered," the water route of the Northwest Passage in 1839. The first crossing was made, partly on foot, by Sir Robert McClure (1807–1873) in 1854.[41]

Sir John Ross (1777–1856) was a Scottish polar explorer who made many important oceanographic discoveries and who accompanied his nephew, Sir James Clark Ross (1800–1862), on many other voyages. Sir James Clark Ross claimed Antarctica for Britain in 1841. Ten years earlier he had discovered the North Magnetic Pole, the existence of which he confirmed by "the total inaction of several horizontal needles in my possession."[42] The South Magnetic Pole was first reached in 1909 by a team of Britons that included the Scottish physician Alistair Forbes-Mackay (1878–1914).[43] Rear Admiral Donald MacMillan, an American who learned to speak Gaelic as a boy while visiting his relatives on Cape Breton Island, was one of Peary's six assistants at the discovery of the North Pole in 1909. A versatile scientist, MacMillan made the first color photographs and the first shortwave transmission in the Arctic.[44]

Robert F. Scott, an Englishman of Scottish descent, rediscovered the South Pole in 1912, only a month after the Norwegian Amundsen's discovery. Compounding this heartbreaking defeat, Scott died, tragically, on the return trip. His ship, the *Discovery*, now lies in state in Dundee harbor.[45] Although Antarctica has few place names of any kind, Scottish names on maps of the continent abound, from the Ross Sea to the Weddell Sea, bearing testimony to the extraordinary enterprise of Scottish explorers.[46]

The Scottish efforts in polar exploration continue right up to the present. On August 17, 1988, Jeff MacInnis, a Canadian whose ancestors came from Skye, completed a three-year crossing of the three-thousand-mile Northwest Passage entirely under sail, a feat never previously accomplished after four hundred years of failed attempts that have cost more lives than Mount Everest.[47]

Also, a most remarkable double has been achieved by the Clan MacNicol. On September 1, 1988, Major Ian Nicholson of New Zealand, a member of the Australian MacNicol Society, planted the clan's banner at the South Pole. Seven months later, on April 11, 1989, an American, Gerald D. McNichols, a member of the Clan MacNicol Society of North America, took a MacNicol banner to the geographic North Pole.[48]

The American Space Program

On July 20, 1969, a young man from Ohio walked a few feet down a flimsy ladder and became the first human being to impress his footprints upon the dusty surface of the moon. His act represented the fulfillment of a dream that mankind had wished for since earliest times. Some called it the greatest event in history. If it was, it was also the greatest event in Scottish history.

Neil Armstrong was followed on the moon by Edwin Aldrin. Both were congratulated by Richard Nixon, the president of the United States, who used the Scottish-invented telephone to bridge the awesome distance of a quarter of a million miles while a worldwide audience gaped at the scene via the Scottish-invented television.

What few people noticed during this most wonderful incident was that both of the principal players, the president and Neil Armstrong, were of Scottish ancestry. Even more interesting, President Nixon's ancestors, who had come to America from Dumfriesshire via Northern Ireland,[49] were members of the Armstrong clan, and therefore the two principal actors in the drama were actually kinsmen![50]

The Scots, of course, noticed. The next day Edinburgh's leading newspaper, *The Scotsman*, carried the headline CLAN PUTS OUT CALL FOR ASTRONAUT NEIL. The Tartan Gift Shop in Edinburgh invited Armstrong and Aldrin to order a kilt each in the tartan appropriate to his ancestry free of charge. Both men, did, Armstrong in the Armstrong tartan and Aldrin in the Ross tartan, exercising the canniness for which Scots are famous.[51] In 1972 Neil Armstrong was given a parade through his ancestral town of Langholm in the Scottish borders.[52]

The American space program has had a Caledonian tinge from its very beginning. Of the original seven astronauts at least five, Malcolm Scott Carpenter, L. Gordon Cooper, John H. Glenn, Jr., Walter M. Schirra, Jr., and Alan B. Shepard, Jr., had Scottish ancestry.[53] At least five of the twelve men who have ever walked on the moon have had Scottish ancestry: Armstrong, Shepard, Alan L. Bean, James B. Irwin, and David R. Scott.[54] In addition, Shepard was the first American in space, Glenn the first American in orbit, and in 1983 Capt. Bruce McCandless won the Wallace Award of the American-Scottish Foundation by becoming the first man to fly free in space. On the second moon landing Alan L. Bean took along a swatch of tartan cloth and later sent pieces of it to various MacBean societies throughout the world.[55] In April of 1991 astronaut Jerry L. Ross wore a Clan Ross patch into space.[56]

In more than twenty years with the space program, Byron G. MacNabb was in charge of launching 207 missiles and ninety spacecrafts, including the Mercury Project, which put Glenn into orbit.[57]

Modern Feats

Throughout the twentieth century the Scottish tradition of exploration has continued. The first airplane flight across the North American continent was made in 1911 by Calbraith Perry Rodgers, a descendant of the Scottish-American naval officer who opened U.S. trade with Japan.[58] The Australian brothers Sir Keith Macpherson Smith and Sir Ross Macpherson Smith made the first flight from England to Darwin in 1919, for which they received a prize of ten thousand pounds.[59] In 1927 a Scottish-American, Lester J. Maitland, the first pilot to fly over two hundred miles per hour, made the first flight from the United States mainland to Hawaii.[60]

In the same year, a more famous American of partly Scottish ancestry, Charles A. Lindbergh, became the first to fly solo from the New World to the Old.[61] The first man to fly solo in the westerly direction over the Atlantic, James Allan Mollison of Glasgow, accomplished this feat in 1932. A year later he also made the first flight from England to South America.[62]

In 1933 Douglas Douglas-Hamilton, fourteenth duke of Hamilton, became the first man to pilot an airplane over Mount Everest. The other pilot in the Scottish-financed expedition was also a Scot, David McIntyre, who later founded the national airlines of Iceland, Belgium, Greece, and Luxembourg.[63]

A Briton of Scottish ancestry, raised in England, may have been the first man to climb Mount Everest. In 1924 Andrew Comyn Irvine, along with George Mallory, perished at or near the summit. Whether they were the first ever to reach the summit is still a matter of speculation.[64]

Publisher Malcom Forbes and his son Robert made the first transcontinental crossing of North America by balloon in 1973.[65] Donald Cameron fell just short (by 110 miles) of making the first transatlantic balloon crossing in 1978.[66] In 1986 Alistair Boyd, a native Briton, parachuted from the top of the Empire State Building in New York, safely reaching the street.[67]

The first solo circumnavigation of the globe without touching land was accomplished from 1968 to 1969 by William Robert Patrick Knox-Johnston, sailing from west to east. He was followed by Chay Blyth, a native of Hawick, who became the first to solo circumnavigate the earth sailing east to west. Blyth sailed the thirty thousand miles in 292 days, 20 days faster than Knox-Johnston.

In 1982 a forty-one-year-old Scottish-American truck driver named Bill Dunlop made a solo west-to-east crossing of the Atlantic in a sailboat only nine-feet, one-inch long, a world record. Asked if he would try for new records, he allowed how he probably would: "You forget all them bad times, all the scarifying things."[68]

In 1990 a seventy-year-old Glasgow sculptor, George Wyllie, sailed what appeared to journalists to be a 120-foot paper boat from London to New York. The vessel was made from an 80-by-120-foot sheet folded on an area the size of a football field. Wyllie's arrival was met by the British consul general and a pipe band.[69]

"Every line of strength in our history is a line
colored by Scottish blood."

—*Woodrow Wilson*[1]

3

The Creation of the United States of America

Colonial Times

The founder of British America, the precursor of the United States, was a Scot—James Stewart—just as surely as King Ferdinand and Queen Isabella were the founders of Spanish America. In 1603, when the Scottish king James VI became James I of England, there was no English presence in America, although Raleigh had tried to establish one earlier. By 1606 James had acted decisively, issuing charters to the London and Plymouth Companies, and in 1607 his London Company established, in Virginia, the first permanent British colony in the New World, naming the settlement Jamestown and the river on which it stood the James, in honor of their Scottish sponsor. The Plymouth Company founded Massachusetts in 1620.

Since Scotland, despite sharing a monarch with England, remained an independent country until 1707, very few Scots were invited to participate in the building of the English colonies in the seventeenth century. Yet among these few were men of prominence. David Thomson was appointed the first acting governor of New England and in 1623 became New Hampshire's first settler.[2] Before 1700 there had been Scottish governors of Rhode Island, New Jersey, and North and South Carolina as well.[3] In 1657 the Scottish Charitable Society, probably the earliest charitable organization in North

18

America, was established in Boston.[4] Andrew Hamilton of Edinburgh was appointed in 1691 as the first postmaster general in the American colonies.[5]

At about the same time the notorious Scottish pirate, Captain William Kidd, the first American folk hero and the son of a Presbyterian minister from Greenock, Scotland, operated out of Long Island. Having been hired by the colony of New York to get rid of pirates, Kidd became one instead.[6] But there may be mitigating circumstances for Kidd's alleged treachery. A legend says that the shares he had promised his low-paid crew were later demanded by high officials in London, including, secretly, the king. When the crew, at sea, discovered their betrayal, they threatened Kidd with death unless he turned the ship into an outlaw vessel. Eventually Kidd was captured and taken to London, where not even the pleas of his wife, a lady who owned property on Wall Street, could save him from the gallows.[7]

It was also in the seventeenth century that Scotland made the mistake, along with Holland and Sweden, of competing with the superpowers of England, France, and Spain as colonizers of North America. Like the Dutch on the Hudson and the Swedes on the Delaware, the Scottish colonial attempts were overwhelmed by their giant adversaries. But unlike the others, the consequences of the Scottish failures were ultimately tragic and devastating.

The first significant Scottish attempt at colonization occurred in 1621, when King James granted a huge tract of land to his fellow Scot Sir William Alexander, whose charter included not only what is still called Nova Scotia (New Scotland), but also much of what was to become Canada and the United States not already occupied by English settlers.[8] This grandiose scheme resulted in two settlements being established, but after only eleven years a treaty gave the Nova Scotia peninsula to the French, and the Scots, mere pawns in a game of international diplomacy, had to leave.

The loss of Nova Scotia proved serious for the Scots. In the new mercantile era foreign trade, colonial trade in particular, were seen as necessities. But although Scotland had the same king as England and was permitted to trade with that nation, she was still a separate country, shut out of all commerce with the English colonies. Desperate, some Scots evaded the law by creating the infamous Newfoundland trade: Pretending that Newfoundland was part of England rather than a colony, they shipped carloads of tobacco north by land from Virginia to be trans-shipped from Newfoundland to Scotland.[9]

But the Newfoundland trade was cumbersome and limited. A real Scottish colony was needed. In 1684 a Scottish settlement was made at Stuart's Town, South Carolina, only to be completely destroyed by Spanish and Indians in a raid in 1686.[10] Another attempt at a Scottish colony was made at East New Jersey in 1683. Seven hundred settlers arrived and founded the town of Perth Amboy, but the proprietors handed over control to the English in 1702.[11]

Meanwhile, even as these measures failed to solve Scotland's economic problems, other concerns, even more debilitating, were plunging her fortunes toward an all-time low. The seventeenth century had seen devastating religious fighting for the establishment of Presbyterianism, the invasions of Cromwell, and the drain of manpower caused by the heavy participation of Scottish mercenaries in foreign wars.[12] Also, the 1600s saw the culmination of centuries of all-out struggle with England. Little Scotland had kept her huge, rich neighbor at bay, but at a staggering cost in resources.[13]

It was these overpowering conditions that drew the Scots into an uncharacteristically emotional and imprudent business venture. Their own genius, William Paterson, the founder of the Bank of England, led them in this last, hopeless attempt to become a colonial power. Paterson had visions of his proposed settlement at Darien on the Isthmus of Panama cutting shipping time to the Orient in half,[14] and he was proved right two centuries later. But the humid jungle at Darien proved hostile to the Scottish settlement, as it has to all comers since. Even as late as 1994, the only part of the Pan-American Highway from Alaska to Chile not completed was at Darien, which remained a dense, sparsely-populated wilderness.[15]

The capital for the calamitous Darien episode was subscribed in a wave of frenzied, patriotic enthusiasm by a broad cross-section of the people of Scotland. It is said that the four hundred thousand pounds ventured represented half of the available money in the entire country. In 1698 five ships sailed for the Central American jungle. The disaster was immediate. Many died on the way, and those who survived the ocean to reach the Isthmus were further decimated by fever.

Predictably, the Spanish attacked, and just as predictably the English refused to help. The little Scottish band fought valiantly, and was reinforced by more boatloads of their countrymen, but inevitably, they were forced to surrender to the vastly superior power of Spain in 1700. Two thousand Scottish lives, including those of Paterson's wife and son, the nation's treasury, and its pride and confidence, had been lost.

It is no wonder that the English soon found enough Scots willing to approve their merger terms after centuries of determined resistance. The government in London actually gave so much sterling to some of the important losers in the Darien fiasco that an English parliamentarian was able to boast that his country had "bought" Scotland.[16]

The union of the parliaments was accomplished in 1707, and the resulting loss of Scottish sovereignty became America's gain, as Scots in substantial numbers began to leave their bankrupt land for the formerly English, now British, colonies in the New World. A wave of immigrants from the Lowlands poured into the colonies usually settling in the area south of Connecticut. The Highlanders, particularly after the disastrous rebellion of 1745, concentrated principally on the Carolinas, where they were led by the famous Flora Macdonald. At one time Gaelic was spoken in six North Carolina counties.[17]

The Ulster Scots, or Scotch-Irish, had become uncomfortable in northern Ireland after several generations of contention with the native Irish Catholics and oppression by the English government. Unable to return to destitute Scotland, the Scotch-Irish came by the boatloads. A few settled in New England, where they founded towns with Ulster names, such as Belfast and Bangor, Maine; Londonderry and Antrim, New Hampshire; Orange County, Vermont; and Coleraine, Massachusetts.[18] But the great majority landed in Philadelphia, usually proceeding to the less settled areas of New Jersey and especially Pennsylvania, where they named places such as Gettysburg, McKeesport, Tyrone, Derry, and Donegal.

In the seven decades before the American Revolution the Scots, scarce in the colonies before 1700, became the most numerous "foreigners" in some places, and their success was so immediate, and so obviously disproportionate to their numbers that they were regarded with suspicion, envy, and even hatred. The pioneer merchant of Baltimore, if not its actual founder, was a Scot, Dr. John Stevenson, and a fellow countryman, George Buchanan, laid out the city's streets in 1730.[19] In Georgetown, Maryland, now part of Washington, D.C., most of the merchants were Scots.

But it was across the Potomac River, in Virginia, that they were the most successful and the least liked. The Scots started in the Virginia tobacco trade later than the English, since they had been effectively barred from emigrating until 1707. Once in the business, however, they quickly took most of it away. They worked harder and did things the English traders would not do: They went across the mountains opening stores to deal directly with the farmers; they paid cash rather than use the English practice of consignment purchase; and they extended credit.[20] Because of the Scottish immigrants the economy of Virginia boomed. It was Scots who first brought Virginia wood, tar, pig iron, and cotton to the market.

Between 1750 and 1775 Glasgow's share of Great Britain's tobacco imports rose from 10 to 52 percent. This was the era of the Glasgow "tobacco lords": the Cunninghame Interests, John Glassford, Alex Spiers and Co., James Buchanan, Neil Jamieson, and many others. William Cunninghame and John Glassford operated twenty-one stores in Virginia and Maryland.[21] In 1771 alone Glasgow received over thirty-five million pounds of Virginia tobacco.[22] As the Scots drove the English merchants from the trade the sentiment against them rose.

The prejudice against the Scots in colonial America is not well-known, but anti-Scottishness had existed in Europe for centuries[23] and had begun in New York even before the arrival of the English. In 1659 there were complaints that the Scots were taking money out of Nieuw Amsterdam, and in 1660 the Dutch government there passed a law restricting Scottish traders. These may have included Sander Leenaerts Glen and his wife Catalyn Doncanson, who came in 1639, and John Hamilton, who arrived in 1660.[24] In the English colonies, from 1697 to 1699, there was actually a prohibition on the elevation of Scots to office.[25]

According to Andrew Hook, the Scots became "certainly the most unpopular national group in the colonies . . . never lost their clannish instincts, always sided together, supported each other, and never really trusted anyone who was not a fellow countryman."[26] In the north, "the prejudice against the Scotch-Irish Presbyterians extended to every part of New England."[27] People like the English author Daniel Defoe were alarmed that the Scots were taking over Virginia.[28] The *Scots Magazine* was concerned about anti-Scottish sentiment in Virginia, and reported of one precinct "that all the Scottish houses in that place have been destroyed by the Virginians, and all their goods and effects distributed among the populace."[29]

Many Americans associated the repressions of King George III with the Scots, inasmuch as his policies were, as we shall see, usually administered by Scottish colonial governors.[30] As anti-Scottish sentiment escalated, a play called *The Patriots* was written in Virginia by one Robert Mumford between 1775 and 1776. Its characters included M'Flint, M'Gripe, and a grasping merchant named M'Squeeze, all presented as stupid and prejudiced. An example of the dialogue follows:

M'FLINT: What is our offence, pray?

STRUT: The nature of their offence, gentlemen, is that they are Scotchmen.[31]

In 1776 John Leacock produced a play in Philadelphia called *The Fall of British Tyranny*, dedicated facetiously to "Lord Kidnapper...Pirates and Buccaneers, and the innumerable and never-ending clans of Macs and Donalds upon Donalds in America."[32] By the time of the American Revolution Scottish merchants were being tarred and feathered, and some were driven out.[33] And when the first draft of the Declaration of Independence was written, a Scot, John Witherspoon, had to demand the retraction of the phrase that complained that the king had sent to America "not only soldiers of our common blood, but Scotch and foreign mercenaries."[34] In 1782 the Georgia House of Assembly actually banned Scots from settling there.[35]

Despite this prejudice, the management of the colonies in the eighteenth century was left largely in Scottish hands. It seems almost incredible, but more than one hundred terms as colonial governor were served by members of the Scottish minority. In the fifty-year period preceding the American Revolution (1725–1775), twelve of the thirteen American colonies that were to become the first American states had Scottish governors. Vermont and Florida also had Scottish governors; and the colonies of New York, New Jersey, Pennsylvania, Virginia, and the Carolinas were governed by Scots most of the time.[36]

Among the more distinguished of these was Alexander Spotswood, who governed Virginia from 1710 to 1722, and for whom the state's Spotsylvania County is named. Born in Tangier, Governor Spotswood helped to bring the frontier under British influence[37] and was "the principal encourager of the growth of tobacco which laid the foundation of Virginia's wealth."[38] After Spotswood came Robert Dinwiddie, who governed Virginia during the French and Indian War, from 1751 to 1758, and for whom the state's Dinwiddie County is named. Dinwiddie, born near Glasgow, "discovered" a young man named George Washington and in 1753 sent him to confront the French military forces in what is now western Pennsylvania—the first important move ever made to establish British rather than French control over the American West.[39]

It is said that even James Oglethorpe, the English founder of Georgia, wore the kilt and plaid, as his mother was Scottish,[40] and near the end of the colonial period Archibald Bulloch, an ancestor of President Theodore Roosevelt, was Georgia's governor.[41] John Cranston, the son of an Edinburgh minister, and the first physician in Rhode Island, was elected its governor in 1678. His son, Samuel Cranston, became governor in 1698 and was reelected each year for twenty-nine consecutive years. Cranston, Rhode Island, is named for him.[42]

George Johnstone, governor of Florida in 1763, brought the controversial translator of Ossian's poems, James Macpherson, to his land for a visit. Macpherson noted, "like most of the other American governors, Johnstone was a Scotchman."[43] Maj. Gen. Robert Hunter was the first of eight Scottish colonial governors of New York, and at various times was also the governor of Virginia, the Jerseys, and Jamaica. Another Scottish governor of New York was Cadwallader Colden, a brilliant scientist who suggested the founding of the American Philosophical Society, and whose grandson was mayor of New York City from 1818 to 1821.[44]

In eighteenth-century America the minority Scots distinguished themselves in three ways that have been characteristic of them wherever they have gone: They wrote and published books and newspapers, they promoted education,[45] and they helped each other. In April 1704, John Campbell, the postmaster of Boston and a native of Islay, published the first issue of the first regular newspaper in America, the *Boston Newsletter*.[46] Another Scot, James Johnston, printed the first newspaper in Georgia in 1763.[47] In 1784 John Wells became Florida's first printer.[48] In the same year John Dunlap made his *Pennsylvania Packet* America's first successful daily.[49]

William Graham produced the first daily newspaper in Baltimore in 1791,[50] and Thomas Dobson, another Scot, published the first American edition of the *Encyclopaedia Britannica* in the same year.[51] John Baine, of St. Andrews, established the first type foundry in America in 1787, and his successors, Archibald Binney and James Ronaldson, both born in Scotland, cast the first dollar sign ever made in 1797.[52] Robert Wells, of Edinburgh and Charleston, published the *South Carolina and American Gazette* before the revolution,[53] while David Hall of Edinburgh printed the *Pennsylvania Gazette* with his more famous partner, Benjamin Franklin.[54] Scottish-born Robert

Aitken printed the first complete English Bible in America and was commended by a resolution of Congress.[55]

In the American colonies south of New England most of the schoolmasters were Scots,[56] and Scottish scholars and administrators were largely responsible for founding four of the first six major American universities, as well as the first three medical schools in America. William and Mary, second in seniority only to Harvard, was founded in 1693 by James Blair, a native of Scotland.[57]

William Tennent came from Armagh, in northern Ireland, to found a rural college, one of the many Scottish "log colleges,"[58] at Neshaminy, Pennsylvania. It was later moved east becoming first the College of New Jersey, and finally Princeton University.[59] Originally a Presbyterian seminary, Princeton was supported by the Church of Scotland, the General Assembly of which passed a resolution requesting every congregation to make a contribution to the building of the college's famed Nassau Hall.[60] In 1754, 3,200 pounds were collected for this purpose at the church doors of Scotland.[61]

The University of Pennsylvania was founded in 1740, and was basically the work of two Scots brought to Philadelphia by Benjamin Franklin. They were William Smith (1727–1803) of Scotland and Francis Allison (1705–1779). Allison came from Ulster but had been educated in Glasgow and Edinburgh.[62] Smith was succeeded as provost by another Scot, John Ewing.[63]

Penn's medical school, founded in 1765 and the nation's oldest, was patterned after that of Edinburgh. Indeed, its emblem is still the Scottish thistle. Four of Penn's first five medical professors had M.D. degrees from Edinburgh.[64] One of these, the famous Benjamin Rush, remotely of Scottish ancestry, was the first chemistry professor in America.[65]

Two presidents of Saint Andrew's Society of the State of New York, Philip Livingston and William Alexander (the earl of Stirling), were among the founders of Columbia University, first called Kings College. Its medical school, America's second oldest, was founded in 1767 by another Saint Andrew's president, Dr. Peter Middleton, a native Scot who performed the first dissection in America.[66] Five of Columbia's first six medical professors had studied at Edinburgh.[67] The third oldest medical school in America was founded at William and Mary in 1779 by Edinburgh-trained Dr. James McClurg.[68]

Scots also had a hand in the founding of many other American colleges.[69] Dartmouth, which started in 1769, succeeded Moor's Indian Charity School, which had been run by Eleazar Wheelock with funds provided from Scotland.[70] In 1768 Joseph Alexander (Princeton, '60) opened the first classical school in North Carolina. It eventually became the University of North Carolina, the first American state university.[71]

Several writers, such as Professor Montague of New York, have noticed that American universities bear a closer resemblance to Scottish universities than to the English. One example of Scottish influence is the "thesis sheet," a tradition developed at Edinburgh that listed students prepared to defend their theses, and that was used from a very early time at Harvard and soon after at Yale, Princeton, the University of Pennsylavnia, and Brown.[72] A contemporary English historian says simply, "If the colonial colleges of the seventeenth century were English, those of the eighteenth century were distinctly Scottish in spirit."[73] In Colonial days, an anonymous Englishman complained, "Can't our universitys [sic] and the whole Kingdom afford an English man qualified to preside over our clergy without being forced to send a Scotchman?"[74]

And the Scots never forgot their own. Between 1729 and 1756 charitable St. Andrew's societies were established in Charleston, Philadelphia, New York, and Savannah, and all are still flourishing today. Saint Andrew's Society of the State of New York, founded in 1756, is the oldest charitable organization in the Empire State. The St. Andrew's Society of Philadelphia, founded in 1749, claims to be the oldest charitable organization in continuous existence in North America.[75]

Toward Revolution

Since they were usually barred from the colonies before the Union of 1707, it was not until the middle of the eighteenth century that Scots became a significant minority in America, and it was at precisely this time that the colonies began to move toward revolution. The coincidence cannot be ignored.

It should not be surprising to discover that the unassimilated Scots, for the most part only recently arrived,[76] should have played a leading role. Unlike the English majority, they had no basic sympathy with an English government. On the contrary, their ancestors had resisted English governments with determined violence for centuries. Many of these immigrants had even come to America because of their disgust with their homeland's recent union with England. Also, their philosophy, as we shall see, was more liberal than that of their English neighbors, more democratic, more egalitarian, more like what America would soon become.

We have seen, too, that these immigrants were thought of as foreign, a condition which led to discrimination against them, something a new democratic government would not allow. Although many of the Scots had risen very quickly in many fields, had vested interests in the status quo, and would become Tories, ridding the colonies of an English government was clearly in the best political and emotional interest of the large majority.

For those Scots who had arrived in America from northern Ireland, the need for the colonies to become independent from England was manifest. The English-dominated government in Ulster had cheated them out of their farms by raising their rents after their labor had made the land valuable; it had discriminated against their Presbyterianism by allowing only Anglicans to hold civil or military office; and it had prohibited the export of linen, the Ulsterman's most valuable manufacture.[77] The Scotch-Irish had arrived in America bearing a hatred of the Hanoverian government, which drove them into the revolutionary movement with a religious fervor. Perhaps their presence in the colonies was even the revolution's principal cause.

In the colonies the Presbyterian church was, in itself, an instigator of the American Revolution. Some historians have said that the widely circulated pastoral letter, issued by the Synod of Philadelphia in 1775 urging the colonists to support the future decisions of their congress was "the chief cause of the colonies' determination towards resistance."[78] The reasons for this relatively small denomination's influence are several. First, most of the Presbyterians were of Scottish or Scotch-Irish descent and therefore, as we have seen, predisposed against English rulers. Only a century before, their recent ancestors had fought a civil war in Scotland to rid both their church and country from English domination. In 1637 King Charles I tried to impose bishops and prayer books on the democratic and plain Presbyterian Church of Scotland. On July 23, a group of ordinary Scottish women rioted when one Jenny Geddes, standing in St. Giles Cathedral, threw her "cutty stool" at the head of the Episcopal dean of Edinburgh, beginning the Presbyterian Revolution, a civil war that was to last several years. The women were protesting English interference in the affairs of their church and country, and were also sending a message to King Charles I that he would need their consent for any actions, religious or political.

The Presbyterian church was founded on the concept of egalitarianism, a much older and stronger concept among Scots than among Englishmen. At the coronation of King James VI, Andrew Melville, a founder of the church, had the temerity to say, "Sirrah! Ye are God's silly vassal; there are twa kingdoms in Scotland; there is Christ Jesus the King of the Kirk, whose subject James VI is, and of whose kingdom he is not a king, nor a lord, nor a head, but a member."[79] Egalitarianism is one of the things the Revolution was about.

But the most important difference between the Presbyterians and the Anglican majority in America was in the organization of their church. Unlike the authoritative Anglican structure of appointed bishops, the Presbyterian church was a democracy, perhaps the most flourishing democracy in the world in the eighteenth century. From the time of its institution in 1560, the general assembly of the Church of Scotland had been "an even more representative body than the Scottish Parliament, and wielded enormous influence on the national life."[80] After the union of the Parliaments in 1707 left Scotland without a representative body, the Church of Scotland became the de facto government of the country. Every member of every parish had a vote to elect the elders of the Kirk Session, a democracy which ran through the local presbyteries and regional synods up to the General Assembly itself. It is obvious that the tiered Presbyterian structure was a model for what would become the precinct, local, state, and national governments of the United States.

One of the early significant events leading toward revolution occurred in 1735, when Andrew Hamilton, a Scottish lawyer from Philadelphia, went to New York to defend a German immigrant printer who was being held in jail on charges of "seditious reflections" and libel against the king. The defendant, John Peter Zenger, was the publisher of the *New York Weekly Journal*, which had printed articles denouncing certain actions taken by the king's colonial government. It appears that four Scottish-Americans, James Alexander, Cadwallader Colden, Lewis Morgan, and William Smith, were the secret owners of the paper and provided the money for Zenger's defense.[81] The judge instructed the jury to decide only whether the paper had made the statements, leaving the decision as to whether they were libelous to the court. But Hamilton's eloquent arguments addressed the broader concepts of free press and the limits of judges, and he encouraged the jurors to decide whether the government had been libeled. When the jury found Zenger not guilty, freedom of the press had been legally established in America. Hamilton and Zenger were heroes, tyranny had been defied, and the colonists' attitudes towards the mother country were never the same again.

Thirty years later, when most Americans still considered thoughts of independence to be seditious, a persuasive and powerful radical in Virginia delivered a speech which became one of the landmarks in influencing the American people towards revolution. Patrick Henry was the son of a Scottish-born judge.[82] Standing in the House of Burgesses, in Williamsburg, he defended his resolutions calling for independent laws for Virginia, closing his speech, "Caesar had his Brutus, Charles the First his Cromwell, and George III..." here he was interrupted by shouts of "Treason! Treason!" but he continued, "...may profit from their example! If this be treason, make the most of it!"[83]

By 1774 the Continental Congress had formed the first government of the British colonies, and on September 5, elected Peyton Randolph, a Virginian of partly Scottish descent, as the first American president.[84]

Americans were now openly discussing separation and meetings were being held in all parts of the colonies. This was particularly true in the remote west, where Scotch-Irish settlers met in several communities in Pennsylvania[85] and in Mecklenburg County, North Carolina, to make resolutions to oppose continued British rule.[86]

On March 23, 1775, Patrick Henry, who Jefferson said was "before us all in maintaining the spirit of the Revolution," gave his most memorable speech. As he declaimed to the Virginia revolutionary conventon in St. John's Church, in Richmond, the magic of his words held his audience entranced. Suddenly Henry stopped speaking, lowered his head and crossed his wrists, appearing to be a shackled slave. Quietly, he then said, "Is life so dear or peace so sweet as to be purchased at the price of chains and slavery?" Then, just as dramatically, he ended with his famous peroration, tossing his head toward the sky, his arms, free of imaginary manacles, wide open. In this posture he shouted, "Forbid it Almighty God! I know not what course others may take, but as for me, give me liberty or give me death!" The American War of Independence began twenty-seven days later, at Lexington, Massachusetts.

The American War of Independence

The "shot heard 'round the world," the first blast that began the American Revolution, was claimed to have been fired by a Scottish-

American, Ebenezer Munro, of the Lexington Minutemen.[87] Its British response (some say it was actually the first shot) was also from a Scot, as Major John Pitcairn discharged his beautiful Doune pistol, now in the Lexington Museum.[88]

With the war underway in earnest, the Scots, who had done so much to bring the Revolution about, were very prominent in it. It has been said that a Presbyterian loyalist was unheard of, and that British soldiers in some areas were instructed to burn farmhouses to the ground if they were found to contain Presbyterian Bibles.[89] But of course, there were many Scots who were loyalists, particularly in the South, where rich Scottish businessmen were intent on preserving the status quo. Even there, though, Scottish physicians and clergymen were usually patriots.[90] In the Carolinas there were many Highlanders who remained loyal despite patriotic appeals addressed to them in Gaelic, and at the end of the war many emigrated to Canada.[91]

The Scottish population in the mid-Atlantic area appears to have been mainly revolutionary. The St. Andrew's Societies of New York and Philadelphia alone contributed six of the fifty-six signers of the Declaration of Independence. Yet the division of loyalties, even in these organizations, was severe enough to cause the suspension of their activities for the duration of the war.

The Scotch-Irish were, according to Gordon Donaldson, "revolutionary almost to a man,"[92] while George F. Black calls them "the most determined revolutionists."[93] T. J. Wertenbaker observes that the Scotch-Irish troops stayed through the bitter winter at Valley Forge while others left.[94] The colonials' most famous battlefield heroine was a woman of Scotch-Irish descent, Mary Hays McCauly, better known to history as Molly Pitcher.[95]

Various sources have identified between one-third and one-half of the American generals in the Revolution as either of Scottish birth or ancestry. Prominent among these were Highlanders Arthur St. Clair, Alexander MacDougall, and Lachlan MacIntosh. Richard Montgomery captured Montreal in 1775 and died in the subsequent assault on Quebec.[96] Hugh Mercer, who had been a surgeon to Bonnie Prince Charlie at Culloden, and later to Washington, was killed at the Battle of Princeton.[97] George Rogers Clark and "Mad" Anthony Wayne made contributions which left them famous.[98] Gen. John Stark commanded eight hundred backwoodsmen at Bunker Hill,[99] and Gen. Henry Knox captured and transported enough artillery to Boston to allow the colonials to drive the British out. Knox participated in nearly every important battle of the war and was in charge of the forces which wrested Trenton from the Hessians on Christmas night in 1776. He succeeded Washington as general in chief in 1783.[100]

John Paul Jones, the son of a Kirkbean gardener, was the first naval officer commissioned by the Continental Congress and is considered to have been the founder of the American navy. He was born John Paul, and added Jones as an alias to avoid arrest on a murder charge. In 1778 he returned to his native shire on the Solway Firth and there led the last foreign invasions of British soil. Although his raids did little damage, they were psychologically disturbing to British morale. In 1779 Jones, commanding the *Bon Homme Richard*, an old French merchant ship equipped with forty-two 18-, 12-, and 9-pound cannon, engaged the British *Serapis*, with fifty-four 18-, 9- and 6-pounders, off Scarborough, England, in one of the world's most famous naval actions. When the battle seemed to be going against the Americans, the British commander called upon Jones to surrender, causing him to shout his immortal reply, "I have not yet begun to fight!" Jones won the battle and became a hero. His extravagant tomb, an ornate sarcophagus, set upon dolphins and situated in a classic marble crypt below the chapel at the U.S. Naval Academy in Annapolis, Maryland, is a national shrine.[101]

George Washington, the most famous revolutionary, the "father" of the country and commander in chief of the victorious American army, was himself remotely descended from the Scottish king Malcolm II. This unusual discovery was made in 1964 by an Englishman, George S. H. L. Washington, and has been accepted by the Garter King of Arms, the official arbiter of English genealogy.[102]

The Declaration of Independence

In the steamy days of Philadelphia's summer of 1776, the representatives of the thirteen American colonies met to decide whether to break completely with Britain. They did so in the Georgian building now called Independence Hall, partly designed by a Scot, Andrew Hamilton, who had once owned some of the square on which it stands.[103] It was in response to the appeal of a Scot, John Witherspoon, that the Declaration of Independence was signed[104] after it had been given to Thomas Jefferson, a descendant of a sister of King Robert I, the Bruce, to draft.[105] The document was written in the handwriting of an Ulster Scot, Charles Thomson, who was secretary of the Congress for all of its fifteen years.[106] The declaration was first printed by another Ulsterman, John Dunlap,[107] and was publicly proclaimed by a third Orangeman, Capt. John Nixon,[108] while Andrew McNair rang the Liberty Bell.[109]

A young Philadelphia seamstress whose husband, John Ross (nephew of George Ross, who signed the declaration) had been killed in the revolution, was engaged to make the first American flag. Her name was Betsy Ross.[110]

Of the fifty-six men who signed the Declaration of Independence, at least twenty-one, or almost 38 percent, have been identified as having Scottish ancestry.[111] But even this figure does not adequately measure the Scottish performance, since there were few Scots living in Massachusetts, Maryland, or Connecticut, and hence no Scottish delegates to the convention from those colonies. Of the men who represented the remaining ten colonies, almost half of those who risked their lives, fortunes and sacred honor, were of the Scottish nation. Even more remarkable, ten of the thirteen colonies had Scottish governors during the ensuing war.[112] And all of this was produced by a people who, according to the 1790 U.S. census, were only 6.7 percent of the white colonial population.[113]

The Constitution

At the close of the Revolution the independence of America had been obtained but not secured, as its government, under the Articles of Confederation, was weak. A meeting to improve commercial relations among the new states was held in Annapolis, Maryland, in 1786. Alexander Hamilton, a half-Scot from New York,[114] drafted a report of the proceedings in which he proposed another convention with much greater powers.[115] Hamilton asked the delegates to meet the following year in Philadelphia to render a "constitution of the Federal Government equal to the exigencies of the union."[116] The Constitutional Convention, thus "called" by Hamilton, met in Philadelphia in May 1787 to write the document upon which the government of the United States is founded. As usual, the Scots were overrepresented.

The convention was opened by a great orator, the thirty-four-year-old governor of Virginia, Edmund Randolph, who, like several others in this book, was descended from the noble Randolphs of Scotland. Randolph spoke for three hours presenting the Virginia Plan, which advocated a strong national government composed of three independent departments: the executive, the judicial, and the legislative, the last of which would have two houses.[117] Although in essence this is the government of the United States today, Randolph's further proposal that the representation of each state be based on that state's population made his plan unacceptable to the smaller states. The response of a northern Scot, William Paterson, was to put forth the New Jersey plan: a one-house legislature in which all of the states would vote equally.

The Great Compromise reached between these two plans gave the states representation by population in the lower house and equal representation in the upper house. James Wilson, a native of Scotland, was one of the most eloquent and frequent speakers at the convention and one of its most influential delegates. He stunned the delegates with the proposal that the executive department should consist of "a single person,"[118] and since his idea and arguments in its favor gained acceptance, Wilson can be said to have created the American presidency.

Previously, we have noted the resemblance of the United States government to the structure of the Presbyterian church, both institutions having their tiers of democracy ranging upward from local through regional and national levels. Some historians have gone so far as to claim that the United States government's structure, as embodied in the Constitution, was copied from the Church of Scotland. This may be true, because the Presbyterian Kirk was indeed a uniquely democratic model among the authoritarian churches and kingdoms of the eighteenth century. Furthermore, Presbyterianism was very well represented at the Philadelphia proceedings. There were nine graduates from Presbyterian Princeton at the Constitutional Convention. Harvard and Yale together had only seven.[119] And one of the Princeton-educated delegates, James Madison, of partly Scottish descent,[120] is generally thought to have been the most instrumental of all the delegates and the master architect of the Constitution.[121] The Bill of Rights, the first ten amendments to the Constitution, also had a Scottish tinge. They were drafted by Madison, and Patrick Henry was largely responsible for their passage.[122]

As he had done with the Declaration of Independence, John Dunlap was the first to print the Constitution.[123] Over the next several years copies were circulated and one by one the states voted to ratify it. Some were very reluctant and might never have done so had it not been for the positive influence of *The Federalist*, a series of essays which explained the benefits of the new government and how it would work. *The Federalist* papers were written largely by Hamilton and Madison, and printed by Scots Archibald and John MacLean of New York. The philosophy of *The Federalist* has been traced to Scotland, and to David Hume in particular.[124]

Scottish Philosophy and the American Revolution

Scottish philosophy was even more important to the creation of the United States than were the distinguished people we have already discussed. But since the thirteen colonies were over 80 percent English and less than 7 percent Scottish and Scotch-Irish, it has been difficult for historians to concede that by far the greater philosophical influence at the birth of the nation was Scottish rather than English. Recently this attitude is changing. In 1986 the American scholar Daniel Bell said that the Scottish enlightenment "emphasized the individual as the unit of society...and came to fruition in Anglo-American society."[125]

English philosophy *had* dominated the colonies in their early years, but, as Esmond Wright says, "this Puritan and Anglican drive was reinforced and then overtaken by avowedly Scottish ideas."[126] Britons on both sides of the Atlantic shared liberal thoughts, particularly those of Locke, who is so often cited as an influence on the Revolution. But, as we shall see, Locke's idea that the people have the ultimate sovereignty and the right to change an unjust government, had been written down in Scotland centuries before him.

Furthermore, Locke's ideas did not directly address the problems of the colonies, as did those of the Scottish philosophers whose writings were based on a fundamental difference between England and Scotland that still exists: England has always been far more class conscious than Scotland. Since America was a new land where class distinctions seemed irrelevant or oppressive, it was Scottish ideas that were embraced. In the half century before 1776, waves of Scottish and Scotch-Irish immigrants came to the colonies, bringing with them an ingrained liberal philosophy that would change the colonists, and indeed the world, irrevocably.

At the time of the American Revolution Scottish ideas were, in fact, being discussed all over the globe, for the last half of the eighteenth century was also the time of the Scottish Golden Age, a magical era when little Scotland burst forth as the intellectual nucleus of civilization. All the arts and sciences flourished in her renowned universities, while those such as Oxford and Cambridge slept.[127]

It was the time when Glasgow held the center stage of the Industrial Revolution, and Scotsmen accumulated vast fortunes supported by the ideas of Adam Smith and the inventions of James Watt and dozens of others.[128] In science, Scots would have won an almost embarrassing portion of Nobel Prizes had the award existed at that time.[129]

It was also the lyric age of Robert Burns, the time when Raeburn and Ramsay were painting their breathtaking portraits, and young Walter Scott was beginning his career as literary wizard. Not since the days of ancient Greece had so much creativity come from such a small place in such a short time. The American physician Benjamin Rush called Edinburgh "the most rational and perhaps enlightened city in the world."[130] Many others referred to the Scottish capital as the "Athens of the North."

This atmosphere of intellectual activity in Scotland produced the philosophers who so greatly influenced the founding of the United States. There was the stimulating skeptic David Hume, considered by many to have been the most important philosopher ever produced by Britain, and the aesthetician Kames. Of paramount importance was the work of the great moralist Francis Hutcheson. And in keeping with the mood of the era, as well as with centuries of Scottish tradition, there was the practical philosophy of Thomas Reid, Adam Ferguson, and Dugald Stewart called Common Sense. This philosophy proceeds from the common sense of ordinary people: that the world, as we experience it, exists, and that hot, cold, color, sound, and so forth are real and need no proof.

So potent was this "sober philosophy," as James McCosh called it, that it would be adopted as the official philosophy of France for half of the next century.[131] But its greatest impact was to be made in America. There the implanted Common Sense philosophy would take root and grow into a political system which would dominate the civilized world.

Scottish philosophy directly addressed the relationship of the colonies to Britain. Long before the Revolution, Francis Hutcheson, whose ideas anticipated Common Sense, had said, "Large numbers of men cannot be bound to sacrifice their own posterity's liberty and happiness, to the ambitious views of the mother country . . . there is something so unnatural in supposing a large society, sufficient for all good purposes of an independent political union, remaining subject to the direction of a distant body of men who know not sufficiently the circumstances and exigencies of this society."[132]

Hutcheson also said that human rights included the right of a people to oppose acts of tyranny by their governors, and the right of colonies to "turn independent" when the mother country resorts to "severe and absolute" policies.[133] Additionally, Hutcheson proposed, "unalienable rights are essential limitations in all governments."[134]

Thomas Reid held that certain moral "truths" were "self evident,"[135] words now familiar to all Americans, while Adam Ferguson believed that Great Britain's colonial subjects in America were endowed with the same natural rights enjoyed by Englishmen.[136] Another prominent Scottish philosopher, Adam Smith, urged Britain to release her American colonies, saying that Britain deserved "nothing but loss" from its restrictions against American businessmen,[137] and argued that Britain would profit more if the colonies were independent.[138] It is obvious that the Scottish philosophers sided with the colonists, and thus no wonder that their fundamental, rational, practical, and egalitarian ideas were widely taught and readily accepted by Americans.

Princeton University was the fount from which this philosophy was broadcast throughout the colonies. It was there that Scottish-born John Witherspoon renounced idealism and preached Common Sense.[139] The American historian Garry Wills, who has uncovered much of the evidence of the Scottish Enlightenment's role in the revolution, calls Witherspoon "probably the most influential teacher in the entire history of American education."[140] His students included:

1 president (James Madison)
1 vice president (Aaron Burr)
3 Supreme Court justices
5 cabinet members
12 state governors
21 U.S. senators
29 U.S. representatives
56 state legislators
6 signers of the Declaration of Independence
9 delegates to the Constitutional Convention
31 Revolutionary Army officers, and more than
100 ministers.[141]

From Princeton the Scottish philosophy "overran the country"[142] and became "the most influential philosophy in America."[143] One reason for this phenomenon was the geographical distribution of Princeton's students. Approximately 90 percent of Harvard men came from Massachusetts, 75 percent of Yale men from Connecticut and almost all of William and Mary's students from Virginia. However, only a quarter of Princeton's graduates came from New Jersey, the rest returning to their homes throughout all of America.[144]

Soon most of the colonial colleges were using Hutcheson's *System of Moral Philosophy* as a basic textbook. The Scot William Smith taught Hutcheson at Philadelphia (now the University of Pennsylvania), while at Kings College in New York (now Columbia University) the study of Hutcheson's moral philosophy took up the final two years of study.[145] Many future American statesmen were exposed to the Common Sense philosophy at Edinburgh, which attracted more colonials than any other British university. There was even a Virginian Club there.[146]

Benjamin Franklin characterized Edinburgh's professors as "a set of truly great men...as ever appeared in one age or Country."[147] Franklin knew the Scottish philosophers personally, and was the intimate of one, Adam Ferguson, with whom in 1771 he spent his last night in Scotland.[148]

Thomas Jefferson drew a clear distinction between Scotland and England, particularly in education: "Why send an American youth to England for education? If he goes to England, he learns drinking, horse-racing and boxing. These are the peculiarities of English education."[149] Jefferson referred to Edinburgh as the finest university in the world[150] and was greatly indebted to Scottish philosophy.

Contrary to what is usually taught, he was probably very little influenced by English philosophy, including that of Locke. And his basic library list contained the most prominent Scottish philosophers.[151] In his early years Jefferson was taught by several Scottish tutors: Samuel Finley,[152] William Douglas of Glencairne,[153] and most importantly by William Small, a native Scot who Jefferson said, "probably fixed the destinies of my life."[154]

James Madison spoke French with a Scottish accent, the result of his having learned the language from his Scottish tutor Donald Robertson, with whom he boarded for five years.[155] Another tutor of young Madison had been Archibald Campbell of Argyll,[156] and the future president later studied under Witherspoon at Princeton.[157] George Mason, author of the Virginia Constitution and its Declaration of Rights was tutored by a Mr. Williams of Glasgow,[158] while Richard Henry Lee, who introduced the resolution calling for independence, had been tutored by William Douglas, Rev. Mr. Craig, and Rev. David Currie of Edinburgh.[159] Alexander Hamilton had a Scottish tutor also: Hugh Knox, a graduate of Princeton.[160]

Perhaps the most pointed illustration of the influence of Scottish philosophy on the American Revolution is the discovery that prior to his emigration to America the radical Thomas Paine had attended lectures of Adam Ferguson in London.[161] When Paine later wrote one of the most influential pamphlets ever published, selling an estimated half million copies in the six months preceding the revolution, he actually called it *Common Sense.*

There is even strong circumstantial evidence that the American founding fathers who drafted the Declaration of Independence and the Constitution actually referred to two antecedent Scottish documents. The *Encyclopaedia Britannica,* perhaps the best general source of conventional wisdom, states that the United States Declaration of Independence "contained the first formal assertion by a whole people of their right to a government of their own choice."[162] This is absolutely untrue. In fact there were two previous such assertions and both of them were Scottish.

The first, The Arbroath Declaration of 1320, in which Scotland declared its independence from England, was addressed to the pope, and like the United States Declaration of Independence, was signed by several dozen representatives of the population, enumerated a long list of grievances against an English king, and unequivocally asserted the country's independence and the people's right to choose their own government.

The second, the National Covenant of 1638, was a declaration of the religious and political independence of Scotland, and in the words of the Anglo-Scottish historian John Prebble, "challenged the King's prerogative, and by implication affirmed that the right to make and change the law rested in parliament only."[163] The National Covenant was copied and carried "to every burgh, parish and university" where it was signed by the "whole people, landed and landless, rich and poor" of Scotland.[164]

Without a doubt, some of the influential delegates on or close to the committees which drafted the documents upon which the United States is based were familiar with these two Scottish declarations. James Wilson and John Witherspoon would surely have studied them as students in their native Scotland. Many of the other leading delegates would have come in contact with them through their Scottish tutors and professors. In fact, a careful comparison of the Arbroath Declaration[165] and the National Covenant against the Declaration of Independence and the Preamble to the United States Constitution readily reveals how the Americans used the words and concepts of the older Scottish documents as models for their momentous works. Some equivalent or nearly equivalent words are italicized for emphasis.

Declaration of Independence Philadelphia, U.S.A. July 4, 1776	**Arbroath Declaration** Arbroath, Scotland April 6, 1320

EQUALITY UNDER THE LAW

all men are created equal	nor distinction of Jew or Greek, Scots or English

THE RIGHT TO LIBERTY AND THE DUTY TO
DEFEND IT WITH ONE'S LIFE

certain unalienable rights, among these are *life, liberty*	we fight for *liberty* alone which no good man loses but with his *life*
we mutually pledge...our lives	we will maintain even to the death

THE PURPOSE OF GOVERNMENT IS TO PROTECT RIGHTS
AND MUST BE CONSENTED TO

that to secure these Rights governments are instituted among Men deriving their just powers from the *consent* of the governed	our...king...(protecting)...our laws and customs...(must reign under)...the succession of right and the due *consent* of us all

WHEN A GOVERNMENT DOES NOT PROTECT PEOPLES' RIGHTS IT IS
THE PEOPLES' RIGHT TO ABOLISH THE GOVERNMENT AND INSTITUTE
A NEW ONE

that whenever any Form of Government becomes destructive of these Ends, it is the Right of the people to alter or abolish it and to institute a new government

But if he (the King of Scots) were to desist from what he has begun...we would immediately endeavour to expel him as our enemy and the subverter of his own rights and ours, and make another our King

WE HAVE BEEN INJURED REPEATEDLY, MOSTLY BY AN ENGLISH KING

The history of the present *King of Great Britain* is a history of repeated *injuries*
death
Desolation

The mighty *King of the English*...perpetrated...*injuries*
slaughters
deeds of violence

He has...sent hither swarms of officers to *harass* our people

...in most unfriendlywise *harassed* our Kingdom

A *prince* whose character is marked by every act which may define a tyrant

...this *prince* perpetrated
...these evils innumerable

merciless Indian *savages*

the most *savage* tribes

in the most *barbarous* Ages

people however *barbarous*

He has *plundered* our seas...*burnt* our towns

plunderings, burnings

an undistinguished Destruction of all *ages, sexes* and conditions

sparing no *age* or *sex*

WE WILL NOT BE GOVERNED BY THE ENGLISH

That these United Colonies are absolved from all allegiance to the British Crown

For so long as a hundred remain alive, we never will in any degree be subject to the dominion of the English

WE APPEAL TO THE ALMIGHTY TO HELP US,
AND TRUST THAT HE WILL

appealing to the *Supreme Judge* of the World for the Rectitude of our Intentions

to Him, as the *Supreme* King and *Judge* we commit the defence of our cause

with a firm reliance on the Protection of *Divine Providence*	(by the help of) *Divine Providence* firmly trusting that He will bring our enemies to nought

Both the American and Scottish declarations are about forty lines long, and are signed by similar numbers of people: fifty-six at Philadelphia and thirty-nine at Arbroath. Each has a signatory named Ross. Jefferson, the author and one of the signers of the Declaration of Independence, was a descendant of Thomas Randolph, a blood nephew of King Robert I, the Bruce. Thomas Randolph had signed the Arbroath Declaration 456 years before 1776.

A comparison of the language between the Declaration of Independence and the Scottish National Covenant shows more similarities:

Declaration of Independence Philadelphia, July 4, 1776	**The National Covenant** Edinburgh, 1638
We...Do...Solemnly...Declare	We...Do...Solemnly Declare
...*usurpations*, all having in direct Object the Establishment of an absolute *tyranny*	...*usurped* authority of...all his *tyrannous* laws
that these United Colonies *are* and of Right *ought to be* Free and Independent States	that the aforesaid Confessions *are* to be interpreted and *ought to be* understood...
with a firm reliance on the protection of Divine Providence	we call the Living God to witness...and bless our proceedings with a happy success
we *mutually* pledge to each *other*	to the *mutual* defence and assistance every one of us of *another*
our lives, our Fortunes	with *our* means and *lives*

The Preamble to the United States Constitution, a masterpiece of concise English, is only fifty-two words long and is printed here in full, below left. On the right are phrases excerpted from the National Covenant and Act ordaining it, which can be read almost if they *were* the Preamble with no change of meaning or spirit whatsoever. Many of the words or phrases are identical or nearly so in both documents, and are italicized.

Preamble to the Constitution of the United States Philadelphia, 1787	**The National Covenant and Act Ordaining It** Edinburgh, 1638 and 1639
We the people of the United States	we noblemen, barons, gentlemen, burgesses, ministers and commons
in order to form a more *perfect union*	considering the great happiness which may flow from a full and *perfect union*
establish justice	judicatories be *established* and ministration of *justice* amongst us
insure domestic tranquillity	procure true and perfect peace
provide for the common *defense*	stand to the mutual *defence*
promote the general welfare	for the common happiness to conduce for so good ends and *promote* the same
and *secure* the blessings of *liberty to ourselves and our posterity*	*security* of said *liberties to ourselves and our posterity*
do ordain and establish this *Constitution* for the United States of America.	*do ordain* the Covenant and *Constitution* of this Kingdom

Several conclusions may be drawn:

That Scotland, not America, was the first country to declare its independence, and did so enunciating the principles of equality under the law, the duty to defend liberty with life, the necessary consent of the governed, and the people's right to change an unjust government 456 years before 1776.

That the Scottish nation was the only nation ever to subscribe en masse to a document which declared that the ultimate political right belonged to the people, and which bound them all to defend that right to the limit, and that it did so 138 years before 1776.

That the brilliant men who drafted the earth-shaking tracts in Philadelphia in the last years of the eighteenth century were often Presbyterians, even more often of Scottish ancestry, and almost all were well acquainted with Scottish philosophy, which was ascendant throughout the world at that time. It appears that they borrowed from two antecedent Scottish documents. That their philosophy was basically Scottish is certain.

The First American Government

The first government of the United States of America had a distinctly thistle hue. Nine of the original thirteen states chose men of Scottish ancestry as their first governors:[166]

Connecticut, Jonathan Trumbull
Delaware, John MacKinley
Georgia, Archibald Bulloch
New Jersey, William Livingston
New York, George Clinton
North Carolina, Richard Caswell
Pennsylvania, Thomas McKean
South Carolina, John Rutledge
Virginia, Patrick Henry

In addition, all of the members of the first American cabinet had Scottish ancestry:[167]

Secretary of State	Thomas Jefferson
Secretary of the Treasury	Alexander Hamilton
Secretary of War	Henry Knox
Attorney General	Edmund Randolph

Of the five original Supreme Court justices one, James Wilson, was born in Scotland and two others, John Rutledge and John Blair, were of Scottish ancestry.[168] The fourth, and perhaps the greatest chief justice, John Marshall, was the grandson of a Scottish minister.[169]

The grand Scottish presence at the beginning of the United States of America was vividly symbolized just after the April day in 1789 when George Washington disembarked on a pier in New York's East River. Amid much pageantry, the American hero walked down Wall Street to begin the nation's first inaugural celebration. A few days later, before a huge, festive throng, this great American, remotely of Scottish royal descent, was sworn in as the first president of the United States on the balcony of Federal Hall, a few yards from where the New York Stock Exchange stands today. The oath of office was administered by the Hon. Robert R. Livingston, L.L.D., in his capacity as chancellor of the state of New York, who was at the same time president of Saint Andrew's Society of the State of New York.

And, perhaps in symbolic commemoration of the Scottishness of the American Revolution and its new government, another member of Saint Andrew's Society, Brig. Gen. William Malcolm, commanded the military escort on this most auspicious American occasion wearing a Scottish-type military uniform, including, of course, a kilt.[170]

The English parliamentarian Horace Walpole said it best: "There is no use crying about it. Cousin America has run off with the Presbyterian parson, and that is the end of it."[171]

Winning the West

The most romantic part of the story of America, that which has captured the imagination of the world, is of the settlement of the more than two million square miles of land that stretches from the Appalachian Mountains to the Pacific. This movement, through which the United States became a world power, is heavily indebted to people of Scottish ancestry.

The westward thrust had begun before the Revolution by trappers, traders, and farmers, the majority of them Scots and Scotch-Irishmen. Forsaking the Georgian beauty of the eastern coastal towns, they worked their way through dark forests then held by a fragile alliance of Frenchmen and Indians, and by the Spanish further west.

These Presbyterian pioneers, more often than not immigrants from the north of Ireland, were uniquely qualified for their particular task. They were rugged and unimpressed by civility, known for their cursing and putting their babies to sleep with whisky-soaked bread. They were self-sufficient, not much concerned with danger, and quite willing to fight. Moreover, they were intelligent, interested in education, and religious, founding churches and schools in the wilderness by the dozens.

They were also realistic, and when the Germans who followed them proved to be better farmers, they simply sold out and went further west, building towns, starting businesses, becoming professionals, artisans, politicians, teachers, and preachers, all of which callings better suited them. They advanced elements of civilization through the frontier and left the flat pronunciation of northern Ireland as their permanent mark on the speech of trans-Appalachian America. The westward movement of their Celtic ancestors, which began in the steppes before recorded history, reached its fullest and final expression in the conquest of the vast North American continent.

By the middle of the eighteenth century the English-speaking settlements in the area, now called western Pennsylvania, were well established and profitable, but they were threatened by the French and their Indian allies. The outcome of the struggle that was to ensue had already been weighted in favor of the British through their peace treaty with the Cherokee Indians. Engineered by the Scottish-born governor of South Carolina, James Glen, the treaty kept the mighty Cherokees out of the French-Indian alliance.[172]

As previously noted, in late 1753 Governor Robert Dinwiddie of Virginia, a native of Glasgow, dispatched young George Washington to the Ohio Valley to warn the French that the British considered the area to be theirs. Soon after, Dinwiddie sent the Scottish-American William Trent to build a fort at the confluence of the Allegheny, Monongehela, and Ohio rivers, the place now called Pittsburgh.[173]

The French, however, easily captured the partly-built fort in April of 1754, finished it, and named it Fort Duquesne.[174] In May of the same year Washington returned to the area and won a small skirmish with the French. The French and Indian War, an aspect of Europe's Seven Years War, had begun. Washington began to build Fort Necessity to the southeast of Fort Duquesne, but in July the French overwhelmed the half-built stockade, and the Virginians surrendered and went home.

In 1755 Maj. Gen. Edward Braddock, born in Perthshire[175] and a loyal commander at Culloden,[176] was named to the command of North America. He arrived in February of that year in Alexandria, Virginia, a town across the river from what is now Washington, D.C. Founded by Scottish merchants William Ramsay and John Carlyle, Alexandria was named for their colleague, John Alexander. Five colonial governors met in Carlyle's mansion to discuss plans for the war against the French as well as the problems of taxation without representation.

The next summer Braddock's 2,200 men marched to within eight miles of Fort Duquesne, almost to the exact spot where Andrew Carnegie would build his first major steel mill a century later. On July 9, 250 Frenchmen and 600 Indians ambushed the British in a ravine and routed them, inflicting heavy casualties. The town of Braddock, Pennsylvania, commemorates the site of the battle and the commander who was killed. Col. George Washington survived to return to Virginia, where four weeks later Governor Dinwiddie made him commander in chief of the newly-formed Virginia Regiment. He was only twenty-three years old.[177]

In 1756 William Pitt, whose paternal great-grandmother was born in Elgin,[178] became the war minister of the British government. Pitt was determined to oust the French from the American West, and assigned the task of taking Fort Duquesne to a Scottish soldier and physician, Gen. John Forbes. In March of 1758 Forbes left Philadelphia with a force of about six thousand, many of them Highlanders, and began cutting a road through the dense Pennsylvania forest, traces of which are still visible. By September the army was so close to the Ohio River that an impetuous Scottish major, James Grant, led eight hundred Highlanders on a reconnaissance of the fort. Seeing its decay and hungry for glory, Grant decided to try to take the fort himself. The result was another massacre by the French and Indians, who decorated stakes outside the stockade with the heads and kilts of the Highlanders.

By November, when the main British force reached Fort Duquesne, the Indians had left to search for food, and the near-starving French surrendered without firing a shot. Forbes, although mortally ill and carried to the frontier on a litter, found the strength to write a letter to his war minister in which he disclosed that he had renamed the place Pittsburgh in his honor. The Scottish *h* in his spelling endures to this day. The next day a Presbyterian minister, Charles Beatty, preached the first sermon. In a few weeks Forbes was taken back to Philadelphia to die, and the new town was left in charge of another Scot, Hugh Mercer.[179] The presence of Britons in the American West had been permanently established.

The French and Indian War continued to be fought in New York, Quebec, and Nova Scotia until France admitted defeat in early 1763 and ceded most of her North American possessions to the British. But things were not settled quite yet. The great Indian chief Pontiac, with the encouragement of French traders, made one last attempt to drive the British back across the mountains. In a short time Pontiac captured eight forts and had Fort Pitt and Pittsburgh under siege. He terrorized and destroyed many settlements until he was stopped on the eastern outskirts of present-day Pittsburgh by a force of Montgomery's and Black Watch Highlanders in the decisive Battle of Bushy Run. The Scots were surprised by the Indians on August 5, 1763, and badly beaten. But they regrouped and routed the Indians the next day. On August 10 the battered Highlanders, marching behind their piper, relieved Fort Pitt. The Indian confederacy collapsed and the vast area between the Allegheny and the Mississippi would speak English forevermore.[180]

Pittsburgh, the gateway to the West, was immediately re-established, and a Scot, John Campbell, laid out the first streets.[181] In 1774 Lewis Morris, a member of Saint Andrew's Society of the State of New York, negotiated a treaty with the Indians securing the safety of the British settlers in the area,[182] and by the start of the revolution over fifty thousand British-Americans lived in the Ohio Valley. So many of these pioneers were Scottish and Scotch-Irish Presbyterians that it is said that John Knox prayed, "Lord give me Scotland," and that God had granted that request and had thrown in Pittsburgh as well.

The Whiskey Rebellion of 1794, the first test of the sovereignty of the United States government, was largely a Scottish affair. On one side was Alexander Hamilton, the first secretary of the treasury, who had proposed the excise with the dual purposes of gaining revenue and establishing federal power. The Presbyterian farmers around Pittsburgh, who produced most of the new nation's spirits, resisted the measure strongly. They refused to pay the tax and were led by a Princeton-educated Scot named Hugh Henry Brackenridge. After a few tar-and-featherings and the burning of a tax collector's home, President Washington ordered thirteen thousand troops towards Pittsburgh, and the rebellion ended. Hamilton's tax, however, is still with us.[183]

After the establishment of Pittsburgh the stream of Conestoga wagons carrying English-speaking settlers across the mountains became a river moving ever farther west and south. Men and women of the Scottish nation continued to be among the prominent and early settlers on the new frontiers. A historical marker near Johnson City, Tennessee, bears eloquent testimony to their bravery: "Near this site Jesse Duncan became the first white man killed and scalped by Indians in this vicinity, 1765."

Capt. William Bean had been the first white man to bring his family to Tennessee. Nashville, the first settlement there, was founded in 1779 by James Robertson.[184] Robert Ferguson produced the first newspaper in Tennessee,[185] and America's most famous whiskey is still made in Lynchburg, Tennessee, by relatives of the Scottish-English Jack Daniel.[186]

In 1789 Elijah Craig made the first batch of corn whiskey in Bourbon County, Kentucky.[187] Other early distillers bore Scottish names, such as Spears, Hamilton, and Stewart.[188] James Crow (1800–1859), a graduate physician from Edinburgh, vastly improved the methods of distilling whiskey with his sour-mash process, and is generally given credit for founding the modern bourbon whiskey industry.[189] Samuel McDowell was head of ten consecutive yearly Kentucky conventions demanding admission to the United States. At the tenth, in 1792, admission was granted and McDowell was named its president.[190]

The Northwest Territory, which became the states of Ohio, Indiana, Illinois, Michigan, and Wisconsin, was brought into the United States through the military efforts of George Rogers Clark who was Scottish on both sides of his ancestry.[191] General Clark fought his part of the War of Independence in the wilderness north and west of the Ohio River almost alone. With a handful of unpaid men he captured the British forts of Kaskaskia and Cahokia, and established such American control over the entire area that it was awarded to the new nation at the peace treaty in 1783.[192]

In 1787 the Scottish-born general Arthur St. Clair presided over the Continental Congress when it established the Northwest Ordinance, and subsequently became the first governor of the Northwest Territory, serving until 1802. St. Clair established civil government and education and oversaw the incorporation of cities such as Cincinnati, which he named, and Detroit. As the largest resident property owner west of the Alleghenies, he advanced money to his new government to guarantee its debts. When the federal government refused to honor the debt, St. Clair lost his entire fortune.[193] George Rogers Clark was similarly treated when the government refused to reimburse him for money he had spent for his army's supplies. Creditors hounded him for the rest of his life.[194]

Throughout the new Northwest, Scots were conspicuous in its development. Among them, David Taylor was a prominent settler in the area which became Columbus, Ohio.[195] In Cincinnati, William Maxwell produced the first newspaper in the territory.[196] Cleveland, Ohio's largest city, was founded by Moses Cleaveland, of Scottish ancestry, in 1796.[197] The Indiana Territory was secured by its first governor, William Henry Harrison, who defeated Tecumseh and his Indians at the Tippecanoe River in 1811.[198] Chicago was founded by Quebec-born John Kinzie (1763–1828), who had changed his name from MacKenzie and fathered the city's first white child.[199]

Matthew Duncan had the first printing press and produced the first newspaper in Illinois.[200] The first printer in Michigan was John McCall, and Alexander and William McComb owned the first press in Detroit.[201] As the settlements pushed further west and south,

Scots continued to lead in literacy. J. A. Aitkenside was Minnesota's first printer and Samuel Irvin and William Hamilton printed the first book in Kansas.[202] Another Scot, Thomas Stenhouse, founded the *Salt Lake Telegraph.*[203]

In predominantly English Georgia an influx of Scotch-Irish pioneers barged in from North Carolina and Tennessee. They were proud, pushy, outspoken, and began to take over things with their hard work. Their own Scottish word *cracker*, a person who boasts, was used against them as an ethnic slur. Now all Georgians are proud to call themselves crackers.[204] The Erie Canal, which played so great a role in opening the West and in making New York America's primary city, was begun in 1817 under its Scottish chief engineer, James Geddes.[205]

Many of the fabulous frontier heroes were of Scottish descent. Daniel Boone (1734–1820), born in Pennsylvania of Ulster Scottish ancestry, was a frontiersman who established the first permanent settlement in Kentucky, at Boonesboro, in 1775. His adventures included the rescue of his daughter and two other girls who had been kidnapped by Indians. Boone was himself twice captured and twice escaped, and in 1778 he was adopted as a son by Blackfish, the chief of the Shawnees.[206]

James "Jim" Bowie (1796–1836) was born in Kentucky of Scottish anecestry. He either invented or popularized the Bowie knife. As a young man he operated a sugar mill in Louisiana, where he introduced steam power, and in New Orleans he learned to speak Spanish and French. About 1828 he went to Texas, receiving land grants from the Mexican governor and marrying his daughter. Bowie joined in the Texas revolution and died defending the Alamo, contesting the leadership of the corps with William Travis.[207]

Christopher "Kit" Carson (1809–1868) was born in Kentucky, the grandson of a Scottish immigrant who had passed through northern Ireland. He had no education and ran away at age fifteen to Taos, where he became a professional frontiersman, Indian agent, and explorer. He was a guide to Gen. Stephen W. Kearney's army in the Mexican War, saving it on one occasion by slipping past the enemy to summon reinforcements. Despite his illiteracy, Carson was made a brigadier general during the Civil War.[208]

David "Davy" Crockett (1786–1836) was born in Tennessee of Scottish ancestry and fought in the Creek War from 1813 to 1815. Even though he had almost no formal education he was elected to the Tennessee state legislature in 1821 and to the United States Congress in 1823, where he became famous for speeches filled with humorous backwoods phrases. Defeated in the election of 1835, he went to Texas to join the American forces and was slaughtered with the rest of his countrymen at the Alamo in 1836.[209]

There were also a number of Scottish Indian chiefs. One of these, Alexander McGillivray, was head of the Creek nation. His father had come from the Isle of Mull and his uncle, a Presbyterian minister, was a member of the St. Andrew's Society of Charleston. McGillivray, whose mother was part Indian, was a brilliant autocrat wielding great power. He negotiated a treaty for the Creeks with President Washington, which was signed in an elaborate Indian ceremony, the last official act of the United States government with New York as capital.[210] Since that time the chiefs of the Creek nation have been McIntoshes and are descended from another Scottish immigrant, who married a Creek princess.

In 1964 the Indian chief McIntosh and the Scottish chief of the Clan Mackintosh posed at the Mackintosh clan gathering in Scotland, each in his full regalia. This ceremony has since been repeated at Highland games in America.[211] With all of these chiefs it is interesting to know that Mackintosh (*Mac an Toiseach*) means "son of the chief" in Gaelic. John Fleming, whose parents were born in Scotland, was the first to put the Creek language into writing.[212]

Chief Lismahago, of the Badger tribe, was born Robert Stobo in Glasgow. He was the designer of Washington's Fort Necessity and when it fell he was taken hostage to Fort Duquesne, where he was able to smuggle out a plan of its defensive positions, which was helpful to his British comrades.[213]

The Scots also have a deep involvement with the Cherokees, who, as the most progressive of all the American tribes, were able to advance from the wilderness to civilization in only one hundred years. In 1740 William Shorey, a Scottish immigrant, married Ghigoo-ie, a Cherokee woman. Their daughter, Annie Shorey, married John McDonald of Inverness. Their daughter, Mollie McDonald, married Daniel Ross of Sutherland, whose son was John Ross (1790–1866). Seven-eighths Scottish, with blue eyes and blond hair, John Ross (Kooweskoowe) was the greatest Cherokee chief. He ruled the Cherokees for thirty-eight years, during which time they became the first Indians to receive formal education and the first to develop their own alphabet. On the two hundredth anniversary of the birth of John Ross a monument to his memory was erected at Talequah, in Cherokee County, Oklahoma.[214] In 1981 the *Ethnic*

Almanac reported a definite tribal descent for fourteen famous Americans. Eleven were Cherokees.[215] And in 1994 the *New York Times* reported that President Bill Clinton had inherited Cherokee blood from his mother.[216]

It appears that many Americans, from the very beginning, had planned for their country to span the continent, and in the first half of the nineteenth century the new nation acquired what is now more than three-quarters of its present territory. Scottish-American soldiers, politicians, and diplomats continued to be responsible for every acquisition, all the way to Hawaii.

In 1801 Thomas Jefferson, in his first year as president, plotted the course to the West Coast by conceiving and promoting the famous expedition of Lewis and Clark. This venture, which returned in 1806 with a wealth of diaries and data, was comanaged by William Clark, the younger brother of soldier George Rogers Clark.

In 1803 Jefferson sent two men to Paris to try to make the Louisiana Purchase. The first to go was Robert R. Livingston, who had sworn in Washington as president. Later he was reinforced by James Monroe, another Scot who would later become president himself. Although they had no authorization, nor any specific instructions, they struck an awesome bargain with the French. Napoleon acknowledged that the trade made the United States a power "forever." Livingston recognized the transaction as his life's "noblest work," and predicted, "from this day the United States take their place among the powers of the first rank." Livingston and Monroe had paid only fifteen million dollars for all of what are now the states of Louisiana, Arkansas, Missouri, Iowa, Nebraska, and most of Oklahoma, Kansas, Colorado, Wyoming, Minnesota, the Dakotas, and Montana.[217] It seems as if the two Scottish-Americans "stole" Louisiana from France, but perhaps there was some justice in it. After all, it was a Scot, the financial wizard John Law who had founded New Orleans in 1718 and promoted Louisiana in the first place.[218]

Livingston continued his efforts in land acquisition when he informed the next president, James Madison, that Spain had ceded West Florida to France in 1800, and it was therefore part of the Louisiana Purchase. As a result, Madison claimed the area.[219] In 1818 the Scotch-Irish fighter Andrew Jackson captured Pensacola, and James Monroe, now president, was able to get Spain to cede all of Florida to the United States the following year.[220]

Most of the rest of the country was acquired during the presidency of another Scotch-Irish Presbyterian, James Knox Polk. Despite a backwoods background and a total lack of formal elementary schooling, at the University of North Carolina he had been the best scholar in his class. Polk actually became president because of his outspoken stance favoring the annexation of Texas and the Oregon country while his rivals straddled or avoided these issues. His campaign slogan was "fifty-four forty or fight!" referring to the latitude of his proposed boundary for the northwestern corner of the United States. In 1845, the first year of his administration, the United States annexed Texas and admitted it to the Union.[221]

The heroes of the Texas Revolution had been mostly Scots. In 1836 the inspiring defense of the Alamo at San Antonio began under the command of Col. Jim Bowie, whose martyred contingent of 189 men included at least 50 Scottish-Americans. Among these were the famous frontiersman Davy Crockett and four native Scots, including bagpiper John McGregor.[222]

The commander in chief of the Texan army was Sam Houston, Scottish on both sides of his ancestry.[223] Houston, who had been governor of Tennessee but left the position to live with the Cherokee Indians, defeated the Mexican army under Santa Ana at the Battle of San Jacinto in 1836, thus winning the independence of Texas. He became president of the republic of Texas the same year, succeeding another Scottish-American, David Burnet.[224] After Texas was admitted to the United States, Houston served Texas as governor—the only man ever to be governor of two different states.

The beginning of the Texas cattle industry was enhanced by the 1,000-mile Chisholm Trail, over which millions of animals were driven northward to the railhead at Abilene, Kansas. The first 220 miles of trail was blazed through the wilderness by the half-Scot, half-Cherokee Jesse Chisholm, the representative of several Indian tribes in their dealings with the government. Chisholm spoke six Indian languages.[225]

The two largest population centers in Texas are both named for Scottish-Americans. Houston, of course, is named to honor Sam Houston, while Dallas is named for George Mifflin Dallas, vice president under Polk.[226] When it opened in 1888, the Texas state capitol was the seventh largest building in the world. It was built by Scottish architects and stone masons.[227]

Not content with acquiring Texas, President Polk acted aggressively to obtain the rest of the West. In 1846 he declared war on Mexico and sent troops to occupy California and New Mexico, while others began an invasion south of the Rio Grande. An early victory occurred on July 9, when the Scottish-American captain John B. Montgomery sailed the sloop *Portsmouth* into San Francisco Bay, raised the American flag in what is now Portsmouth Plaza, and claimed the territory for the United States.[228]

But most of the initial results of the Mexican campaign disappointed Polk, who then ordered the Scottish-American general Winfield Scott, the grandson of a veteran of Culloden,[229] to take command. In March 1847, Scott landed an army at the port of Veracruz and captured it after a siege of three weeks. On September 14 he entered Mexico City, effectively ending the war with astonishing speed. The Duke of Wellington called Scott's campaign brilliant.[230]

In early 1848 the United States and Mexico signed a treaty under which Mexico received fifteen million dollars in exchange for all or part of what are now the states of California, New Mexico, Colorado, Utah, Arizona, Wyoming, and Nevada.

In 1846 Polk effectively made good on his campaign slogan, as Britain ceded what are now the states of Washington, Oregon, Idaho, and parts of Montana and Wyoming to his government. His Scotch-Irish secretary of state, James Buchanan, negotiated with the British, settling the border between Canada and the United States at the 49th parallel, as it remains today.[231]

James Knox Polk was an extraordinary, if little known, president. He founded the U.S. Naval Academy, authorized the Smithsonian Institution, and created the Department of the Interior. During his administration the United States acquired over one-third of its present territory and spanned the continent. Three months after leaving office, James Knox Polk died at the age of fifty-four, apparently from exhaustion.[232]

By the end of the Polk administration, fleets of Conestoga wagons were creaking through the wide prairie as Americans by the thousands poured into the West. Many of the more interesting participants were of Scottish ancestry. Alexander McNair was the first governor of Missouri[233] and Alexander Ramsey the first governor of the Minnesota Territory.[234] Judging by his middle name and the names of his immediate ancestors,[235] Zebulon Montgomery Pike, an army officer who discovered Pike's Peak in 1806, appears to have been of Scottish ancestry.

Elley Orum, "Queen of the Comstock Lode," was born in the Highlands. She made a million dollars in the Nevada gold rush of the 1850s, spent it all and went broke, only to win back her mansion in a raffle![236] Law and order were maintained on one part of the frontier by the famous marshall of Dodge City, Wyatt Earp, who was of Scottish ancestry.[237] Both the good guys and the bad guys used the famous 45-caliber revolvers made by Samuel Colt, who was Scottish on both sides.[238] And recent excavations at Arizona's Fort Apache turned up old stone bottles which once contained McEwen's Ale, imported from Edinburgh.[239]

Large amounts of Scottish capital funded the expansion of the West. In fact, there is evidence to suggest that more capital was obtained in tiny Scotland than in any other country. By 1890 as much as two hundred million dollars had been invested in cattle, land, mining, and railroads—fifty dollars for every person in Scotland. In addition, Scottish mortgage and investment companies, made loans to thousands of American farmers.[240]

One company, the Scottish American Investment Trust, founded in 1873 in Dundee by Robert Fleming, channeled money into cattle ranches, fruit farms, mining companies, and railways, mainly in Arizona, Nevada and Texas. The largest cattle ranch in America, the Matador Land and Cattle Company, was run out of Dundee until 1951.[241] The Swan Land and Cattle Company, sold in Edinburgh in 1882 by Alexander Swan, stayed in Scottish control until 1925.[242]

Dr. John McLoughlin, the "Father of Oregon," was born in Canada of Scottish descent.[243] Fur traders from the heavily-Scottish North West Company established the trading post that became Spokane, Washington.[244] One of the founders of Portland, Oregon, was Captain William Irving of Annan, Dumfriesshire.[245] The famous Oregon Trail, traveled from Missouri to the Pacific by tens of thousands of settlers, was first traversed by the Scottish-born Robert Stuart, who discovered the south pass through the mountains in 1812. Traveling eastward, he reached St. Louis on April 30, 1813, and was hailed as a new Lewis or Clark. Later, he built the first brick house in Detroit.[246]

Only fifty Scots lived in Hispanic California, but they became prominent. John Gilroy (born Cameron) was the first non-Spanish or Indian resident of California, after having been "left" at Monterey in 1814. Gilroy, California, now the "garlic capital of the world," is named for him. Mary Anderson was the first "foreign" woman in California, and with George Kinlock parented the first "foreign" child, George David Kinlock.[247]

Hugh Reid, born in Scotland and a former Cambridge student, became the Scottish *paisano* (fellow countryman) when he came to

Los Angeles in 1834. After marrying the daughter of an Indian chief he opened a store and a boy's school, and became a member of the Los Angeles City Council, styling himself Don Perfecto Hugo Reid. He acquired the huge Rancho Santa Anita, comprising about one-half of present-day Pasadena and including the site of the Santa Anita racetrack and Hugo Reid Park, in what is now Arcadia, California.

In 1849 Reid was one of forty-eight members of the California State Convention, and spent the last two years of his life, having lost most of his fortune, writing an account of the Gabrieleño Indians, his wife's tribe. The Reids' adobe house (c. 1840) was rebuilt as an official state landmark in 1961.[248] Don Jaime McYntoch was the *alcalde* (mayor) of Sonoma and San Rafael. David Spence, a Scottish sailor, was several times *alcalde* of Monterey, and John Sinclair was *alcalde* of Sacramento. The merchant firm of Scott and Wilson was the most prominent in Santa Barbara.[249]

In 1848 James Wilson Marshall, a Scottish immigrant, discovered gold at Sutter's Mill, creating the California gold rush of 1849, which led to a fantastic increase in population.[250] By 1873 another Scot, Andrew Halladie, had introduced his cable cars to San Francisco, where they remain the symbol of the city to this day.[251]

The last territorial addition to the lower forty-eight states was made in 1853, when Secretary of War Jefferson Davis, of Scottish descent on his mother's side,[252] advocated the purchase of the southern parts of Arizona and New Mexico. A surveying error at the end of the Mexican War had cost the United States this land and Davis felt it was an important route for a transcontinental railroad. He was right. From El Paso, Texas, to California, the Southern Pacific Railroad runs entirely through the Gadsden Purchase today.

Alaska was bought from Russia in 1867 under the administration of another Scots-blooded president, Andrew Johnson. And another Scot, L. N. McQueston, called the father of Alaska, built the first settlement on the Yukon in 1879 and later owned a saloon and trading post at Circle City that grubstaked many prospectors in the gold rush.[253]

Hawaii, which had been discovered by the Anglo-Scottish Captain Cook in 1778, had henceforth been claimed by Britain. But Daniel Webster, the American secretary of state, who was of Scottish descent,[254] paved the way for the annexation of the island kingdom when he formally recognized its independence in 1843. There were many colorful Scots in Hawaii's early history. Archibald Campbell, a

Scottish sailor, arrived in 1809 and stayed to become King Ka-mehameha's sail maker. He was probably the first teacher in the islands and wrote an English-Hawaiian vocabulary.

There were also Scottish engineers, agriculturalists, scientists, doctors, and government officials, many of whom advised the Hawaiian monarchy. The most famous was Archibald Scott Cleghorn, a successful merchant who married Princess Likelike, King Kalakaua's sister, and who fathered Kaiulani, Hawaii's most beautiful and revered princess. Cleghorn's skill as a landscape artist can still be seen in Kapiolani Park in Waikiki and at the Royal Iolani Palace.[255]

Archibald Menzies (1754–1842), a surgeon and botanist, was probably the first person, certainly the first *haole* (white person), to climb 14,000-foot Mauna Loa. His feat stood unchallenged for forty-one years, when it was equalled by another Scot, David Douglas. Menzies imported and planted the seeds for most of the species of Hawaiian orange trees. Nineteen varieties of Hawaiian flora are named after him.[256]

In 1864 Eliza Hutchinson Sinclair (1803–1895), a native of Scotland, bought the island of Niihau. It is still privately owned by her descendants and is called the forbidden island. There are no tele-phones, and only island-born people are permitted to live there. Those who marry non-Hawaiians are banished. The two hundred residents still speak the Hawaiian language and practice native customs along with Christianity. Mrs. Sinclair's descendants are treated like gods.[257] James Campbell (1826–1900; Kimo-ona-milliona, or James the millionaire) was born in Londonderry of Scotch-Irish parentage. He was a leading figure in the development of the Hawaiian sugar cane industry and brought in the first artesian well there. During his illustrious career he talked cannibals out of eating him and San Francisco kidnappers out of shooting him.[258]

The first newspaper in Hawaii, the Sandwich Island *Gazette and Journal of Commerce* (1836–1839), was produced by Samuel Mackin-tosh.[259] Between 1845 and 1865 Robert Crichton Wyllie, a Scot,[260] served as minister of foreign affairs of Hawaii and guided her destiny towards the United States. Finally in 1898, under the Scotch-Irish-American president William McKinley, the Hawaiian Islands were annexed and the territory making up the fifty United States as we know it today was geographically completed.

In 1903 President Theodore Roosevelt achieved some sort of vindication for a Scottish ancestor, Rev. Alex Stobo,[261] a survivor of the Darien debacle, when he acquired the Canal Zone and began to direct the building of the Panama Canal. The first chief engineer on the project was the Scottish John Findlay Wallace.[262] The spirit of the "manifest destiny" of the American people had reached its high point.

We could, of course, go on. Several writers often cited here, George F. Black, Charles A. Hanna, and William A. Taylor, have done so, naming dozens of American Supreme Court justices, cabinet members, senators, and governors of Scottish descent who have made their marks. They have identified hundreds of counties and thousands of towns in America which bear Scottish names. To go into such detail in this book is not practical, but more information is provided in the appendices at the end.

In 1990 the U.S. Bureau of the Census issued a report on ethnic background which showed that eleven million, or 4.4 percent of the 249 million Americans claimed either Scottish or Scotch-Irish ancestry.[263] In the first census taken in 1790 the figure was 6.7 percent.[264] Although higher estimates have been made at various times, these are the official figures and it is clear that the Scots in America are now and have always been a very small minority.

Yet, as we have seen, it was Americans of Scottish birth and descent who, more often than not, played major roles in the creation of the United States. The land was originally colonized by the design of a Scottish king, and was usually administered by Scottish governors, at least south of New England. Scottish merchants contributed heavily to the colonial economy and were so successful that they were sometimes persecuted. Scots promoted literacy and were the pioneer printers in many places. They founded four of the first six major American colleges, all of the first three medical schools, and many other institutions.

Scottish philosophy motivated the American Revolution and Scottish fighting men played a major part in delivering it. The Declaration of Independence and the Constitution were largely the work of Scots and drew heavily on antecedent Scottish documents and of the experience of Scottish Presbyterians, with their tiers of democracy.

At the beginning of the western trek, Scottish colonial soldiers were the principal defenders of the English-speaking settlers, the better part of whom were Scottish and Scotch-Irish, and together they established an irrefutable claim to the American West. All of the land of postcolonial America was acquired by soldiers, diplomats, and statesmen of Scottish ancestry.

The first president and his entire cabinet were all men of Scottish ancestry, and since that beginning more than three-quarters of the American presidents have had at least some Scottish blood.[265] Since people of Scottish ancestry make up only 4.4 percent of the American population they are thus overrepresented in the presidency more than seventeen times. Except for six months in 1881, all of the presidents from 1865 through 1928, from the Civil War through the Roaring Twenties, had Scottish ancestry. During this period of unprecedented prosperity the population quadrupled. No wonder the band plays the old Scottish song "Hail to the Chief" when the president arrives!

During the War of 1812 a man named Sam Wilson, whose parents had come from Greenock, lived in Troy, New York, where he operated a food business. One of his customers was the U.S. Army, and when he shipped beef to the troops he stamped "U.S." on the barrels. Sam Wilson's workers gently derided their employer and called these barrels Uncle Sam's beef. The soldiers receiving it, however, did not know Sam Wilson and thought Uncle Sam was new slang for the United States government. The world has used the name ever since. But it is fitting that we perpetuate this error. Uncle Sam is not usually thought of as being particularly Scottish, but he surely is.[266]

"Perhaps the moon is shining for you in a far country,
  But the skies there are not island skies.
You will not remember the salt smell of the sea,
  And the little rain."
—*Agnes Muir Mackenzie (1891–1955), Scottish author*

4

The Construction of the British Empire

Time and distance are measured from the London borough of Greenwich, a fact which indicates the nineteenth-century world's acquiescence in the domination of the British Empire, the largest and grandest in history. But this acknowledgment of the achievements of the Britons, brought about in 1884 by the international agreement creating Standard Time, was not the work of an Englishman, as might be supposed, but as was so often the case, the initiative of an enterprising Scot, in this case Sir Sandford Fleming.

Although the rise of the British Empire is coincident with England's amalgamation with Scotland, the Scots cannot claim to have been the empire's builders, despite their greatly disproportionate contributions. Empires are developed by powerful nations with profound cultures such as England's, not by small countries like Scotland, which before the union had demonstrated an inability to plant even one successful colony on its own.[1]

While it is overreaching, therefore, to refer to the Scottish Empire, as some patriotic writers have done, it is nevertheless clearly appropriate to contend that without the participation of the Scots the empire could not have been constructed. As the Arabs relied on their Jewish minority for unique but essential contributions to the Muslim Empire, so the English relied on the Scots.

The nineteenth-century English statesman Sir Charles Dilke wrote, "In British settlements from Canada to Ceylon, from Dunedin to Bombay, for every Englishman that you meet who has worked himself up to wealth from small beginnings without external aid, you find ten Scotchmen.[2]

In effect, the British Empire was, founded by a Scot, the same James Stewart of Edinburgh who, as King James I, should also be given credit as the founder of English-speaking America. When James ascended the English throne in 1603 there were no British colonies anywhere. At the end of his reign, only twenty-two years later, the British Empire was well established with plantations operating or underway in northern Ireland, Nova Scotia, New England, Virginia, Bermuda, Newfoundland, Guiana, the East Indies, and India.[3] James was the interested promoter of all the early colonial schemes, and their success is in no small part due to his policies and encouragement. In 1613 he even became the first king to write a letter to the emperor of Japan.[4] With remarkable prescience, James also observed that his fellow Scots were particularly well suited for the business of planting colonies.

When James was crowned in Westminster Abbey in 1603 he became the first King of Scots in over three centuries to sit upon the ancient coronation stone, the sacred Lia Fail, the Stone of Destiny. Legend suggests the Lia Fail is Jacob's pillow carried by the prehistoric Scots in their wanderings through Egypt, Spain, Ireland, and finally to Scone, in Perthshire. It was at Scone that all their kings were crowned upon the stone until 1296, when the English king Edward I stole it and removed it to England, placing it under the coronation chair. In his rage at the independent-minded Scots, Edward (the Hammer of the Scots) is said to have had a prophecy erased from the stone, which in Latin read:[5]

> Ni fallat vatum,
> Scoti hunc quocunque locatum,
> Invenient lapidem,
> Regnare tenentur ibidem.

This is from an earlier oracular verse in Gaelic:

> Cinnidh Scuit saor am fine,
> Mur breug am faistine,
> Far am faighear an Lia-Fail,
> Dlighe flaitheas do ghabhail.

Or as it was rhymed in English by Sir Walter Scott:

> "Unless the prophets faithless be,
> And Seer's words be vain,
> Where'er is found this sacred stone,
> The Scottish race shall reign."

As the prophecy predicts, the royalty of the Scottish race has followed the stone, and through James and his descendants continues to reign over England, as it has over the British Empire and Commonwealth from their beginnings to the present.

The Scots in England

The Scots have never had a large presence in England owing, in early times, to almost constant warfare and serious prejudices between the two nations, and to better opportunities for Scots overseas in the modern era.

As early as A.D. 973 Kenneth, King of Scots, was given a palace in London for use on his visits to England, and the land on which it stood is still called Scotland Yard. But as late as 1567 the total population of Scots in London was only forty souls. By 1571 even that number had been reduced to thirty-two.[6]

English prejudice against the Scots is recorded as early as the thirteenth century in the *Chronicle of Lanercost*, which calls the Scots "deceitful," a "perfidious race," and "madmen." Even Shakespeare contributed:

> "For once the eagle England being in prey,
> To her unguarded nest the Weasel Scot
> Comes sneaking and so sucks her princely eggs,"
>
> —*King Henry V, Act I, scene 2*

With the accession of King James to the English throne in 1603, Scots began to come to England in significant numbers for the first time, many invited by the founder and self-styled king of Great Britain (the latter term one which James was the first to use).[7] Soon London was aswarm with hard-working Scots[8] who took over a great deal of economic activity while keeping to their own. By 1611 the "Scots Box" for the relief of the "poor brethren" had been established in London.[9] The more formal Royal Scottish Corporation succeeded the Scots Box in 1665, and still distributes twenty-two thousand pounds to ditressed Scots annually.[10]

A wave of racial prejudice swept against the immigrating Scots[11] and by the eighteenth century it had developed into hatred. Leading the anti-Scottish attack was one John Wilkes, whose paper, "The North Briton," questioned the loyalty of all Scots, even the first Scottish prime minister, Lord Bute, who held the office in 1762. To the average Englishman the Scots appeared to be "growing fat at the expense of their neighbors, the suspicious clannishness of the Scots was constantly referred to, and the partiality of Scot for Scot was now seen at work in the highest levels of the country's political life."[12]

In *Old England*, an anonymous author wrote, "The Scots have poured in upon us like swarms of locusts... The Army abounds with them, in unequal Proportions to our own Countrymen... and even the Law, which used to be pretty clear of them, begins to abound with dissonant notes... And where there is any thing to be got you may be sure to find a number of Scotchmen conven'd, like hounds over a Carrion, or Flies in a Shambles."[13]

It appears that John Gay, the English author of *The Beggar's Opera*, chose the name of his thievish leading man, MacHeath, as an ethnic slur. And Charles Lamb wrote in an essay:

"Are you a Jew?"

"No; I am one of your imperfect sympathies—a Scotsman."[14]

Even Swift and Johnson joined in the chorus against the Scots.[15] Boswell, of course, converted Johnson in the end by taking him to Scotland, but he was so upset by the anti-Scottish prejudice which he himself felt in London (he had heard shouts of "No Scots! No Scots! Out with them!" at Covent Garden) that he became a sort of one-man Anti-Defamation League. Boswell is the apparent author of a pamphlet published in Philadelphia in 1769 defending the Scots.[16] There is no doubt that prejudice was a factor that led Scots to emigrate elsewhere instead of to England, where they have always been a tiny minority among their Saxon neighbors. In 1921 they amounted to only one percent of the population of the London Administrative County.[17] Today the Scots in England number in the millions, but still remain a small minority.[18] Nevertheless, they have left their mark on the country.

SCOTS AND THE POLITICS OF ENGLAND AND GREAT BRITAIN

By 1762 John Stuart, the earl of Bute, had become the first Scottish prime minister. But his nationality caused riots in London, and until

1868 the only other prime ministers to have Scottish blood were the earl of Aberdeen and William Pitt, the latter being only one-eighth Scottish. However, for the next hundred years, ten different Scots and part-Scots occupied 10 Downing Street most of the time—about sixty-seven years.[19]

One of these, William Ewart Gladstone, was the greatest British statesman of the nineteenth century, the height of the empire. Although born in Liverpool, Gladstone was of purely Scottish ancestry. He served a record sixty-one years in the House of Commons and is the only man to have been prime minister four times, having been chosen for his last term at age eighty-two.

Another Scot, Sir Henry Campbell-Bannerman, had the distinction of being the first constitutionally recognized prime minister.[20] Churchill, the defender of Western civilization in the 1940s, was remotely Scottish on his mother's side.[21] His wife, born Clementine Hozier, was a descendant of Scottish nobility.[22]

In the century-and-a-quarter between 1756 and 1880 three Scots, Lord Mansfield, John Campbell, and Alexander Cockburn held the post of lord chief justice more than half the time.[23] In 1987 Lord Mackay of Clashfern (James P. H. Mackay), the son of a Scottish railwayman, was appointed lord chancellor, the head of the British judiciary.[24] He succeeded several other Scots in that august post: Alexander Wedderburn (1793–1801); Thomas Erskine (1806–1807); Henry Brougham (1830–1834); John Campbell (1859–1861); Hugh McCalmont Cairns (1868; 1874–1880); Robert Threshie Reid (1905–1912); Richard Burdon Haldane (1912–1915; 1924); Robert Bannatyne Finlay (1916–1918); and David Patrick Maxwell (1954–1962).[25]

The British Labour party was effectively founded by two Scots, Kier Hardie, the first Labour member of Parliament, and Cunninghame Graham.[26] Ramsay MacDonald was the first Labour prime minister. John Anderson (Viscount Waverley) was perhaps the last Independent to be in a cabinet (Churchill's).[27] Wallis Warfield Simpson, a woman of Scottish descent,[28] almost brought down the British government when she decided to marry the king in 1936, causing the monarchy's only abdication.

In the 1980s the heads of all three opposition parties were Scots. Labour was headed by Neil Gordon Kinnock, whose great-grandparents migrated from Scotland to Wales,[29] while the Liberals were led by David Steel, a Lowlander.[30] Robert Adam Ross Maclellan was the leader of the Social Democrats.[31] In 1992 Labour chose still another Scot, John Smith, as its leader. Smith built a commanding lead in the polls but died suddenly, in 1994, at the age of fifty-five.[32] The Labour party's response to this tragedy was to select yet another leader with a Scottish name, Tony Blair.[33]

SCOTS AND ENGLISH EDUCATION

In 1263 Devorguilla Balliol of Scotland founded the famous Balliol College at Oxford, only fourteen years after University College, giving Scotland one-half share in England's oldest university at that time.[34] Seven centuries later businessman-philanthropist Sir Isaac Wolfson (1897–1991), born in Glasgow to a Jewish immigrant cabinet-maker, became the second Scot to found a college at Oxford.[35] Scots have always been overrepresented in English education. By the eighteenth century, for instance, the four best private medical schools in England were all run by Scots: William Cullen's School for Internal Medicine; Joseph Black's School for Chemistry; William Smellie's School for Obstetrics, and William Hunter's School for Anatomy and Surgery.[36]

London University was founded in 1828 by two Scots, Thomas Campbell[37] and Henry Brougham (Lord Brougham)[38] on the model of a Scottish university. The London School of Economics was founded by the Fabians, which were, in turn, founded by Thomas Davidson, the illegitimate son of a Scottish shepherd.[39]

In 1924 A. S. Neill (Alexander Sutherland Neill) founded the influential Summerhill School in England, where children were allowed to develop at their own pace. His system was revolutionary and far-reaching, and still provokes controversy.[40]

SCOTS AND ENGLISH RELIGION

A Scot, King James I, is the first person mentioned in most English Bibles, as he was the promoter of the scholarly project which translated the Bible into a style which could be understood by ordinary people. The result is a jewel of the English language, The King James Version. The Scots have had a very large effect on the Church of England, even though fewer than 2 percent of their people are Episcopalians. Since 1868 four Scots have been archbishop of Canterbury, holding this highest Anglican position more than half the time:

Archibald Campbell Tait (1868–1882)[41]
Randall Thomas Davidson (1903–1928)[42]
Cosmo Gordon Lang (1928–1942)[43]
Robert Alexander Kennedy Runcie (1980–1991)[44]

George Basil Cardinal Hume, at this writing the archbishop of Westminster and head of the English Roman Catholic church, is the grandson of an Edinburgh physician.[45] Coventry Cathedral, destroyed by the Germans in World War II, was rebuilt on the design of a Scot, Sir Basil Spence, and decorated with the seventy-foot-high tapestry of another, Graham Sutherland.[46]

MISCELLANY

Since the Union of 1707 the English have relied upon the Scots for talent in many fields, from the legions of Scottish "nannies" who raised so great a part of their aristocracy, to the Scottish Queen Mother who produced their second Elizabeth, the monarch with the most British ancestry of any since 1625. Lady Diana's Highland ancestry has added more Scottish blood to the royal family.

England has obtained from Scotland much of its most important engineering. London Bridge, built from 1824 to 1831, was designed by John Rennie, who also built the Waterloo, Lambeth, and Southwark bridges.[47] Rennie and his sons also constructed the London and East India docks in London, as well as docks in Leith, Plymouth, Liverpool, Dublin, and Portsmouth.[48] Blackfriar's Bridge was built by Robert Mylne, of Edinburgh.[49] The steelwork for the London Tower Bridge is the work of Sir William Arrol, who also constructed the Tay Bridge and the famous Forth Bridge in his native Scotland.[50]

The notoriously poor roads of Great Britain in the mid-1700s were vastly improved by the work of two Scots. The first was Thomas Telford, who was orphaned from his shepherd father at age one. Telford built roads, bridges, and canals all over Britain and in 1820 became the first president of what is now the Institution of Civil Engineers. John Loudon McAdam emigrated to New York in 1770 and in 1783 returned to Scotland with a fortune.[51] There, at his own expense, he developed a system of repairing roads which led to his becoming general supervisor of roads in Great Britain. From this position he paved the streets of London, Edinburgh, and Dublin, along with hundreds of miles of highways, with the smooth waterproof surface which is still called macadam after him in France and elsewhere. It is now usually referred to as *tarmac* (after "tar-macadam") in America.[52]

In later years Sir Patrick Abercrombie was the "architect" of the Greater London Plan.[53] Owing to the work of two Britons of Scottish ancestry, the centuries-old dream of a tunnel between England and France has become reality. Sir Alistair Morton is the chairman of the Channel Tunnel Group Limited, which since 1987, raised the billons necessary to fund the project. Colin Kirkland, who has been associated with the tunnel scheme since the 1950s, is its technical director.[54]

In subsequent chapters there will be discussions of many more Scots in England whose success in business, the military, science, the arts, and literature has gone far beyond what would be expected of a small minority. Even in symbols the Scottish presence has tended to be authoritative since the early days of the Union. The colloquial name "limey," by which Englishmen are known all over the world, is due to the reputation of British seamen for drinking lime juice, a practice instituted by two Scottish naval physicians, Sir Gilbert Blane and James Lind, in the interest of preventing scurvy.[55] The model for Britannia on British pennies was Frances Stuart (La Belle Stuart), granddaughter of Lord Blantyre.[56] And "Rule Britannia," that confident hymn to the glory of the empire, was written by a Scottish poet, James Thomson.[57]

The Scots in Ireland

"I love Highlanders and I love Lowlanders, but when I come to the branch of our race that has been grafted on to the Ulster stem, I take my hat off in veneration and awe."

—*Lord Roseberry, prime minister of Great Britain*
(1894–1895)[58]

It is difficult to see how, through the dark mists of the industrial and spiritual malaise of modern Northern Ireland, any present-day British statesman could be moved to salute anything in that unhappy province except, perhaps, the almost heroic determination of its people to survive. But near the end of the nineteenth-century, at the time of Lord Roseberry, the northeastern part of Ireland was a great success story and enjoyed "a record prosperity quite unlike anything shewn" by the rest of the island.[59] The industrialization of

Ulster was accomplished largely by Scots in the face of the great hostility "of the native population, and the jealous tyranny of the English government."[60]

Only a dozen miles separate the coast of Ireland from the Mull of Kintyre, in Argyll. Since long before historical times people have been traveling between the two countries. In the early Christian era the movement was largely from Ireland to the north, and resulted in the founding of Scotland by the eponymous Ulster race, the Scots. By the fourteenth century this tide had reversed and the powerful Clan Donald was sending settlers from the Scottish Isles to tend the glens of Antrim and Down.

Then, in the early seventeenth century, the English government in Ireland set out to break the Irish clans through a variety of trumped-up charges and legal tricks. First, in direct contravention of Ireland's ancient Brehon Laws, they claimed that the property rights of the clan chiefs were absolute and that the clansmen had no permanent tenure. Then they ruled that if a chief were found to be a traitor all his lands were forfeit, a scenario which would leave the clansmen on the land as mere intruders. All the English needed then was a charge of treason, and this they concocted with forged "evidence" against Ulster's two most prominent chiefs, the O'Neill earl of Tyrone and the O'Donnell earl of Tir Conaill. The earls, recognizing the un-tenability of their situation, fled to the Continent in 1607.

The Irish still lament the Flight of the Earls, as their departure changed Ireland forever and destroyed her ancient heritage. Their absence was treated as a confession of their "treason," their estates were forfeit, and their clansmen became, as the English lawyers had ordained, "illegal" occupants on their ancestors' lands. In this disgraceful manner the native people of Ulster were deprived of their birthrights and their homeland was made available for exploitation.[61]

In this, its darkest hour, the government of King James I, in 1609, then moved to "plant" the vacated Ulster estates with Britons, the large majority of whom were Scots. Despite a poor start, the colonization of Ulster became successful under the direction of two Scots, Hugh Montgomerie and James Hamilton,[62] and by 1641 there were over one hundred thousand Scots and twenty thousand English settlers in the north of Ireland.[63] Not surprisingly, these mostly Presbyterian intruders met with hostility from the native Irish Catholics, an animosity which carries on today.

Many, if not most of the Scotch-Irish, left Ulster for America after a short sojourn, but some stayed to become the founders of the province's spectacular nineteenth-century industrialization. John Barbour, of Paisley, began the modern Irish-linen industry. Ulster's cotton industry was started by William and John Orr and Robert Gemmill, and her chemical industry by Francis Home.[64]

The Scots in Ireland, as elsewhere, have pursued their interest in education. In 1911 Presbyterians had the lowest rate of illiteracy in all counties of northern Ireland, a rate about half that of Episcopalians and about one-third that of Catholics.[65]

When the province separated from Ireland in 1920 the first prime minister was Edinburgh-educated James Craig, whose tenure lasted until 1940.[66] In the late twentieth-century Northern Ireland retains a Scottish presence, despite considerable assimilation. The Presbyterian church claims 29 percent of the population as members.[67] In fact, a Presbyterian minister with the doubly Scottish name of Ian Paisley has been the usual spokesman for the Unionists who resist integration into Ireland.

The marvelous achievement of the Ulster Scots in industrializing Northern Ireland is now remembered by few, and in view of the economic deterioration there seems almost irrelevant, amidst the violence and hatred of the present day. The situation begs for a dynamic leader to overcome the bigoted legacy of social, political, ethnic, and religious conflict. But while the Scotch-Irish branch has yielded American presidents of quality, such as Jackson, Polk, Wilson, and Truman, it has not yet been able to produce a redeemer in its homeland. Awaiting such deliverance, the ugly mood of Ulster has been seen scrawled on a wall:

> "Then it's down with the future,
> And up with the past,
> May the Lord in His mercy,
> Be kind to Belfast."

The Scots in Canada

> "From the lone shieling of the misty island,
> Mountains divide us, and the waste of seas;
> Yet still the blood is strong, the heart is Highland,
> As we in dreams behold the Hebrides:
> Fair these broad meads, the hoary woods are grand;
> But we are exiles from our fathers' land."
>
> —*David Macbeth Moir (1798–1851), Scottish poet.*[68]

No words have ever better expressed the nostalgic, resigned feeling of the Scottish immigrant than those just quoted. They must have seemed particularly pertinent in the vast wilderness of Canada, retained by Britain at the end of the American Revolution. This place, situated in a difficult environment, thinly populated by a suspicious French-speaking majority, mixed with unreliable Loyalist refugees from the newly-formed United States, must have seemed like the end of the world. In 1783 who would have predicted that wild, underpopulated Canada, opposed by four million Americans whose victorious new government was eager to "liberate" and annex it, would be a success?

Yet here she is today—a world industrial power, an agricultural giant which feeds herself easily and has plenty left over to supply other lands, a country which absorbs immigrants at a rate which allows the language spoken on a single Toronto street to change from Italian to Portuguese to Chinese within a generation, a nation which, despite its ethnic controversies, is a model of peace, enjoying one of the highest living standards and lowest crime rates of any nation in history.

Canada is one of the most Scottish-influenced countries in the world. About 10 percent of all Canadians report to the census that their paternal immigrating ancestor came from Scotland,[69] and allowing for intermarriage, perhaps one in six Canadians has at least some Scottish blood.[70]

But the Scottish prominence in Canadian history far exceeds the proportion of Scots in the Canadian population. It would be extravagant to claim that the Scots built Canada, but it is not immoderate to say that Canada could not have been built without them. They have had, in fact, a longer and more consistent connection with the country than any other European ethnic group. This can be demonstrated by citing the westward voyages of mariners through Canada.

As early as A.D. 1010 two Scots are reported among the crew that Thorfinn Karlsevni sent to explore Vineland (presumably Newfoundland and Nova Scotia).[71] As we have seen in chapter 2, Prince Henry Sinclair reached Nova Scotia in 1398. In 1542 Jean Rotz, born in Dieppe, France, but the son of David Ross, a Scot, became one of the first to map the mouth of the St. Lawrence River.[72] In 1619 William Gordon, a Scot, was mate and ice pilot of the Danish attempt to find a northwest passage.[73] Duncan McTavish, an early Canadian explorer, conceived of trade from the orient through Canada.[74] Sir Robert McClure commanded the first expedition to complete the

Northwest Passage in 1854.[75] And in 1969 the first commercial passage was accomplished by Captain Roger A. Steward, who with staff captains Arthur Smith and Donald Graham, all fitted out in Royal Stewart tartan Tam-o'-Shanters, piloted the *Manhattan* through the McClure Strait. The American ship was accompanied by a Canadian ice-breaker, the *John A. MacDonald*, and at a party for the crews a piper played "Auld Lang Syne."[76]

SCOTS IN THE FOUNDING OF QUEBEC

By the middle of the seventeenth century there appeared in the embryonic French colony of Quebec an apparent Scot, specifically styled as Abraham Martin *dit l'Écossais*. Some say that he was the pilot of the *Don de Dieu* as it sailed up the St. Lawrence to found French Canada. Others merely contend he was the king's first pilot on the river. Whatever the case, Martin was awarded for his service the Heights and Plains of Abraham near Quebec City, from which General Wolfe launched his famous victory over the French in 1759. Thousands of French Canadians trace their ancestry back to Martin today.[77]

British Canada was established in 1759 by Wolfe's Fraser Highlanders, who were guided up the Heights of Abraham by Maj. Robert Stobo, of Glasgow,[78] whom we have already discussed as an aide to Washington in western Pennsylvania and as a sometime Indian chief. The battle for Quebec had an interesting twist, as the aide-de-camp of the losing French General Montcalm was the Chevalier Johnstone, a Scot who had fought at Culloden with many of those he had *opposed* at Quebec.[79]

Since Wolfe was killed during the battle, the citadel of Quebec was surrendered to the Scottish general James Murray, who shortly after became the first British governor of Canada. The keys to the city gates were handed over by Lt.-du-Roi Jean-Baptiste-Nicholas Roch, who was descended from Claude de Ramezay, a Frenchman of Scottish ancestry who had been made commanding general of the troops of New France in 1699. De Ramezay was governor of Montreal from 1704 until his death in 1724, and for a time was Governor *par interim* of Canada. He was awarded the highest French military distinction, the Cross of St. Louis.[80]

The treaty of 1763 opened the door to settlers from the British Isles who began to descend upon the little French colony of some sixty-five thousand souls. The small Scottish contingent of immigrants separated itself from the rest and at once began to distinguish itself. Almost immediately they became "the dominant group in most forms of commerce."[81] Among these, John Richardson of Banff was chairman of the committee which prepared the articles for the establishment of the Bank of Montreal, and most of the early directors were also Scots. Richardson was also the founder and first president of Montreal General Hospital.[82] Other Scots founded the Board of Trade.

William Brown and Thomas Gilmore published Quebec's first newspaper, the *Quebec Gazette*, in 1764.[83] John Buchanan founded the first newspaper in Montreal.[84] Much later, in 1869, the *Montreal Star*, "the establishment newspaper," would be founded with one hundred dollars by Hugh Graham.[85]

In early Quebec, or Lower Canada as it was called, the Chateau Clique, a group of powerful men, ruled the province's politics. It was, in turn, so dominated by Scots that it was often referred to as the Scotch Party.[86] Pierre Berton, writing of Scots in early Quebec, says simply, "The Irish outnumbered them as did the English, but the Scots ran the country. Though they formed only one-fifteenth of the population, they controlled the fur trade, the great banking houses, the major educational institutions, and, to a considerable degree, the government."[87]

SCOTS IN THE FUR TRADE

In early Canada the fur trade was by far the dominant economic activity, and by the time the Scots arrived it had already been well established by the French of Quebec and the English of Hudson's Bay. However late in their start in the trade, the Scots quickly caught up. At the beginning of the eighteenth century we have no record of any Scots in the fur trade. By the end of that century they so dominated it that Elaine Allan Mitchell says, "It would be almost impossible to over-emphasise the pre-eminent position which Scots of every stripe, Highlander, Lowlander and Islander, attained during the eighteenth and nineteenth centuries in the North American fur trade."[88]

The Scots had many advantages over the English, who they rapidly displaced in the Hudson's Bay Company. First, their lack of class consciousness allowed them to treat the Indians, French, and *métis* (those of mixed French and Indian blood), with whom they dealt in the endless forests, with much good will. Also, after centuries of the Auld Alliance the *esprit* between Frenchmen and Scots must have given the Scots a great advantage over the English, the Frenchman's traditional enemy.

The Scots were better educated than the English, and much more used to harsh living conditions, particularly in regard to climate. A further element may have been that many of the Scots were bilingual, especially the Highlanders, and therefore more adept at learning French and the various Indian languages which were necessary on the frontier.[89] Whatever the reasons for their success, by 1799 four out of every five employees of the Hudson's Bay Company were Scots, the majority from the Orkneys.[90]

Meanwhile, Highlander Simon McTavish had founded the Montreal-based North West Company in 1783 in direct competition with the Hudson's Bay Company.[91] McTavish preferred and hired mostly fellow-Scots, and as the new company boomed some of the non-Scottish population of Quebec began to be bitterly resentful of the Scottish success.[92] An English competitor complained, "The country is overrun with Scotchmen."[93] By the time of McTavish's death in 1804, forty of the forty-six partners of the North West Company were Scots.[94]

Inevitably, fierce rivalries arose among the proud Scots who dominated the Canadian fur trade. The "Nor' Westers" eventually encroached upon the Hudson's Bay Company's Red River colony, which had been founded by another Scot, the earl of Selkirk, who at that time was in control of the company. The Baymen in turn struck back at the upstart Montrealers and there was bloodshed on the frontier, followed by bitter court battles.

Gradually the better-organized and capitalized Hudson's Bay Company put enough pressure on the wild Nor' Westers to force a merger. In 1821 the largely Scottish Hudson's Bay Company absorbed the almost entirely Scottish Northwest Company, and not surprisingly, a Scot, George Simpson, became overseas governor of all the merged companies' territories. His tenure, lasting to his death in 1860, marked the height of the company's power and prosperity.[95] Under Simpson the Hudson's Bay Company became the largest corporate landowner in history. Its realm encompassed nearly three million square miles—ten times the size of the Holy Roman Empire at its height. It was a vast domain that comprised much of the present United States and most of Canada. The company had 110 forts across the continent, and even over the Pacific to Siberia and the Philippines.

During his term the red-haired Simpson traveled one hundred thousand miles in a canoe "sitting in state wearing his beaver top hat," with his personal piper beside him ready to pipe him into the forts. He was the first man to travel around the world by land[96] and in Norway was toasted as "head of the most extended dominions in the known world—the Emperor of Russia, The Queen of England and the President of the United States excepted."[97]

In the nineteenth century the giant Hudson's Bay Company had become the vehicle through which modern Canada was being constructed. During this period the Scots, who had started out as frontier employees shivering in their remote outposts, were now the principal owners and managers of the vast enterprise. It is estimated that between 1821 and 1870, the year the company's lands became part of Canada, 171 of a total of 263 commissioned officers of the company, or 65 percent, were of Scottish origin.[98] One of these, Donald Alexander Smith (Baron Strathcona), who had started out as an apprentice in 1838, became the company's principal shareholder and was its governor until his death in 1914.[99]

Perhaps the Scottishness of the company reached its peak on the day when the governor general of Canada, the marquess of Lorne, himself a Scot, while making a tour of wilderness posts asked a manager to introduce him to a typical Indian. The Bayman motioned for the fiercest-looking brave to come forward saying, "Would ye come here for a minute Macdonald?"[100]

The Hudson's Bay Company is one of the oldest commercial enterprises still in existence. Its current principal shareholder is a Canadian Scot, Kenneth Thomson.[101]

SCOTS IN THE FOUNDING OF NOVA SCOTIA

As we have previously observed, the Scots have had an off-and-on presence in Nova Scotia for a thousand years, and that in 1621 they attempted to colonize it, bequeathing the province its name, New Scotland, but losing the colony to the French in 1632. Revenge came in 1758, when the Fraser Highlanders, used as shock troops for the British army, took part in the capture of the French fortress of Louisbourg on Cape Breton Island, permanently establishing British, if not Scottish, control.[102] Soon after, boatloads of Scottish immigrants such as those on the *Hector*, a sort of *Mayflower* of Scottish Canada, began to arrive, and by 1843 Nova Scotia was one-third Scottish.[103]

From the beginning Scots were leaders of the colony. Lord William Campbell, son of the duke of Argyll, was lieutenant governor from 1766 to 1772.[104] In the same period Charles Inglis, a Loyalist from New York, became the first Anglican bishop of the diocese of British North America.[105] Samuel Vetch was Nova Scotia's first governor general.[106] Scots are still prominent in the province's government. In recent years the province's premier has been John M. Buchanan, and the leader of the opposition, A. M. "Sandy" Cameron.

In the late twentieth century the Scots in Nova Scotia have been reduced to a small but still very distinct minority. Nowhere outside Scotland have Scottish traditions been so well maintained as in Nova Scotia, particularly on Cape Breton Island. There, several thousand people still claim Gaelic as their mother tongue and a college exists to teach the language, music, and the old crafts. Visitors from Scotland are astonished to find piping, dancing and Gaelic song of the highest quality being performed routinely on Cape Breton Island by people whose families have not seen the Highlands in two centuries.

SCOTS IN THE FOUNDING OF ONTARIO

When the American Revolution broke out many Highlanders, newly arrived in New York's Mohawk Valley, went to Canada to serve in the British army. At the war's end, 1,500 of these Loyalists were given land in Glengarry, in what is now eastern Ontario, and after several years of hardship made the wilderness bloom. The success of this Gaelic-speaking community attracted hundreds of immigrants from around Glengarry in Scotland, and the new Glengarry became the most important settlement in early Ontario.[107]

Many more Scots soon immigrated to what was then called Upper Canada, and by 1800 comprised a significant minority. Somehow they managed to dominate its politics, maintaining a government by the few until the 1840s through what was called the Family Compact. Like the Chateau Clique in Quebec, the Family Compact controlled the legislative and executive bodies in Upper Canada for decades and was made up mostly of Scots. It was led by John Strachan, who had left Aberdeen as a poor schoolmaster to become the first Anglican bishop of Toronto, and founded both Kings College, now the University of Toronto, and Trinity College. Another Aberdonian, William Allan, attended to the business side of the Family Compact promoting "ambitious projects in land settlement, banking and canal building" and becoming, along the way, the first president of the Toronto Board of Trade, the first governor of the British America Assurance Company, and the first president of the Bank of Upper Canada.[108]

Even the opposition to the Family Compact was Scottish in the persons of Robert Fleming Gourlay and William Lyon Mackenzie, the latter of whom became the first mayor of Toronto in 1834.[109] In 1837 Mackenzie led a rebel band against the Family Compact in Toronto but was routed by the forces of another Scot, Allan MacNab, leading volunteers. Mackenzie fled to Navy Island in the Niagara River and proclaimed a Canadian republic, but MacNab pursued him, sending the republic's schooner, which belonged to American "symphathisers," over the falls in flames. The Duke of Wellington said that Sir Allan MacNab had saved Canada "for the British Crown."[110]

Another influential Scot in the making of Ontario was Rev. Alexander Macdonell, who helped save Upper Canada for the British Empire during the War of 1812. Macdonell sent out the Fiery Cross to muster men to arms and acted as field chaplain. In 1826 he became the first Roman Catholic bishop of Upper Canada.[111]

George Brown of Edinburgh founded what became Canada's national newspaper, the Toronto *Globe*, in 1844.[112] When confederation came in 1867, John Sandfield Macdonald became Ontario's first premier.[113]

SCOTS IN THE FOUNDING OF NEW BRUNSWICK

The harbor at St. John was first surveyed by a Scot, named Bruce, in 1761.[114] Four years later William Davidson, "Canada's first lumberman," came from Inverness to found the huge lumber industry along the Miramichi.[115] Among the founders of St. John were Capt. Archibald McLean, Charles McPherson and Hugh MacKay.[116] The main business street in St. John in the 1790s was known as Scotch Row, and the center of commercial activity on the street was McPhail's Tavern.

By 1790 fifteen Scottish mercantile firms dominated the trade of New Brunswick, especially the houses of the Pagans, Blacks, Johnstons, and Andrew Crookshank. By 1798 there was a St. Andrew's Society.[117] Pollock and Gilmour, established in 1804 with 1,500 pounds capital, had, by 1832, one hundred vessels employing five thousand sailors with fifteen thousand men cutting down trees in the New Brunswick forest for shipment. The business of this firm, only one of many such Scottish enterprises, is remarkable for the scope of its operations in this era, especially in a semiwilderness.[118]

SCOTS IN THE FOUNDING OF NEWFOUNDLAND

The colonization of Newfoundland was attempted in 1583 by England but was not successful. In 1637 all of Newfoundland was transferred to an Englishman of Scottish descent, Sir David Kirke, who became the colony's first governor and its actual founder. The arms of present day Newfoundland are those of Kirke.[119]

Before 1707 the quasi-legal trade between Virginia and Scotland through Newfoundland[120] became a major factor in the development of the colony, and many Scots were attracted to it as settlers. Between 1740 and 1794 a Graham, a Duff, a Campbell, and a Wallace were governors of Newfoundland.[121] In 1824 a Scottish physician, William Carson, led a movement that caused Parliament to recognize Newfoundland as a British colony. He was Speaker of the Assembly in 1837.[122] In 1946 Sir George Gordon Macdonald became governor of Newfoundland, and in 1949 guided the colony into the Canadian confederation as a province.[123]

SCOTS IN THE FOUNDING OF PRINCE EDWARD ISLAND

Canada's smallest province is largely a Scottish creation. In 1758 Lord Rollo, a Scottish peer, captured the sparsely-populated island from the French and awarded the land by lot to sixty-seven British subjects, most of whom were Scots.[124] The colony was separated from Nova Scotia in 1769 and a Scot, Capt. Walker Patterson, was appointed as the first governor.[125] Other early Scottish governors were Charles Douglas-Smith, Sir Donald Campbell, Sir A. Bannerman, and George Dundas.[126]

In 1803 Thomas Douglas, earl of Selkirk, established a successful settlement of some eight hundred Highlanders, and by the 1860s Prince Edward Island was more than half Scottish.[127] Although this percentage is now far lower, the Scottish presence remains significant.

SCOTS IN THE FOUNDING OF BRITISH COLUMBIA

The Scottish connection in British Columbia goes back to 1776, when Capt. James Cook repaired his ships on what is now Vancouver

Island. In 1793 another Scot, Alexander Mackenzie, became the first European to visit the area by land.[128] A few years later two other Scots were in the vicinity. Simon Fraser discovered and named the Stuart River, and in 1808 was the first to descend the Fraser River, the principal waterway of British Columbia, to the sea to where the city of Vancouver now stands.[129] About the same time fur traders from the North West Company traced the Columbia River to its source.[130]

Fort Vancouver was founded by John McLoughlin in 1824,[131] and in 1843 James Douglas, the "father" of British Columbia and chief agent of the Hudson's Bay Company west of the Rocky Mountains, sent a fellow-Scot named Finlayson to what is now Victoria to purchase the site from the Indians.[132] Archibald MacDonald founded the first school in Vancouver, in 1834.[133] Robert Dunsmuir (1825–1889), who went to British Columbia as a common coal miner, became Vancouver's first major capitalist. At his death he was one of the richest men in North America.[134] Of the eight men who served on the legislative council of Vancouver in its first decade (1850–1859), it appears that no less than six were Scots.[135]

In 1866 Vancouver Island was united with the mainland territory under the name of British Columbia. Sir James Douglas, the governor of Vancouver Island, was appointed governor of the united colony.[136] In British Columbia's first century as a province at least eight Scots have served as premier, holding the office almost half the time.[137]

SCOTS IN THE FOUNDING OF MANITOBA

Manitoba was created by Scotsmen, Englishmen, Frenchmen, and *métis*. From the beginning, it was the Scots who had the largest impact.[138] As we have noted, the North West and Hudson's Bay companies were both very active in the area in the eighteenth century, and both were largely Scottish.

But the first real settlement was entirely Scottish. Thomas Douglas (Lord Selkirk), the sponsor of the Red River settlement, is regarded as the founder of both Winnipeg and Manitoba. Selkirk was on the verge of becoming an important figure in the British government, but his concern for the plight of the Highlanders of the time "prevented him from pursuing this goal."[139] In 1810 he acquired control of the Hudson's Bay Company, which granted him a vast tract of land in the Red River valley.[140] Selkirk brought out his first Scottish settlers in 1811, but the rival North West Company destroyed the colony. In retaliation, the Hudson's Bay Company leveled the Nor' Westers fort.[141] Ruinous court battles followed in which Selkirk lost both his fortune and his health. However, his Highland settlers held on and more joined them, and when he died in 1820 Selkirk had, in effect, established Manitoba.[142] The first school in Winnipeg was begun by Archibald MacDonald.[143]

Further west, the first farmer at Portage la Prairie, in 1862, was John McLean, and in 1867 Thomas Spence became president of the abortive "Republic of Portage la Prairie."[144] In 1868 Simon Dawson, a civil engineer from Scotland, opened communications between Canada and Red River by what became known as the Dawson route.[145] In 1872 Winnipeg General Hospital was founded as a gift to the city, then with a population of 1472, by two Scottish traders, Andrew McDermot and A. G. B. Bannatyne.[146] In 1873 Robert Gerrie opened the first furniture store west of the Great Lakes, in Winnipeg.[147] William and John Ogilvie were the pioneer wheat buyers of Manitoba, and with other Scots founded the Winnipeg Grain and Produce Exchange in 1887.[148]

In the fifty-eight years between 1812 and 1870, Scots held the position of governor of the district forty-two years.[149] In 1869 the first quasi-governor of the new western province of Manitoba was William McDougall, a Scot, as were the first two official governors, Adams G. Archibald in 1870 and later Alexander Morris, who was also the province's first chief justice and the founder of the University of Manitoba.[150] John Norquay, born in the Orkney Islands, became Manitoba's first premier (1870–1879).[151]

SCOTS IN THE FOUNDING OF SASKATCHEWAN

French and English explorers were the first Europeans to see what is now Saskatchewan, but the first pioneers were the Scottish merchants Thomas Curry and James Finlay.[152] In 1774 Orkneymen built the first permanent settlement.[153] Lieutenant governor Alexander Morris of Manitoba and the Northwest Territories served as the principal commissioner in negotiating the three Indian treaties which covered "virtually all of what became the settled areas" of Saskatchewan and Alberta. All of the other commissioners were Scots too.[154]

Scots were also prominent in founding Saskatchewan's world-famous agriculture. Archibald Wright imported the first Holstein cattle to western Canada and grew the first sweet clover there. John

Rutherford became the first dean of agriculture at the University of Saskatchewan, and A. J. McPhail was the first president of Saskatchewan Co-operative Wheat Producers, Ltd.[155] Scottish capital, from Dundee in particular, financed huge farms, just as it had south of the border.[156]

The first two mayors of Regina were Scots, David L. Scott from 1884 to 1885 and Daniel Mowat from 1886 to 1887. At that time many of the people of substance in the town were Scots, including merchants, lawyers, the schoolteacher, and the deputy sheriff.[157] In 1905 the first ministry of the province of Saskatchewan was composed entirely of four Scots named Calder, Scott, Lamont, and Motherwell. Walter Scott was the first premier, and of the first seventy years of the office the premiership was held by Scots for more than fifty years.[158] T. C. Douglas, born in Falkirk, was elected premier five consecutive times and held the office from 1944 to 1961.[159]

SCOTS IN THE FOUNDING OF ALBERTA

In 1788 Alexander Mackenzie and his cousin Roderick set up a fur trading post on Lake Athabasca at Fort Chippewyan and actually "contrived the foundation of a library" in the wilderness.[160] In 1795 William Tomison, a native of Scotland, began the building of the city of Edmonton.[161] Calgary, the Houston of the North, was founded in 1875 as a fort for the Northwest Mounted Police by Col. James F. Macleod, who named the place after his wife's hometown on the Island of Mull. A statue of King Robert I, the Bruce, looks out on the downtown.[162] In 1905 Alex Rutherford became Alberta's first premier and at least five other Scots have followed him in that office.[163]

SCOTS IN THE FOUNDING OF THE YUKON AND NORTHWEST TERRITORIES

The Scots contributed heavily to the opening of the Canadian Arctic. In 1834 John McLeod reached the headwaters of the Sitkine River, and in 1838 Robert Campbell discovered the upper parts of the Yukon. John Bell established Fort McPherson on the Peel River. Alexander Hunter Murray built Fort Yukon in 1847. Thomas Simpson and John Rae, both Scots employed by the Hudson's Bay Company, completed the survey of the Arctic coastline between 1837 and 1854.[164]

George M. Dawson, the "greatest of Canadian geologists" made the pioneer geological surveys of the Yukon and later directed the

Geological Survey of Canada. Dawson City is named for him. It was, in turn, surveyed by another Scot, William Ogilvie, who also drew the line between the Yukon and Alaska.[165]

The government of John A. Macdonald created the romantic Northwest Mounted Police. Its early leader, Col. James F. Macleod, was given three hundred men to police a territory as wide as Europe.[166]

SCOTTISH GOVERNORS GENERAL

As had been the case in the American colonies, many of the governors of Canada were Scots. In fact, the first British governor in what is now Canada was Sir William Alexander, the Raleigh of Scotland. James VI and the Scottish Parliament appointed him the hereditary lieutenant of Nova Scotia in 1621. As Raleigh had been unsuccessful in founding English America, so Alexander was the first to try and first to fail at founding Scottish America.[167] The second British-Canadian governor was also a Scot, Sir David Kirke, who established the colony of Newfoundland.[168] Gen. James Murray became the first actual British governor in Canada in 1763.[169]

In the nineteenth century, when the form of Canadian government was being determined, Scots and part-Scots held the office of governor general more than half the time:

James Craig (1807–1811)[170]
The Duke of Richmond (1818–1819)[171]
The Earl of Dalhousie (1819–1828)[172]
Sir James Kempt (1828–1830)[173]
Lord Gosford (1835–1837)[174]
Lord Cathcart (1845–1846)[175]
The Earl of Elgin (1846–1854)[176]
Lord Lisgar (1868–1872)[177]
The Earl of Dufferin (1872–1878)[178]
The Duke of Argyll (1878–1883)[179]
The Earl of Aberdeen (1893–1898)[180]
The Earl of Minto (1898–1904)[181]

The greatest of these was James Bruce, eighth earl of Elgin, who brought Canada through her most difficult years. It has been observed that Elgin is not better known because his business was not war, but the prevention of it. His legacy is Canadian self-government.[182] Elgin had already served as governor of Jamaica during the difficult period just after the end of slavery there. He arrived in

Canada to find intense racial animosity between the British and French Canadians. In addition there were demands for self-government to deal with as well as acute economic problems and poor relations with the United States.

In 1849 Elgin upheld the Canadian Parliament against the very Scottish Family Compact and equally Scottish Chateau Clique, a decision which caused extensive Tory riots, the burning of Parliament buildings, and his lordship's name to be struck from the list of members of the St. Andrew's Society of Montreal. But Elgin persevered and succeeded in establishing responsible government. Racial tensions were eased and in 1854 a treaty was signed with the United States.[183] James A. Roy says, "Under a governor of less tact, understanding, and patience, Canada might well have been lost to the Empire."[184] According to William J. Rattray, "Lord Elgin stands out in Canadian history...as by far the greatest and most conspicuous figure."[185]

THE FATHERS OF CONFEDERATION

Thirty-six men attended conferences in 1864 and 1866 that resulted in the confederation of the British North American colonies into the Dominion of Canada. About half were of Scottish origin. But more importantly, except for two delegates, George E. Cartier and D'Arcy McGee, the remaining eight of the ten main "Fathers" of Confederation were Scots.[186] John A. Macdonald was the most important delegate. In 1864 his Quebec Resolutions became the basis for the creation of modern Canada, and his vision and political skills made him the de facto leader of the conferences.[187]

Another, George Brown, the owner of the "Scotchman's Bible," the Toronto *Globe*, used his pages to lend support to compromise. Alexander Galt gave his financial expertise. William McDougall and Oliver Mowat worked out the division of powers between the local and federal governments. In New Brunswick Peter Mitchell and John Hamilton Gray were the key delegates in favor of confederation. In Nova Scotia, Adams George Archibald made the arguments which brought that province into the confederation.[188]

THE GOVERNMENT OF CANADA

The first two Canadian prime ministers were both native-born Scots, John A. Macdonald and Alexander Mackenzie.[189] Macdonald was recognized as the new nation's principal founder and as its master politician. During his administration, Canada spanned the continent and added the provinces of British Columbia, Manitoba, and Prince Edward Island, while keeping repeal-minded Nova Scotia in.

One of Macdonald's greatest achievements was his successful promotion of the Canadian Pacific Railway, an outstanding feat of engineering and finance that he believed was necessary for the continuing unity of his vast, thinly-populated nation. The syndicate formed to build the railway was entirely Scottish and included Donald Smith, his cousin George Stephen of the Bank of Montreal, Duncan MacIntyre, Robert B. Angus, and John Rose, who had been Macdonald's finance minister but who was in a London bank at that time. The brilliant engineer of the project was Sandford Fleming, also a Scot.

Smith and Stephen became the principal members, and as time went on and funds ran short they sold their personal assets and borrowed heavily. As the project neared completion they were driven almost to bankruptcy. At one point Stephen cabled Smith from London, "Stand Fast Craigellachie," remembering the inspiring slogan of Clan Grant, from whose territory they had both come. At last, on November 7, 1885, Smith drove the last spike into the completed roadbed at Craigellachie, British Columbia. The next summer John Macdonald, his vision of a permanently united transcontinental Canada now a reality, rode the cowcatcher of a Canadian Pacific locomotive at age seventy-one, his beautiful wife by his side.[190]

Despite their minority status, since the confederation of 1867, eight men and one woman of Scottish ancestry have been prime minister of Canada more than two-thirds of the time:

> Sir John A. Macdonald (1867–1873; 1878–1891)[191]
> Alexander Mackenzie (1873–1878)[192]
> Sir Mackenzie Bowell (1894–1896)[193]
> Sir Robert Laird Borden (1911–1920)[194]
> Arthur Meighen (1920–1921)[195]
> W. L. Mackenzie King (1921–1926; 1926–1930; 1935–1948)[196]
> John G. Diefenbaker (1957–1963)[197]
> Pierre Elliott Trudeau (1968–1979; 1980–1984)[198]
> Kim Campbell (1993)[199]

Mr. Trudeau, despite his French name and ancestry, seemed to delight in confirming the Scottishness of the office by wearing the Elliott tartan Highland dress of his mother's family to numerous Scottish affairs.[200] There have been dozens of Scottish premiers and cabinet members, far too numerous to note. But three Scottish-Canadian women deserve special mention: Kim Campbell, the first female prime minister (1993); Agnes Campbell Macphail, the first woman elected to the House of Commons (1921), and Cairine Mackay Wilson, the first woman appointed to the Senate (1930).[201]

CANADIAN UNIVERSITIES

Wherever they have gone the Scots have contributed heavily to education, and nowhere more impressively than in Canada, where five different Scots founded five of the first six colleges:

University of New Brunswick	1785	Sir William Dawson[202]
Kings College (Nova Scotia)	1789	Rev. Charles Inglis[203]
Dalhousie University	1818	Lord Dalhousie[204]
McGill University	1821	James McGill[205]
University of Toronto	1827	John Strachan[206]

In addition, Scots founded McMaster University,[207] St. Francis Xavier University,[208] Victoria College for Women,[209] Queens University,[210] and dominated in the early days at others. The first principals at McGill, McMaster, Queens, Dalhousie, and for generations all of the presidents of the University of Toronto, were Scots.[211]

No matter where one goes in Canada the presence of Scotland is felt. For instance, at Ogilvy's department store in Montreal, founded in 1866 by James Angus Ogilvy of Kirriemuir, the lunchtime crowd is entertained every day by an Ogilvy-tartaned piper.[212] Perhaps the piper plays a song, "The Maple Leaf Forever," written by a Canadian Scot, Alexander Muir, which in 1867, the year the dominion became a reality, enabled Canadians to articulate their newly-won nationhood.[213] Or perhaps, he plays "O Canada!" written by another Canadian with a Scottish name, R. Stanley Weir.

The Scots in India

The East India Company was formed in London in 1600 to break the Dutch monopoly in the spice trade. Since this was more than a century before the Union of 1707, the company employed no Scots. But even after the union, the English did not immediately invite Caledonian participation in their enterprise on the subcontinent. In 1784, however, the prime minister, William Pitt, unhappy that the English monopoly had failed to establish paramount control over

India after almost two centuries of effort, called out the Scots, creating a board of control for Indian affairs dominated by his close friend, the Scotsman Henry Dundas. Dundas (Viscount Melville) was president of the board from 1793 until 1801 and during his tenure was responsible for encouraging many Scots, whom he preferred, to seek their fortunes in India.[214] One of these was Sir David Baird, who conquered Mysore, a state larger than Scotland, in 1799.[215]

The first appointed Scottish governor general, Sir John Macpherson, derisively called Johnny McShuffle, was dismissed as corrupt.[216] But after him, it was largely Scots who were prominent in making and keeping India British. Jonathan Duncan was an enormously successful governor of Bombay (1795–1811) after having founded the first Sanskrit university in 1788,[217] and by 1805 Charles Grant had become chairman of the board of directors of the East India Company.[218] As early as 1792 Grant had been the first Briton to express a concern for the welfare of the Indians and to propose the teaching of the English language, Western science, and other reforms.[219] From 1806 to 1813 Gilbert Elliot (earl of Minto) was governor general, and during his reign French influence declined.

Britain added a great deal of territory and became the paramount power on the Indian subcontinent as a result of winning the third Maratha war (1817–1819). Two Scots, Mountstuart Elphinstone and John Malcolm, both of whom were really diplomats, nevertheless played decisive roles as fighters commanding troops in the war.[220] But these Scots were even better at peace than war. In 1819 Elphinstone was made governor of Bombay and was succeeded by Malcolm in 1827. Elphinstone introduced method and system during his term, and twice refused the governor generalship. John "Boy" Malcolm, so-called because he had been commissioned at age thirteen, made central India prosperous during his tenure. These two Scots were well liked by the Indians. Another Scot, Sir Thomas Munro, governor of Madras (1819–1827), carried southern India forward from a system of corruption to a model of rent and tax collection using Indian civil servants instead of British ones.[221] Sir Charles Napier conquered the Sind in 1843. As governor there Napier established a model police force, expanded trade, and began work on a reliable water supply for Karachi.[222]

In 1848 one of the most remarkable of empire builders became governor general of India. He was James Andrew Broun Ramsay, first marquess and tenth earl of Dalhousie, and only thirty-five years old. In his first year this young leader put down a Sikh rebellion and annexed the Punjab. By the time his seven-year term ended he had added lower Burma, Oudh, and many smaller states, built India's first few thousand miles of railway, four thousand miles of telegraph, and sent the Koh-i-noor diamond to the Queen. Dalhousie organized India into a modern state. He promoted public works, created a post office, built roads, and emphasized and expanded education. He was ruthless and driven, but using his Scottish egalitarianism to great advantage, he drew the map of India. His own words testify: "My lady gave...a ball...and to this I caused the native officers to be invited. Some of the old school and some of the young gentlemen did not like this I believe. I mean to make it the rule."[223] But Dalhousie's rapid westernization programs and iron rule had offended traditional Indians. His departure in 1856 created a vacuum in which their discontent flourished.

The year 1857 brought the great Indian Mutiny, a full-scale rebellion the Indians refer to as a war of independence, in which Britain stood to lose all it had won on the subcontinent. Scots played the major roles in all of the important events of the uprising, but credit for the eventual British victory must first be given to Gen. Sir Colin Campbell (Baron Clyde), the son of a Glasgow cabinetmaker, and commander in chief of Her Majesty's troops in India.[224]

Two Ulster-Scottish brothers, Henry Montgomery Lawrence and John Laird Mair Lawrence (Baron Lawrence), were extremely important in the British success against the mutiny. First, they had been such good administrators that the Sikhs of the Punjab, the best soldiers in India, remained loyal, a feat which swung the balance in favor of Britain from the outset. John Lawrence then made an immediate and successful move against Delhi, the old capital, which was in the control of the Indian rebels. With the aid of another Ulster Scot, John Nicholson, who commanded a Sikh army, Delhi was recovered. For these efforts John Lawrence is known as "the Savior of India."

His brother, Henry Lawrence, brilliantly organized and provisioned the British residency at Lucknow, thus enabling it to resist the subsequent Indian siege against it until relief came. Henry Lawrence died during the siege and is remembered as "the Hero of Lucknow." The rebels were finally beaten at Lucknow on March 21, 1858, by Campbell and the Scottish general Sir James Outram, who were commanding Black Watch, Sutherland, and Cameronian troops. In just two days at Lucknow Scottish soldiers won six Victoria Crosses. Whittier, the American poet, wrote in "The Relief of Lucknow" that "the tartan clove the turban."[225]

But the war was not yet over. In central India, Gen. Hugh Rose (Baron Strathnairn) conducted the most difficult, vigorous, and successful operations of the rebellion. Rose, in effect, reconquered the heart of India, and ended the Indian Mutiny on June 20, 1858.[226]

After their victory, the British decided to rule India directly instead of through the East India Company. The awesome task of managing a resentful people, while at the same time creating a new civil government where only a corporate one had existed, fell to another Scot, James Bruce, the eighth earl of Elgin, who had already distinguished himself in Canada. Lord Elgin became viceroy and governor general in 1862. His new government in place, he died in bad health in the Punjab in 1863 and was succeeded by John Lawrence. Victor Bruce, ninth earl of Elgin, was viceroy from 1894 to 1899.[227]

Most of the lawyers in colonial India were Scots, and much Anglo-Indian legislation is more like the Scottish legal style than the English. The origins of Indian democracy and the Congress party, which ultimately won independence for India, are the work of a Scot, Allan Hume, the founder of the first Indian Congress, in 1885.[228] Since that beginning, the Congress party has ruled the world's second largest nation most of the time.

As elsewhere, the Scots in India made unusual contributions to education. Mountstuart Elphinstone founded the system of state education in India.[229] Alexander Duff built schools, was a founder of the University of Calcutta, and advised on the founding of the city's medical college and hospital.[230] David Hare founded the Hindu College in Calcutta. Jonathan Duncan founded the College of Benares, and other Scots founded Elphinstone College in Bombay, the Bethune College for girls in Calcutta, and the College of Madras. Sir William Muir (1819–1905) started Muir College and the university at Allahabad.[231] "Everywhere in India," said an Indian visiting Edinburgh, "the young have been brought up at the feet of Scottish schoolmasters."[232]

Around 1800, John B. Gilchrist, assisted by fellow-Scot William Hunter, worked with two Indians, one a Hindu and the other a Moslem, to develop the systematizing of a grammar and dictionary of the Hindustani language, the lingua franca of the Hindus and Moslems. Greatly facilitating commerce, the development of Hindustani brought order out of the linguistic chaos of India. It is the language of India's gigantic cinema industry today.[233] John Wilson deciphered the Ashoka Brahmi script, enabling others to recover India's lost classical past.[234]

Beginning in 1859, India's first finance minister, James Wilson, founder of the *Economist*, introduced paper currency and income taxes and greatly strengthened the economy. He was succeeded in the post by another Scot, Samuel Laing of Edinburgh, in 1860.[235] The first Indian census was planned and carried out under the direction of Sir William Hunter in 1872.[236] In 1823 Maj. Robert Bruce discovered indigenous tea in India. Dr. Hugh Falconer (1808–1865), of Forres, made the first experiments for growing tea in India. He became head of the Calcutta Botanical Garden, introduced quinine, and recommended its (later) successful cultivation as a commercial crop.[237] William Jameson was the first to cultivate a tea plantation.[238]

The Scots in Australia

A few intrepid sailors from Europe had seen parts of Australia as early as 1605, but the first to visit its east coast or any part of the continent suitable for settlement was the Yorkshire-Scottish Capt. James Cook, who made land on April 20, 1770.[239] The next month an unlucky member of the crew, Forbes Sutherland of Aberdeen, became the first Briton to be buried in Australian soil.[240] Cook's visit aroused the first real British interest in Australia[241] and by 1786 the Pitt government had enacted legislation allowing the "transportation" of criminals to New South Wales.[242] Colonization began soon after and was backed up by a great deal of exploration, most of it by Scots.

By 1824 Allan Cunningham, Hamilton Hume, and Thomas Mitchell, all Scots, had been among the most prominent early explorers of substantial parts of what are now New South Wales, Victoria, and Queensland. Hume's journey was the most important. He was the first to cross the Blue Mountains, first to reach Australia's greatest river, now called the Murray, and the first to cross what is now Victoria.[243] In 1836 Thomas Mitchell descended the Darling to the Murray and then trekked across Victoria to the sea.[244] Soon afterwards Angus Macmillan, a native of Skye, discovered Victoria's fertile Gippsland.[245] Another Scot, John Forrest, was the first to cross the desert region from Perth to Adelaide.[246]

The two most significant Australian explorers were Charles Sturt and John MacDouall Stuart. Sturt, an Englishman whose parents were of Scottish ancestry,[247] discovered the Darling River in 1828, and later descended the Murray to its mouth. In 1845 he neared the center of the continent.[248] John MacDouall Stuart, a native of Fife, was the first to reach the center (in 1860) and the first to cross the continent, which he accomplished in 1862.[249]

John Hunter, who in 1795 became the second governor of Australia, was a Scot,[250] and upon his arrival found a countryman, John Macarthur (1767–1834), living in what has been described as Australia's oldest house[251] and raising crossbred Bengal and Irish sheep.[252] Seeking some industry upon which an economy could be based, Hunter encouraged Macarthur to pursue his enterprise, and by 1796 Macarthur had introduced the Merino sheep, completing the breed upon which Australia's early prosperity was based. Macarthur is generally considered to be the founder of Australia's wool industry.[253] In 1817 he founded another industry by planting Australia's first vineyard.[254] Another Scot, Robert Campbell, broke the East India Company's trading monopoly, and in 1798 became Australia's first merchant.[255] He owned the land on which the capital, Canberra, later rose, and in 1840 built the first church in that area, which is still standing. One of his homes now serves as the Royal Military College mess, the other as a residence for important visitors, including the queen.[256] James Chisholm ran the first saloon in Sydney, the Thistle Tavern.[257]

John Macarthur soon became, by far, the most powerful man in Australia, and when his friend Hunter left he began to run the country to his advantage. In 1805 the British government sent an Englishman, William Bligh (previously known for his heavy hand as captain of H.M.S. *Bounty*) to be Australia's fourth governor. Bligh arrested Macarthur, but Maj. George Johnston, another Scot, assumed the governorship (perhaps on Macarthur's orders), released Macarthur, and arrested Bligh, deporting him—to England![258] It was clearly time for responsible government in Australia. In 1810 it arrived in the person of a Highlander, Lachlan Macquarrie. The new governor must have been shocked at the first sight of his new domain, a raw continent populated by only a few thousand white people, almost all of whom were convicts, living in primitive conditions with practically no organized government.[259] It took him only a decade to bring Australia into a permanently civilized state, and when he left in 1821 he had become "the father of Australia."[260]

Macquarrie believed that a convict's former condition should not be held against him forever and encouraged these "transported" people to become productive in his realm. He used his broad authority, backed by the seventy-third Highlanders, of which he was commanding officer, to create a nation. He was a harsh governor, quickly restoring order and introducing strict Sabbatarian rules, but he got results. During his tenure towns, roads, bridges, schools, markets, banks, churches, and parks were built. More than a dozen Australian place names memorialize his stature.[261]

So it is that two very different Scots are thought of as the cofounders of Australia, inasmuch as they did more than anyone else to establish the country on a firm foundation: John Macarthur for his vigor and personal ambition as founder of two thriving industries, and Lachlan Macquarrie for giving the colony balance, government, and its essential public facilities.[262]

The next governor, Thomas Makdougall Brisbane, also a Scot, encouraged the immigration of free settlers, established freedom of the press, and introduced tobacco plants and sugar cane. The city of Brisbane is named for him.[263] Also during Brisbane's term, the Leith Australian Company was formed in Scotland with capital of 138,000 pounds. It was the first public company begun in Great Britain to operate in Australia.[264]

In 1827 Captain James Stirling, a native of Lanarkshire, sailed into the Swan River and founded Western Australia, naming the capital Perth, after the city in central Scotland. He was the first lieutenant governor of Western Australia.[265] Another Scot, George Fife Angus, was the founder and "father of South Australia."[266] The first chief justice of Australia (from 1823 to 1827) was also a Scot, Francis Forbes.[267] The Ebeneezer Church, the oldest ecclesiastical building in Australia, was built by Scots and is forty miles from Sydney.[268] The beautiful little landmark synagogue at Hobart (1845), the first in Tasmania, was designed by the Scottish architect James Alexander Thomson, who had been "transported" in 1825 for a minor offense. Not knowing how a synagogue should look, he used a picture of Herod's temple at Jerusalem as a guide.[269] By 1860 the Scots amounted to only 5 percent of Australia's population, but it was observed that all over the country, particularly in Melbourne and Adelaide, they "controlled affairs and gave the prevalent tone to the community."[270]

For his work in 1900, George Houston Reid, a Scot and the leading politician of New South Wales, has been called the architect of the commonwealth of Australia.[271] The first government was sworn in on January 1, 1901, by the first governor general, also a Scot, John A.

Louis Hope, seventh earl and first marquess of Linlithgow.[272] He has been followed as governor general by other Scots, including Baron Stonehaven, Sir Alexander Ruthven, whose term coincided with World War II, and later W. S. Morrison.[273] In 1975 governor general Sir John Kerr, at the center of one of Australia's most bitter disputes, dismissed the Labor party government.[274]

Despite their small numbers, during the first nine decades of the commonwealth, Scots have been prime ministers of Australia more than half the time:

Sir George Houston Reid	(1904–1905)[275]
Andrew Fisher	(1908–1909; 1910–1913; 1914–1915)[276]
Stanley Melbourne Bruce	(1923–1929)[277]
Robert Gordon Menzies	(1939–1941; 1949–1966)[278]
Sir John McEwen	(1967–1968)
John Malcolm Fraser	(1975–1983)[279]

Among these, Andrew Fisher has the most interesting biography. A coal miner, he left Scotland for Queensland, where he became a labor organizer, then married the mine owner's daughter. He was elected to Parliament only nine years after quitting the mine in Ayrshire.[280] As a politician, Fisher was ahead of his time. Under him Australia made social progress long before America and Europe. His regime also saw the founding of the new capital, and Fisher declined his cabinet's suggestion that it be named after him.[281]

Robert Gordon Menzies, the prime minister who has been called Australia's most successful politician, took the country, an empty part of the British Empire at the end of World War II, and made it into an expanding, industrializing, cosmopolitan nation with its own identity. A scholarship student who won top honors in law, Menzies claimed to be "a reasonably bigoted descendant of the Scottish race," and explained, "I have a respect for the rights of the top dog, and no use for the foolish doctrine of equality between the active and the idle, the intelligent and the dull, the frugal and the improvident." Thus steeped in Scottish philosophy, Australia's postwar, capital-oriented society boomed.[282]

There have, of course, been many other Scottish politicians in Australia far too numerous to detail. Just let it be shown that Australia has already had numbered among its premiers a MacPherson, a MacAlister, a MacIlwraith, a McCulloch, a Maclean, and a MacKenzie.[283]

Alexander Macleay created the Australian Library in 1826 and helped found the Australian Museum in 1828.[284] And, of course, the Scots have been overrepresented in Australian education. The Rev. James Forbes, a native of Aberdeen, founded the famous Scotch College in Melbourne in 1851. The first rector was Robert Lawson of Perth.[285] Forbes is thought of as Australia's first public educationist. Sir Walter Hughes, of Fife, founded Adelaide University, and two of the three largest benefactors were Scots. Queensland University was founded by two Scots, William Kidston and Sir William MacGregor, the latter serving as its first chancellor.[286]

A Scottish-Australian, James Harrison, invented an ice-making machine with the idea of exporting beef. Harrison failed, but in 1880 the Scots-built *Strathleven* made the first shipment of Australian beef to Britain using Harrison's technique, radically enhancing the country's economy.[287] Nat "Bluey" Buchanan, "King of the Drovers," blazed new trails after 1880 and founded many cattle stations, including Victoria River Downs, claimed as the world's biggest.[288]

The newspaper business was, as usual, very Scottish in early Australia, as it was elsewhere in the English-speaking world. The first newspaper in Melbourne, the *Argus*, was published by William Kerr in 1846, and later by Wilson and Mackinnon, until 1936. The Melbourne *Age* was owned by the Syme family from 1856 to 1948. The Sydney *Bulletin* was developed by W. H. Traill and William Macleod. The first newspaper editor in Southern Australia was also a Scot, George Stevenson.[289]

Andrew "Banjo" Paterson, the son of a Scottish immigrant, wrote the hauntingly beautiful song of Australia, "Waltzing Matilda."[290]

The Scots in New Zealand

"O thugaibh buidheachas do Dhia"
(O give ye thanks to the Lord)

—*Rev. Norman McLeod,*
Scottish Moses

In 1769, the Scoto-English captain James Cook became the first European to set foot in New Zealand and is considered to be its founder. Cook stayed the winter making good relations with the native Maoris, whom he described as intelligent. He recorded the culture of the people, noted the islands' suitability for settlement, and through his writings convinced many Britons to form plans for colonization. On March 9, 1770, a few weeks before Cook returned to

Britain, New Zealand's first haggis was served aboard his ship, the *Endeavour*, on the occasion of a Scottish officer's birthday.[291]

Scots were very prominent in the colonization of New Zealand. George Bruce became the first recorded settler in 1809.[292] The first organized attempt at settlement was by the New Zealand Company, headed by James Herd, a Scottish seaman whose 1825 expedition left a few men behind.[293] James Busby, a Scot who landed in 1833, was the first representative of the British government to arrive in New Zealand. The first major settlement was made at Petone, near what is now Wellington, by 162 Scots in 1840. Thistle was ceremoniously planted at a St. Andrew's Day picnic on November 30 of that year.[294]

Two Scots, John Logan Campbell and William Brown, owned the first ship to sail directly from England to New Zealand.[295] Campbell is considered to be the "father" of Auckland, and in 1844 sent the first cargo of New Zealand produce, including sawn timber, to the English market.[296]

In 1842 George Rennie conceived of an entirely Scottish colony at Otago, complete with a Presbyterian church and schools. By 1849 his colony existed and included a library. Otago became a model for the prosperity and high educational standards which prevail to this day in New Zealand.[297] By the time the English began their first independent colony, at Canterbury in 1850, the Scots were firmly established at Otago, and were exporting to Britain.[298]

In 1852 an extraordinary "Scottish Moses," Sutherland-born Rev. Norman McLeod, ended thirty-five years of wandering in the wilderness and began to bring his flock to a "Promised Land" at Waipu. McLeod had taken his people from Scotland to Nova Scotia in 1817, but after having battled the climate for thirty years decided to move his group to New Zealand. In 1852 he led the first of them to the North Island, which he thought would be particularly suitable, since his people would be almost alone and could form a self-contained Gaelic-speaking community. McLeod's entire assemblage moved from Nova Scotia to Waipu from 1852 to 1859 in six ships built, manned, and provisioned by themselves.[299]

By 1861 there were thirty thousand Scottish-New Zealanders, most of them at Otago and Waipu, in a non-Maori population of ninety-nine thousand.[300] Among the early leaders of the Otago colony was the Rev. Thomas Burns (1796–1871), a nephew of Robert Burns, Scotland's "national bard."[301] Donald Sutherland (1835–1919) discovered Sutherland Falls, the highest in the country.[302] William Brown, of Dundee, started the early newspaper the *Southern Cross*.[303]

Most significantly, two Scots, William Davidson and Thomas Brydone, made the first shipment of frozen meat to Britain in 1882, revolutionizing New Zealand's economy.[304]

The Scots have always been active in the politics of New Zealand. For instance, Sir Bernard Fergusson, governor general in the mid-twentieth century, was also the son of a governor general, and both of his grandfathers were governors general.[305] David Munro was an early Speaker of the House of Representatives, and Sir Robert Stout, born in Shetland, was an early prime minister (1884–1887) and chief justice (1889–1930).[306] John Mackenzie, born in Ross-shire, became minister of agriculture in the 1890s and instituted vast land reform.[307] The prime minister during World War II was Scottish-born Peter Fraser,[308] and in the 1970s Norman E. Kirk, also of Scottish descent, became prime minister.[309]

By 1901 the Scottish percentage of British-born New Zealanders had declined to 24 percent,[310] but as late as 1982, 18 percent of the population were still listed as Presbyterians.[311] The Scottish influence remains important in New Zealand. Perhaps this helps to explain why New Zealand high school seniors ranked first in a 1973 survey of nineteen countries in reading comprehension, literature, and science, just ahead of second-place Scotland and also ahead of such distinguished nations as the United States, England, Israel, Italy, Sweden, and the Netherlands.[312]

The Scots in British Africa

SOUTH AFRICA

The development of southern Africa was facilitated by the exploration of two Scots in the service on the Netherlands, Robert Gordon and William Paterson. The two men discovered and named the principal river of the region, the Orange, in 1778–1779.[313] Soon afterwards Scots became Britain's main instruments in taking South Africa from the Dutch. In 1795 Gen. Sir James Craig, supported by Admiral George Keith Elphinstone, conquered the tip of the continent with five thousand troops. Craig remained as governor until 1797. His administration was marked by increased prosperity and an end to the Dutch practice of torturing criminals. Craig was followed, with less distinction, by a series of Scottish governors named MacArtney, Dundas, and Yonge and, as a result of the Treaty of Amiens, the cape became Dutch again for a brief period in the first years of the nineteenth century. In 1806, however, the British sent yet another Scot, Sir David Baird (1757–1829) to conquer the land once more, and this time, with a Highland charge the key point in a rather even-sided battle, the influence of Britain at the cape became permanent.[314]

In the early days of British South Africa there were very few Scots, but, as usual, we find them in the forefront of all activities.[315] The first governor was the earl of Caledon, who ruled from 1807 until 1811.[316] In the latter year Lt. Col. John Graham, for whom Grahamstown is named, gained a great deal of fertile land for settlement.[317] An extremely successful early farmer was Robert Hart, who landed in his kilt in 1795 as a member of the Argyll Highlanders. Hart became the unquestioned political head of the Somerset East district, elected by the English and Afrikaans-speakers alike. William Anderson, the son of an Aberdeen merchant, was a missionary who sowed the first wheat and fathered and raised the first white children north of the Orange. Andrew Geddes Bain, a self-taught engineer, built most of the early roads of South Africa.[318] Duncan Campbell was among the founders of the South African wool industry.[319] The three brothers of war hero "Shipka" Campbell sold their unproductive diamond claim to a man named De Beer. It is now called the Kimberley Deep and is the base of the South African diamond industry.[320]

The first newspaper in South Africa, the *Capetown Gazette and African Advertiser*, was published briefly in 1800 by Alexander Walker and John Robertson.[321] George Greig is considered to have been South Africa's first printer, and published the first successful newspaper, the *South African Commercial Advertiser*, in 1824.[322] Thomas Pringle, of Edinburgh, with John Fairbairn, founded the first literary magazine, the *South African Journal*, which made a determined stand for freedom of the press. The governor, Lord Somerset, hated the magazine and suppressed it, but Pringle went to London and exposed the misdeeds of Somerset, who was recalled and forced to resign in 1827.[323] David Dale Buchanan published the first regular newspaper in Natal, the *Natal Witness*, in 1846.[324]

James Rose Innes, born in Banff, is considered to have been the founder of the educational system of South Africa. Since the Afrikaners had made very little provision for education, the British government selected Innes as the first superintendent of the Cape Colony in 1839, on a budget of 3,640 pounds per year. Almost all of the early teachers were Scots. Rose had to write the first textbook himself but retired in 1859, leaving a flourishing system.[325]

South African College was founded in 1829 by two Scots, John Fairbairn and James Adamson. It grew into the University of South Africa, University of Capetown, and many others.[326] Among the early professors at Stellenbosch, the most prestigious Afrikaans-speaking university, were several Scots, including a Macdonald and a Mackenzie.[327]

The greatest Afrikaner prime minister, Jan Christian Smuts, had this to say of the Scottish minority: "South Africa can never forget what Scotland and the Scots have done. It would be difficult to do justice to the work which Scotsmen have done in the upbuilding of our country."[328]

RHODESIA-ZIMBABWE

In 1857 Robert Moffat, the father-in-law of Dr. David Livingstone, was the first missionary in what is now Zimbabwe.[329] Sir Leander Starr Jameson, a physician from Edinburgh, became a close friend and collaborator of Cecil Rhodes as he began the development of Rhodesia and later served as president of the British South Africa Company.[330]

Ian Douglas Smith, a son of a Scottish immigrant, was the most famous prime minister of Rhodesia. As a boy, Smith was captain of his school's cricket, tennis, and rugby teams. An RAF pilot in World War II, he was shot down twice and returned to Rhodesia a hero. As prime minister he resisted calls for majority rule, declared independence from Britain in 1965, and in 1978 negotiated a majority rule government with safeguards for the white minority.[331]

BRITISH EAST AFRICA

The Imperial British East Africa Company was founded by Sir William Mackinnon in 1888 and included as directors A. L. Bruce, the marquess of Lorne, John Kirk, Sir Donald Stewart, and Sir George Mackenzie, who remarked, "Thank God we are all Scotsmen here."[332] Kirk explored with Livingston and in 1873 became consul general in Zanzibar. His successful dealings with its sultan built the foundation on which British power in eastern and central Africa was based.[333]

Some of the early explorers and missionaries in the area were named Keith, Johnston, Stewart, and Mackay.[334] Joseph Thomson, who opened up the country around Lakes Nyasa and Tanganyika, was a skillful diplomat who "laid the foundation of the colonies to come."[335]

WEST AFRICA

Zachary Macaulay, his father a Hebridean minister and his son the famous historian, was an early governor of Sierra Leone.[336] Macgregor Laird (1808–1861), a man opposed to slavery, founded the African Steamship Company, which pioneered legitimate trade in western Africa. Laird sponsored expeditions, the most successful of which was headed by a fellow-Scot, William Balfour Baikie, who in 1854 pushed two hundred miles farther up the Niger than anyone had gone before. These two men opened up a large area for commerce. Without them, the largest and richest territories in western Africa would not have been British.[337]

Mary Slessor, a Scottish missionary who was officially consul, ruled the province of Okoyong in Nigeria almost as a queen near the turn of the last century.[338] Sir John Macpherson, governor of Nigeria (1948–1956), "was a major factor in framing the constitution that paved the way for self-government" for that African state.[339]

Corners of the Empire

THE ANDAMAN AND NICOBAR ISLANDS

The Scottish influence is easy to detect in these islands, situated between Burma and Sumatra. Port Blair is the largest town and features the Aberdeen Bazaar. Ross Island, modeled on a Scottish village, served as the administrative headquarters in the nineteenth century.[340]

CORSICA

Gilbert Elliott, first earl of Minto, was viceroy of Corsica in 1794.[341]

THE CARIBBEAN

The first Briton, Simon Gordon, landed on Barbados in 1620 and found the island to be uninhabited. James Hay, earl of Carlisle, received a hereditary grant from King James I of all of the "Caribee Islands," then called the Carlisle Islands, which included Barbados. The grant, upheld by Charles I in 1627, gave the Hays almost unlimited power in the area, but subsequently they lost it to the crown.[342]

In the eighteenth century Robert Hunter and Sir Archibald Campbell were among the Scottish governors of Jamaica,[343] and James Philip was governor of the Leeward Islands and of St. Martin.[344] Sir Ralph Abercromby took Trinidad for Britain in 1797.[345] The nineteenth chief of Clan Gregor, Sir Evan MacGregor of MacGregor (1785–1841), was governor of Dominica and the Windward Islands.[346]

In 1980 Edward P. Seaga, of Scottish, Lebanese, and Jamaican ancestry, was elected prime minister of Jamaica, probably saving that nation from the grip of Castro's Cuba.[347]

TRISTAN DA CUNHA

William Glass, a Scot from Kelso, was the colony's founder and its first governor.[348] As late as 1961 the islanders celebrated the Scottish New Year's "first footing."[349]

THE COCOS ISLANDS

From 1827, when Queen Victoria gave the Clunies-Ross family a 999-year lease, until 1984, the Cocos-Keeling Islands were "ruled by the descendants of a Scottish sea captain like a medieval estate. Among the lush coconut and banana plantations, the Malay indentured labourers were paid in stones or plastic tokens, forbidden to leave or communicate with outsiders, and refused education beyond the primary level."

John Clunies-Ross, the fifth and last so-called King of the Islands and the great–great grandson of the sea captain was still "the chief of the court of the supreme power, owner of all the land and the houses, and the sole maker of laws" in 1984, by which time charges of slave labor had forced him to sell out his leasehold to the government of Australia for four million pounds. In the king's white rambling mansion, where "servants pad in and out with gin fizzes, there are dark portraits of ancestors on the walls," including one of the sea captain who found the islands uninhabited and imported the first Malay laborers. "The tables are covered with old copies of the *Times* and the *Illustrated London News*."

The last King of the Cocos explained in an interview, "We always dress for dinner. I mean we put on shoes and a tie. You could let your standards slip in a place like this."[350]

THE SOUTH SEAS

In 1842 Admiral Erskine stated that most of the missionaries among the islands of the western Pacific "belonged to the Presbyterian Church." This was certainly true in Fiji and New Guinea, and in 1857 the Presbyterians were given total responsibility for the New Hebrides.[351] In 1874 Britain proclaimed Fiji a British possession, and in 1875 Arthur Gordon became governor and high commissioner of the western Pacific. He favored the Fijians and would not allow their exploitation.[352]

In 1883 Thomas MacIlwraith, the prime minister of Queensland, seeing German designs on New Guinea, defied the London government and annexed the island in the name of Great Britain. From 1887 to 1897 Sir William MacGregor created a government as administrator of Papua. During his tenure agriculture was developed, native rights and customs were protected, and native policemen were employed.[353]

James Chalmers, the Livingstone of New Guinea, was born in Ardrishaig, Argyll, which he described as "a fearful place for whisky" and left to become a missionary. In 1878 he and his wife were the only white people on the mainland, which was then a savage, cannibalistic place. Chalmers civilized large sections of the population and discovered the Purari River in the process, but he ended up being eaten in 1901.[354]

THE EAST INDIES

Lord Minto, Sir John Malcolm, and General Ochterlony, all Scots, were put in charge of adding Nepal to the British Empire. Under Ochterlony the Ghurkas were subdued and Nepal conquered.[355]

Hugh Cleghorn, a professor of history at St. Andrews and an erstwhile soldier-of-fortune, provided the scheme which took Ceylon from the Dutch. He audaciously walked into the enemy camp and demanded that the Dutch governor hand over his troops. The bluff worked, and shortly thereafter the remaining Dutch forces on Ceylon were subdued, and it was added to the British Empire almost without loss of life.[356]

In 1703 a Scottish ship captain, Alexander Hamilton, called at Johore near Singapore and pronounced it a good site for a commercial port. When the British East India Company took Singapore in 1819 a Scot, Maj. William Farquhar, who had led the small invasion force, was left in charge and became First Resident. He was succeeded by another Scot, John Crawfurd, who took over in 1825. A third Scot, John Turnbull Thomson, was Singapore's official surveyor. Alexander Laurie Johnston founded the first European firm in Singapore and became the first chairman of the city's chamber of commerce. John Cameron was the influential editor of the *Straits Times*.[357]

CHINA

In 1774 two Scots, George Bogle and Alexander Hamilton, were the first British visitors to enter Tibet, the first Britons to cross the Tsanpu in its upper range, and the first to cross the Himalayas. They befriended the Panchen Lama and, because of them Britain became the first European country to establish official relations with Tibet.[358]

James Bruce, eighth earl of Elgin, laid the groundwork for greatly expanded trade with China by negotiating the Treaty of Tientsin in 1858.[359] The British presence in China was menaced by the T'ai P'ing rebellion in 1863, but an Englishman of Scottish descent, Charles George "Chinese" Gordon, in command of a motley peasant band, protected the European settlement at Shanghai. In a year and a half of fighting, Gordon proved to be one of the greatest commanders of irregular troops in history and crushed the rebels.[360] For thirty years Robert Hart, a Scot, served as the head of the Chinese financial system and opened many Chinese ports to commerce.[361]

The Noble House of Jardine Matheson was founded in Canton in the 1820s by two Scots, William Jardine (1784–1843), the original Tai-Pan, and James Matheson (1796–1898). They may have been the most influential Europeans in Chinese history, and were certainly that in the history of Hong Kong. When they moved their business there, after the opium wars, they became the colony's principal creators. Nine Hong Kong streets are named for different Tai-Pans. The Princely Hong, once the world's largest property owner, still turns over billions each year and employs over 220,000 people in more than thirty countries. Yet a few years ago the chairman, still a descendant of a founder, claimed that Jardine Matheson was just "an old-fashioned Scottish business," complete with an annual St. Andrew's Day party with pipes, haggis, and whisky. The thistle with Chinese characters remains the company's logo.[362]

The Hong Kong and Shanghai Bank was founded in 1864 on a prospectus drawn up by Thomas Sutherland (then the Hong Kong superintendent of the Scottish-owned Peninsula and Orient Steamship Company, and later Sir Thomas), which promised the new bank would be operated on sound "Scottish banking principles." As a result of Sutherland's effort, most of the money in circulation in present-day Hong Kong bears the bank's symbols, and it is by far the most influential bank in Asia and the most profitable bank in the world. The bank opened in Shanghai in 1865 under David McLean. The present chairman is a Scot, John M. Gray, as is the chairman of the holding company in London, Sir William Purves.[363]

In 1898 Sir James H. S. Lockhart acquired Hong Kong's New Territories and was their first special commissioner.[364] There have been many Scots involved in Hong Kong's government, including governor general Sir Henry Pottinger[365] and more recently Sir Murray MacLehose, who was governor general for ten years, longer than any of his predecessors. When he retired in 1982, "thousands came to the pier to wave goodby as he and his wife boarded a ferry for the airport at Kowloon."[366] One of the last British governors was the Scottish-born Oxfordian, Sir David Wilson.[367]

The Scots have always made spectacular contributions to education wherever they have gone. Sir Patrick Manson (1844–1922) "founded a school of medecine which became the University and Medical College of Hong Kong."[368] An almost unknown and unsung Presbyterian minister, Robert Morrison (1782–1834), in 1818 founded the Anglo-Chinese College at Malacca, Malaya, which was transferred to Hong Kong in 1843. In China Morrison translated the entire Bible into Chinese, and between 1815 and 1823 produced the first Chinese grammar and the first English-Chinese dictionary.[369] Another Scottish teacher, Reginald Johnston, was the faithful tutor to Pu Yi (1906–1967), the last emperor of China. He was the only European ever made a mandarin of the first rank. In the 1987 film *The Last Emperor*, Peter O'Toole played the part of Johnston.[370]

The End of the Empire

Following the end of World War II the British Empire was dismantled. The transition to the commonwealth was in no small part directed by the skillful work of Scottish-descended Lord Duncan-Sandys, who negotiated the independence of Jamaica, Trinidad and Tobago, Cyprus, Malta, Malaysia, Nigeria, Kenya, Uganda, Malawi, Tanganyika (now Tanzania), and Sierra Leone.[371]

That the empire's reach continues is demonstrated daily by the awesome power of the English language. Spoken by only about seven million people on a small island when King James VI and I unified it, the legacy of the empire he founded now finds one billion people using English and one hundred million more studying it in China. Over half the world's telephone calls, 75 percent of the telegrams and letters, and 80 percent of computer data are in English. When Italian pilots flying Italian planes between Italian cities converse with Italian air traffic controllers, they speak in English. So does every pilot on every plane in the world.[372] Even the new definitive dictionary of the Yiddish language is being written with English "glosses," or equivalents.[373]

The triumph and achievements of British civilization belongs, of course, to all Britons, not just Scots. Yet the empire could not have been created without the special breed of northerners whose exceptional works cover these pages. As Sir James Barrie said, addressing the students at St. Andrew's University when he was rector: "You come of a race of men the very wind of whose name has swept to the ultimate seas."[374]

Oh Lord, we do not ask you to give us wealth—
But show us where it is!
                                    —*Scottish joke*

Nae sweat, nae sweet.
                    —*Scottish proverb*

5

The Industrial Revolution

The Industrial Revolution did not begin in Scotland, but by the middle of the eighteenth century the little land in the north had become its center. By that time "Scotland did not merely share in a universal process...at last Scotland was leading the world."[1]

In this era Scotland possessed, at the same time, Adam Smith, David Hume, Joseph Black, and James Watt. "It is a matter of historical fact," says Lord Clark, "that these were the men who, soon after the year 1760, changed the whole current of European thought and life."[2] We have already seen how Hume and other Scottish philosophers at that time, notably Hutcheson and the Common Sense school, were affecting America and the world at large. Black and Watt discovered that heat, and in particular steam, could be a source of power. Watt soon produced the world's first independent power source, the practical steam engine, the pivotal invention of the entire Industrial Revolution.

It would be hard to overestimate the influence of Adam Smith on the Industrial Revolution. He was its apostle, the ideologist of free trade, and the first economic philosopher. Smith's fundamental idea is "that a democratic society, driven by the self-interest of its people competing against one another, can generate more wealth than the same society, ruled by a government that tries to regulate the minute details of economic life." "It is Adam Smith's greatest contribution that he recognized in the social world of economics, what Isaac Newton had recognized in the physical world of the heavens: a self-regulating natural order."[3] Smith's famous book, *The Wealth of Nations*, calls that order "the invisible hand." As a result of the work of Adam Smith the world abandoned mercantilism and became capitalist.

For most of the twentieth century, Smith's influence was profoundly affected by the ideas of Karl Marx, whose wife was, incidentally, half-Scottish.[4] But as the twentieth century comes to a close, Marx, whose system has been tried and found wanting all over the world, is now in disrepute, while Smith's ideas are on the ascendance from Angola to Britain, Poland to China, and even in Russia itself. In 1987 the *New York Times* observed: "As the world becomes more competitive, capitalist and communist countries alike are turning to Adam Smith."[5]

The people of Scotland immediately took to the new philosophy with unparalleled vigor, its workers, artisans, entrepreneurs, and inventors reconstructing sleepy Glasgow into a metropolis known for a while as the second city of the empire and the richest city in the world. At the time of the Union of 1707, Glasgow had only twelve thousand residents. By 1782 she had the world's first chamber of commerce and was the world's leading tobacco-importing port. By 1886 she produced more locomotives than any city in Europe, more steamships than any city in the world, had become the second city in the world, after London, to construct a subway, and was called home by a million people.[6]

But Scotland was not big enough for the enterprising Scots. Tens of thousands of emigrants took their philosophy and talents to all parts of the world and were consistent promoters of free trade and capitalism. In Canada, for instance, Professor T. W. Acheson has shown that between 1880 and 1885, 20 percent of Canada's industrial elite was born in Scotland and 28 percent had fathers born in Scotland, a total of 48 percent, while only 3 percent of the population of Canada, as a whole, were first and second generation Scots.[7]

In addition to philosophy, the contribution of the Scots to the Industrial Revolution involves two subjects: invention and business.

Invention and the Scots

The contribution of the Scottish nation to the industrialization of the world through the practical science of invention is almost certainly greater than that of any other people, regardless of size. Indeed, it is difficult to identify a major invention which does not have some Scottish component. The following is a presentation of the highlights of the Scottish genius for invention. As extensive as it is, it represents only a small fraction of the total.[8]

BASIC INVENTIONS

The most important invention of the entire Industrial Revolution is that of the practical steam engine, by James Watt. Watt conceived of the idea of a separate condenser on a walk across Glasgow Green. "He saw that by a system of valves the steam could make the piston return to the top of the cylinder as well as descend." Later he adapted his engine to rotary motion and devised the flywheel and the governor for control.[9]

An incredible string of lucky circumstances brought Watt's invention to the market. Dr. William Small, the tutor of Jefferson, left America for Birmingham with a letter of introduction from Benjamin Franklin to the English industrialist Matthew Boulton, who helped Small set up as a physician there. It was Small who told Boulton about Watt's machine, and on June 1, 1775, Watt and Boulton entered into their partnership and changed the world.[10] From that time on, factories did not have to be built at waterfalls and powered travel on land and sea became inevitable.[11]

The subsequent advancement of heavy industry was aided by the basic inventions of four Scots. The hot blast furnace, in which the blast of air is heated before being forced into the furnace under pressure, was the creation of James Beaumont Neilson in 1828. It was the pivotal development of the iron and steel industry, vastly increasing output. Neilson's invention reduced the fuel costs of making iron by more than two-thirds.[12] The steam hammer was invented by James Nasmyth of Edinburgh in 1839. Nasmyth also invented the pile driver and the dentist's drill. But his most important invention was the creation of standardized, automatic machine tools, which made mass production possible.[13] In 1850 Sir William Fairbairn invented the crane[14] and in the middle of the nineteenth century James Young (1811–1883) founded the petroleum industry by producing paraffin from oil shale in the Lothians of Scotland. He coined the word "cracking," still used by the world's oil-refining industry to mean the chemical process by which various products such as gasoline are extracted from crude oil. By 1858 Young was the world's largest producer of coal oil, his patents on license to twenty firms in the United States.[15]

Photography was not discovered by any one person. It was rather a continuous process, in which three Scots played important roles. David Octavius Hill and Robert Adamson, of Edinburgh, were the first to recognize the artistic potential of the new medium, making the first artistic photographs in 1843.[16] And George Eastman was able to produce his first Kodak camera by purchasing a patent for a visible film indicator from Peter Houston, a Scottish immigrant to America.[17]

The long march from the abacus to the computer relates to Scots at least as early as 1615, when John Napier (1550–1617), the Scottish inventor of logarithms, built what is regarded as the world's first mechanical computing device. A series of numbered rods (Napier's bones) were used to facilitate multiplication and division.[18] In 1843 Ada Byron, the daughter of the half-Scottish poet Lord Byron, wrote a list of instructions for a hypothetical computer theorized by the Englishman Charles Babbage, thus becoming the world's first computer programmer. Others go farther and call her the world's first computer scientist. In 1979 the U.S. Department of Defense named its new standardized computer language ADA in her honor.[19]

In 1916 James Graham Johnston, born in Scotland, and Thomas J. Watson, an American of Ulster-Scottish ancestry on both sides,[20] developed a practical tabulating machine—a prototype computer—for the debt-ridden Computing-Tabulating-Recording Company, which Watson was managing, later to become IBM.[21] Both men became millionaires, and in the mid-twentieth century Johnston returned to Scotland in triumph to open the IBM facility at Greenock.[22]

In the 1930s Alan Mathison Turing, a resident of England of Scottish ancestry, built the Turing Machine, an early computer. Turing, a mathematical genius, believed that all concrete mathematical calculations could be programmed on his machine, perhaps the most important idea leading to the computer revolution. It may turn out, says one expert, "that when a future historian of automation looks back..." the computer revolution "will have much more to do with the...abstract ideas of Alan Turing than everything else."[23]

During World War II Turing built a decoding machine[24] that has been called the world's first electronic digital computer.

An American, Howard H. Aiken, presumed to be Scottish by his surname, is credited with producing the world's first automatic sequence computer, in 1939.[25] He was assisted in his research by Grace Murray Hopper (1906–1992), a scientist who won the Legion of Merit and over twenty honorary degrees. Hopper retired from the navy in 1986 as a rear admiral, the highest-ranking woman and the oldest American naval officer. Amazing Grace, as she was called, was the coinventor of the early computer language Cobol, and also coined the word "bug," meaning a defect in a machine or system. She was, like the others, of Scottish ancestry.[26] The pocket calculator, perhaps the most widely used computer, was first produced by Clive Sinclair, an Englishman of Scottish descent.[27]

It is said that the transistor has "changed the world's industry more than any invention since James Watt's steam engine." The senior member of the team of three Americans who received the Nobel Prize for its invention was Walter H. Brattain, of Scottish ancestry.[28] The transphasor, an optical switch pioneered at Herriot-Watt University in Scotland, may someday replace the electronic switches now used universally in the world's computers. It is predicted that transphasors will eventually lead to photonic, or optical switch, computers capable of calculating thousands of times faster than electronic computers.[29]

Scottish interest in electricity goes back at least to May 1793, when Prof. John Robison built a Voltaic pile—an electric battery. Volta's discovery appears to have been made in August 1796.[30] A Scottish-American, Joseph Henry, built the first electromagnet of insulated wire and the first with spool winding, in 1829. His electromagnet "is essentially the one used since then in modern generators and electric motors."[31] Electric welding was invented in 1877 by Elihu Thomson, an American of Scottish ancestry who was born in Manchester, England.[32]

The uncomfortable and fearsome darkness in which mankind had always lived was ended in Scotland by the invention of gaslight. William Murdock, an associate of James Watt, lit his own house in 1792.[33] In 1834 James B. Lindsay, of Dundee, astonished his neighbors by illuminating his home with electric lamps. And in 1878 J. W. Swan, a Briton of Scottish ancestry, exhibited and patented a carbon incandescent lamp that he had made nine years earlier.[34] The first complete incandescent lighting system was demonstrated at Menlo

Park, New Jersey, in 1879 by Thomas Edison, whose mother, Mary Elliott, was of Scottish ancestry.[35] In 1913 another Scottish-American, Irving Langmuir, invented the tungsten filament and developed the use of inert gasses inside the lightbulb, greatly increasing its efficiency.[36]

Edison, the "Wizard of Menlo Park," was the peerless inventor, amassing 1,098 patents.[37] Among his most famous basic inventions are the stock ticker (1870) and the mimeograph (1876), which was the first practical duplicating machine.[38] In 1877 he produced the phonograph, and a year later the wax phonograph record.[39] He is also credited with the invention of motion pictures, in 1894,[40] and talking motion pictures in 1913.[41]

AGRICULTURAL INVENTIONS

David Fife, a Canadian Scot, developed the first hard spring wheat in North America,[42] and John Mackintosh produced the famous apple variety.[43] But it is through five mechanical inventions that the Scots have made their largest contribution to agriculture. Before 1743 Michael Menzies of Scotland was credited with inventing a threshing machine which "could do the work of six."[44] However, the first successful threshing machine is credited to another Scot, Andrew Meikle, in 1786.[45] In 1780 James Small, also of Scotland, gave farmers the first scientific plow—the improved swing plow—by inventing the curved cast-iron mould board.[46]

In 1827 the Rev. Patrick Bell of Carmyllie invented the reaper, tested it successfully, and was awarded fifty pounds by the Highland and Agricultural Society. But Bell did not patent his invention, and in 1834 an American Scot, Cyrus McCormick, reinvented the reaper, patented it, founded the International Harvester Company, and became fabulously rich.[47]

Later on in the century Robert Dalzell, an American Scot, invented the grain elevator.[48] The milking machine was invented in Scotland by William Murchland, in 1891.[49]

COMMUNICATIONS INVENTIONS

The four principal communications inventions—the telegraph, telephone, radio, and television—are all largely credited to men of the Scottish nation, and their contribution to these creations is well documented. The idea of the telegraph goes back to 1753, when Charles Morrison, writing anonymously as "C. M." to *Scots Maga-*

zine suggested a way to build the first practical telegraph.[50] In 1831 the American Scot Joseph Henry built a working telegraph but did not patent it. Within a few years another American of Scottish ancestry, Samuel Finley Breese Morse, had built a working telegraph and invented the Morse code. In 1844 he constructed the world's first practical telegraph system between Washington and Baltimore, and tapped out the first message in Morse code: "What hath God wrought."[51]

Lord Kelvin, another Scot, invented the electric apparatus for the first transatlantic cable, supervised its construction, and sent the first signals between Europe and America.[52] Sir Sandford Fleming produced the Pacific cable between Canada and Australia.[53] The fax machine, at this writing becoming a common appliance, is thought to be a relatively new invention. Actually, the first patent on fascimile transmission by wire was issued to Alexander Bain of Scotland in 1843, just a few years after the basic technology was produced by Henry and Morse.[54]

Almost everyone knows that a Scot invented the telephone. Alexander Graham Bell was born in Edinburgh and moved to Canada for his health in 1870. Two years later, to train teachers of the deaf, he opened a school in Boston where he gave lessons in the mechanics of speech. This interest in sound and speech caused him to conceive of a telephone and led to years of experiments to construct one. On March 10, 1876, Bell pronounced the first telephone message to his assistant, Thomas A. Watson, who was in the next room: "Mr. Watson, come here; I want you."[55]

Again, almost everyone knows that Marchese Guglielmo Marconi was the inventor of radio, but few know that his mother was Anne Jameson, the daughter of Andrew Jameson, an Irishman of Scottish descent. It was Marconi's mother who encouraged his experiments, and in 1896 he filed his first patent in England, for which he is universally recognized as the inventor of practical radiotelegraphy.[56] Radio detecting and ranging, or radar, was perfected during World War II by the British scientist Sir Robert Watson-Watt, a direct descendant of James Watt.[57]

The principles of modern electronic television were formulated by a Scot, A.A. Campbell Swinton, who, in 1908, proposed the use of magnetically reflected cathode ray tubes at both the camera and the receiver.[58] But few men have ever done more to change the habits of the human race than John Logie Baird, a native of Helensburgh and the actual inventor of television. Baird was the first to achieve television over any distance. He reproduced objects in outline (1924), transmitted recognizable human faces (1925), and on January 26, 1926, at 22 Frith Street in London, before a distinguished audience of members of the Royal Institution of England (mainly writers, scientists, and radio engineers) he demonstrated the first true television. The following day the *Times* of London, which had covered the event, gave Baird rave reviews.[59]

According to R. M. Bowes of Oakville, Connecticut, television was invented in 1918 when Bowes, who worked in a shipyard with Baird, became his "Mr. Watson." Baird took the young Bowes to his flat to show him his experimental equipment and told him to go into an adjoining room to see if an image would appear on a makeshift screen. When one did, Baird told Bowes that he was the first person ever to witness television and gave him a penny as a memento which Bowes still has.[60]

In 1927 Baird demonstrated television between London and Glasgow, and in 1928 demonstrated the first practical color television. In the same year he invented the video disc, sent the first pictures from London to New York and the first from shore to ship. By 1929 Baird had launched his first television service via BBC transmitter and was broadcasting until 1935. In 1930 he marketed the first television sets, the Baird Televisions, and set up the first big screen in the London Coliseum.[61]

Baird also invented phonovision, a talking picture telephone, noctovision, which enabled sight in the dark, and three dimensional television. Handicapped throughout his life by ill health and poverty, he had to try many things to keep economically afloat. He was the sometime producer of Osmo boot polish, Speedy Cleaner soap, and Baird's Trinidad Jam, among other things. While employed at a power plant he even tried to turn coal dust into diamonds. Baird brought a great deal of energy to bear on the coal dust, fuses were blown, Glasgow was blacked out for eleven minutes, and Baird was fired.[62]

TRANSPORTATION INVENTIONS

The five principal inventions relating to transportation—the steam railway, steamboat, bicycle, automobile, and airplane—all have distinctly Scottish components.

William Murdock, the inventor of gaslight and an associate of James Watt, built the first experimental model of a locomotive in 1785 but did not obtain a patent. Richard Trevithick of England saw Murdock's prototype and received his patent in 1802.[63]

The Kilmarnock and Troon Railway "experimented with steam power in 1816 or 1817."[64] But the builder of the first practical locomotive and the "inventor and founder of railways" was George Stephenson, an Englishman of Scottish parentage. In 1823 Stephenson was invited to build a railway in England from Stockton to Darlington. (The route for the line had been surveyed by the Scottish lighthouse engineer Robert Stevenson, the grandfather of author Robert Louis Stevenson.)[65] George Stephenson persuaded the directors to use a steam locomotive instead of horses for power. He designed and built the railway and it opened, triumphantly, on September 27, 1825. On that day the first practical steam locomotive in the world pulled the first public passenger steam railway train in the world.[66]

In 1830 Peter Cooper, an American of Scottish descent, built the first American steam locomotive, the Tom Thumb.[67] The world's first railway ferry, between Granton and Burntisland, opened in 1847, connecting Edinburgh with the north of Scotland.[68]

In 1786 James Rumsey, born in Virginia to Scottish parents in 1754, made the world's first demonstration of a steamboat on the Potomac River in the presence of George Washington and hundreds of spectators.[69] On October 14, 1788, Patrick Millar (or Miller) and William Symington (1764–1831) ran the first steam-driven boat in Europe on a loch near Dumfries not far from where the poet Robert Burns farmed. Some say that Burns, a tenant of Millar, was actually on board and that he excitedly described the experience to others.[70]

In 1801 Symington operated the world's first practical steamboat, the *Charlotte Dundas*, on the Clyde River at seven miles per hour. Robert Fulton (1765–1815), the son of an Ayrshire farmer, is said to have been one of the spectators.[71] Two years later Fulton built what some claim was the world's first reliable steamboat, a seventy-four-foot sidewheeler, which he demonstrated on the Seine before cheering Parisians.[72] Fulton, with the help of Robert Livingston, the Scottish-American purchaser of Louisiana, launched the first practical American steamboat, the *Clermont*, on the Hudson in 1807. In the same year, between New York and Albany, Fulton and Livingston established the first commercial steamboat service in the world.[73]

Still another Scot, Henry Bell, had the first commercial steamboat success in Europe when his *Comet* made her first trip with passengers from Glasgow to Greenock in 1812.[74] Sir William Fairbairn built the first iron steamship in the world, the *Lord Dundas*, in 1830.[75]

Along with the invention of the steamboat, Scots have made many other significant marine innovations. Robert Stevenson planned and built over twenty lighthouses and invented and installed flashing lights.[76] Lord Kelvin completely reinvented the mariner's compass and produced the tidal gauge, the tide predictor, the mirror galvanometer, and an advanced sounding apparatus.[77] Robert Wilson of Scotland invented the screw propeller in 1827. The screw propellor was first patented by the Scoto-Swedish John Ericsson in 1836.[78] The modern system of shipping in sealed containers was developed in the mid-twentieth century by an American Scot, Malcolm McLean, and has completely changed world commerce, dramatically lowering freight costs and transforming the appearance of ports all over the world.

Some sources say that the pedal-driven bicycle was invented in 1835 by Gavin Dalziel of Lesmahagow, Scotland,[79] but most standard authorities credit Kirkpatrick "Daft Pate" Macmillan, in 1839.[80] On June 11, 1842, this article appeared in the *Glasgow Courier*: "On Wednesday a gentleman who stated that he came from Thornhill, in Dumfriesshire, was placed at the Gorbals public bar, charged with riding along the pavement on a velocipede to the obstruction of the passage, and with having, by so doing, thrown over a child. It appeared from his statement that he had, on the day previous, come all the way from Old Cumnock, a distance of forty miles, bestriding the velocipede, and that he performed the journey in the space of five hours. . . . The child had not sustained any injury, and under the circumstances the offender was fined only five shillings." The article then states that the judge asked for a demonstration and Daft Pate performed several figure eights in the courtyard, and concludes, "This invention will not supersede the railroad."[81] Although this prediction proved correct, the bicycle is still the principal means of transportation for millions of people. The two-stroke engine, the precursor of today's motorcycle and lawnmower engines, was invented by Sir Dugald Clerk, a Glaswegian, in 1879.[82]

James Nasmyth (1808–1890) built and operated a steam horseless carriage carrying eight passengers on Queensferry Road, Edinburgh, "in his late teens."[83] The development of the automobile was enhanced in 1817 by Rev. Robert Stirling's invention of the first gas-sealed internal combustion engine.[84] Sir Dugald Clerk pioneered the development of internal combustion engines and built his first gas engine in 1876.[85] The first oil engine was patented by Ackroyd Stuart in 1890, two years before the patent of Rudolph Diesel.[86]

Alexander Winton, a penniless Scottish immigrant to America, built the first automobile in Cleveland and one of the first in America in 1896. His cars were the class of the time. In 1900 Winton drove one of his cars fifty miles in one hour, seventeen minutes, and fifty seconds, to establish a world record. A later Winton was the first to break seventy miles per hour, beating a Mercedes in a race. In 1903 a Winton that is now in the Smithsonian became the first car to cross America, making the trip from San Francisco to New York in two months. Winton also made diesel engines and sold this business to General Motors, where it became the basis for GM's diesel division.[87]

The principal of the double tube pneumatic tire was patented by Robert Thomson of Scotland in 1845.[88] In 1888 John Boyd Dunlop, a native of Scotland living in Belfast, Ireland, reinvented the pneumatic tire and founded the Dunlop Rubber Company to produce it.[89] The speedometer was invented in Scotland by Sir Keith Elphinstone (1864–1944).[90]

The invention of the airplane can be claimed by Scots even though the Wright brothers did not have any Scottish ancestry. Alexander Graham Bell and Samuel Langley launched a manned, powered, heavier-than-air flight on the Potomac River in Washington, D.C., in 1903. Their airplane flew but suddenly crashed. Nine days later the Wright brothers made their famous flight at Kittyhawk, North Carolina. The Smithsonian Institution called the Bell-Langley plane "the first flying machine in the history of the world capable of flight with a man," and displayed this plane and *not* the Wright brothers' plane until 1948.[91] Bell continued his interest in flight at his home, Beinn Bhreagh at Baddeck, Nova Scotia, where he founded the Aerial Experiment Association. It was there, in 1909, that the Scottish-Canadian James Alexander Douglas McCurdy made the first successful flight in the British Empire.[92]

MILITARY AND NAVAL INVENTIONS

In 1776 a Scot, Maj. Patrick Ferguson of the British army, patented the first practical breech-loading rifle. Demonstrations proved Ferguson's rifle to be more powerful and more accurate than those then in use. It was far faster to reload and thus increased firepower three or four times. It could be loaded in a prone position and would therefore save many lives, and it could operate under wet conditions.

It could even be reloaded during an advance.

The Ferguson rifle's first use in battle occurred on September 11, 1777, at the Battle of Brandywine during the American War of Independence. As expected, the new weapon proved to be extremely effective. However, for some reason which has never been explained, the British general Howe packed up the vastly superior rifles after the battle and never used them again for the balance of the war.

During the battle Ferguson, the best marksman in the British army and holding the best weapon in the world, declined, on moral grounds, to shoot an American officer in the back at close range. The officer, he later found out, was Washington. It is interesting to speculate on whether the outcome of the war would have been different had Ferguson pulled the trigger that day, and had Howe continued to use the Ferguson rifle.[93]

In 1805 a Scottish clergyman, Alexander John Forsyth, revolutionized all firearms theory by inventing the percussion lock. To do this he developed a percussion powder which would explode when struck by a hammer. Separate priming powder and free sparks were no longer necessary. He then enclosed the powder in metal, thus laying the basis for the cartridge. Forsyth's invention was almost as important as that of gunpowder itself.[94]

Further developments in firearms continued to come from Scots. William Malcolm invented telescopic sights[95] and in the 1880s Archibald Barr was coinventor of the range finder.[96] James P. Lee, born in Scotland, was the inventor of the Lee-Enfield rifle. This rifle was faster to fire and held twice the number of cartridges as the Mauser and Springfield rifles, and became famous in World War I.[97] An American, Samuel Colt, Scottish on both sides of his ancestry, in 1833 perfected the first handgun with a revolving breech.[98] Later Colt pistols, such as the legendary Colt .45, were the standard side arms of the U.S. Army from 1846 to 1985.[99]

Several naval inventions are credited to Scots. The gunboat *Monitor*, with its rotating turret, was used against the Confederacy during the American Civil War. She was the first ironclad warship in the world, and was designed and named by John Ericsson, a Swede whose mother was of Scottish descent.[100] The duke of Montrose invented and designed the aircraft carrier during World War I.[101] And Robert Fulton, of steamboat fame, invented and named the torpedo in 1804.[102] It would be another half-century before torpedoes were self-propelled and in common use.

The Scots in Business

BANKING

> One Scot is a store.
> Two is a church.
> Three is a bank.
>
> —*Saying in pioneer America*

Banking has always seemed attractive to Scots. In fact it was Scots who founded the central banks of three major countries: England, France, and the United States.

The Bank of England was founded in 1694 by William Paterson, who was born on a farm in Scotland. Paterson gave the world a new banking system, which would consist of a central bank with certain privileges and powers over the many private banks. Paterson's bank was the beginning of modern banking.[103] He was also the promoter of the ill-fated Darien scheme.[104]

"Solid as the Bank of England" is a phrase still appropriate today, but certainly not to the central bank that another Scot founded in France. John Law (1671–1729), a financial genius, was born in Edinburgh and fled Scotland after he had killed someone in a duel. He became known as the Scottish wizard, and in 1716 founded the Banque Générale, the first central bank in France. His bank issued paper money against deposits of coin, which resulted in a wave of prosperity in France. Law then combined his bank with the Louisiana Company, which had the exclusive rights to develop the Mississippi Valley. Under his direction New Orleans was founded and, initially, his development scheme in America produced even greater prosperity for France, but owing partly to political intrigue that was not his fault, and frenzied speculation in the bank's securities, the "Mississippi Bubble" burst in 1720, bankrupting many of the French aristocracy. Law, once the darling of royalty, was ruined and mobs threatened his life. He fled France with this comment: "Last year I was the richest individual who ever lived. Today I have nothing, not even enough to keep alive." Law died in poverty in Venice and is not well remembered in France, where a verse about him is still recited:

Cet Écossais célèbre,
Ce calculateur sans égale,
Qui par les règles de l'algèbre,
A mis France à l'Hôpital.

This celebrated Scot,
This schemer without equal,
Who by the rules of algebra,
Has put France in the hospital. [105]

Alexander Hamilton, a half-Scot from New York, was appointed as the first secretary of the treasury of the United States by George Washington. During his term he created the country's first central bank and organized its treasury.[106] Hamilton also founded New York's first bank, the Bank of New York, in 1784. Of its first eight directors at least four, Hamilton, William Maxwell, Gen. Alexander MacDougall, and William Seton, were Scots. Maxwell, a president of the Bank of New York, was also one of the founders of the city's chamber of commerce.[107] In 1799 Hamilton and Aaron Burr (who later killed Hamilton in a duel) were responsible for founding the company which became Chase Manhattan, America's largest bank.[108] The first savings bank in America was founded in New York by Archibald Gracie, in whose mansion the mayor of New York City now resides. Gracie was a fabulously rich Scottish immigrant who is given the largest measure of credit for developing New York as a great seaport.[109]

The first bank in Baltimore was organized by Robert Gilmour,[110] and the first in Chicago by George Smith, of Aberdeen. Smith, also founded a bank in Milwaukee with another Scot, Alexander Mitchell.[111] One of the most important banks in the industrial history of the United States was founded in 1870 by Thomas Mellon, an Ulster Scot born in County Tyrone. Mellon left his parents, who were scratching out a bare existence from the western Pennsylvania soil, and moved to Pittsburgh, where he became a judge and founded the Mellon Bank. His son, Andrew, built the bank into one of the greatest fortunes in America and financed the founding of Gulf Oil, the Aluminum Company of America, and many others. In the 1920s Andrew Mellon became secretary of the treasury and was probably the richest man in the country.[112]

In Baltimore, in 1800, Alexander Brown, born in Ballymena, Ulster of Scottish ancestry, founded the oldest investment bank in the United States, which still bears his name. He also began Brown

Brothers in New York. Founded in 1818, Brown Brothers Harriman and Company is the largest and oldest surviving private bank in America today.[113] Also in Baltimore, Alexander E. Duncan founded Commercial Credit, America's largest factoring firm, in 1912. He died in 1972 at the age of ninety-three, leaving his business with four billion dollars in assets.[114]

After a Scot had founded the Bank of England it was only natural that some of his countrymen would follow his success in the south. The prestigious London banking firm of Robert Fleming and Company, as well as Barclays Bank, one of England's largest, are examples of this.[115] In 1755, in London, two Scots, Thomas and James Coutts, founded Coutts and Company, bankers to the royal family for two hundred years, plus Pitt, Scott, Dickens, Thackeray, and many other notables. In the *Gondoliers*, Gilbert and Sullivan wrote:

> The aristocrat who hunts and shoots,
> The aristocrat who banks with Coutts.[116]

The Bank of Scotland was founded in 1695, only a year after Paterson had founded the Bank of England. Scottish banks pioneered many of the practices of modern banking, and by the beginning of the nineteenth century had developed the most advanced system in the world.[117] By 1878 there was one banking location in Scotland for every 4,036 people, compared with one for every 12,493 in England and Wales, and one for every 13,994 in Ireland.[118] As of 1973 the Royal Bank of Scotland had more assets than the largest bank in many much larger nations, including Argentina, Egypt, Iran, Korea, Pakistan, Peru, Portugal, Taiwan, Thailand, and Turkey.[119] The world's first savings bank was founded in Scotland in 1810 by the Rev. Henry Duncan, the parish minister of Ruthwell, a village in Dumfriesshire. All of his parishioners, no matter how poor, were encouraged to save.[120]

Perhaps because of this early start there are almost two hundred thousand people employed in banking, insurance, and finance in present-day Scotland, a huge number for a country of only five million. Financial institutions unique to Scotland are the Scottish trusts. These are powerful combines in which patient fund managers take the long-term view and have a reputation for spending most of their time sitting before a fireplace in the company of a dog, thinking. By 1990 Edinburgh's fund managers were running about eighty billion pounds, more than any other European city except

London and Zurich.[121] Firms such as Murray Johnstone, Ivory and Sime, Martin Currie, Edinburgh Fund Managers, Walter Scott, Dunedin, and Baillie Gifford avoid fads, preferring to play the big trends. "We're not racists," a portfolio manager said in 1987. "We do employ the odd English interloper."[122]

SHIPBUILDING

The business for which Scotland is most famous is shipbuilding, a calling at which it excelled long before the age of steam. Scotts of Greenock, the oldest private shipbuilding firm in the world, was founded in 1711.[123] In addition to the Scottish development of the steam engine and its subsequent application to navigation, Thomas Wilson gave Scotland another ingredient to become dominant in shipbuilding when, in 1818, he regularly ran his *Vulcan* on the Forth and Clyde Canal. This was the world's first iron passenger vessel.[124] In the same year David Napier designed the *Rob Roy*, which showed that steamboats could sail on the ocean.[125] Many other innovations came throughout the nineteenth century by men such as Napier and his cousin Robert, Charles Randolph, John Elder, James Howden, and Dr. A.C. Kirk, all of whom made continuous improvements on marine engines which became world standards, made the Clyde the most important shipbuilding river in the world, and the employment of thousands of legendary Scottish chief engineers on ships everywhere necessary.[126]

The earliest crossing of the Atlantic by a power vessel was by the Dutch flag *Curaçao*, a 127-foot wooden paddle boat of 438 tons, which had been built in Scotland in 1826.[127] The brothers John Laird and MacGregor Laird pioneered iron shipbuilding in order to promote commerce on the Niger River. Their hope was that legitimate commerce would prove more profitable than the slave trade, which they hated, and would thereby adversely affect it. In 1832 they sent the *Alburkah*, designed by MacGregor Laird, from Liverpool to the Niger. It was the first iron vessel to make an ocean voyage. In 1838 Laird sent the *Sirius* from England to New York. It was the first ship to cross the Atlantic under continuous steam power.[128] The pinnacle of the Clyde's hegemony came in the 1930s, when the Clydebank works of John Brown and Company, using Cunard designs developed by Sir James McNeill and Dr. John Brown (no relation to the owner of the yard) produced the *Queen Mary* and the *Queen Elizabeth*.[129]

It must not be forgotten that the rise of the steamship coincided with the glory age of sail. Once again it was Scots, but this time usually on the other side of the Atlantic, who made the greatest contributions. The first clipper ship, the 500-ton *Ann McKim*, was built in Baltimore in 1833 by Isaac McKim.[130] The greatest of all the clipper builders was the Canadian-American Donald McKay, who made the largest and fastest sailboats the world has ever seen. His ships recorded twelve of the thirteen times any sailing vessel surpassed four hundred nautical miles in twenty-four hours. His *Great Republic*, 320 feet in length, was the largest clipper ship ever built. In 1854 McKay's *Flying Cloud* established a New York to San Francisco speed record of eighty-nine days and eight hours, which stood for 135 years until broken by a small yacht in 1989.[131] In the Great Tea Race of 1866 Scotland showed off her maritime prowess. Sixteen ships left Foochow for London in May. The first three to arrive, after ninety-nine days and sixteen thousand miles, the *Taeping*, the *Ariel*, and the *Serica*, were all from Steele's yard in Greenock and all were sailed by Scots: Captains Keay, MacKinnon, and Innes, respectively.[132] In 1869 the Dumbarton firm of Scott and Linton contributed the magnificent record-breaking tea clipper *Cutty Sark*, perhaps the fastest sailing ship ever for sustained speed over long runs in all types of weather.[133] The *Cutty Sark* sits proudly today in her berth in Greenwich, England.

SHIPPING

Since the Scots were so involved in building ships it is not surprising that they started many of the famous shipping lines.[134] The most notable of these is the Cunard Line, begun by Samuel Cunard, a Canadian of Scottish ancestry who came to Britain for financing and expertise. Among those who joined in the founding of the firm were David MacIvor, James Donaldson, and a Glasgow minister's sons, George and James Burns, who were already shipping between Glasgow and Liverpool. One of the great Scottish engineers, Robert Napier, joined with the others in 1839 and designed and built the first four Cunarders for the North Atlantic.[135]

Scottish women joined with the men in advancing navigation. Betsy Millar (1793–1864) of Ayr was the first woman to be registered with Lloyd's as a ship captain.[136]

RAILROADS

Many of the important railroads of North America were begun by Scots. The greatest of these railroad barons was James J. Hill, a Canadian-American of mainly Scottish ancestry. Hill owned and/or controlled the Great Northern Railroad, the Northern Pacific Railroad, and the Chicago Burlington and Quincy Railroad.[137] During the age of steam Glasgow was the leading builder of locomotives in the world. One company, North British Locomotive, closed in 1962, after having built almost twenty-seven thousand units.[138]

AIR TRANSPORT

Scots have been prominent in the development of airlines, but it is in the construction of aircraft that their efforts have been truly amazing. At the end of World War II three out of the four major American aircraft-building companies had been created by Scots. The first was Lockheed, a company founded in 1926 by the Loughead brothers, Allan and Malcolm, which still survives today and is valued in the billions.[139]

Few men have ever attained the dominance in any calling as Donald Wills Douglas did in the building of airplanes. At one time Douglas planes carried 95 percent of all United States passenger traffic. In fact, in 1935 the DC-3, also known affectionately as the Gooney Bird, launched the era of commercial aviation as the first plane ever to make money carrying only passengers. The DC-3 is also the most durable plane ever built. Out of 10,629 produced between 1935 and 1946, more than 1,500 were still flying in 1985 and one of these had logged eighty-seven thousand hours, the equivalent of ten years in the air.[140]

James S. McDonnell, Jr., started making planes in 1939 at age forty, beginning with capital of only 165,000 dollars. McDonnell delivered the first carrier-based jet fighter in 1946 and later built the Mercury spacecraft, which carried the first American into orbit. The company eventually took over the business of Douglas, and in 1989 McDonnell Douglas had sales over fourteen billion dollars and 133,000 employees.[141] The Scottish-born aeronautical engineer Sir James Arnot Hamilton (1923–) was the principal creator of the first supersonic passenger aircraft, the British-French Concorde.

RETAILING

The United States   The chain store seems to be a creation of Scots in colonial America. William Allason operated a chain at Falmouth, Virginia, around the time of the Revolution and the Cunninghame interests operated seven units in Maryland as well as fourteen in Virginia. In the nineteenth century A. Swan Brown organized a chain of Scottish dry-goods stores called the Syndicate Trading Company. Each firm was owned, run, and staffed by Scots. Some examples are:

> Providence—Callender, McAuslan and Troup
> Buffalo—Adam, Meldum and Anderson
> Hartford—Brown, Thomson and Co.
> Springfield, Massachusetts—Forbes and Wallace
> Worcester—Denholm and McKay

The Syndicate also had stores in Rochester, Reading, Salem, Minneapolis, and Kansas City.[142]

A. T. Stewart was the largest store in the world when it opened at Ninth and Broadway in New York City in 1862. Its owner, Alexander T. Stewart, is credited with the invention of modern retailing and the one-price system—prices clearly marked, no discounts for certain classes of customers, and no bargaining.[143] Chicago's great store, Carson Pirie Scott, was begun by Scots who number among their descendants actor Bruce Dern and poet Archibald Macleish.[144] In the late nineteenth century Donaldson's Glass Block, a great department store, dominated retailing in Minneapolis. It was built by a Scottish immigrant, William Donaldson (1849–1897).[145] New York's best furniture store, W. and J. Sloane, was started by William and John Sloane, whose family had emigrated from Edinburgh in 1834.[146] W. T. Grant, a high school dropout, founded his first store with one thousand dollars. At his death in 1972 there were 1,176 Grant stores, with sales over one billion dollars.[147]

The department store Santa Claus was the creation of James Edgar, a native of Edinburgh, who opened a department store in Brockton, Massachusetts. During the Christmas season of 1890 Edgar went to the store in costume, playing the part of Santa himself. Within days of his original appearance trains were bringing children to Brockton from as far away as Boston and Providence. Within a few years Santa was appearing in stores all over the United States, just as he does today.[148]

Canada In addition to their influence in the Hudson's Bay Company, a major Canadian retailer already discussed in chapter 4, Scots founded two other giant Canadian retail firms. Simpson's was begun by Robert Simpson and Eaton's by Timothy Eaton, who was born in Ulster of Scottish Presbyterian ancestry.[149]

Great Britain In the 1970s Harrod's, the largest store in Britain, and 136 other stores were controlled by Hugh Fraser, whose great grandfather started in business with a fabric shop in Glasgow.[150] The Argyll Group, a leading British retailer headed by James Gulliver, the son of a small town Scottish grocer, made history in 1985. Gulliver bid 2.74 billion pounds for Distillers Company, proposing to move its headquarters back to Scotland. Although his bid failed it was the largest take-over bid up to that time in British history.[151]

ACCOUNTING

Although its origins go back to Babylonian times, modern accounting developed in Scotland. George A. Watson (b. 1645) of Edinburgh was the first full-time public accountant in western Europe. By 1697 Alexander Herreot of the same city was established as a teacher of bookkeeping.[152]

LABOR

Alexander Macdonald, born in Lanarkshire, became the first president of the National Mineworkers in Britain.[153] Philip Murray, born in the town of Blantyre in the same shire, became the head of the United Steelworkers of America.[154] Also born in Blantyre was William B. Wilson, the first U.S. secretary of labor.[155] William Pollock, general president of the United Textile Workers of America, was born in Philadelphia of Scottish parentage.[156]

In the last years of the twentieth century several of the most influential labor leaders in America have been Scottish. Douglas Fraser, a self-described "Scottish immigrant kid," became president of the United Automobile Workers of America, the management of which, he always reminded people, had never sustained a jail sentence. As the first American labor leader to sit on the board of a major American corporation, Fraser was able to help Chrysler restructure its labor costs while getting a good deal for his workers. His role in the rebirth of the company, a modern industrial miracle, proved significant.[157] In 1992 the 1.5 million–member Teamsters

Union, America's largest, chose former truck driver Ronald Carey, of Scottish, Irish, French, and American-Indian ancestry, as president.[158]

Lane Kirkland, a Scottish-American, retired in 1995 after sixteen years as president of the A.F.L.-C.I.O., the most powerful union position in America. Kirkland used his presidency to project American unions as strongly anti-Communist. A forceful advocate of Lech Walesa's Polish Solidarity movement, Kirkland even created a clandestine section in the A.F.L.-C.I.O. which actually smuggled supplies behind the Iron Curtain.[159]

SCOTTISH BRAND NAMES

Throughout the world products are sold bearing dozens of Scottish-originated brand names.[160] The whisky companies alone would make an essay, but are too well-known to require one. Among the more famous Scottish brands is Avon Products, the world's largest cosmetics company, which was founded by David McConnell, an American of Scotch-Irish ancestry.[161]

Buick cars were the creation of David Dunbar Buick, who emigrated from Scotland to the United States in 1856 and built the first Buick in 1903, featuring an unprecedented valve-in-head engine.[162] Illness forced Buick to sell his company to William C. Durant, who used it as the base to found General Motors, now the company with the largest sales in the world.[163] David Dunbar Buick died in poverty, his name almost unknown, as millions of Buicks and other G.M. cars rolled off the assembly lines.[164]

Burpee Seeds is the work of W. Atlee Burpee, whose mother, Lois Torrance, was born in Tiberias, Palestine, the daughter of a Presbyterian minister from Glasgow.[165] Burpee copied the modest success of Scottish-American farmer John Rennie, who was the first to grow flower seeds in California's Lompoc Valley. Rennie, in turn, had planted his seeds at the suggestion of John Smith, a Scot who visited him in 1907. Today the Lompoc Valley produces more than half the world's flower seeds.[166]

Campbell's Soups was created by Joseph Campbell, who was born in 1817 in Bridgeton, New Jersey, to James and Hannah Campbell, two strict Presbyterians. The Campbell plant at Camden, New Jersey, was at one time unquestionably the greatest industrial canning plant in the world.[167]

Holiday Inns was founded by Charles Kemmons Wilson, an

American of Scottish descent whose father died when he was nine, leaving him and his mother poor. Wilson's response was to buy a fifty-dollar popcorn machine on credit, paying one dollar down, one dollar per week, while placing it productively in a movie theater in Memphis, Tennessee. From that start he now owns the largest hotel chain in the world, with almost two thousand hotels in all fifty states and on every continent but Antarctica.[168]

Lipton's Tea was the creation of Sir Thomas Johnstone Lipton, who thought of himself as Irish but was, in fact, born in Glasgow and was at least partly Scottish, owing to his Irish Protestant Johnstone ancestors. He went to New York at age fifteen with eight dollars in his pocket and returned to Glasgow six years later with enough money to open a grocery store. His use of flamboyant advertising made him the owner of twenty stores and a millionaire at a very early age. He then went to Ceylon and bought distressed tea estates at a time when tea was a very expensive drink, and only for the rich. Lipton's cost savings on volume purchases made tea cheap, and it soon became the British national drink. As a yachtsman, Sir Thomas tried and failed to win the America's Cup five times.[169]

The Marriott hotel chain was started in Washington, D.C., by J. Willard Marriott, an American of partly Scottish ancestry. He began the business with a root beer stand during the Depression.[170]

Mount Gay rum is the product of the Ward family, whose ancestors came to Barbados from Scotland and Africa. At this writing the owners of Mount Gay Distilleries, Ltd., are Darnley D. Ward and Lisle Ward. Another member of the family, Sir Deighton H. L. Ward, was governor general of Barbados in the 1980s.[171]

James Purdey and Sons, Ltd., the world's most exclusive firearms manufacturing establishment, was founded in London in 1814 by James Purdey, who claimed Scottish ancestry.[172] Today the company still makes only sixty-five to seventy weapons a year, which it sells to kings, world leaders, and celebrities like Khrushchev, Franco, and Bing Crosby for about forty-five thousand dollars per copy. Buyers wait two and a half years for delivery.[173]

Rolls Royce, a name which speaks for itself, was cofounded by Charles Stewart Rolls, a Briton of Scottish ancestry. His father was John Allan Rolls and his mother was Georgiana Maclean, a daughter of Fitzroy Maclean, ninth baronet.[174]

Scotch Tape, always sold with its tartan design, was developed at the 3M Company by Scottish-American William L. McKnight, who joined the firm as a bookkeeper and sold part of his shares for fifty million dollars in 1975. The McKnight family are Americans of Scottish descent and still own millions of 3M shares.[175]

The products of France's giant Thomson S. A. are well-known, particularly in Europe. The firm produces, among many other things, more television sets than any company in the world including those in Japan. It was founded by Elihu Thomson (1853–1937), a Connecticut inventor-businessman who held more than seven hundred patents. Thomson was born in England of Scottish ancestry.[176]

THE VERY RICH

As accumulating wealth is a goal of capitalism, it is to be noted that Scots have excelled in this regard. This has been particularly true in the United States, where a laissez-faire attitude has prevailed more than in most countries, class has been of little concern, and a relatively "level playing field" has existed for all comers. That the Scots have been among the very rich in the United States was demonstrated in a 1968 *Fortune* magazine article that uncovered the most affluent people in the country. Of the richest thirteen, at least seven were of Scottish ancestry. They were: J. Paul Getty, then the richest man in California and, some said, the world; Ailsa Mellon Bruce, the richest woman in both New York and America; her relatives Paul Mellon and Richard King Mellon, at that time the richest people in Virginia and Pennsylvania, respectively; John D. MacArthur, perhaps the richest man in both Illinois and Florida; William L. McKnight, perhaps the richest man in Minnesota; and Charles Stewart Mott, perhaps the richest man in Michigan.[177]

Of course, in the three decades since, all this has changed due to deaths, estate changes, and the vagaries of the marketplace. Yet a glance at any such list will continue to show people of Scottish background among the very wealthy. In 1988 *Forbes* magazine added many new names, among whom were John Murdoch Harbert III, the richest man in Alabama, with an estate of more than a half billion dollars and a winner of the Wallace Award of the American-Scottish Foundation.

It also disclosed that the Scotch-Irish McCaw family, founded by the late John Elroy McCaw, was the richest in the state of Washington. McCaw left his four sons an embryonic business when he died in 1969 and they built it into the world's largest cellular communications network. The four young McCaw brothers, Bruce R., Craig O., John E., and Keith W. sold their shares in McCaw

Cellular Communications, Inc., to the American Telephone and Telegraph Company in 1993 for almost three billion dollars. The chairman, Craig O. McCaw, was forty-four years old.[178]

By then the McCaws had been eclipsed as Washington's richest by thirty-eight-year-old William H. Gates III, the founder of Microsoft, the company which makes the operating systems for the world's IBM computers. Gates, with a net worth estimated at fourteen billion dollars, may be America's richest person. His mother, born of Scottish descent as Mary Maxwell, was an excellent businesswoman as well, serving on the boards of several prominent companies. It was, in fact, with the help of his mother that Bill Gates got his first contract with IBM.[179]

All throughout the history of the United States Scots have been among the richest. In New York, the business capital of the nation, this can be shown in all periods. Archibald Kennedy was the largest property owner in colonial New York but tried to stay neutral during the revolution. He found himself accused as a Loyalist and had most of his property confiscated. His townhouse at 1 Broadway was appropriated by George Washington and served as his headquarters in 1776.[180]

When John Jacob Astor arrived in New York in 1783 he found Robert Bruce to be the city's richest man.[181] Archibald Gracie, the banker previously mentioned, was among the city's most affluent in the early nineteenth century. He was also a president of Saint Andrew's Society of the State of New York. When James Lenox died in 1880 he was described as one of the five richest New Yorkers. He owned twelve square blocks of what has become the city's swankiest neighborhood, Lenox Hill. He was a founder of Presbyterian Hospital and left enough books in his estate to supply one of the three principal founding collections of the great New York Public Library. His father was a president of Saint Andrew's Society.[182]

When department store owner Alexander T. Stewart died late in the nineteenth century he was reputed to have had the largest probate estate ever filed in the United States up to that time. And when the McAlpin brothers opened the McAlpin Hotel on Thirty-Fourth Street in 1896 it was the largest in the world.[183] In the same era Alexander Graham Bell founded the American Telephone and Telegraph Company in New York and was, with his wife, the owner of 1,507 of the 5,000 shares of what became the world's second largest company.[184]

In the twentieth century the name of Malcolm Forbes stands out as one of the richest men, not only in New York City, but in the United States. In 1985, the publisher of *Forbes* gave a cocktail party for one hundred guests, including Princess Margaret. They were piped aboard Forbes's 126-foot yacht *Highlander IV* by his personal piper. As the party toured New York Harbor, consuming caviar, the publisher was asked why he was exchanging his four-year-old yacht for a new 151-footer. Mr. Forbes replied, "the ash trays were full." Forbes topped even this affair in May 1987 when he threw an extravaganza for 1,100 rich and famous people at his estate in Far Hills, New Jersey. The guests consumed almost a ton of Scottish salmon, and were entertained on the lawn by 140 pipers marching through a Scottish baronial stage, complete with artificial mist. Forbes, dressed in a proper black-tie kilt outfit and standing under his chief's crest, greeted his guests while escorting Elizabeth Taylor.

To celebrate his seventieth birthday, Forbes chartered airplanes to fly six hundred guests to his palace in Tangier, Morocco, for a two-million-dollar bash. Once again he wore the kilt, escorted Elizabeth Taylor, and employed pipers. Mr. Forbes, a longtime member of Saint Andrew's Society of the State of New York, died in 1990.[185]

As the century comes to a close, the most visible of New York's money-makers is Donald Trump, whose mother, Mary MacLeod Trump, was born in Scotland. By 1987 Trump, then only forty-one years old, owned huge real estate projects in New York as well as casinos in Atlantic City and had bought the yacht *Nabila*, its original cost one hundred million dollars, from the sultan of Brunei. Since that time he has acquired New York's landmark Plaza Hotel, but as real estate values have plummeted, his worth, once calculated as high as the billions, has shrunk considerably.[186] It must be mentioned that all of this activity in New York has been accomplished by a Scottish-American population which is minuscule.

A city which has always had a substantial Scottish presence is Pittsburgh, perhaps the only American metropolis with a Presbyterian aristocracy. It is not surprising, therefore, to discover that its two most famous businessmen were Scots. Andrew Carnegie, it can be argued, was the greatest businessman as well as the greatest philanthropist of all time. A Scottish immigrant who started with nothing at all, Carnegie became the "richest man in the world," according to J. P. Morgan, who put together the group which bought him out. When Carnegie sold his industrial interests in 1901, creating the United States Steel Corporation, he collected some 350 million dollars, a sum which would today be reckoned in quite a few billions. He then gave almost all of it away, creating, among other things, 2,800 libraries in the United States and Britain.

The other Pittsburgh dynasty is the Scotch-Irish Mellon family, previously mentioned as the founders of the Mellon Bank. Andrew Mellon was reputed to have been the richest man in the United States in the 1920s. His stock in Gulf Oil alone was worth more than the entire Ford Motor Company, and the Mellons also owned the Aluminum Company of America (ALCOA), the Koppers Company, and many others.

Marcus Alonzo Hanna, a Scotch-Irish-American, was the richest and most powerful businessman in Ohio in the nineteenth century. He made a vast fortune in coal, iron, banking, and shipping and was directly responsible for engineering the election of fellow Scotch-Irish-American-Ohioan William McKinley as president of the United States.[187] In the twentieth century, John W. Galbreath, of Columbus, was one of Ohio's richest men, owning a large real estate empire along with race horses and the Pittsburgh Pirates baseball club.[188]

Even in Texas the Kelton-Mathes family is considered to be rich. Jane Mathes Kelton and her son Andrew Kelton, heirs of Scottish-American television magnate Curtis Mathes, are currently developing an entire 340-acre "city" at a cost of more than one billion dollars. Situated between Dallas and Fort Worth, the project is called the Highlands and displays a thistle logo.[189] Another Texan, H. Ross Perot, of French and Scotch-Irish ancestry, has become one of America's richest by providing computer services to others.[190] In 1992, Perot, trying to reform a stagnant government, ran for president and won almost a fifth of the votes.

But it is the legends of the oil business for which Texas is most famous. Ross. S. Sterling, the chief promoter of Humble Oil Company, was born in 1875 of Scottish and Irish ancestry. In the 1920s he sold out to Standard Oil for twenty-eight million dollars and built himself a replica of the White House for the then immense sum of 1.4 million dollars. Later he almost went broke.[191]

Clint Murchison, one of the richest of the "wildcatters," was born in 1885, the descendant of Presbyterian pioneers.[192] One of the last of the great Texas oilmen was W. A. Moncrief, who died at the age of ninety in 1986. His son, W. A. Moncreif, Jr., succeeds him in the managing of a half-billion-dollar estate.[193]

J. Paul Getty, a modern oilman, at one time was the richest man in America—some said in the world. His mother was Sarah Catherine

McPherson Risher, whose ancestors had fled Scotland after the Battle of Culloden. Getty's paternal ancestors were Scotch-Irish Presbyterians who founded Gettysburg, Pennsylvania. His son and heir, Gordon Getty, was the richest man in America in 1984, with an estimated 4.1 billion dollars, double the next richest at the time.[194]

By far, the greatest of all the oilmen, however, was John Davison Rockefeller (1839–1937), whose name is synonymous with wealth. At age twenty and with a nine hundred dollar stake, he founded what became the largest industrial company in the world, Standard Oil. Its descendants are many and include Exxon, by itself the world's largest industrial company, which operates in one hundred countries and creates billions in annual profits. In his time Rockefeller was the world's richest man and one of the great philanthropists, giving away 750 million dollars, a world record. His mother was Eliza Davison, a strong disciplined woman of Scottish descent who drilled him in honesty, sobriety, industry, thoughtfulness, altruism, and a fervent religious faith.[195]

In agriculture the Scots in America have done almost as well as they have in oil. James Johnston was the largest planter in the United States upon his death in North Carolina, in 1865.[196] The Irvine Ranch, eighty thousand acres in Orange County, California, was in 1971 the single largest in the state and worth well over a billion dollars. It was assembled in the late 1800s by James Irvine, of Ulster-Scottish parentage.[197] The Garvey family, reputedly the richest in Kansas in the 1960s, owns grain elevators and huge tracts of land. At an ethnic display in Wichita they loaned a tartan cloth which their immigrant ancestors had brought with them.[198] Paul DeBruce, of Kansas City, owns DeBruce Grain, one of the largest agricultural businesses in the world and one of the largest privately owned enterprises in America. Malcolm McLean, the inventor of containerized shipping, is the son of a farmer and mail carrier. He started McLean Trucking with a 120-dollar secondhand truck in 1934 and ended up owning the largest private plantation in the United States. Situated in eastern North Carolina, it contained 360,000 acres, which is almost six hundred square miles.[199]

In the heartland, David Eccles, a native of Scotland, was described as the wealthiest citizen of Utah upon his death in 1912.[200] In 1935 John D. MacArthur, a minister's son, acquired the Chicago-based Bankers Life and Casualty Company, a small bankrupt insurance business, for 2,500 dollars, and turned it into a giant. He was the brother of Charles MacArthur, who was coauthor of the famous

American play *The Front Page*. In later years John MacArthur, who died in 1978, was called the "accessible billionaire," conducting business in a MacArthur tartan jacket in the coffee shop of a hotel he owned near Palm Beach. With one hundred thousand acres, he was the largest landowner in Florida.[201] In 1968 *Fortune* magazine called Charles Stewart Mott, the largest stockholder in the world's biggest manufacturing concern, General Motors, America's twelfth richest person. His mother had the musical Scottish name of Isabella Turnbull Stewart.[202]

Two of the largest private companies in American history have had Scottish roots. *Reader's Digest*, the largest circulation magazine in the world, was founded in 1922 by a Scottish-American couple, DeWitt and Lila Acheson Wallace. At the time of their deaths in the 1980s, the Wallaces owned all the stock of the company. When Reader's Digest Association, Inc., finally went public in 1990 the company was valued at over two billion dollars.[203] Cargill, Inc., of Minneapolis, founded by William Wallace Cargill, is rated as America's largest private company. Over thirty members of the Cargill and MacMillan families own the forty-seven-billion-dollar agribusiness giant, which handles 25 percent of America's grain exports, among many other activities. Cargill has six hundred plants and forty thousand employees in forty countries.[204]

Outside the United States, John M. Templeton sold his mutual funds in 1992 for 913 million dollars, the largest amount ever paid for such a business. In 1972 this devout Presbyterian founded the Templeton Prize for Progress in Religion with the goal that it would be more valuable than the Nobel Prize. The annual winner receives more than one million dollars. Sir John was born in the United States and is based in the Bahamas, but all four of his grandparents came from Scotland.[205]

Retailing and energy have made Paul Fentener van Vlissingen, of partly Scottish ancestry, a multibillionaire, and one of the three richest men in the Netherlands.

In 1988 *Fortune* magazine noted that three Canadian families were among the nine richest in the world. Two of these had Scottish origins. The Irving family of New Brunswick, headed by Kenneth C. Irving, owned over four hundred companies with a worth of 6.2 billion dollars.[206] The Thomson family, headed by Kenneth Thomson, the second Lord Thomson, are owners of newspapers, oil properties, and the Hudson's Bay Company, and are worth an estimated six billion dollars. The *Fortune* article also pointed out that a very well-known lady of largely Scottish descent, Queen Elizabeth, the international Chief of Chiefs of the Scottish nation, was worth 8.7 billion dollars, making her the fourth richest person and the richest woman in the world.[207]

That the Scots have been good at making money and running businesses is not a new discovery. But formal recognition was lacking until 1975, when *Fortune* magazine elected the first nineteen Americans to its Business Hall of Fame. At least seven of those had Scottish ancestry. Between 1976 and 1982 another fifty-eight were chosen and at least eighteen of these had Scottish ancestry. In all, a total of seventy-seven Americans were elected to the *Fortune* Business Hall of Fame through 1982, of which twenty-five, including the only two women, were of Scottish ancestry, making up about 33 percent of the list as compared to the approximately 5 percent of the general population of the United States which is Scottish.[208]

Despite their parsimonious stereotype, Scots are also good at giving money away. As of 1993, thirteen of the twenty-one largest charitable foundations in the United States, their assets totalling over twenty five billion dollars, had been started by the following Scottish-Americans:[209]

W. K. Kellogg	Charles Stewart Mott
J. Paul Getty	De Witt Wallace
John D. MacArthur	William L. McKnight
John D. Rockefeller	Andrew Carnegie
Andrew W. Mellon	Richard King Mellon
James Buchanan Duke	Lila Acheson Wallace
Doris Duke	

'S ann as an tir 's eachdraidh a chineas spiorad cogail.
Martial spirit grows out of the land and history.

6

Scottish Soldiers
and Sailors

Nineteen centuries ago the Roman Empire had conquered and pacified the entire Mediterranean basin and most of northern Europe, including what is now England. Then, in A.D. 81 in what is now Scotland, the Roman general Julius Agricola engaged a people called Caledonians and later Picts, who resisted him with a fury that Rome had seldom, if ever, encountered before. The Romans occupied Pictland at times, but were never able to subdue these fierce northerners or pacify their misty kingdom. In fact, the Picts continuously attacked the Romans as if to prove that they would not be part of the peaceful province of Britannia.

To contain the Picts, the Romans built two great walls, parts of which are still visible. The first was Hadrian's Wall, 73 miles long, constructed from 122 to 128 between the Tyne and Solway. It was a stone rampart eight to ten feet thick, and was sustained by seventeen forts, eighty castles, and over a hundred signal towers. In front of its nineteen-thousand-man garrison was a ditch ten yards across. Hadrian's wall was a formidable tribute by the greatest empire the world had ever known to the resolve of the enemy it was meant to contain.

But the Pictish attacks on the wall were so constant that the Romans were forced to advance their frontier after a decade, this time building the Antonine Wall, named after the emperor Antonius Pius, from Forth to Clyde, a distance of 37 miles. But this new barrier, which would prove to be, gloriously, the ultimate northern boundary of the Roman Empire, was subjected to raging attacks, and about A.D. 186 the Romans drew back to their more southerly bastion. By 197 the Picts had practically destroyed Hadrian's Wall and were raiding what we now call northern England.[1] These valiant ancestors of the Scots, about whom we know so little, have bequeathed their military tradition to all of the succeeding generations of the Scottish people.

It is not within the plan of this book to detail the blood-soaked history of Scotland itself. We are concerned here with the impact that Scots have had on the rest of the world, and therefore, we must pass over the dim heroics of Arthur, the consolidating victories of Kenneth and Malcolm, the heroism of Wallace, the military genius of Bruce and Montrose, the romantic battles of Bonnie Prince Charlie, and the deeds of countless outnumbered Scottish knights in their successful thousand-year struggle against the might of haughty England. It is enough to say that despite continuous attacks and invasions, Scotland remains unconquered after two thousand years.

Therefore, it is not surprising that the Scots, who have had so much experience in warfare, should have played a large part in the military and naval histories of many lands. We have already discussed the critically important Scottish military and naval contributions to the creations of the United States and the British Empire. This chapter examines the Scottish component in the service of maintaining the interests of these two entities as well as the occasional, but remarkable, Scottish military and naval presence in lands which are not English-speaking.

Scottish Soldiers and Sailors in the British Empire

1707–1815

Scotland always did far more than its share in defending the empire, sending soldiers to the various fronts in numbers greatly disproportionate to its population. And it was a Scot, the military genius Sir David Dundas (1735–1820) who, as author of *Rules and Regulations for His Majesty's Forces* and *Rules and Regulations for the Cavalry*, introduced the theory of strategy based on the Prussian tactics of the school of Frederick the Great, which achieved so much for Britain.[2]

Two interesting footnotes to the American Revolution involve

Scots. Lt. Gen. Sir Charles Kerr was appointed to lead the British army in the American colonies in 1775 but declined as a result of a petition signed by one hundred Kerrs in America requesting that he not accept the assignment.[3] In 1776 Col. Allan MacLean successfully defended Quebec against an American force under Richard Montgomery, thus preventing the Americans from acquiring a fourteenth state.[4]

Another Scot, George Elliot, with only a handful of men, managed to hold Gibraltar against the might of France and Spain, enduring a four-year siege (1779–1783) and saving the Rock for Britain.[5] Between 1793 and 1799 Britain fought a war against Holland that featured the signal victory of Adm. Adam Duncan (First Viscount Duncan) over the Dutch at Camperdown in 1797.[6] Sir Ralph Abercromby (1734–1801) restored discipline and prestige to the British army during this period. He was ordered to defeat Napoleon in Egypt in 1801 and organized the fight to do so, but fell, mortally wounded, in the hour of victory.[7] Adm. George Keith Elphinstone (Viscount Keith) assisted Abercromby in Egypt. From then until 1807 he bore the main responsibility for defending Britain's shores against the invasion plans of Napoleon.[8]

Several other Scots made extraordinary contributions in the wars against Napoleon. Adm. William Carnegie (Lord Northesk) was third in command at Trafalgar, in 1805, and later became first sea lord.[9] In the Peninsular War, Lt. Gen. Sir John Moore successfully evacuated twenty-six thousand British troops that had been trapped by eighty thousand French at La Corunna in 1809 and died in the battle.[10] Thomas Graham (Baron Lynedoch) was second in command to Wellington, and in 1813 commanded the left wing of the army in the advance to Vitoria and the decisive victory there.[11]

At Waterloo, Gen. Sir James MacDonnell won the five-hundred-pound prize offered by Wellington to "the bravest man in the British army" and gave the money to his sergeant.[12] Highland troops made a difference at Waterloo, and it was Ensign Ewart of the Royal Scots Greys who captured the French eagle standard.[13] Surveying the lost battlefield, Napoleon is said to have muttered, "The brave Scots."[14]

1815–1914

The Crimean War had many Scottish heroes. Among these was Robert Lindsay (1836–1901; Lord Wantage) who rallied his regiment at Alma after it had been thrown into confusion by a mistaken order.

For this, Lindsay received the first Victoria Cross ever awarded by the army.[15] The war's most famous soldier was Colin Campbell (Baron Clyde), the Glasgow-born commander of the "thin red line" of kilted Scots at the pivotal Battle of Balaklava in 1854. The defense of the vital British, French, and Turkish supply port at the town of Balaklava was threatened by Russian cavalry positioned in the heights above the town. As several thousand mounted Russians thundered down on the defenders, Campbell called out to his Highlanders, "Remember men, there is no retreat from here—you must die where you stand!" The Russians were repulsed.[16]

During the Crimean War the Black Sea Fleet was commanded by Admiral J. W. Dundas,[17] while the British naval forces in the Baltic were commanded by Adm. Sir Charles Napier, a native of Stirlingshire.[18]

A Scoto-Englishman, Charles George Gordon, became governor general of the Sudan in 1877, acquiring sole responsibility for a million square miles of land inhabited by savage and hostile people. This was the same "Chinese" Gordon who had protected the European interests in Shanghai two decades before. In 1884 he was asked by the British government to defend Khartoum against a powerful *fakir*, the Mahdi, or "expected one." Gordon arrived in Khartoum in February 1884, and managed to evacuate two thousand women, children, sick, and wounded before the forces of the Mahdi closed in. Despite the British government's vacillation, which prevented any timely reinforcement, Gordon performed one of the remarkable feats of military history, defending Khartoum for almost a year with a weak Egyptian garrison, without staff or confidants, until January 26, 1885, when he and his troops were massacred. The British relief force arrived three days later.[19]

In 1898 the British army, under the Anglo-Irish general Kitchener, avenged Gordon's death, completely overwhelming the dervishes at Omdurman. The British, very nearly defeated at the battle's outset, were saved by the tactics of the Highland officer Col. Hector MacDonald, whose brigade turned the tide. Kitchener, however, got the credit due to class differences, MacDonald being one of the very few soldiers ever to rise all the way from private to general. One young second lieutenant who was there, Winston Churchill, wrote "All depended on MacDonald."[20]

During the nineteenth century the inspector general of the British army hospitals, "Dr. James Barry," was found, upon her death in 1865, to have been a Scottish woman and an Edinburgh graduate of unknown parentage.[21] In 1872 Sir Houston Stewart was made admiral of the fleet.[22]

Gen. Joseph M. Gordon, the main organizer of the Australian army prior to 1914, was born in Jerez to the Scoto-Spanish sherry wine family as José Maria Jacobo Rafael Ramón Francsico Gabriel Del Corazón De Jesús Gordon y Prendergast.[23]

World War I
1914–1918

"In Flanders Fields the poppies grow,
Beneath the crosses, row on row..."

John McCrae, Canadian soldier, 1915[24]

The chief of the imperial general staff, that is, head of the entire British army, during the greater part of the World War I was Sir William Robert Robertson, an Englishman of Scottish ancestry. It is believed he was the only British soldier to rise from private to field marshal.[25] Likewise, the British commander in chief of the forces in France and Flanders during most of World War I was Edinburgh-born field marshal Douglas Haig (First Earl Haig). Haig's troops, the largest British army that had ever taken the field, bore the brunt of the fighting in the war, and ultimately defeated what was then the mightiest war machine in the world.[26] Another Scot, Sir David Henderson, had been a founder of the Royal Flying Corps.[27]

On the front lines, Lt. Col. Sir Iain Colquhoun, the Chief of the Colquhouns, became the lightweight boxing champion of the British army and killed a Prussian officer with a revolver, and five Bavarians with an improvised club. Colquhoun also kept a lion, reportedly reasonably tame, in the trenches, was wounded more than once, and won the D.S.O. (Distinguished Service Order) and bar. After the war he became chairman of the National Trust for Scotland and Lord Rector of Glasgow University.[28]

Lt. Col. T. E. Lawrence (Lawrence of Arabia), a dashing figure in Arab garb, had been a scholar working in the Near East at the war's beginning. Lawrence completely revitalized the Arab army into its efforts against the Turks. He was not the actual head of the army, but as its "moving spirit" helped it make a major contribution in the war, including the captures of Aqaba in 1917 and Damascus in 1918. Lawrence, whose mother was Anglo-Scottish, mysteriously enlisted in the R.A.F. in 1922 as John Hume Ross, and was enough of a scholar to translate Homer's *Odyssey* into English verse.[29]

Adm. J. R. Jellicoe (First Earl Jellicoe), an Englishman, won the Battle of Jutland in 1916, rendering the German fleet ineffective for the rest of the war and the same year was made first sea lord, or commander of the entire British navy. He was descended from the Fife-born Admiral Patton, second sea lord at the time of Trafalgar.[30] Admiral R. J. B. Keyes (First Baron Keyes) planned and directed the raid on the enemy base at Zeebrugge, Belgium, in 1918, which closed the straits of Dover to German submarines. His grandmother was the Scotch-Irish Mary Anne Patton, of County Donegal.[31] Admiral Rosslyn Erskine Wemyss (Baron Wester) was admiral of the fleet, and first sea lord in 1917. He signed the armistice on behalf of the allied navies after World War I. The German fleet surrendered, almost in sight of Castle Wemyss and its famous caves in Scotland. The name Wemyss is derived from the caves, which in Gaelic is *uaimh*.[32]

Interwar Period

1918–1939

Between the world wars the Scottish minority's participation in the military affairs of Britain had reached the point where the London Caledonian Society could boast that the army's command by 1928 was actually dominated by Scots, offering the following lineup of command:[33]

Chief, Imperial General Staff	Gen. Sir George Milne
Chief, Indian General Staff	Maj. Gen. Sir Andrew Skeen
Aldershot Command	Lt. Gen. Sir David Campbell
Eastern Command	Gen. Sir Robert D. Whigham
Commanding First Division	Maj. Gen. Sir John Duncan
Commanding Second Division	Maj. Gen. Sir Edmund Ironside
Commanding Third Division	Maj. Gen. Sir J. Burnett-Stuart
Commanding Fourth Division	Maj. Gen. Sir A. R. Cameron

It was also during this period that Sir Basil Liddell-Hart, descended from Scottish Borderers, campaigned for the mechanization of the British army and was called the undisputed leader among British military thinkers of the twentieth century.[34]

Scottish-American Soldiers and Sailors

THE WAR OF 1812

1812–1815

The War of 1812 was fought between Britain and the United States largely over British trade restrictions and diplomatic misunderstandings, and ended with the newer nation having gained none of its objectives against the overwhelmingly superior British navy. Nevertheless, the war induced in Americans a heightened sense of nationhood and left them claiming victory, largely because of the successful activities of a few Scottish-Americans.

As had been the case in the American Revolution, the distinction of firing the first shot of the War of 1812 went to a soldier of the Scottish nation, in this case to the Maryland-born son of a Scottish colonel, John Rodgers.[35] Gen. Winfield Scott was largely responsible for securing the Niagara frontier for the Americans, and Oliver Hazard Perry became a national hero in 1813 when he regained control of Lake Erie at the Battle of Put-in-Bay. It was the first time in the history of the British navy that an entire squadron was lost. Perry, whose mother, Sarah Wallace Alexander, was a Scotch-Irish immigrant, sent the immortal message to Brig. Gen. William Henry Harrison: "We have met the enemy and they are ours."[36] Another Scotch-Irish-American naval officer, Thomas MacDonough, defeated the British at Lake Champlain in 1814, saving New England from invasion.[37]

In 1814, Francis Scott Key wrote the national anthem, "The Star-Spangled Banner," upon seeing the battered American flag still waving over Fort McHenry the morning after the United States Army repelled the British naval forces in Baltimore harbor. The song inspired the nation. Key was a descendant of John Ross, a Maryland planter who was Lord Baltimore's deputy agent. In addition to his Ross ancestry, two genealogists say that his English Key ancestors were originally Scottish Mackays.[38]

In early 1815, the Scotch-Irish Andrew Jackson, the future president, then a major general, defeated a British force at New Orleans, a hugely popular victory. Neither side knew that the peace treaty had been signed in Belgium two weeks before.[39]

The Civil War
or
The War Between the States
1861–1865

As Lincoln said, the Civil War tested whether the United States could endure as a nation. The answer to the president's implied question is that this great convulsion did indeed secure a permanent political bond, but the price was a bitter and bloody struggle. Scottish-Americans were divided from the beginning. William Steel, a noted antislavery advocate and one of the organizers of the Underground Railroad, which conveyed slaves to freedom in the North, was born in Lanarkshire.[40] On the other hand, Mark Twain asserted in his *Life on the Mississippi* that it was the romantic impact of Sir Walter Scott "on the South that produced the Civil War."[41] And when the time came to elect a president of the rebel Confederate States of America, Jefferson Davis, Scottish on his mother's side, was the unanimous choice.[42] Perhaps it was auspicious that the first state to secede, South Carolina, voted to do so at the hall of the St. Andrew's Society in Charleston.[43]

At the beginning of the war, Gen. Winfield Scott, too old to fight actively, was Lincoln's chief military advisor.[44] The commander in chief of the Union Army in 1861 was General George B. McClellan, only thirty-four years old. He was the victor at the Battle of Antietam, which prevented Lee's advance on Washington. In 1877 he became governor of New Jersey and was a charter member of the St. Andrew's Society of Illinois.[45]

The Union commander at the First Battle of Bull Run (called First Manassas by the Confederates) was the Scottish-American general Irvin McDowell.[46] But the victor was the southerner general Joseph E. Johnston, who was called by Grant the ablest of the Confederate commanders. Johnston's grandfather was born in Scotland and his mother was a niece of Patrick Henry.[47] The popular hero of Bull Run is still Gen. T. J. "Stonewall" Jackson, whose brigade stood "like a stone wall" against the Union troops. In the early battles of the war Jackson was Lee's right hand, and they seemed to be an invincible duo. But the Scotch-Irish Jackson was killed by his own men's fire at the victory at Chancellorsville, and the South was never able to replace him.[48]

The financier of the of the Civil War for the Union government was

Salmon Chase, who was descended from Janet Ralston, the daughter of a Scottish settler.[49] Chase became U.S. secretary of the treasury during the war, and refined the national banking system. Before the war he had been a lawyer who defended "conductors" on the Underground Railroad, governor of Ohio, and a U.S. senator. His ambition to be president led Lincoln to fire him from the cabinet, but Lincoln later named him chief justice of the U.S. Supreme Court.[50] Allan Pinkerton, born in Glasgow, left his detective agency to organize the secret service division of the U.S. Army in 1861.[51] Historians hold this to be the first U.S. intelligence agency.[52]

Gen. Arthur MacArthur became a colonel in the Civil War at age twenty. He was wounded three times and cited for "gallant and meritorious service" in ten battles, and received the Congressional Medal of Honor at Missionary Ridge. Later, as military governor of the Philippines, he paved the way for the Philippine Republic, introducing habeas corpus and a free school system. He was the father of Gen. Douglas MacArthur.[53]

Gen. J. E. B. "Jeb" Stuart was a Confederate soldier known for his daring cavalry raids. He was descended from Archibald Stuart whose family moved from Scotland to Ulster in the seventeenth century.[54]

Franklin Buchanan was the only full admiral and senior officer of the Confederate navy. He also became the first commander of an ironclad ship to engage an enemy in warfare when, in 1862, he gave the U.S. Navy the worst defeat of its time, commanding the *Virginia*, previously named the *Merrimack*. However, the day after this success the Union's *Monitor* held the Confederates at bay, resulting in a great swing of morale in the war. The *Monitor* had been designed by the Scoto-Swedish John Ericsson. Buchanan was of Scottish ancestry, and before the war, in which he was twice wounded, had been the first superintendent of the U.S. Naval Academy. After the war he became president of the Maryland Agricultural College, a bankrupt, institution with only a handful of students, and turned it into the University of Maryland.[55]

The greatest naval hero for the Union, who captured both New Orleans and Mobile, was David Glasgow Farragut, who was of Scottish ancestry.[56] The victory at New Orleans was the most important against the Confederates in the west, as it later helped Grant at Vicksburg. At Mobile Farragut decided to cross a minefield, yelling his famous, "Damn the torpedoes!"[57]

The Union's second most important soldier, Gen. William

Tecumseh Sherman, was of Scottish ancestry on his mother's side.[58] Sherman is remembered for marching sixty thousand men from Atlanta to Savannah, Georgia, in 1864, leaving desolation in his wake. He is also famous as the man who said, "War is hell." Sherman became commanding general of the army in 1869.[59]

The head of the Confederate army, Robert E. Lee, had some Scottish ancestors.[60] Lee was the victorious commander at the Second Battle of Bull Run (Second Manassas), at Fredericksburg, and at Chancellorsville. He led his troops into Union territory but was defeated at Gettysburg. A gentlemanly soldier, Lee fought with dignity and skill against overwhelming odds.

The commanding general of the victorious Union army was a Scottish-American, Gen. Ulysses S. Grant. His campaign at Vicksburg was one of the most brilliant of the war and cut the Confederacy in half. Grant took Richmond, the Confederate capital, and forced and received Lee's surrender at Appomattox Court House.[61] After the war he dissuaded politicians who wanted to try Lee for treason. Grant became president in 1869 and was instrumental in founding the National Parks Service. Upon his death he stood as one of America's foremost heroes. The design of his tomb was debated for a decade, and his funeral in New York was attended by more than a million people.[62]

Continental Wars
1865–1940

In the 1870s, Brig. Gen. Ranald Mackenzie ended a century and a half of Indian terror in Texas by defeating and pacifying the Comanches, led by their brilliant chief Quanah Parker. Ironically, Parker became a successful businessman and federal judge, while Mackenzie died insane.[63]

Lt. Col. George Armstrong Custer, who made his "last stand" at the Little Big Horn in 1876, was descended from the Cursiter family of the Orkney Islands, according to one source.[64] Although this has been disputed, his middle name also points to Scottish origins. Among those massacred at the battle were at least seven Scottish soldiers.[65]

Commodore Winfield Schley, partly Scottish, commanded the "flying squadron," which blockaded the entrance to the harbor at Santiago, Cuba, during the Spanish-American War of 1898.[66] Adm. William S. Sims improved naval gunnery, ship design, and fleet tactics to the point that it is said he influenced the navy "more than any other man who ever wore the uniform." Sims was commander of U.S. naval forces operating in European waters in World War I and was descended from John Simm, who came from Scotland to Pennsylvania in 1793.[67] The first American-trained air ace in World War I was Douglas Campbell, who shot down a German airplane on his first day of combat, just a year after he had left Harvard.[68]

Gen. William "Billy" Mitchell was the grandson of a poor Scottish immigrant, Alexander Mitchell, who became the "Rothschild" of Milwaukee. Billy Mitchell was fluent in five languages and, at eighteen, the youngest officer in the Spanish-American War. In World War I he was the only flying general. Between the world wars, as commander of an air force which scarcely existed, he became a consistent and strident advocate of American air power, and predicted the debacle at Pearl Harbor seventeen years before the event. His abrasive personality got him court-martialed for his views. The public supported him, particularly the American Legion, but he was found guilty anyway, his boyhood friend Gen. Douglas MacArthur casting the only dissenting vote. Milwaukee named its airport Mitchell Field.[69]

World War II
1939–1945

"There is only one thing wrong with Scotsmen,
there are too few of them."

—*Winston Churchill, addressing the House of Commons*[70]

World War II was the pivotal event of the twentieth century, with the fate of civilization in the balance. The Nazis had been allowed to gather enormous military advantages during the 1930s and seemed to be prepared to end the Age of Reason, as Hitler himself had proclaimed. But in the end the Germans and their Japanese allies were resisted, beaten back, and finally routed. The Scottish nation provided a very small, but crucially important, fraction of the heroes.

As the war began a defiant tone was set by the proudly Scottish queen of Great Britain (at this writing she is the Queen Mother) when she was asked, as the bombs fell, whether she or her children would flee the country. Her answer should have told her enemies something: "The children will not leave unless I do. I shall not leave unless their father does, and the king will not leave the country in any circumstances whatever."[71]

At the beginning of the war the chief of the British imperial general staff was Field Marshal William E. Ironside, a native of Aberdeenshire.[72] He was succeeded by an Ulster Scot, Field Marshal Sir John Greer Dill, who became chief of the imperial general staff, and chief military advisor in Britain in 1940. Later Dill served as the British military representative in Washington, where he died in 1944. He is buried in Arlington National Cemetery.[73] Sir Ralph Cochrane was air chief marshal in World War II, and from 1936 to 1939 the first commander of the Royal New Zealand Air Force.[74] Sir Alexander Hood was director general of the British Army Medical Services from 1941 to 1948.[75]

Victor Alexander John Hope (second marquess of Linlithgow) was the Scottish-born viceroy of India, who in 1939 declared war on Germany without consulting the Indian politicians.[76] Philip Henry Kerr (eleventh marquess of Lothian) was, from 1939 to 1940, an extremely important British ambassador to the neutral United States who was able to negotiate much for the British war effort, including fifty destroyers.[77]

In 1940 the aerial Battle of Britain prevented a planned German invasion, radically affecting the outcome of the war. As Churchill said, "Never in the field of human conflict was so much owed by so many to so few." Radar was an important aid to the R.A.F. against the Luftwaffe, and the first practical system was developed by a Scottish scientist, Sir Robert Watson-Watt (1892–1973).[78] John A. Dawson, chief engineer, coastal command, for the air defense of Britain from 1940 to 1948, was born in Aberdeen.[79] The "architect" of the Battle of Britain, who directed the fighter command with skill and determination, was Air Chief Marshal Hugh C. T. Dowding (Baron Dowding), born in Moffat, Scotland.[80]

Archibald "Archie" McKellar of Glasgow shot down the first German plane during the Battle of Britain and was killed himself after being credited with a total of sixteen kills.[81]

Air Commodore Aeneas MacDonnell (twenty-second *Mac Mhic Alasdair*, or twenty-second chief of the MacDonnells of Glengarry) was one of the heroic fighter pilots who won the Battle of Britain, commanding a Spitfire squadron. He was credited with shooting down twelve enemy aircraft and was himself downed over the English Channel in 1941. He spent the rest of the war as a prisoner.[82] Sir Douglas Bader was a British air ace who, despite the handicap of flying with *two* artificial legs, was credited with downing twenty-four Nazi planes from 1940 to 1941. He was shot down and captured, yet despite his handicap, escaped from the Germans in France. His mother was Jessie McKenzie.[83]

Westminster Hall is the finest medieval hall in Europe, its hammer-beam roof having been constructed in the late fourteenth century, when Chaucer was minister of works. The hall was saved from conflagration by two Scots on the night of May 11, 1941. Col. Walter Elliot, M.P., was fighting a fire caused by German bombs in a neighboring street when he noticed that the roof was ablaze. He hurried to the spot and arranged with Chief Superintendent C. P. MacDuell to use all available pumps to save the structure where William Wallace, the thirteenth-century Scottish patriot, was sentenced to death.[84]

A decorated soldier in World War I, Field Marshal C. J. E. Auchinleck, an Ulster Scot on both sides of his ancestry, was appointed head of British forces in the Middle East in World War II. In Egypt he successfully ended Britain's string of reverses against Rommel but, protecting his men, who were in need of reinforcements, was fired by Churchill for refusing an order to counterattack immediately when Rommel stopped near Cairo.[85] Gen. Sir Archibald P. Wavell was a British soldier of Scottish ancestry who served in the Black Watch in World War I. In 1940 and 1941 he routed the Italian armies in Libya, and liquidated the Italian Empire in East Africa, liberating Ethiopia.[86]

Air Marshal A. W. Tedder (Baron Tedder) commanded all of the allied forces in the Middle East in 1941 and played a large part in the Normandy invasion. He was born in Glenguin, Scotland.[87] Field Marshal H. R. L. G. Alexander (Earl Alexander of Tunis) has been called by authorities "unquestionably the greatest British field commander of the Second World War."[88] He commanded the rear guard at Dunkirk, then coordinated the Allied advances in North Africa, which led to the German surrender at Tunis in 1943. He also commanded the forces of many nations that drove the Germans from Sicily, forcing the Italian army to surrender, and eventually liberated all of Italy. Of Ulster-Scottish stock, he had probably directly descended from Scotland's Royal House of the Isles.[89]

The most famous British soldier of modern times was Field Marshal Bernard Law Montgomery (Viscount Montgomery). His 1942 victory over Rommel at El Alamein is considered one of the decisive battles of history. Up to that time the Nazis had never lost a major battle, afterwards, they never won one. He received the German surrender in 1945. Montgomery was born in London of Ulster-Scottish ancestry, the first Montgomery having left Scotland for Ireland in 1623.[90]

The commander of the Allied naval forces on D-Day, 1944, was Adm. Bertram Ramsay.[91] Leading one of the attacks on a Normandy beach, his piper Bill Millin by his side, was Simon Fraser, the seventeenth Lord Lovat, and twenty-second chief of Clan Fraser of Lovat (twenty-second *MacShimi*). Lord Lovat, the famous commando leader, was grievously wounded during the war. But it is for audacity that he is best remembered. Although it was against the rules for pipers to march into battle due to heavy losses in World War I, Lord Lovat told Millin to do so anyway. He told his men to walk across a bridge rather than run, practically strutting into the enemy with their piper playing away. Hitler was so outraged that he put one hundred thousand marks on Lovat's head. Each year Millin, now heavily decorated, returns to France at the request of the French people to recreate the events. In the film *The Longest Day* Peter Lawford played Lord Lovat and Bill Millin played himself.[92]

Maj. Gen. Robert E. Urquhart was the British commander at the heroic but ill-fated Battle of Arnhem in the Netherlands in 1944. As his troops tried to take the bridge over the Rhine they were overwhelmed by German forces who had captured their battle plans. Nevertheless, they fought bravely for nine days. Urquhart was played by Sean Connery in the 1977 film *A Bridge Too Far*.[93] The minister of the Scots Kirk in Paris, Dr. Donald Caskie, was a French resistance hero and saved the lives of many Jews.[94]

Lt. Gen. Lesley James McNair directed the training of American ground combat troops during the mobilization for World War II. This "son of a Scotsman" was killed in Normandy in 1944 and was the highest-ranking officer to die in the field. His only son, Col. Douglas McNair, was killed in Guam the same year.[95]

Gen. George S. Patton, "Old Blood and Guts" to his troops, was one of the most colorful and successful soldiers in American history. He became interested in tanks in World War I and continually advocated their use between the wars. Patton commanded the U.S. Seventh Army in Sicily and took Palermo. In France his Third Army swept through the Germans with a relentlessness that will be remembered forever. Patton's most important feat, however, was in rapidly mobilizing his troops and rushing them to the relief of

Bastogne, snuffing out the Germans' offensive in the Battle of the Bulge. When asked by General Eisenhower how soon he could get his forces ready, Patton answered, "As soon as you're through with me." His paternal ancestor, Robert Patton, was a native of Scotland. On his mother's side he was descended from the Scottish-American revolutionary war hero General Hugh Mercer.[96]

As the war in Europe neared its end, Lord Malcolm Douglas-Hamilton, the much decorated R.A.F. group captain, discovered the German V-2 rocket base at Peenemünde.[97]

The only infantry division to follow Montgomery all the way from El Alamein to Berlin was the Fifty-first Highland Division, drawn from a handful of regiments which are, perhaps, the most famous in the world: the Black Watch, the Argyll and Sutherland Highlanders, the Gordon Highlanders, the Seaforth Highlanders, and the Cameron Highlanders. In World War I a captured German document listed it as the most *furchtbarkeit*, or most feared, of all British divisions. In World War II, when it fought with such distinction that it was praised by leaders of Britain, France, Canada, the United States, and even the German general Rommel, it numbered eleven clan chiefs among its members.[98]

Fleet Adm. W. F. "Bull" Halsey was the American whose task force beat the Japanese at Guadalcanal in 1942 and who led the U.S. naval operations in the last months of the war. He was a great–great grandson of the rich Scottish immigrant Archibald Gracie.[99] Adm. Ernest J. King, another prominent American naval officer in the war, was of partly Scottish ancestry.[100]

Alistair MacLean, a mild-mannered school teacher and later a famous novelist, was busy during the war blowing up Japanese supply bridges. He was captured and his Japanese torturers pulled out all of his teeth. Undaunted, he and a friend stole guns and blasted their way out, enabling MacLean to fight against the Germans, who wounded him twice.[101]

Andrew Browne Cunningham (Viscount Cunningham), commander in chief in the Mediterranean at the beginning of the war, fought a series of battles which crippled the Italian navy. He was first sea lord from 1943 to 1946. Adm. Sir Bruce Fraser (Baron Fraser of the North Cape) was commander in chief of the British home fleet and responsible for keeping the sea lanes open to Russia. On December 26, 1942, aboard his flagship, he challenged and sank the German battleship *Scharnhorst* off the North Cape of Norway, greatly boosting Allied morale. In 1944 he was commander in chief of the British fleet in the Pacific. From 1948 to 1951 he was first sea lord, and chief of naval staff.[102]

The Japanese advance which had overrun Singapore and most of Burma was stopped decisively by Gen. Sir Philip Christison, a Gaelic enthusiast who beat the enemy at Rangoon, a turning point in the Eastern theater. Sir Philip, the highest-ranking British officer in Southeast Asia, took the surrender of all Japanese forces in that area on September 3, 1945. He lived to be one hundred and died at his home in Melrose in 1993.[103]

Gen. Douglas MacArthur was supreme commander of the Allied powers in the Pacific, and one of the great military figures of his day. The son of Gen. Arthur MacArthur, he graduated first in his class from West Point and was a heavily-decorated foot soldier in World War I. Ordered to retreat to Australia at the beginning of World War II, he saved that country from invasion, and by his island-hopping technique steadily defeated the tenacious Japanese, operating over a vast theater without the resources allocated to the Allies in Europe. He reentered the Philippines in 1944, making good his famous promise "I shall return," and received the Congressional Medal of Honor, as his father had eight decades earlier. For the next five years MacArthur was supreme commander in Japan, supervising that nation's recovery and converting its government to democracy. In 1950 he was called to Korea, where his skill saved American troops from impending disaster, particularly with his famous Inchon landing, deep behind enemy lines. His challenge to presidential authority led to his dismissal by President Truman in 1951. Relieved of command, he returned to America to an unparalleled hero's welcome.[104]

Scots from many nations made outstanding and diverse contributions to the war effort. William Sholto Douglas (first baron Kirtleside) was a marshal in the R.A.F.[105] Robert Leckie was chief of staff of the Royal Canadian Air Force.[106] Capt. Colin Purdie Kelly, Jr., a bomber pilot shot down and killed on December 10, 1941, was the first American hero of World War II. Despite his Irish-looking surname, Captain Kelly was of Scottish Presbyterian ancestry.[107] In 1942 Mildred McAfee became the first director of the WAVES, the womens' reserves of the U.S. Navy.[108] Gen. Andrew G. L. McNaughton, Canada's most famous soldier of the twentieth century, commanded his country's forces overseas during the war and was minister of defense in 1944.[109] Alexander Johnstone was the founder of the Malaysian Air Force.[110]

Sir Archibald Clark Kerr, born in Australia to a native Scottish father and a mother of the same ancestry, was the British ambassador to Russia whose rapport with Stalin made him important in the war, especially at the "Big Three" meeting in 1943. After the war he became ambassador to the United States.[111]

Sir Fitzroy Maclean, the "Balkan Brigadier," parachuted into Nazi-occupied Yugoslavia in 1943 to command the British mission to Tito's partisans. Maclean knew Ian Fleming during the war and is undoubtedly a model for James Bond.[112]

Lt. Col. David Stirling was the Scots Guards officer who created the British Special Air Service, a commando-type group which played havoc with German supply lines between 1941 and 1943. Stirling was captured in 1943, but not before his unit had destroyed 250 German airplanes and much else. He made four escape attempts, but at six feet, six inches tall he was too obvious to succeed. The unit may still be in existence, but as it is secret, we do not know.[113]

Maj. Gen. Sir Ronald MacKenzie Scobie became the liberator of Greece in 1944.[114] The American movie star Brig. Gen. James Stewart flew twenty-five missions as a bomber pilot over enemy territory in World War II. His bombardier called him "a first rate flier, a better flier than an actor."[115] Robert Alexander Kennedy Runcie, a decorated Scots Guards tank commander during the war, later became archbishop of Canterbury.[116]

Gen. George C. Marshall, chief of staff of the U.S. Army at the time of Pearl Harbor, directed the organization and training of American land and air forces during World War II. After the war he became secretary of state and created the Marshall Plan, which aided Europe in its recovery. His term saw the recognition of Israel and the beginnings of NATO. Like Thomas Jefferson and Chief Justice John Marshall, George Marshall was a descendant of Scotland through the Randolphs of Virginia. His mother came from the Stuarts of Pittsburgh.[117]

The defeat of Hitler in western Europe was accomplished in large part by the successful Allied execution of three crucial phases of the war: the alert to the awesome danger posed by the German rearmament in time for Britain and America to begin preparations; the winning of the Battle of Britain, which prevented what surely would have been a catastrophic German invasion; and the successful invasion of France against the strongest military defense ever assembled. In each of these phases the balance was swung in favor of the Allies by superior British intelligence, and was largely the work of a handful of Scots belonging to several countries.

Many people wonder why Churchill, and later Roosevelt, were so sure of Hitler's intentions before the war while most of their countrymen were not. The answer is that Churchill knew what Hitler's plans were, while almost everyone else was guessing. He obtained his information from a Canadian Scot, William Stephenson, whose intelligence career had begun when he delivered a report after his escape from a German concentration camp in World War I. Stephenson, whose business interests had taken him to pre–World War II Germany, observed that German steel production had turned to armaments, and later discovered the Nazi plan to conquer Europe and rule the world. Churchill called him by the code name Intrepid, and as such he became, prior to the war, head of a private intelligence network for the future prime minister.

Chamberlain did not have the information and sought appeasement, while Churchill decided to inform Roosevelt of Germany's designs and enlisted his cooperation by sending Intrepid to America as his agent, bypassing the cabinet and Parliament and receiving consent for his actions from the king instead.

In 1940 Stephenson moved to New York, where he directed the formation of the American offensive intelligence agency, the O.S.S., the forerunner of the C.I.A., while continuing as Churchill's liaison with Roosevelt and de facto general of the Anglo-American clandestine war against Hitler.[118] It is largely because of these brave, legally questionable actions that Britain and the United States did not face the enemy totally unprepared.

In Britain, both Adm. Sir Hugh Sinclair and Col. Sir Stewart Graham Menzies served as chiefs of the famous MI-6.[119] Their Scottish-American counterpart was David K. E. Bruce, the chief of the O.S.S. in the European theater.[120]

Throughout the war British intelligence was able to read coded messages dispatched by the German cipher machine Enigma because of the Ultra project, which deciphered Enigma's codes. The British effort had been helped immeasurably when, in the summer of 1939, Polish intelligence, realizing that their country was about to be invaded by Germany, presented British intelligence with a working model of the Enigma machine, which was carried to

England by British and French agents. Ultra used a machine (actually the world's first electronic digital computer) developed by the Scoto-Englishman Alan Mathison Turing, a mathematical genius who called it Colossus Mark I.[121] Turing's work was the subject of the 1987 play *Breaking the Code*, starring Derek Jacobi.[122]

A German invasion of under-prepared Britain would have been catastrophic in 1940, and partly because of Ultra it was prevented. The British were able to learn that Hitler had decided not to try an invasion that year unless he had first gained air superiority over Britain. They also learned when and where the Luftwaffe would attack. This information was crucial in the Battle of Britain, which the R.A.F. won by downing several German planes for every one it lost. Also, because Ultra told them exactly where the German fleet would be, the British were able to get increasing numbers of ships past the U-boats to provide supplies. Hitler could not obtain air superiority in 1940, and the invasion of Britain was prevented.

In similar fashion, Ultra told the British everything they had to know about the deployment of troops and materiel by the Germans prior to the D-Day invasion, upon which the Allies would invest the bulk of their material and human resources. To prevent the Germans from concentrating troops in France the British engaged in a massive deception to convince Hitler that they might invade Norway first, forcing them to garrison four hundred thousand men there. This was project Skye, a fantastic operation run from Edinburgh Castle by Col. R. M. Macleod in which he "commanded" the "British Fourth Army," which never existed. Using radio broadcasts, wireless messages, and newspaper reports complete with "Fourth Army football results," Macleod created the image of a powerful army in Scotland massing enormous quantities of materiel for an attack on Norway. Ultra, of course, gave him continuous information on what the German high command was believing about his phantom army, and ultimately told him that they were convinced that it was real. Another Scot, Gen. Colin McVean Gubbins, a Hebridean by birth, commanded a network of thousands of spies and saboteurs behind the German lines prior to D-Day.[123] Ian Fleming was not being chauvinistic when he told his readers that James Bond was a Scot.

The war against Japan was shortened considerably by the atomic bomb, which forced Japan to surrender without being invaded, saving tens of thousands of lives. Sir George P. Thomson, a British physicist of Scottish descent, headed the wartime committee which reported to the Allies that it was possible to build the bomb.[124] The

American physicist Harold M. Agnew, a son of a Scotch-Irish stonecutter, had helped build the first nuclear reactor in a Chicago squash court in 1942, and then went to Los Alamos to help build the atomic bomb. On May 6, 1945, he autographed the first atomic bomb and flew in the Hiroshima mission as an observer. Although he was only twenty-four years old, he was the only person to witness the entire procedure, from the pile in Chicago, to the building of the bomb, to the bombing of Hiroshima.[125]

The concluding event of World War II was held under an overcast sky on the morning of September 2, 1945, as Allied military and naval leaders packed the decks of the U.S.S. *Missouri*, triumphantly anchored in Tokyo Bay. It is fitting that the small nation of Scots, which had done so much to win the war, was well represented at the ceremony. The flagship itself was under the command of the Scottish-American admiral "Bull" Halsey. Signing the document for Britain was Adm. Sir Bruce Fraser. Signing as the supreme commander of the Allied powers was Gen. Douglas MacArthur. The sun broke through the clouds, as if on cue, as MacArthur ended World War II by stepping to the microphone and saying simply, "These proceedings are now closed."

Scottish Soldiers and Sailors in Other Lands

DENMARK

In the early sixteenth century Scottish soldiers were found in the service of Denmark, and in 1520 helped the Danes capture Stockholm.[126] But Scottish mercenaries never forgot who they were. When a Danish king refused to allow them to carry their St. Andrew's flag, they all threatened imminent departure.[127]

FINLAND

A soldier known as Teet of Pernå (Tait of Pirn) conquered Finland for the king of Sweden in 1250. He built Pernå church in Finland and lived as an important man in the country.[128] Hans Ramsay, born in 1550, became captain of all horse, and chief of the Finnish "company of nobles."[129] Arvid Forbes, born in Ånäs, Finland, in 1598, became a major general in the army of Gustavus Adolphus, and in 1648 was governor of Pomerania.[130] John Gustaf Lagerbjelke was chief admiral of Finland in 1809. He was born in 1775, a descendant of John Fistulator of Scotland, who was ennobled as Lagerbjelke.[131] Anders Ramsay was commander in chief of the Finnish military forces in the late 1800s.[132]

FRANCE

"I do not think that a Frenchman has ever been able to come to Scotland without feeling something very special."

—Gen. *Charles de Gaulle, addressing the the Scottish nation in Edinburgh, 1942*[133]

The Scots Guards As early as the reign of Louis IX (1226–1270), the monarchs of France had Scottish bodyguards.[134] In 1418 a contingent of Scottish archers was raised as a *garde du corps* for the king.[135] The Moncreiffes furnished archers for the guards and were ennobled for it.[136] One of the first of the *Gendarmes Écossais* was John Stewart, earl of Buchan, who won a signal victory for France at Baugé in 1421, personally killing the duke of Clarence, the English commander. Buchan was made constable of France, with precedence next after the king himself, and commander in chief of the French armies.[137]

In 1424 Archibald Douglas, fourth earl of Douglas, arrived in France and was made duc de Touraine. He liberated Ivry, which had been besieged by the duke of Bedford, and was made *lieutenant général du roi* (the supreme commander) by King Charles VII.[138] Both Buchan and Douglas were killed at Verneuil in the same year, and the king created the Scots Guards in their honor. The subsequent king, Louis XI, said the guards, "held in their hands the fortune of France."[139] He was probably referring to the two events in which Scots saved him from imminent death.[140]

The first official mention of the guards occurred in 1425, when Robert Pattilok (Pittilloch) recovered Bayonne and Bordeaux for France, ending up with fame and fortune as the "Little King of Gascony."[141] The guards also fought for France in Normandy and Italy, and held the post of honor as guards of the royal person under a long succession of French kings. A low point came in 1559, when King Henry II was killed in a jousting tournament by Gabriel de Montgommery of the guards. Montgommery himself was killed by the queen, the former Catherine de Médicis.[142]

The Scots Guards continued with distinction even past the time of Napoleon. Eight guards carried the coffin of Louis XIII in 1643, and they were used at the funeral of Louis XVIII in 1824.[143]

Scots with Joan of Arc   It is said that Joan of Arc "first raised the standard of nationalism in the Western world." But Joan was not the first. William Wallace, the outlaw knight, had shown her the way a century before when he began the Scottish war for independence in the late thirteenth century.[144] Following his example, Joan, a seventeen-year-old peasant girl who believed herself to be divinely inspired, revived France during the Hundred Years War upon her relief of the besieged city of Orleans. What is well known, but seldom said, is that France's most beloved heroine was conducted into Orleans by a contingent of five hundred Scottish soldiers marching to the music of "L'air des Soldats de Robert Bruce," and under the command of Sir Patrick Ogilvy, vicomte d'Angus. Even Joan's standard had been painted by a Scot living at Tours, Hames Polvoir (Hamish Polwarth).

This Franco-Scottish triumph, which provided provisions to the starving town, proved to be the turning point of the war, dramatically improving the morale of the French army, resulting in the ultimate expulsion of the English troops and the securing of France's independence. On May 8, 1429, when the siege was raised, Joan headed a procession of thanksgiving through the churches of the town. At her side was another Scot, the bishop of Orleans, John Kirkmichael. After Orleans King Charles VII gave many Scots land and titles, provoking great resentment among the French.[145]

Later Heroes   Bernard Stuart, *maréchal de France* and a cousin of the earl of Lennox, captured Genoa and conquered all Lombardy in 1499 with an army that included many Scots.[146] John Hepburn, *maréchal de France*, took Heidelberg for the French during the Thirty Years War. Hepburn, who had previously fought for Sweden, died fighting in Alsace in 1636, at the head of his own *régiment d'Hebron*, which included the famous *Garde Écossaise*. Cardinal Richelieu said that Hepburn's death made him "inconsolable," and a monument to this Scottish soldier was erected by Louis XIV. The epitaph reads, "To the best soldier in Christendom."[147]

Napoleon   According to G. S. H. L. Washington, "it was not until he was about to put the crown of France on his head that Napoleon revealed the astonishing fact that he was of royal blood." A detailed genealogy shows that in 1745 the emperor's grandmother, Mme. Maria Buonaparte (née Paravicini) had an *affaire de coeur* in Ajaccio, Corsica, with Prince Joseph Stuart (1722–1783) a scion of the French house of Rohan Stuart. Therefore Napoleon was actually a Stuart rather than a Buonaparte, and the great-great-great-grandson of King Charles II of Great Britain.[148]

One of Napoleon's generals was Jacques Étienne Joseph Alexandre Macdonald, *maréchal de France* and *duc de Tarente*, the son of Scottish Jacobite refugees.[149] Frederick Maitland, the Scottish captain of the ship *Bellerophon*, captured Napoleon and brought him to England.[150] The Scottish admiral George Keith Elphinstone supervised the emperor's transfer to the *Northumberland*,[151] and aboard that ship the Scottish admiral Sir George Cockburn conveyed Napoleon to his final exile at St. Helena, which was then under the command of another Scot, Adm. Sir Pulteney Malcolm. The emperor died there in 1821, perhaps from stomach cancer, as a Scottish physician, Archibald Arnott, tried to save his life.[152]

GERMAN-SPEAKING EUROPE

As early as the fourteenth century there were Scottish soldiers in Germany fighting with the Order of the Teutonic Knights.[153] In 1577 the city of Danzig hired a regiment of seven hundred Scots to defend themselves against Poland.[154] The most famous Scoto-German soldier was Field Marshal James Keith, who became Frederick the Great's closest friend and most important warrior. He was the brother of George Keith, Earl Marischal of Scotland.[155]

Walter Leslie, of Aberdeenshire, fought for the imperial (Catholic) side during the Thirty Year's War, although he was a Protestant. He took part in the plot to murder Wallenstein, the imperial commander, and in 1650 was made field marshal of the empire. He became a diplomat and received the Order of the Golden Fleece, the emperor's highest honor, in 1665.[156] Freiherr (baron) Gideon Ernst von Laudon (1717–1790) was one of Austria's greatest soldiers and was descended from Scottish Loudons. In 1760, during the Seven Year's War he was in command in Bohemia, Moravia, and Silesia. In 1789, in the Turkish War, he captured Belgrade, and Emperor Leopold II made him commander in chief of the Austrian armed forces, *Feldzugmeister* (field marshal), and *generalissimo*.[157]

In 1945, just before the end of World War II, Helmuth James Count von Moltke, scion of a proud German military tradition, was sentenced to death and executed by the Nazis for being a key member of the Kreisau Circle, a group of responsible Germans working from the inside to defeat the Third Reich. Count von Moltke was a grandson of, and named for, Sir James Rose Innes, a Scottish chief justice of South Africa.[158]

HOLLAND

Scottish soldiers arrived in Holland as early as 1570, and soon played a prominent part in helping the Dutch throw off their Spanish yoke. The Scots Brigade wore distinctive red uniforms and fought so well that they were given preferential treatment over Dutch troops. By 1576 the Spaniards were gone. It is said that the Scots Brigade "rocked the cradle" of the infant Dutch republic. They stayed in Holland generation after generation, and both Highlanders and Lowlanders kept their discipline and their Scottish nationality. In present-day Holland some Scottish surnames survive in their Dutch forms. Among them are Boguenan (Buchanan), Sidderlan (Sutherland), and Verbaas (Forbes).[159]

ISRAEL

A Scottish-English soldier, Gen. Orde Charles Wingate, became a legend in Israel as *hayedid*, the "friend." From 1936 to 1939 he trained the special Jewish night squad of the *Hagana*, constantly urging his fighters on. Yisrael Galili, a former head of the *Hagana*, said, "Wingate not only taught us military matters, he also taught us Zionism." At one point he asked a timid Zionist, "Did your people suffer in exile for two thousand years to become like any other nation?" American Jews honor Wingate at an annual memorial ceremony in Arlington National Cemetery, where he is buried.[160]

MOROCCO

In the late nineteenth century Sir Harry Maclean was commander in chief of the army of the sultan of Morocco, which, at least as late as 1970, continued to use the Maclean tartan on its pipe bags.[161]

NORWAY

Axel Mowat (1593–1661) was one of the richest men in Norway and an admiral in the Norwegian-Danish fleet in the seventeenth century.[162]

PERSIA

In the nineteenth century John Malcolm was sent on a mission to Persia. The shah made him a general in the Persian army. Sir Henry Lindesay-Bethune, one of Malcolm's staff, later commanded the shah's army against the Russians. He was over seven feet tall.[163]

POLAND

There were many Scottish soldiers in the service of Poland in the seventeenth and eighteenth centuries. They were preferred as bodyguards for the king and his nobles.[164]

PORTUGAL

Sir Charles Napier (1786–1860), admiral of the fleet which restored Queen Maria II of Portugal, was born in Falkirk. The Miguelite army, commanded by another Scot, Ranald MacDonnell, had opposed Napier.[165]

RUSSIA

Sir Alexander Leslie was one of the first of many famous Scottish soldiers in Russia. In addition to achieving the rank of general, he became governor of Smolensk and chief of the permanent Foreign Legion. He died in 1661 at the age of ninety-five.[166]

Gen. Patrick Gordon (1635–1699), born in Aberdeen, was one of the giants of Russian history and did more, perhaps, than any man save Peter the Great to construct the Russian Empire. He defeated the Turks for Russia at Tschigirin in 1677. In 1687 he was made a full general, received the name Patrick Ivanovitch, and the right to be addressed in the third person. By 1694 he was also an admiral and the chief military advisor to the tsar. At this point he was Peter's right-hand man and was left in charge of the Kremlin during the tsar's famous trip to the West (1697–1698), putting down a rebellion of the *streltsy*, the military nobility attached to the crown, in 1698. Peter wept at Gordon's deathbed a year later, and personally closed his eyes with his own hand.[167]

Field Marshal George Ogilvy was the planner of many of Peter the Great's battles.[168] In 1721 Field Marshal James Bruce (Yakov Vilemovitch Bruce; 1670–1735) negotiated the cession of the Baltic provinces to Russia at the peace of Nystadt. By this time he had become the second Scottish right-hand man to Peter the Great, directing the tsar's schools of navigation, artillery, and military engineering, and had become a count and a senator. His brother, Lt. Gen. Roman Vilemovitch Bruce, was commandant at St. Petersburg and one of the builders of the city. Around 1700 he drove the Swedes away from St. Petersburg three times and is considered to have been the city's savior. In 1984 his remains were reinterred with great ceremony. Count James Bruce was also an astronomer. At the coronation of the Empress Catherine I in 1724 he carried the crown, while his wife, the countess of Bruce, followed as one of the train-bearers to the empress herself.[169]

"I had sooner lose ten thousand of my best soldiers than Keith," said the Empress Anna (1730–1740) of the Scottish-born soldier Gen. James F. E. Keith (1696–1758), who became governor of the Ukraine. In the Russian war against Sweden he was both commander in chief and minister plenipotentiary to Sweden. Keith might actually have become tsar. It appears that the Empress Elizabeth wanted to marry him, and in a letter she called him "the only man who can bring up a future heir of the throne in my mind and in the footsteps of Peter the Great."

But Keith could see that a formidable lady, soon to be known as Catherine the Great, had many powerful allies who intended to see *her* succeed Elizabeth. He wrote to a friend, "The Empress is resolved to raise me to a height which would cause my ruin as well as her own." Fearing the wrath of Russia if he accepted the marriage and that of Elizabeth if he refused, Keith (no doubt with a vision of Siberia in mind) fled in 1747 to Prussia, where Frederick the Great immediately made him a field marshal and governor of Berlin.[170]

Some say that the Russian navy was founded by the Scottish admiral Thomas Gordon, who captured Danzig for Russia in 1724.[171] Others call Adm. Samuel Carlovitch Greig (1735–1788) the "father" of the Russian navy. Greig, born at Inverkeithing, was commodore of the Russian fleet and the chief instrument in the conquest of the Crimea when, in 1770, he destroyed the Turkish fleet. When he died in 1788 Greig was given a state funeral by Catherine the Great. In 1970 the Soviet Union issued postage stamps commemorating the Russian victory over the Turks under Greig.[172]

On the advice of Thomas Jefferson, John Paul Jones, the Scottish-born founder of the American navy, agreed to succeed Greig in the post of supreme commander of the Russian navy under Catherine the Great in her war against the Turks. However, ethnic prejudice, allowed subordinates to dispute his authority, and his victories were credited to others. Jones soon left for Paris, where he died in 1792, dispirited, at age forty-five, at 19 rue de Tournon.[173]

The most important Russian soldier in the Napoleonic wars, perhaps the greatest soldier in all Russian history, was Prince Mikhail Bogdanovich Barclay de Tolly (1761–1818), born in Russia but descended from the Barclays of Towie in Aberdeenshire. Barclay de Tolly fought for Russia against Turkey, Sweden, and Poland from 1788 to 1794. In 1808 he made a daring invasion of Sweden across the ice of a frozen sea and was named governor of the new Russian duchy of Finland. In 1814, during the Napoleonic wars he played a key part in the invasion of France and was made a field marshal in Paris. He was commander in chief of the Russian army which invaded France in 1815, helped finish Napoleon, and was made a prince.

But for all this, Barclay was slighted by Russia. He had been the commander of the army at the beginning of Napoleon's thrust into Russia in 1812 and was really the chief architect of his country's heroic defense against, and expulsion of, the Grand Army. Because of his foreign name and lineage, his brilliant strategy of calculated retreat was criticized, even to suggestions of treason, and he was relieved in favor of General Kutuzov, who successfully used the same tactics. Later Tolstoy and Stalin, continuing the prejudice, gave credit for the salvation of Russia to Kutuzov. However, Marx and Engels, concluded that Barclay "was beyond question the best of Alexander's generals," and Pushkin, like many others, changed his mind and wrote:

> How often in his passing may a man be seen,
> At whom a blind and hectic age will vent its spleen,
> But whose exalted face, within a generation,
> Draws poets in rapt and loving contemplation.[174]

SOUTH AMERICA

Simon Bolivar had some Scottish help in his liberating activities in South America. Sir Gregor MacGregor was one of his generals. The chief of the Munros, Gen. Sir Charles Munro (ninth baronet of Foulis) commanded a division of the Colombian Revolutionary Army under Bolivar at the decisive battle that freed the continent of South America from Spanish control. Gen. John MacPherson, known to some as "the illustrious procurer of the independence of Venezuela" and Bolivar's right-hand man, rose to be commander in chief of the Venezuelan army, as did his son, also Gen. John MacPherson.[175]

Adm. Thomas Cochrane (tenth earl of Dundonald) became one of the greatest seamen of all history. His early career was marked by controversy and included a court martial for disrespect, as well as a duel. In 1801, commanding a brig with a crew of only fifty-four men, he boarded and captured the Spanish frigate *El Gamo*, which carried a crew of 319 men and thirty-two heavy guns, a feat unparalleled in naval history. He continued this career, commanding frigates, winning a fortune in prize money, and successfully defending Trinidad Castle against the French. In 1806 he became a member of Parliament, a platform from which he began to demand naval reform. His resulting unpopularity with the admiralty led to his conviction, on trumped-up charges, of securities fraud, and he was removed both from Parliament and the navy. The voters believed in his innocence and reelected him, but he had to serve his year in jail anyway.

In 1817 he accepted the invitation of Chile to command its fleet, and subsequently played a major part in the liberation of both Chile and Peru, particularly by his capture of the Spanish flagship *Esmeralda*. In 1823 Cochrane took command of the Brazilian navy and was a large factor in that country's struggle for independence from Portugal. In 1827 he took command of the Greek navy in that country's war of independence.

Cochrane finally returned to England, and in 1832 was restored to the navy, where his reform plans then found sympathetic ears. He was an early advocate of the use of steamships, and his novel plans for smoke screens were filed and kept secret for a century. He died in London in 1860, and, reputation restored, was buried in Westminster Abbey.[176]

SWEDEN

"First they took my brothers twain,
Then wiled my love frae me:
Oh, woe unto these cruell wars
In low Germanie!"

—*Scottish song*[177]

The first Scottish troop was established in Sweden in 1563, and by 1604 Hans Stuart had become ennobled, and was inspector general of all foreign troops there.[178] For the most part, however, the Scottish experience in Sweden in this era marked a low point in the history of Scottish mercenary soldiers. Archibald Ruthven's army crossed to Sweden in 1573 and was cut down by its German allies in Estonia in 1574, with King Johan III accusing the Scots of treason.[179] And in 1612 Scottish mercenaries defied their own government, landed in Norway en route to Sweden, and were massacred.[180]

But the years of glory soon came with the Scottish participation in the Swedish army of Gustavus Adolphus, who intervened briefly but decisively on the side of the Protestant cause in the Thirty Years' War (1618–1648). To the Swedish army, Scotland contributed troops variously estimated at twenty to forty thousand men, by far the greatest levies of any country and a substantial percentage of that small country's population.[181] The Scots morale was raised above that of the common mercenary because of a feeling of loyalty to the king of Bohemia, whose wife was the daughter of their own King James VI, and it is said that they were willing to live on roots and carrots to fight for Protestantism. Thus they were entrusted with the most perilous tasks, and invariably stood firm.[182]

It seems certain that Gustavus Adolphus could not have gained his victories without his Scots. More than sixty of them were made governors of castles and towns in the conquered provinces of Germany, including Maj. Gen. Sir D. Drummond, governor of Stettin; Maj. Gen. Sir James Ramsay, governor of Hanau; and Maj. Gen. W. Legge, governor of Bremen.[183]

In the Thirty Years' War Scotland contributed, in addition to those above, the following officers in the service of Sweden:

Field marshals: Sir Robert Douglas; Hugo Hamilton; Sir Alexander Leslie, governor of the Baltic provinces; and Sir Patrick Ruthven, governor of Ulm.

Generals: George, earl of Crawford-Lindsay; James, marquess of Hamilton; Malcolm Hamilton; Andrew Rutherford, earl of Teviot; and Sir James Spence.

In addition to these were Lt. Gen. Alexander Forbes, tenth Lord Forbes; Vice Admiral Richard Clark; at least nine major generals; and forty-one colonels.[184] Special mention must be made of some. Donald Mackay (Lord Reay) raised the famous Mackay's Regiment, which fought with much distinction, and Robert Munro, of Foulis, was a close confidant to the king.[185] William Philip retired as commander in chief of the Swedish army in 1658.[186] Alexander Erskine was minister of war to Gustavus Adolphus and represented Sweden at the conference that resulted in the Treaty of Westphalia (1648), ending the Thirty Years' War.[187] Robert Douglas began his career as a page to Gustavus Adolphus and rose to field marshal. His dashing courage at the decisive Battle of Jankovitch, near Prague in 1645, "was mainly responsible for the downfall of the Imperialists."[188] His descendant, Gen. Archibald Douglas, was commander in chief of the Swedish army during World War II.[189]

Col. John Hepburn participated in battles all over Germany. His Scots Brigade, with a drummer sounding the feared "March of the Scots," led the advance at one of the decisive battles in world history, the Battle of Breitenfeld, near Leipzig, which opened southern Germany to the Swedes. Hepburn took possession of Leipzig in September 1631. Munich fell to him in 1632 when the Scots Brigade, piped in by Mackay's Highlanders, were the first to enter. Hepburn was made governor of Munich, and his men, much to the disgust of the Swedes, were entrusted to guard the person of the king. Despite all of this, when Gustavus quizzed Hepburn as to why his armour was so splendid and why he was a Roman Catholic, the insulted Scottish hero at once sheathed his sword and left the Swedish service for France, where he was immediately made a field marshal.[190]

Field Marshal Alexander Leslie was largely responsible for Russo-Swedish military cooperation as Sweden's envoy to Russia.[191] He had also been the Swedish commander who relieved the besieged town of Stralsund in 1628. On July 18 he forced his way into the town, and on August 3 the siege was lifted. According to George A. Sinclair, "All historians, including Carlyle...are agreed...that if the city had fallen, Sweden and Denmark would have been excluded from further interference in Germany."[192] Eventually Leslie succeeded Gustavus Adolphus in command of the Swedish army.[193]

Historians have often wondered how Sweden, a country not much known for military prowess before or since, became the decisive military power in seventeenth-century Europe.

Conclusion

During the Russo-Turkish War of 1877 Alastair Campbell, a British war correspondent, took over a disorganized Turkish combat group and defeated a much larger Russian force at Shipka Pass, in Turkey. He was decorated by the Turkish government and always called Shipka Campbell afterward.[194] Perhaps this is the source of the oft-told story, probably apocryphal, of two generals commanding, respectively, Russian and Turkish armies in the mid-nineteenth century. A truce is called, and the generals begin to negotiate an armistice, speaking in French. The bargaining proceeds at a slow pace, and at length the Russian general, exasperated with the Turk, mutters under his breath, "Och, ye auld futer" ("Oh, you old contemptible bungler"). Whereupon the Turk wheels and glares, "Hoot! Wha ca's me auld futer?" It turns out they are both from Kilmarnock, embrace, and an armistice is quickly arranged.

Undoubtedly, scenes like this have actually occurred, as Scots have been fighting for a very long time in many lands. Their history has made them regard military service as the norm, and even when they have found fellow Scots opposing them in some army, somewhere, they have treated them with respect and have given better treatment to Scottish prisoners than to others.

The Scottish ability in warfare can be shown statistically by analyzing *A Concise Biography of Military History*,[195] which lists two hundred significant names in land warfare in the last one thousand years. There are twenty-nine men named, almost fifteen percent, who are at least partly Scottish. Since people of Scottish ancestry make up only about one-half of one percent of the world's population, they are overrepresented thirty times.

> Abercromby, Sir Ralph
> Alexander, H. R. L. G. (Earl Alexander)
> Auchinleck, Field Marshal Sir C. J. E.
> Bruce, King Robert I, the
> Campbell, Colin (Baron Clyde)
> Custer, Lt. Col. George Armstrong
> De Gaulle, Gen. Charles
> Gordon, Charles George "Chinese"
> Graham, James (Marquess of Montrose)
> Graham, Thomas (Baron Lynedoch)
> Grant, Gen. Ulysses S.
> Haig, Douglas (Earl Haig)
> Jackson, Gen. Thomas J. "Stonewall"
> Lawrence, Col. T. E. "Lawrence of Arabia"
> Lee, Gen. Robert E.
> Liddell-Hart, Sir Basil H.
> MacArthur, Gen. Douglas
> Marshall, Gen. George C.
> Montgomery, Bernard Law (Viscount Montgomery)
> Moore, Sir John
> Patton, Gen. George S.

Scott, Gen. Winfield
Stirling, Sir David
Stuart, Gen. J. E. B. "Jeb"
Taylor, Gen. Zachary
Wallace, Sir William
Washington, Gen. George
Wavell, Archibald P. (Earl Wavell)
Wayne, Gen. "Mad" Anthony

On the level of the common foot soldier the U.S. Army provides an astonishing proof: although few immigrants have been American soldiers, and even fewer of these have been Scots, thirty-eight Congressional Medals of Honor, more than one percent of the total of the nation's highest award, have been bestowed upon soldiers and sailors *born* in Scotland.[196]

In recent times there has been a peaceful trend running through the Scottish nation. Although Maj. Gen. Ian Ross Campbell commanded the forces of Australia in Korea,[197] it was the Scottish-American General Alexander Haig who assisted in ending the Vietnam War.[198] It was Andrew Carnegie who donated the Temple of Peace in the Hague, and from 1919 to 1933 James Drummond, sixteenth earl of Perth, was the first (and almost only) secretary general of the League of Nations. John D. Rockefeller, Jr., gave the land for the United Nations in New York.

But it seems likely that if the situation calls, the Scots will rise again. What else can anyone make of a people who would fight such a battle as that of *Blar na Leine* (shirt field), where on July 3, 1544, three hundred Frasers opposed five hundred Macdonalds and Camerons, most of whom had discarded their shirts against the summer heat. At the end there were only four Frasers and eight of their opponents left standing.[199]

One of the reasons the Scots fight so well is that their nobility has never shirked the call of duty or the anxiety of combat. As early as 1390 Sir David Lindsay, the champion of Scotland, met the English knight, Lord Welles, who had disparaged Scots, on a colorfully decorated London Bridge before a multitude of spectators, including the king and queen of England. The Scot overwhelmed the Englishman in a jousting match and in the hand-to-hand combat which followed he lifted Lord Welles on his dagger point and threw him to the ground. Lindsay spared Welles' life, returned to a hero's welcome in Scotland, and eventually became the earl of Crawford.

In the course of this chapter we have seen how the Scottish nobility has carried on the tradition of combat through all of Scotland's wars, and this has been of great inspiration to the entire population. One small family, the Campbells of Cawdor, provides an unparalleled example by itself. Sir Ian Moncrieffe said, "in the last hundred years, descendants of the Campbell thanes of Cawdor have been awarded no less than twelve mentions in despatches, three brevets, three French croix de guerre (one with palm and star), the Legion of Honour four times," and twenty-three other medals, including three Victoria Crosses.[200]

The Scottish aptitude for warfare continues right up to the present. In the 1980s, before the end of the cold war, the security of the free world was entrusted to the Scottish-American admiral, W. L. McDonald, the supreme allied commander in the Atlantic, whose "responsibility in the event of war" would have been, quite simply, "to lead the combined military forces of the sixteen member nations to victory."[201] In 1991 the American general Colin Powell led twenty-eight nations to victory as the architect of Desert Storm in the Persian Gulf War. General Powell's mother is of Scottish descent.[202] Serving under Powell, an Edinburgh-born U.S. marine, Robert B. Johnston, was central command chief of staff in the Persian Gulf War. The following year Lt. Gen. Johnston was named to lead all forces in the United Nations expedition to restore order in Somalia.[203] At about the same time the commander of the United Nations forces in Bosnia was Maj. Gen. Lewis W. MacKenzie, of Canada.[204]

"It has been my lot to have found myself in many distant lands. I have never been in one without finding a Scotchman, and I never found a Scotchman who was not at the head of the poll."

—*Benjamin Disraeli*[1]

7

Civilian Scots Abroad

From very early times the Scots traveled to the continent, since they were not welcome in England. The Scots in the Middle Ages thought of themselves as Europeans, while the English thought of themselves as English. The insular Englishman pronounced Latin in a unique way. The Scots said their Latin like everyone else.[2]

At first Scotland sent scholars to many parts of Europe. But starting around the fourteenth century Scottish traders came as well. Scottish "factors" were soon seen in places like Elsinore, Danzig, Stockholm, and Bruges. These factors were independent Scots who aided the flow of commerce for their countrymen, giving advice on what and where to buy, price information, currency rates, market conditions, and warnings on crime in exchange for commissions, such as 2.5 percent.[3]

As the centuries have passed the expatriation of Scots has continued far beyond Europe, to all parts of the world. In this chapter we shall discuss Scottish influence in foreign lands which has not been covered in other chapters.

Africa

Following the enormous Scottish contribution to the exploration of Africa in the nineteenth century, several people of the Scottish nation have left their mark in other ways. Thomas Buchanan, a cousin of the American president James Buchanan, was the first governor of Liberia in 1836.[4] One of the oddest pipe bands in the world is kept by a tribal chief in Uganda and is called the Mac-scotchers.[5] Sir John Macpherson was governor of Nigeria in 1948 and paved the way for that nation's independence. As this is written, the undisputed head man of Ghana is the half-Scottish, half-Ghanian flight lieutenant Jerry Rawlings, who led a successful coup in 1979.[6]

Baltic Lands

From the fifteenth through the eighteenth centuries there were colonies of Scottish merchants in the Baltic, especially at Memel and Tilsit, in what is now Lithuania, and at Riga in what is now Latvia.[7] Joachim Wolthers gennant von Fersen, descended from Scottish Macphersons, was Sweden's governor of Livonia, roughly equivalent to today's Estonia and Latvia, in 1670, a time when there were many Scottish traders in the area. Fabian von Fersen, Otto Wilhelm von Fersen, and Axel von Ferson were all general officers in the eighteenth century.[8] In 1681 Johan Lichton (John Leighton), the son of a Scottish immigrant, was governor of Reval and Estonia and became president of the Superior Court of Justice in 1687.[9] By the eighteenth century most of the trade of Lithuania was in the hands of Scots, and they are remembered by the word *szātas*, the ordinary word for peddler, derived from the German *Schotte*.[10]

Belgium

One of the ancestors of the present Belgian royalty is Baron William Gunn. (See German-speaking Europe, below.)[11]

Denmark

Records of Scots in Denmark go back to the late fifteenth century, but their enterprise there does not appear to have been long-lasting, perhaps because of their immediate success and the Danes' consequently harsh and prejudicial reaction to it. There were Scots in the town of Malmö, a part of Scania which is now in Sweden but then belonged to Denmark, as early as 1520.

The *Skotter* there originally peddled directly to the people in the countryside, causing a loss of business to the town merchants. Since this trade was very profitable, there were soon so many Scots in Scania that the word *skotter* came to mean a small trader. It was not long before the enterprising Scots were accused of all sorts of things, including the export of coin, cornering the town property markets, and unscrupulous methods, including the bribery of royal officials. The *Skotter* were also considered to be unreliable in time of war.[12] In 1534 the Ystad magistrates and council complained of the Scots trafficking to the great loss of all old, established businesses and soon after they were barred from the town.[13] In 1578 the people of Lund were warned against dealing with non-Lutheran strangers, "especially Netherlanders and Scots." But by 1627 there were over nine thousand Scots in Denmark, and before their demise the *Skotter* were commemorated with place names such as these at Elsinore: Skotterbakken, Skottehuset, and Skottestraede.[14]

Not all of the Scots in Denmark were traders. Peter Davidson, also known as Peter Skotte and Petrus David de Scotia, became one of the founders of the University of Copenhagen in 1478. Davidson was made the first dean of its faculty of arts in 1479 and later elected president of the university no fewer than six times. Other Scottish professors soon followed Davidson to Denmark.[15] David Cochran (d. 1529) became Danish king of arms, that is, the highest-ranking heraldric officer, and served King Hans as ambassador to Poland and Russia.[16] From 1513–1523 Alexander Kinghorn was physician to King Christian II of Denmark, and in 1517 rector of the University of Copenhagen. John MacAlpin, also known as Johannes Machabaeus, was rector of the university in 1544 and a member of the committee to draft the first complete Bible in Danish.[17]

Sander Leiel, born Alexander Lyell, became one of the richest Danish merchants of his time. He also served as *borgmester* (mayor) of Elsinore in 1536, advisor to the king and godfather to one of his sons. David Thomson was also a *borgmester* of Elsinore.[18]

Thomas Lummesden (b. 1528), also known as Thomas Scotus, served as the Danish ambassador to Scotland from 1505 to 1522, and Andrew Sinclair (1555–1625) was Danish ambassador to what King James VI and I was calling Great Britain.[19] Denmark's greatest hymn writer was Bishop Thomas Hansen Kingo (1634–1707), who was of Scottish extraction.[20] Andrew Mitchell introduced the steam engine into Denmark in 1790.[21] John Gordon (d. 1807) was physician to the king of Denmark for the West Indies and lived on the island of St. Croix.[22]

The Far East

During the nineteenth century the Church of Scotland and American Presbyterians established churches all over the world. Apparently they met with their greatest success in Korea where, out of a total population of forty million in 1984, there were nine million Christians, of whom five million were Presbyterians. This is almost equal to the number of Presbyterians in the United States, Canada, and Scotland combined.[23]

A Scottish sea captain, Robert Hunter, found himself in Thailand in 1824 and became the first white man to observe the phenomenon of Siamese twins. In the 1970s a Thai physician, Mechai Viravaidya, whose mother is Scottish, became the most successful birth control advocate in the Far East. In four years his super-salesman techniques reduced Thailand's pregnancies by 41 percent and changed the Thai word for condom to *mechai*.[24]

The cool refuge of the Cameron Highlands in Malaysia was first charted by surveyor William Cameron in 1885. The oldest hill station in the Highlands is Maxwell's Hill, and Fraser's Hill is just south. Kuala Lumpur still has a St. Andrew's Society.[25]

Japan was opened to the West, both for the United States and for Britain, by Scots in the nineteenth century. In 1853 Commodore Matthew Calbraith Perry, an American of partly Scottish ancestry, commanded a fleet which was sent to try to initiate diplomatic relations with Japan. Perry, confronted by Japan's traditional isolation, decided that only a show of force would open the country and demanded "as a right...those acts of courtesy which are due from one civilized country to another." He refused Japanese orders to leave and sent his documents ashore with Adm. Franklin Buchanan, who would later head the Confederate navy during the Civil War. Buchanan took his barge straight in and, jumping into the surf ahead of his crew, became the first American ever to set foot on Japanese soil. Perry returned the following year with more ships, enough to convince the Japanese to conclude the first treaty between Japan and the United States.[26]

James Bruce, eighth earl of Elgin, negotiated Britain's first treaty with Japan at Yeddo in 1858.[27] Richard Henry Brunton (1841–1901), born in Scotland, went to Japan in 1868 as chief engineer in constructing almost fifty lighthouses. He also played a major role in developing the port and city of Yokohama. Samuel M. Bryan, an American of Scotch-Irish ancestry, introduced the Western postal system into Japan and served as postmaster general there for more than a decade.[28] Henry Dyer (1848–1918), born in Bothwell, greatly aided in the industrialization of Japan in the late nineteenth century when he became the first principal and professor of engineering at the (then) new Imperial College of Engineering, in Tokyo. When he left in 1882, what had come to be called Dyer's College, the emperor awarded him the Order of the Rising Sun.[29]

Thomas Blake Glover, a Scot practically unknown in his native land, is famous in Japan. Every year more than two million Japanese visit the magnificent Glover mansion and gardens overlooking Nagasaki's beautiful harbor. Glover was born in Fraserburgh in 1838, and at age twenty-one was sent to Nagasaki for the famous Scottish trading company of Jardine Matheson. Two years later he started his own company and became very rich. He was the catalyst for bringing Japan out of feudalism and into the industrial world. Among other things, he brought the first steam locomotive to Japan, opened the country's first coal mine, ordered the first full-scale dock (built in Aberdeen), and founded the Japanese navy with three ships ordered from Alexander Hall and Co., in Scotland.

Glover went bankrupt in 1870, but Mitsubishi took over his interests and retained him as a consultant. In 1908 the emperor awarded him the Order of the Rising Sun. Thomas Glover had a colorful life and fathered several children. One of these affairs, with a woman now known only as Maki Kaga, gave him a kind of immortality as their story became the prototype for Puccini's opera *Madama Butterfly*.[30]

From 1946 to 1950 Elizabeth Gray Vining was tutor to the then crown prince and present emperor of Japan, Akihito. Her father, John Gordon Gray, was a native of Aberdeen and a maker of scientific instruments, including some of those taken by Peary to the North Pole. Elected president of the St. Andrew's Society of Philadelphia in 1912, he conceived that organization's successful effort to erect the famous Scottish-American War Memorial in Edinburgh, with its Tait McKenzie sculpture.

Elizabeth Gray Vining, whose story parallels that of *The King and I*, was the first foreigner permitted inside the living quarters of the Imperial Palace and was, perhaps, closer to Akihito than anyone else outside the imperial household. As this is written, the emperor still keeps in touch with Mrs. Vining. His father, the late Emperor Hirohito, said of her, "If ever anything I did has been a success it was bringing Mrs. Vining here."[31]

Finland

Gustaf Otto Douglas, only thirty years old, was made governor general of Finland in 1717. He was the grandson of Field Marshal Douglas of Sweden, and an ancestor of Archibald Douglas, who was commander in chief of the Swedish army during World War II.[32] The noble Finnish Thesleff family, with many civil and military leaders to its credit, is of Scottish origin. So also is the noble Finnish family of von Wright, with many artists and civic leaders among its ranks. The von Wright's are descended from George Wright, who fled Scotland at the time of Cromwell.[33]

France

"But there's a saying very old and true,
'If that you will France win,
Then with Scotland first begin.'"
—*Shakespeare*, Henry V, *Act I, scene 2*

According to the historian Hector Boece (c. 1465–c. 1536), Franco-Scottish alliances go back to the time of Charlemagne, Holy Roman emperor from 800 to 814, when the emperor "entered into a league with Achaius" (in Gaelic, Eochaid IV), the king of Scots at that time. Charlemagne's purpose was to induce talented Scottish professors to help him establish a vast system of imperial education.[34] In 848, according to the *Chronicon Normaniae*, King Kenneth I, MacAlpin, extended relations to King Charles the Bald, of France: "Rex Scotorum ad Carolum, pacis & amitiae gratia, legatos cum muneris mittit & c." (The king of Scotland to Charles, for peace and friendship's sake, sendeth ambassadors with presents & c.) There were almost certainly other treaties before the 1295 document between Balliol and Phillip the Fair (which refers to an alliance already existing for centuries), and the 1326 treaty of Robert I, the Bruce, and Charles the Fair, since the latter alluded to "a friendship of long standing between our predecessor kings." There were more treaties in 1359, 1371, 1390, and 1407.[35] In 1419 the duc de Vendome was sent to Scotland to renew the *"anciennes alliances,"*[36] and in 1436 Louis XI married Margaret, the daughter of the Scottish king James I, further cementing the relationship.[37]

Still more treaties followed in 1428, 1448, 1484, 1492, and 1512.[38] In 1513 Louis XII granted French nationality to all Scots, *"Pour tout la nation d'Écosse,"* as the grant read. Soon Scotland reciprocated, thus creating a Franco-Scottish nationality while preserving two distinct national identities, an arrangement unique in European history.[39] Within a few years the King of Scots, James V, had married, successively, two French ladies.[40] In 1558 Henry II, in honor of the marriage of the Dauphin Francis to Mary, Queen of Scots, extended the grant of dual nationality, and again it was reciprocated by the Scots.[41]

The Auld Alliance was ended, in effect, by the mutual agreement of Scotland, France, and England at the Treaty of Edinburgh in 1560.[42] Yet the dual nationality of Scots and Frenchmen was reconfirmed in 1599, 1612, and 1646, these last two *after* the union of the Crowns of England and Scotland.[43] The declaration in 1646 by Louis XIV reaffirmed the mutual rights of Frenchmen and Scots "without taking out any letters of naturalization."[44] And right up until the revolution in 1789, Scots were exempted from the French *droit d'Aubane*, under which the effects of a foreigner dying in France were seized by the crown.[45] This dual nationality may still exist, as the grants do not seem to have been officially cancelled by the *Code Napoleon*.[46]

The Auld Alliance was of much more than politico-military value to both countries. For the Scots the open door to the civilization of France was an opportunity to employ skills which were in oversupply in their own country and which could not be used in hostile England. For the French, the alliance brought talented men to their land, not only soldiers but also scholars, educators, merchants, and administrators, a constable of France, governors of provinces, and a host of noblemen: Maxuels, d'Espences, Locarts, Tournebulles, Montcrifs,[47] and a Hamilton, the *duc de Châtelherault*, who is still, from the royalist point of view, the premier duke of France.[48]

France was, in fact, thoroughly impregnated with Scottish blood, as thousands of Scots married into the local population over the centuries becoming completely French. Their contributions to this most civilized of nations was very significant, yet although they came to France not as mendicant or marauder, but to be teachers and leaders, they were often reproached by the native French. As one commentator has said, "the evil of their presence" was "their ambition and haughtiness."[49]

It was in education that Scotland left its biggest mark on France. The Scots College in Paris was founded in 1326 under the auspices of

King Robert I, the Bruce, and is the oldest institution of higher learning connected with the name of Scotland, predating the establishment of St. Andrews by almost a century. The French king Charles the Fair presented property to David, Bishop of Moray, to found this center for Scottish scholars in the French capital.[50] *Le Collège des Éccossais* was moved to 65 rue du Cardinal Lemoine in 1662. Now housing a Dominican order, it still stands proudly, its façade and ornate Scottish chapel protected by the French government.[51]

Sir John Sinclair has put forth the brave claim that the University of Paris itself had Scottish beginnings.[52] Whatever the merits, Fischer tells us that in Paris Scottish scholars attained the dignity of rector, the head and premier elected officer of the university, no less than thirty times.[53]

There was also a Scots College in Douai that lasted until 1793.[54] It is said to have possessed priceless ancient Gaelic manuscripts, now lost. At the University of Louvain John Lichton was unanimously elected rector in 1431. John of Scotland was secretary in 1447.[55] David Wauchoip was procurator of the Scottish nation at the University of Orleans in 1502.[56]

One of the greatest of all Scottish educators was George Buchanan (1506–1582), the humanist who spent much time in France and became tutor to Michel de Montaigne. He also exercised great influence as tutor to Mary, Queen of Scots, and to her son James VI and I, the founder of Great Britain, British America, and the British Empire.[57] At the academy of Sedan, between 1611 and 1622, Andrew Melville found himself among a cosmopolitan staff, a third of whom were Scots. The principal himself was the eminent Walter Donaldson.[58] In 1647 William Davidson became the first professor of chemistry in France.[59]

France's most glorious monarch, Louis XIV, had Scottish ancestors, "and it is ironical to reflect," said Sir Iain Moncreiffe, "that when the exiled Stuarts [the heirs of Bruce] fled to refuge in France, the then heir of Balliol and of the Red Cummin [the enemies of Bruce] was their host, King Louis XIV himself."[60] Jean Baptiste Colbert (1619–1683), one of the greatest of all French statesmen, ran almost every department of the government for Louis XIV in this, the nation's greatest era. For twenty-five years Colbert reconstructed the French economy and its tax system, rejuvenated the navy, promoted the arts, beautified the architecture of the country, founded royal societies and schools, and encouraged the settlement of New France. He claimed to have been a descendant of Richard Colbert, a native of Inverness, and left this inscription on his ancestor's tomb:

> "En Écosse j'eus le berceau,
> Et Reims m'a donné le tombeau."

> (In Scotland I had my cradle,
> And Rheims has given me my tomb.)[61]

On July 11, 1789, at the very beginning of the French Revolution, the Marquis de Lafayette presented the first draft of the Declaration of the Rights of Man and the Citizen, which he had written with the help of Thomas Jefferson. The ideas he expressed contained many from the Declaration of Independence, which, as has been shown in chapter 3, relied heavily on Scottish philosophy and antecedent Scottish documents. Thus, Scottish philosophy had a large presence at the founding of modern France.

During the Revolution a Swedish count of Macpherson ancestry played a key role in the demise of the French monarchy. Hans Axel von Fersen was the representative of Sweden in Paris who had fallen in love with the queen, Marie Antoinette. It was Fersen who financed and organized the disastrous attempted escape of Louis XVI and his queen from the country in 1791.[62]

The infamous symbol of the French Revolution, the guillotine, was actually invented in Scotland before 1567. The original model, the "Maiden" can still be seen in the National Museum in Edinburgh. Ironically, the instigator of the Maiden, the earl of Morton, got caught up in Scotland's changing fortunes and became one of its first victims.[63]

The oldest family business in the Bordeaux wine trade was founded in Bordeaux in 1734 by Nathaniel Johnston, a Scotch-Irish immigrant. Nath. Johnston & Fils is operated today by his descendant, also Nathaniel Johnston, and his sons Denis and Archibald, who are the ninth generation.[64]

In 1816 the French government adopted Scotland's Common Sense philosophy, which had spawned the American Revolution, as the official philosophy of France, maintaining this designation until 1870.[65] In the same era Eugénie, the last empress of France and wife of Napoleon III, discovered Biarritz, then a sleepy Basque village, and brought the emperor for a vacation. As a result, Biarritz became the posh resort it is today. Eugénie was the great granddaughter of

William Kirkpatrick, a Scottish wine merchant of Malaga, Spain.[66]

In similar fashion another Scot, the author Tobias Smollett, had "discovered" the Côte d'Azur when, on a May day in 1764 he had himself carried in a sedan chair to the water's edge and waded into the Mediterranean. Smollett noted the year-round blossoms and that the daily weather, of which he kept records, was far better than in Britain. He wrote a book about it all and the royal family followed, making the place fashionable.[67]

Yet the Mediterranean littoral was still underpopulated and Cannes almost unknown when another Scot, Lord Brougham, decided to settle there in 1834. Because of Brougham, British society began to visit the Riviera in large numbers and it became the prosperous place it is today.[68] The presence of Scotland in nineteenth-century France was formalized with the dedication of the Scots Kirk in Paris in 1874.[69]

In the twentieth century, Franco-Scottish tradition has been guarded by the presence of Harry's New York Bar. This Paris saloon was founded by two Americans in 1911 but was soon sold to a bartender, Harry MacElhone of Dundee, who made it into an institution. Joyce and Hemingway drank there. Gershwin played the piano. Scott and Zelda fought, while Sartre and de Beauvoir sulked. The Bloody Mary was invented there in 1921. Harry died in 1958, but his son Andy and grandson Duncan continue.[70]

Charles de Gaulle, the greatest French statesman of the twentieth century, was partly of Scottish ancestry.[71]

German-Speaking Europe

Scottish monks (some were probably from Ireland) founded twelve monasteries in Germany between 1067 and 1215. The monastery at Ratisbon (Regensburg) was founded by St. Marianus from Dunkeld in the eleventh century, and in 1152 King David I of Scots was approached "in order to collect further sums for the building of a new church" in Germany. It appears that the monasteries gradually became largely Irish in their makeup until about the fifteenth century, by which time they had fallen into disrepair and were, basically, abandoned. The Scottish monastery at Vienna was handed over to German Benedictines in 1418, while in 1530 the one in Constance simply ceased to exist. Weih St. Peter at Ratisbon was razed. In order to halt this decay, Pope Leo X (1513–1522) decided to return St. James at Ratisbon to the Scots and appointed James

Thomson abbot with the phrase "since he is Scottish by birth and not an Irishman."[72]

This decision by the pope encouraged the Scottish king James V to demand that all Scottish monasteries in Germany be returned, as he put it, to "his" people.[73] In 1578 Mary Queen of Scots made a similar request, granted by Emperor Rudolph II, who sustained the claims of the Scots to the monasteries at Ratisbon (now Regensburg), Würzburg, and Erfurt, since, he said, they were the "original owners." For the next two centuries many Scots came to Germany to reclaim and restore their monasteries. But after the union of the crowns, which gave Scots opportunities in their own British Empire, there was less reason for Scots to be on the continent. By the middle of the nineteenth century the Scottish monasteries in Germany had died.[74]

The most important of all the clerical Scots who came to Germany was John Duns Scotus (c. 1265–1308), by far the most prominent British theologian of the Middle Ages. He is responsible for the doctrine of the Immaculate Conception and died in Cologne, where his monument states:

Scotia me genuit,	Scotland bore me
Anglia me suscepit,	England received me,
Colonia me tenet.	Cologne holds me.[75]

Trade between Scotland and Germany goes back to before 1297, when Sir William Wallace, the Scottish hero, sent a letter to the senates of Lübeck and Hamburg letting it be known that German ships were safe in Scottish ports "because the Kingdom of Scotland has, thanks be to God, by war been recovered from the power of the English." The letter goes on to ask for the resumption of courtesies for Scottish merchants in Germany.[76]

For the next several centuries Scotland engaged in a lively trade with Germany, sending wool and woolen cloth and returning with cargoes of beer, iron, soap, and hemp. The most important destinations were Aberdeen and Danzig, in the latter of which a suburb, Alt Schottland was founded. But there are also records in many other ports including Lübeck, Bremen, Hamburg, and Königsburg, and on the other side, Leith, Perth, St. Andrews, and Dundee.

The Scottish government promoted this trade and, fortunately, also provided for the inspection of ships, ordering advanced quarantine procedures which enabled Scotland to escape the worst of the pandemic plague, which decimated the population of Europe through the seventeenth century.[77]

The Scots were very successful in Germany. As evidence, Alexander Gibsone, a shipowner, was elevated to president of the chamber of commerce and also of the town council of Danzig. And Germany in the Middle Ages was teeming with prosperous Scottish (and Jewish) peddlers. The word *Schotte* was used to mean "peddler" in Germany as early as 1330. Other words showing Scottish influence are *Schottenkram, Schottenhandel, Schottenpfaffe,* and *Schottenfrau.*[78]

But the hard-working and clannish Scots were as envied and disliked in Germany as they had been and were to be elsewhere. They imported their wives from Scotland. They maintained their own language, schools, churches, charities, and hospitals. And, of course, their great sin was that they made money. In 1539, in Rügen, there was a complaint against "illegal" trading by *Schotten.*[79] A threat to naughty children in Prussia was *"Warte bis der Schotte kommt,"* or, roughly, "Look out, the Scot will get you."[80]

The Scottish and Jewish peddlers in Germany had to endure near-Russian winters, wolves, many recorded murders at the hands of the peasantry, harsh discriminatory laws, confiscation of merchandise, jail terms, and the strong and continuous opposition of the guilds. Near the end of the seventeenth century the guild merchants of Königsburg prayed in a successful petition "the Scots skim the cream off the milk of the country" and even if they were German-born, Scots were afterward forbidden to peddle there and the town gates were shut against them. In 1683 orders were given to banish them but they were protected from this calamity by a sympathetic duke.[81]

As time passed things began to change. The creation of the British Empire provided opportunity for Scots in their own English-speaking world, and Scottish immigration to Germany stopped. In Danzig many of the more integrated and better-established Scots were themselves the instigators of a petition against Scottish peddlers. The Scots in Germany were, through intermarriage, becoming Germans, changing their names and adopting local manners. It was not long before they were no longer classified with the Jews as non-German, and finally, they assimilated completely into the German nation. Fischer says, "the increase in strength and industrial capacity which this Scottish admixture instilled into the German was of the very highest importance."[82]

Of course, there have been more than Scottish clerics and traders in Germany. In the fifteenth century the University of Cologne had two Scottish rectors, two professors of theology, and two professors of law.[83] Carl Aloysius Ramsay, a scholar in seventeenth-century Germany, was a pioneer of shorthand.[84] Immanuel Kant (1724–1804), one of the most important philosophers in history, was the grandson of Richard Cant, an immigrant Scottish innkeeper in Prussia.[85] Johann von Lamont (1805–1879), born John Lamont in Braemar, the son of the earl of Fife's forester, studied at the Scottish Benedictine monastery near Regensburg and stayed to become astronomer royal of Bavaria. He became director of the Bogenhausen Observatory in 1835 and professor of astronomy in Munich in 1852.[86]

Elizabeth Stewart, daughter of King James VI and I and the grandmother of George I, was crowned queen of Bohemia in 1619.[87] Sir William Gunn was created a Baron of the Holy Roman Empire in 1649. About the same time Col. Iain Gunn (Johann Gunn) was governor of Ohlau, in Silesia.[88] At the end of World War II John J. McCloy, an American of Scottish ancestry, was appointed military governor and high commissioner of West Germany and, with the powers of a dictator, directed the rebuilding of Germany's industry and commerce.[89]

Greece

Lord Byron (George Gordon Byron), the half-Scottish poet, was the most famous Briton in the world in 1824, the year the Greeks asked him for help in their war of independence against the Turks. Byron, who had visited Greece previously and was enchanted by it, arrived with nine servants, a dozen small cannon, and colorful military uniforms. All Europe was impressed and began to support the Greek cause and contribute money to it. When Byron died of fever he became a mythical figure, and his is one of the few foreign names bestowed upon Greek children.[90]

Ireland

As all Scots have Irish ancestors, it is not surprising that there are many things in common between the two people. Both share a common and mutually intelligible language, Gaelic, which few people realize was once spoken over the whole of both countries. In addition they are the only two people who have names beginning

Guysborough Harbor, Nova Scotia—the probable spot where a Scottish expedition, which left a written record, landed in the New World, June 2, 1398, almost a century before the first voyage of Columbus.

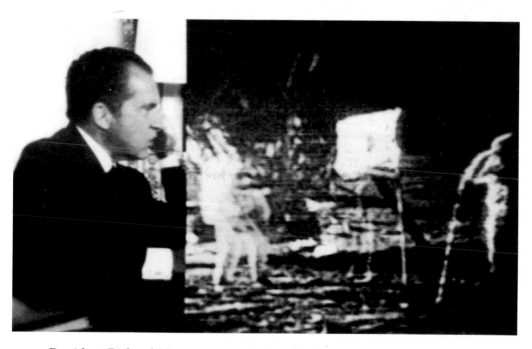

President Richard Nixon congratulating the first men on the moon, 1969. Perhaps the biggest moment in world history and in Scottish history as well, as both the president and astronaut Neil Armstrong belonged to the same clan. *AP/Wide World Photos*

The Arbroath Declaration of 1320. Its philosophy and wording inspired the writing of the American Declaration of Independence four and a half centuries later.
The Scottish Record Office, National Archives of Scotland

The inauguration of George Washington as first president of the United States, New York, 1789. Washington, of royal Scottish descent, was sworn in by the president of Saint Andrew's Society of the State of New York. Another member of the society commanded the military escort in Scottish dress. *Museum of the City of New York*

THE ACQUISITION OF THE TERRITORY OF THE UNITED STATES OF AMERICA

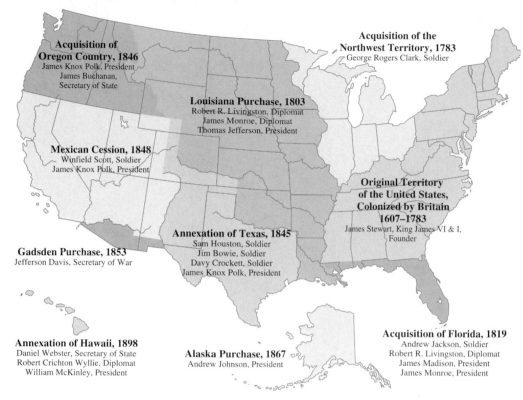

Acquisition of Oregon Country, 1846
James Knox Polk, President
James Buchanan, Secretary of State

Acquisition of the Northwest Territory, 1783
George Rogers Clark, Soldier

Louisiana Purchase, 1803
Robert R. Livingston, Diplomat
James Monroe, Diplomat
Thomas Jefferson, President

Mexican Cession, 1848
Winfield Scott, Soldier
James Knox Polk, President

Original Territory of the United States, Colonized by Britain 1607–1783
James Stewart, King James VI & I, Founder

Gadsden Purchase, 1853
Jefferson Davis, Secretary of War

Annexation of Texas, 1845
Sam Houston, Soldier
Jim Bowie, Soldier
Davy Crockett, Soldier
James Knox Polk, President

Annexation of Hawaii, 1898
Daniel Webster, Secretary of State
Robert Crichton Wyllie, Diplomat
William McKinley, President

Alaska Purchase, 1867
Andrew Johnson, President

Acquisition of Florida, 1819
Andrew Jackson, Soldier
Robert R. Livingston, Diplomat
James Madison, President
James Monroe, President

The acquisition of the territory of the United States of America, showing the names of prominent people of Scottish ancestry who played crucial roles in the process. *Map by Bernard Adnet*

The adobe house, built around 1840, of Don Perfecto Hugo Reid, born in Scotland as Hugh Reid. As proprietor of the huge Rancho Santa Anita, Reid became one of the founders of American California.

Kaiulani, Hawaii's most beautiful and revered princess, daughter of Scottish-born merchant Archibald Scott Cleghorn and Princess Likelike, sister of King Kalakaua.
Hawaiian Historical Society

Adam Smith, possibly the most influential Scot ever. His 1776 book *The Wealth of Nations* gave a philosophical basis to the Industrial Revolution and free trade, and continues to do so.
AP/Wide World Photos

Scottish surnames and proprietors abound on the wines and spirits of many places. *Left to right:* Grant's Scotch Whisky (Scotland); Laird's Apple Jack (New Jersey); Mount Gay Rum (Barbados); Johnston's Wines (Bordeaux); Old Crow Bourbon Whiskey (Kentucky); Jameson Irish Whiskey (Ireland); Graham's Port (Portugal); Stewart and Stewart Sherry (Spain); Jack Daniel's Sour Mash Whiskey (Tennessee); Gordon's Gin (England); and MacNaughton Canadian Whisky (Canada).

Grant's Tomb, New York City. Gen. U. S. Grant, the commander of the forces that preserved the union, was one of America's greatest nineteenth-century heroes. His funeral was attended by a million people.

The leaders of the Western Alliance in World War II, Franklin D. Roosevelt, Charles de Gaulle, and Winston Churchill, at Casablanca, 1943. All three statesmen had Scottish ancestors. *AP/Wide World Photos*

Gen. Douglas MacArthur making good on his promise "I shall return" at Leyte, Philippines, 1944. *AP/Wide World Photos*

Le Collège des Écossais (The Scots College), Paris. Founded in 1326 under the auspices of King Robert I, the Bruce, it was the first institution of higher learning connected with Scotland, preceding the establishment of the university at St. Andrews by almost a century. The present building was erected in 1662.

(*Above*) Some newspapers founded or later owned by people of Scottish ancestry in five different countries. (*Below*) Some magazines founded by people of Scottish ancestry in several different countries.

Foreign Office,
November 2nd, 1917.

Dear Lord Rothschild,

I have much pleasure in conveying to you, on behalf of His Majesty's Government, the following declaration of sympathy with Jewish Zionist aspirations which has been submitted to, and approved by, the Cabinet.

"His Majesty's Government view with favour the establishment in Palestine of a national home for the Jewish people, and will use their best endeavours to facilitate the achievement of this object, it being clearly understood that nothing shall be done which may prejudice the civil and religious rights of existing non-Jewish communities in Palestine, or the rights and political status enjoyed by Jews in any other country".

I should be grateful if you would bring this declaration to the knowledge of the Zionist Federation.

The Balfour Declaration, 1917. Arthur James Balfour, head of the British Foreign Office and a native Scot, decided in favor of Zionist aspirations and wrote the document that enabled the creation of Israel. *By permission of the British Library 41178#f3*

Alexander Graham Bell, Scottish-Canadian-American inventor of the telephone. Bell could also claim some credit as coinventor of the airplane, was the first to advocate treating cancer with radium, and was the de facto founder of the National Geographic Society and its world-famous magazine. *AP/Wide World Photos*

Alexander Calder, creator of the mobile and one of the great artists of the twentieth century. *AP/Wide World Photos*

At the Wallace Award Dinner of the American-Scottish Foundation, Inc., New York, 1988, the author with awardees Cliff Robertson and Hugh Downs. *David Gould*

Dame Joan Sutherland,
Australian-born "voice of the
century." *Patrick Jones*

Elizabeth Taylor, two-time winner of
the Academy Award for best actress.
Bruce Weber

Arnold Palmer, one of the
greatest golfers in history.
His charging style began
the transition of the old
Scottish game into a big-
time international sport.
Arnold Palmer Enterprises

Otto Graham, whose records make him, arguably, the best American football player of all time. *Otto Graham*

Bill Monroe, creator of blue-grass music and a descendant of President James Monroe. *Jim McGuire*

John Davison Rockefeller at age ninety-four. He was perhaps the richest man in the world in 1933 when this picture was taken. His mother, Eliza Davison, was of Scottish descent. *Photofest*

Marchese Guglielmo Marconi, the inventor of radio. His mother, Anne Jameson, was of Scottish descent. *Photofest*

Edvard Grieg, Norwegian composer whose parents were of Scottish descent. *Photofest*

American painter Anna Robertson "Grandma" Moses, shown in 1955 with some of her most famous paintings. *Photofest*

Scottish-born Annie Lennox, pop/soul diva and multiple Grammy Award Winner *Photofest*

Jackie Stewart, Scottish auto racer, won twenty-seven Grand Prix races in ninety-nine starts, a record. *Photofest*

Hall of Fame pitcher James Augustus "Catfish" Hunter pitching for the New York Yankees *Photofest*

Rock in British Columbia inscribed by Sir Alexander Mackenzie, Canada's greatest explorer and the first man to cross North America at its full width. It reads: "Alex Mackenzie, from Canada, by Land, 22 July, 1793." © *Kevin Fleming*

Sir John A. Macdonald, the principal founding father of Canada, shown here with his wife aboard a Canadian Pacific transcontinental train in 1886. The railroad, which unified Canada, was one of Macdonald's many achievements and was mostly the work of fellow Scottish-Canadians. *Canadian Pacific Limited 10217*

Thomas J. Watson, Sr. and Thomas J. Watson, Jr. — father and son — led the world's computer revolution, building the greatest industrial corporation of the twentieth century, IBM. *IBM Archives*

Mel Gibson, born in New York and raised in Australia, was winner of the 1996 Academy Award as best director for his Scottish epic *Braveheart*. *Photofest*

with "Mac," and even today, the popular music of Ireland and Scotland is virtually interchangeable.

The Irish and the Scots also share Saint Patrick, the patron saint of Ireland, who appears to have been born in Scotland. Scots say his birthplace is in their town of Kilpatrick. Muirchú, an Irish writer in the seventh century, says Patrick was born in Britain at "Ventre." It seems possible, then, that the town of Fintry, only twelve miles from Kilpatrick is therefore the birthplace of the saint.[91] Patrick was once a common Christian name in Scotland, its use diminishing after the Irish immigration to the Lowlands during the Industrial Revolution, when unfortunate ethnic and religious overtones caused the Scots to drop it. It is interesting that the surnames Paterson, Patrick, Patton, and Pate are usually Scottish rather than Irish.

Edward Bruce, the brother of King Robert I, the Bruce, had a brief but important role in Irish history. The impetuous brother of Scotland's greatest monarch, it was he who, much to the king's dismay, challenged and provoked the English to try to relieve Stirling Castle, a chivalric flourish which, though fraught with the danger of a pitched battle the Scots could ill-afford, resulted in the decisive triumph at Bannockburn. The dashing Edward was then invited to assist in a nationalist cause in Ireland. He landed at Larne in May 1315 and was crowned high king of Ireland on May 2, 1316.[92] It may have been that the Bruces were trying to restore a Celtic kingdom on both sides of the Irish sea, complete with Gaelic and the Celtic Church.

Whatever their plan, it was dashed when Edward was killed in a battle near Dundalk in the north of Ireland, on October 14, 1318. Although his invasion was a military failure his mission was not. Ireland was thrown into chaos, English allegiance was renounced, Norman primogeniture cancelled, and Celtic tanistry, whereby chiefs were elected, restored. From that time on Ireland would always think of herself as a separate nation, the Irish liberation movement was ignited, never to be extinguished, and the Gallowglass tradition (in Gaelic *gall-òglach*, or "foreign soldier"), in which Scottish mercenary soldiers helped the Irish against the English, was born.[93]

During the reign of Queen Elizabeth I, Sorley Boy MacDonnell (Gaelic *Somhairle Buidhe*, Blond Sorley) an Irish chieftain of Scottish ancestry, augmented with reinforcements from Scotland, led the Irish clans to enough victories against the English that the position of the clans and their chiefs was reestablished.[94]

Charles Stewart Parnell (1846–1891) became the great Irish states-man who took the subject of Irish nationalism out of academia and into practical politics and inspired later generations. He was a descendant of Commodore Charles Stewart of the U.S. Navy, who was born in Philadelphia to Ulster-Scottish parents.[95] In the twen-tieth century Frank Aiken, whose ancestors came to Ulster from Scotland during the Plantation, was cofounder (with Eamon de Valera) of Fianna Fail, Ireland's largest political party. He was also IRA chief of staff from 1923 to 1925, and foreign minister from 1951 to 1969.[96]

Israel

"His Majesty's Government view with favour the establishment in Palestine of a national home for the Jewish people. . . ." Thus wrote the head of the British Foreign Office, Arthur James Balfour, a former prime minister and native Scot, on November 2, 1917. Abba Eban calls the Balfour Declaration, which opened the way for the creation of Israel, "the authentic turning-point in Jewish political history."[97]

Ruhiyyih Rabbani, the spiritual leader of the world's four and a half million Bahai faithful, is based in Haifa, Israel. She is the daughter of the distinguished Canadian architect William Suther-land Maxwell.[98]

A beautiful blue and white building in Jaffa houses the Tabeetha School, founded in 1863 by Jane Walker Arnott of Glasgow. The school teaches Christian, Jewish, and Muslim children, and is run by the Church of Scotland.[99]

Italy

Scots have been in Italy for a long time. The aristocratic Scotti family claims to trace their roots to William Douglas, who they say served under Charlemagne in the ninth century and stayed on.[100] After the Battle of Pavia in 1525, some Scots, who had fought a losing battle for Francis I of France, tried to get home by way of the Val Cannobina, Julius Ceasar's road from Cis-Alpine to Trans-Alpine Gaul, and were stopped by blizzards at the town of Gurro, short of the Simplon pass. Today Gurro is populated by their descendants, who have names like Patritti (Patrick), Tenenti (Tennant), and Gibi (Gibb). The people of the town still use tartan cloth and say *slante* (in Gaelic *slàinte*, "health") when proposing a toast. In 1971 the people of Gurro were given rights as members of the Clan Gayre by its chief, Lt. Col. R. Gayre of Gayre and Nigg, and in 1973 a memorial was dedicated in the town with great ceremony to Sant' Andrea degli Scozzesi.[101]

Etruscology, the study of the Etruscans, Italy's ancient people, became a separate branch of scholarship four hundred years ago when Thomas Dempster (1570–1625), a Scot who had a distinguished career at Pisa and Bologna, published *De Etruria Regali*.[102]

Scottish support for the *Risorgimento* in the nineteenth century was much greater than in the rest of Britain. Factory workers in Glasgow went without pay to make munitions for Garibaldi, who was carried on a Scottish ship, the *City of Aberdeen*, with two thousand men the day before the Battle of Milazzo. Many Scots enlisted and fought for the Italian cause.[103]

In 1862 the Rev. J. R. MacDougall built the Scots Church in Florence. There have been other Scots churches in Italy, such as that founded by Dr. John Ker at San Remo in 1872, but only those at Genoa and Rome remain.[104]

The Knights of Malta, whose full name is the Sovereign Military Hospitaller Order of Saint John of Jerusalem, Rhodes and Malta, is based in Rome and insists on sovereignty, maintaining diplomatic relations with fifty nations. In 1989 Fra Andrew Bertie, a Scot, became the seventy-eighth grand master and the first Briton to hold the post since 1277.[105]

Latin America

The first Briton to be associated with Latin America was Thomas Blake, a Scot who reached Mexico City before 1536. As Tomás Blaque he was a member of Coronado's expedition to what is now Arizona in 1540, thus becoming the first Briton to set foot on what is now the American Southwest.[106]

Among the Scots who assisted Bolivar with his liberating activities was Dr. Samuel Forsyth, one of the founders of Peru.[107] Sir Gregor MacGregor was a distinguished general in the Venezuelan revolutionary army, married Bolivar's niece, and then created a "kingdom" for himself on the Mosquito Coast in what is now Nicaragua. Styling himself as His Serene Highness Gregor I, Prince of Poyais, he presented his credentials at the court of St. James in 1820, issued worthless bank notes printed in Edinburgh, but finally retired on a hero's pension to Venezuela.[108] Alexander MacGregor trained the

Brazilian army after the Peninsular War. Later, he founded Mac-Gregor's Bank in Rio de Janeiro.[109]

The first successful British colony in Argentina was founded in 1824 by John and William Robertson of Roxburghshire, at Monte Grande, six leagues from Buenos Aires, on sixteen thousand acres that they had purchased. About two hundred fifty Scots left Edinburgh in May 1825, and when they debarked from the ship *Symmetry* on August 8 the entire assembly drank a toast of whisky and sang "Auld Lang Syne." By 1829 there were 514 Scots in the colony, but a civil war plunged Argentina into chaos and brought an end to Monte Grande. The Robertsons were ruined but the Scottish colonists dispersed and founded many pioneer *estancias*, opening Presbyterian churches and schools wherever they went. The St. Andrews Church at Buenos Aires, the first Presbyterian church in South America, was opened with an entirely Scottish congregation in 1835.

Most significantly, John Miller, said to be from Elgin, imported a pedigree shorthorn bull to his *estancia*, La Caledonia, significantly improving the Argentine breed. The immense Argentine beef industry of today is in no small part due to these early Scottish settlers. Descent from one of the *Symmetry* Scots is still a matter for boasting along the River Plate. La Caledonia and many other Scottish-founded *estancias* still exist.

In Patagonia, the vast plain as big as Texas, many of the richest sheep farmers have been Scots and have played a large part in making Argentina one of the world's richest countries. In Patagonia occasional reference is still made to a sign in Gaelic or a kilted rancher playing his pipes.[110]

The origin of the term *gringo*, often used in Latin America to refer to people from the United States, has sometimes been ascribed to the Spanish word for Greek, *Griego*. A more likely derivation is that during the Mexican War rowdy American soldiers bestowed the term on themselves as they swaggered through the bars of Mexico singing repeated choruses of "Green Grow the Rashes, O!" by Robert Burns. In support of this theory it is observed that the French around Norman seaports called their English occupiers *Goddons* because of the way they swore.[111]

William Walker (1824–1860), an American whose father was born in Inverness, was, in turn, a physician, lawyer, and journalist before he became an adventurer in Latin America. Starting in San Francisco with a small force in 1853 he landed at La Paz, Mexico, proclaiming an independent republic in Lower California and

Sonora. The Mexicans forced him out in 1854. In 1855 he was invited by revolutionaries to Nicaragua, where he landed with fifty-six followers, quickly made himself master of the country, and became its president. His government was recognized by the United States in 1856, but in 1860 he was arrested by the British navy and executed by Honduras. Walker's career was the subject of the 1987 film *Walker*. So far, he is the only American citizen to serve as president of a foreign country.[112]

Very few Europeans had ever landed on Easter Island before 1868, when a Frenchman and a Tahiti-based Scottish family, the Branders, arrived. Soon the Frenchman was murdered by *indigènes*, and until 1893 the Branders, who grazed sheep, were in effective control. In the mid-1890s they sold most of the island to the Valparaiso-based Scottish firm of Williamson and Balfour, which grazed as many as forty thousand sheep as late as 1952. Therefore, for almost a century Easter Island was a Scottish-owned company state, employing managers from New Zealand, Australia, Patagonia, Tierra del Fuego, and Scotland, with names like McKinnon, Munro, and Murdoch.[113]

In this century a Scottish Presbyterian missionary, Thomas Paine, discovered the Inca ruins at Machu Picchu in 1911.[114] In Chile the Scots have continued their interest in education. The MacKay School at Viña del Mar and the St. Andrews School at Santiago are considered among the best preparatory schools in the land. Both were started by Scots, and Scottish customs are maintained.[115]

George Price has been the dominant political figure in Belize, formerly British Honduras, the only English-speaking country in Central America, from the 1950s to the present. The *New York Times* described Price, the country's first prime minister, as "a tall scripture-quoting seminarian of Scottish and Mayan ancestry."[116]

At the time of this writing Ronald Maclean, a descendant of eighteenth-century Scottish immigrants and the former mayor of La Paz, the principal city and de facto capital of Bolivia, is that country's foreign minister.[117]

Many of the men who were employed in building the Panama Canal were Scots, and following its completion in 1914 settled in nearby Colombia in the ports of Barranquilla and Cartagena, where they married into the local communities and became prominent citzens.[118]

In 1975 Robert Laughlin, a descendant of Ulster-Scots and the curator of Middle-American Ethnology at the Smithsonian Institution, published his *Great Tzotzil Dictionary of San Lorenzo Zinacantán*, with thirty thousand entries. This is the most attention given to a Mayan language in hundreds of years, and has allowed the Indians of the troubled Mexican state of Chiapas to read and write their language for the first time. Mr. Laughlin is an advocate of justice for the Indians and his work has helped them to preserve their culture.[119]

Madeira

Scotland has had an influence on the Portuguese island of Madeira, off the coast of Africa. The island's legendary hotel, Reid's, was founded in the nineteenth century by William Reid twelve years after he had left Kilmarnock with five pounds in his pocket.[120] Cossart Gordon and Co., Ltd., the esteemed Madeira wine producer, was founded in 1745 by Francis Newton, a Scot. The firm owes its present name to Thomas Gordon, another Scot, and to William Cossart, an Irishman who joined the firm later.[121]

Muslim Lands

Helen Gloag was born in Perthshire in the middle of the eighteenth century, the daughter of a blacksmith. When she turned eighteen she booked passage for America, but at sea her ship was attacked by pirates who killed all the men and took all the women to the slave market in Algiers. There she was purchased for the emperor of Morocco, who became so infatuated with her beauty that he made her his principal wife, and later empress.[122]

Another youthful Scot who suffered a similar experience and turned the tables was Thomas Keith, a twenty-one-year-old soldier serving with the British army in Egypt. Keith was taken prisoner and enslaved by the Turks in 1807. In rapid order he took the name of Ibrahim Aga, embraced Islam, fought a duel, was sentenced to death, then escaped and became a general in charge of the Marmeluke horsemen, the most barbarous unit in the pasha's army.

In 1812, at age twenty-six, he was made treasurer, the second highest post in the court of the pasha. In the same year Keith was the first man to breach the walls in the conquest of Medina and was made governor of this, the holy city where Mohammed is buried. A few years later he was hacked to death in an ambush, but not before he had killed four of his adversaries. He died not yet thirty years old.[123]

William Murdock (1754–1839), the inventor of gas lighting, was proclaimed a deity by Nassr-ed-din, shah of Persia, who believed him to be a reincarnation of Merodach or Marduk, the god of light.[124] James Baxter (1886–1964) was financial secretary and economic expert to the Egyptian government from 1924 to 1929 and 1943 to 1946.[125]

The possibility of building a canal at Suez occurred to the French, who made a survey in 1801. But an error in their work showed the Red Sea to be ten meters higher than the Mediterranean, making the construction of a canal difficult. In 1830 the British government commissioned a survey by an Ulsterman, F. R. Chesney, who found only a slight difference in the levels, proving that a canal was feasible.

The first technical study was made in 1841 by a company headed by Arthur Anderson, the Scottish founder of the P&O shipping lines. It confirmed Chesney's work and made a strong impression on world opinion. But the British did nothing. The French then began work but soon got stuck, sending for help to the Scottish firm of Neilson and Company, whose owner, Walter Neilson, was the son of the inventor James Beaumont Neilson. Frenchmen went to the Clyde to study Scottish dredging and excavation methods. Teams of Scottish engineers and workmen went to Egypt. In 1865, with completion assured, the French head of the Suez Canal Company, de Lesseps, made a deal with Neilson allowing the French to get credit for what was basically a Scottish-engineered project.[126]

The giant oil industry of Kuwait was begun in 1927 when the Scotch-Irish-American banker Andrew Mellon backed a concession arranged by a New Zealander.[127] Malcolm Kerr, president of the American University of Beirut, and father of Chicago Bull's star Steve Kerr, was murdered by Islamic militants in 1984.

The Netherlands

By the early years of the thirteenth century there was a Scottish settlement at Bruges known as *Scottendyk*, and since 1291 a street called Scotland.[128] In the mid-sixteenth century Veere (Dutch for ferry) replaced Bruges as the center of trading and in 1541 the Scottish Staple, a sort of monopoly trading port community, was formed there by the Scottish and Dutch governments. The Scottish Staple, under the control of a Scottish lord conservator, became a thriving colony, and the Schotsehuizen at Veere still stands today. By the late seventeenth century trade had moved to Rotterdam, where the first Schotse kerkje (Scottish church) there was established in 1642. By 1700 there were about one thousand Scots in Rotterdam alone and their presence in Holland had become so ordinary in the country that the term *Schots koopman* was used to mean a small trader, regardless of nationality.[129]

Gilbert Jack (c. 1578–1628), a Scottish professor, was the first to teach metaphysics at Leyden.[130] In the nineteenth century Baron Aeneas Mackay became prime minister of Holland. His great-grandson, the fourteenth Lord Reay, is presently the chief of the Mackays, as well as Baron Mackay, in the peerage of the Netherlands.[131]

Norway

As in the Netherlands and other countries, there were so many Scottish traders in Norway that by the sixteenth century the word *schotser* had come to mean all small traders, not just Scots.[132] Out of these, Axel Mowat (1593–1661) rose to become one of the richest men in Norway.[133] Prince Henry Sinclair, mentioned in chapter 2 as the leader of the first voyage of discovery to America that left the written record of a participant, was earl of Orkney and the premier noble of Norway.[134]

Poland

"Poor as a Scots peddler's pack."
—*Polish proverb*

Poland's Golden Age was the sixteenth century, according to the Polish poet and Nobel laureate Czesław Miłosz.[135] It may not be entirely coincidental that this was also the century of the greatest Scottish influence on Poland, a time when there were thirty thousand prosperous Scots in the country.[136]

It is not certain how far back Polish-Scottish trade goes, but it is clear that a boom of sorts started in 1454, when Poland recovered Gdansk (Danzig) from Germany.[137] Between 1474 and 1476 twenty-four Scottish vessels entered the harbor at Gdansk,[138] and it was not long before the Scots realized that Poland had practically no commercial people, except the Jews, and that the country was a gold mine of opportunity with very little competition.[139]

Swarms of Scots emigrated to Poland, fanning out from Gdansk to establish communities in Cracow, Poznan, Lublin, Warsaw, and Lwow.[140] The Scots became extremely successful in Poland but most started, as they had elsewhere, as humble peddlers. The word *szot* meant a commercial traveler of any nation in the Polish literature of the sixteenth and seventeenth centuries, and continues to have the same meaning today in the language of the Pomeranian Kashubs.[141]

The Scottish immigrants followed the same route that the German Jews would take three centuries later in the United States: from peddler to shopkeeper to moneylender to banker. By the late 1700s this pattern had produced Philipp Bernhard von Fergusson-Tepper, called the second banker of Europe.[142] However, the Warsaw bank of Tepper-Fergusson failed when it loaned the king five million ducats that he did not repay.[143] Many Scots were ultimately ennobled, such as the Barons Von Skene, Gordon, Gibson, Drummond, and de Bonar. One of the de Bonars, St. John Isaiah, was canonized in 1483.[144]

At the height of their influence the Scots formed the Scottish Brotherhood, with twelve branches, and built Presbyterian churches everywhere.[145] King Stephen Batory (1576–1586) appointed eight Scots as exclusive purveyors to the Court, each to be replaced by another Scot when he died. This privilege continued under successive monarchs until 1697.[146] Various Scots held the positions of prime minister to the Crown, premier lay senator, lord chief governor, and lord high treasurer.[147] Alexander Czamer (Chalmers) was four times elected mayor of Warsaw in the 1600s.[148] Dr. William Davidson was senior surgeon to King John Casimir in the mid-seventeenth century.[149]

But their success and clannishness were to cause great difficulties for the Scots. Their achievement in Poland was so obvious that in 1606 even in England an opponent of union with Scotland, speaking in the House of Commons, could say, "if we admit them into our liberties we shall be overrun with them... witness the multiplicities of the Scots in Polonia."[150] When many noble estates had been mortgaged to Scots the prejudice grew, and in 1594 King Sigismund III issued a mandate against "Jews, Scots and other vagabonds," and similar edicts were issued in various cities.[151]

Because of this, and for economic reasons, including better opportunities in the new British Empire, the Scots began to leave Poland in the eighteenth century.[152] As a final heroic flourish they would claim Stanislaw II, the last king of independent Poland, as one of their own, as he was the great-grandson of Lady Catherine Gordon, daughter of the marquess of Huntly.[153] Of course, many Scots remained in Poland and, unlike the Jews, married into the general population, and became invisible as a people. They left some surnames, such as Loson (Lawson), Wajer (Weir), Ridt (Reid), Machlajd (Macleod), and Napierski.[154]

It seems quite possible that the spokesman of Solidarity, Lech Wałesa, the recent hero of Poland, the Gdansk electrician who ignited the peaceful revolution against communism in the 1980s in Eastern Europe, and who says his ancestor came to Poland with a fortune from "somewhere in Western Europe," is really a Wallace.[155]

Portugal

During one of the wars which shut off the supply of French claret to England, an alternative source was sought in Portugal. A Scottish surveyor, James Forrester, had opened the Douro River to navigation and was made a *barão* (baron) for his contribution to the wine trade.[156] But the Portuguese wine was too bitter for British tastes until some now-forgotten Scot created what we now know as port by adding brandy to "Red Portugal" wine to stop the fermentation process and maintain a higher sugar level.[157]

From the beginning the production of "the Englishman's wine" has been more Scottish than either English or Portuguese. Of the seven firms which have dominated the industry, four have Scottish names: Cockburn, Dow, Graham, and Sandeman. The Scottish Symington family, which at this writing has thirty-four members living in Oporto, is the largest independent firm and markets the Dow, Graham, and Warre brands. One of their relatives was U.S. senator Stuart Symington.[158] Other brands with Scottish names are: Campbell, Forrester, Mackenzie, Menzies, Robertson, and Tait.[159]

Vintage port is also a Scottish creation, the first historically accepted shipment of Sandeman in 1790 having been made by George Sandeman, who came from Perth.[160] The Sandeman family sold the company in 1979 but still run it. The current head is also George Sandeman, the seventh generation of the family in the business.[161]

The famous Scottish architect Robert Adam (see Chapter 10) was invited to plan the new city of Lisbon after the disastrous earthquake of 1755.[162] For some reason, not apparent, Portuguese peasants often wear clothes with tartanlike designs.

Russia

A Scot may have been the founder of the Romanovs, the ruling dynasty of Russia. Andrei Kambila, the ancestor of the Romanovs, is recorded as a *boyar* in the mid-fourteenth century. The *boyars* were the ruling class and often included newcomers.[163] It has been alleged that Andrei Kambila was a Scot, Andrew Campbell.[164]

By the 1700s there were already many Scottish merchants in St. Petersburg and the Court banker was named Sutherland. But there were never enough Scots in vast Russia to provoke the repression they faced in Germany, Poland, and other places where they were more numerous and more obvious among smaller populations. Nevertheless, their success was held against them and was "irksome" to the Russian people.[165]

Only fragmentary evidence remains of the civilian Scottish presence in Russia, but some highlights can be found. In the seventeenth century Gen. William Drummond was made governor of Smolensk.[166] William Bruce of Clackmannan also emigrated to Russia in the seventeenth century. His son James was made Count Bruce by Peter the Great, and his house near Moscow is now a Bruce family museum.[167] In the eighteenth century, from 1781 to 1786, Count James Alexandrovitch Bruce was governor of Moscow.[168]

In the nineteenth century a Scottish traveler was surprised to find a remote colony of his nation living in Karass.[169] In the same century William Carrick of Edinburgh, now regarded as one of the founders of photography in Russia was, with his partner John MacGregor, making their St. Petersburg studio prominent. Carrick took thousands of photographs of ordinary Russians, many of which survive, providing an extraordinary glimpse of the past.[170]

The outlook and education of Russia's greatest ruler was heavily influenced by two Scottish teachers. Madame Artamon Matveeva, who was born a Hamilton, educated her sister's niece, Nathalia Narishkina, who became the mother of Peter the Great. It was Nathalia who "instilled the desire" in Peter to westernize Russia. Until he became tsar in 1682, Peter was tutored by Paul Menezius, who had been born in Scotland as Paul Menzies.[171]

Dr. Robert Erskine (1677–1718) was the first of many Scottish physicians to the tsars, and was put in charge of all medical services in Russia. His great library became the core of the library of the Russian Academy of Sciences, and Peter the Great carried a torch at his funeral. During his tenure the emperor of China needed a physician, so Erskine recommended another Scot in Russia, Dr. Thomas Garvie, who accepted the post and became the first Briton to travel to China across Siberia.[172] The explorer John Bell was also physician to Peter. Sir Alexander Crichton was physician to Alexander I for twenty-four years (1801–1825). Dr. James Mounsey of Lochmaben was physician to the Empress Elizabeth. Dr. John Rogerson of Dumfriesshire was physician to Catherine the Great, as were Dr. James Guthrie, Dr. Matthew Halliday, and Dr. James Wylie. Dr. Wylie was also imperial physician to Emperor Paul, and the only other person present at the historic meeting of Paul and Napoleon.[173]

Andrew Muir and Archibald Mirrielees founded Moscow's great department store Myur Meriliz, on Theatre Square near the Bolshoi. Called the Selfridges of Eastern Europe, it served forty thousand customers each day. Chekhov bought ink and Countess Tolstoy shopped for lace. The store was confiscated and looted in 1917 and became the Central Universal Stores (TsUM), a name it retains today. It was reprivatized in 1993.[174]

Spain

Michael Scot (D. C. 1235) was a Scottish scholar known as the Wizard for his renown as an astrologer and alchemist. His most important work was done in Toledo, as one of the principal revivers of Greek knowledge in the West. He is best known for his translations of Aristotle from Hebrew and Arabic sources. The Scots College in Madrid was founded in 1627 by William Semple and in 1771 moved to Valladolid, where it still exists. In the past two centuries it has educated three hundred priests for Scotland.[175]

There are fifteen families who dominate the sherry trade in the Andalusian town of Jerez de la Frontera. Among the names appearing in Jerez society and on the labels of its famous wine are Duff, Gordon, Sandeman, and Ferguson. The Scots came early to Jerez and, contrary to the insular British stance they have maintained in Portugal, married into the community. In the 1970s the patriarch of the "Sherry Barons" was Manuel Maria Gonzalez Gordon, chief of Gonzalez Byass bodegas. Diego Ferguson, a member of the Harvey family, was manager of its bodega in the same period.[176] Sherry, not surprisingly, is passionately imbibed by Britons. Sir Alexander Fleming, the Scottish discoverer of antibiotics, said, "If penicillin cures illnesses, sherry resuscitates the dead."[177] The first large shipment of brandy from Jerez was shipped by J. Gordon and Co. in

1798.[178] In the early twentieth century Rafael Gordon succeeded his grandfather, Carlos Pedro, as count of Mirasol in Spain and as laird of Wardhouse in Scotland. He was also mayor of Madrid.[179]

Sweden

Scottish businessmen began to arrive in Sweden in the late sixteenth century, and by 1624 there were about 1,200 in the country. They were concentrated principally in Göteborg, a city founded officially in 1619 by King Gustavus Adolphus to promote trade. The earliest evidence of a Scottish presence is revealed on the 1579 tombstone of one Jacobi Reid. Dutch traders predominated in the earliest days of Göteborg and there were Englishmen, Germans, and Belgians as well.

But it was the Scots who really got things going. One of the first to arrive was John Maclean, one of the principal builders of the city, who made himself a large fortune in the process. He was ennobled by Queen Christiana in 1649 under the name Makeleer and was royal banker to the queen. His son, also John, was president of the Göteborg Court of Justice.[180] By 1678 John Spalding, born in Scotland, was president of the Court of Justice and in 1697 Andrew Spalding was *borgemästare* (mayor) of the city. In the same era Gabriel Spalding was also a *borgemästare*.[181]

There were two principal engines leading to the permanent prosperity of Göteborg: the Swedish East India Company and the Göta Canal.[182] Each of these brought separate, distinct waves of prosperity and were principally the work of several Scots. Colin Campbell, who had fled his creditors in Britain, was the cofounder, with Niklas Sahlgren, of the Swedish East India Company, which was begun in 1730. Campbell accompanied the first ship to China and brought back enormous wealth both to Göteborg and himself before his death in 1757.[183] Thomas Telford engineered the construction of the Göta Canal, which allows passage through Sweden from the North Sea to the Baltic. The canal, opened in 1832, links Göteborg with Stockholm, and brought important economic activity to Sweden. The canal was actually built by the Trollhätte Canal Company, of which Daniel Fraser was the technical leader. William Chalmers was a director of the firm.[184]

David Carnegie, founder of Sweden's famous Carnegie brewery, was the grandson of a fugitive from Culloden.[185] A relative of his, Susan Carnegie, gave money to bring drinking water into Göteborg in 1785. The system still carried water to fifteen public taps in the city as late as 1957. Many other Scots gave large bequests to Göteborg, such as the park donated by the Keillors and the working-class housing provided by the Dicksons.[186] William Chalmers (1748–1811), the founder of the city's famous Chalmers Technical College, was a rich textile man whose father had come from Scotland.[187] Thomas Erskine founded the Bachelor's Club, considered to be the world's fifth oldest club, in Göteborg in 1769. Erskine was member number one and the other eighteen initiates included an Innes, a Greig, a Lyall, a Scott, and a Fraser. The Bachelor's Club in Tarbolton, Scotland, was founded by Robert Burns and others in 1780.[188]

Andrew Boy changed his name to Boij, and in 1663 became one of the several Scottish *borgemästare* of Stockholm.[189] The most famous was Blasius Dundee, a rich Scottish *borgemästare* who led the deputation to welcome the king and queen on their entry into Stockholm in 1593. The Blasieholmen, a broad peninsula facing the royal palace in Stockholm on which the National Museum and other public buildings stand, was named for him.[190]

As usual, the Scottish prominence did not go unnoticed, and in 1635 the magistrates of Stockholm were complaining that the Scots "did oust all native competition. All the best trade they draw to themselves."[191] Despite this, by 1700 a Kurck was president of the Swedish Board of Commerce, a Hamilton was president of the Royal Patents and Registry Office, and a Spens was president of the Board of Mining.[192] In addition, over one hundred Scots had changed their names and joined the Swedish nobility. Some of the names are: Crafoord, Erskein, Haij, Livensten, Pfeif, Bryssz, Mackeij, Crokat, Leijel, Cahun, Fersen (Macpherson), Lagergren and Lagerström (Maclaurin), and Duwall (Macdougal).[193]

How rapidly the Scots had risen in distinction could be seen very plainly in 1660 at the funeral of King Charles X Gustavus. On that occasion Baron Forbes led Princess Maria Euphrosyna; Colonel Hamilton was one of the bearers; and in the procession walked the Barons Lichtone, John Clerk, and Jacob Spens. John A. Stuart bore the banner of Ravenstein, a Forbes that of Holland, and a Duwall that of Götland.[194]

Two Scots are credited with saving the lives of successive Swedish kings. Casten Ronnon, the son of Magnus Dunbar, shielded King Charles XI from an unexpected Danish patrol by hiding him in a chimney.[195] William Bennet, a Scottish sergeant who rose to become a major-general in 1717, personally saved the life of King Charles XII when the impetuous king ventured too far forward and was surrounded by the enemy. Bennet appeared with a small band and cut a way of retreat through overwhelming forces. Later he became governor of Malmö and a baron. The mantel of Charles XII was carried at his coronation by Carl Magnus Stuart.[196] Jacob Robertson, a native of Struan who was ennobled in 1635, served as royal physician to Gustavus Adolphus, Sweden's most famous king.[197]

Other Scoto-Swedish nobles included Robert Finlay, who came to Sweden from Russia in 1744, became rich, and was ennobled as Finlaij only eleven years later.[198] Count Fredrik Axel von Fersen (1719–1794), of Macpherson ancestry, was elected *lantmarskalk* (speaker of the first estate, the nobility) in 1756. His son, Count Hans Axel von Fersen (1755–1810), arranged the abortive escape of Louis XVI and Marie Antoinette from France in 1791. He was made *riksmarskalk* (earl marshall) of Sweden in 1801.[199]

Thomas Lewis, a native of Scotland, erected the first crucible steelworks in Sweden at Esta, becoming a founder of that nation's famous quality steel industry.[200] Hanna Ouchterlony founded the Swedish Salvation Army, and also that of Norway.[201]

The Crafoord Prize, on the magnitude of the Nobel Prize, is awarded annually, usually in the presence of the king of Sweden, for astronomy, mathematics, and other sciences not covered by the Nobel. The prize was established by Holger Crafoord, an adopted son of Sweden's distinguished Crafoord clan, who are descended from Crawfords in Scotland. Carl-George Crafoord was Sweden's ambassador to Spain in the 1980s.[202]

8

The Printed Word

Scotland is a Celtic nation and, as a result, nourishes a deep respect for the word, as do Ireland and Wales. In the Celtic world an agile turn of phrase, the sound of the words, and their choice are often thought to be almost as important as their meanings. For many centuries people on the Celtic fringe have been taught to speak and write artfully. There is not even a word to express a simple "yes" in Gaelic. To the Celtic mind it would be totally barbarous to answer a question with anything other than a complete sentence.

The influence of the Celtic strain on Scotland is shown by the country's veneration of its two best authors. In Scotland's capital the most prominent statue is not of a politician or even a military figure, but rather of Sir Walter Scott, a writer. While the poet Robert Burns has no comparable representation, he scarcely needs it, as his birthday is practically a national holiday and is celebrated not only in Scotland but all over the world. Burns is revered by Scots as is no other person.

British Authors

Soon after the union of Scotland with England, Scots began to produce literature in English exceeding, both in quantity and quality, what would have been expected from such a small part of Britain. And even before the union there were signs that this would be so. As an example, Gavin Douglas, the bishop of Dunkeld, became the first person to translate Latin classics into English (a work of Ovid and the *Aeneid* of Virgil) around 1500.[1]

Of course, the most prominent Scottish writer was Sir Walter Scott (1771–1832), the creator of the historical novel. Scott was the first

British novelist to become a famous public figure, and such works as *Ivanhoe*, *Rob Roy*, and *The Bride of Lammermoor* will live forever.² In honor of his Waverley novels, devotees in New York successfully petitioned the city to name a street Waverley Place.³

Soon after the union of the Parliaments two Scots made their way to London and fame. Tobias Smollett (1721–1771), a novelist, was best known for *The Expedition of Humphrey Clinker*, published in 1771.⁴ James Boswell (1740–1795) was one of the greatest diarists and biographers of all time. His most famous work was his *Life of Johnson*, published in 1791. His subject, Dr. Samuel Johnson, was an anti-Scot whose virulence Boswell had somewhat softened during their tour of Scotland some years earlier. The book is considered by some to be the best biography ever written. Boswell left so many letters and diaries that perhaps more is known about him, than any other eighteenth-century man. A "Boswell factory" at Yale employs several people, full-time, sifting through the papers.⁵

The next century produced two of Britain's best historians. Thomas Carlyle (1795–1881) was born in the village of Ecclefechan in Dumfriesshire, in a house, still standing, which had been built by his stonemason father. He rose to become the most important British man of letters of his time. In 1834 he moved to London and wrote the two works upon which his fame rests, *The French Revolution* and *Life of Frederick the Great*. He declined to be buried in Westminster Abbey as was offered, directing, as his last request, that his body be returned to Ecclefechan.⁶

Thomas Babington Macaulay (1800–1859) was the grandson of a Hebridean minister. His reputation was secured with his *History of England*, published in 1848. Macaulay wrote his first history at age eight, became a member of the bar at twenty-six, a member of Parliament at thirty, wrote the Indian penal code at thirty-four, and was secretary of war at thirty-nine. Throughout his life he maintained an anti-Scottish prejudice and always sought to hide his Highland ancestry.⁷

John Stuart Mill (1806–1873) was born in London, the son of the Scottish intellectual James Mill, who had Anglicized the family name from the Scottish Milne. John Stuart Mill was a prolific writer on many subjects, including politics and economics, and he had a great impact on Victorian thought. Perhaps his most important work was *On Liberty*, the classical liberal statement on the importance of individual freedom. Mill defended "absolute freedom of opinion, nearly absolute freedom of expression [the qualification turning on circumstances where expression constitutes 'a positive instigation to some mischievous act'] and freedom of action so long as it does not harm others."[8] Mill was educated entirely by his demanding father. By age eight he had read Plato, Aesop, Herodotus and other Greek classics in the original and was beginning Latin, Euclid, and algebra. A 1976 study estimated his I.Q. between 190 and 200, the highest in history.[9]

Robert Louis Stevenson (1850–1894) was the most popular Scottish author of the late nineteenth century. His *Treasure Island*, *Kidnapped*, and *The Strange Case of Dr. Jekyll and Mr. Hyde* are classics. He was born in Edinburgh to a family of distinguished lighthouse engineers but declined to enter the profession.[10]

John Ruskin (1819–1900), "who more than anyone else influenced the public taste of Victorian England,"[11] was the grandson of John James Ruskin, an Edinburgh merchant, and had Tweedale, Adair, Ross, and Agnew ancestors.[12] *Leaves From a Journal of Our Life in the Highlands*, which the Scottish-descended Queen Victoria wrote in 1867, made her the most popular ruler-writer since Julius Caesar.[13]

Sir Arthur Conan Doyle (1859–1930) wrote his first Sherlock Holmes story in 1887 and became one of the most famous of Britain's authors. His first career was in medicine and he was probably his own prototype for the bumbling Dr. Watson. So ingenious were his methods that they actually furthered the advance of criminology. Sir Arthur was born in Edinburgh but, almost unique in this book, had no apparent ancestors from the old Scottish national stock. It appears that his people were entirely Irish.

In the twentieth century Scoto-English writing proliferated. Rudyard Kipling (1865–1936), his mother a Macdonald with ancestral roots in Skye,[14] published *Kim* in 1901. Kipling, born in Bombay, was best known for his short stories concerning India but also wrote children's books, such as *Just So Stories* and the *Jungle Books*. He was awarded the Nobel Prize for literature in 1907.

Sir James Matthew Barrie (1860–1937) was born in Kirriemuir, Angus, the son of a weaver. He was already a well-known novelist when, in 1904, he authored the play *Peter Pan*, which made him famous.

Bertrand Russell (1872–1970), the British philosopher and mathematician, was of partly Scottish ancestry and actually claimed descent from King Robert I, the Bruce.[15] His championship of individual freedom has been compared to that of Voltaire in the eighteenth century and to that of John Stuart Mill in the nineteenth.

He was awarded the Nobel Prize for literature in 1950.

Also claiming descent from Scotland's warrior king was Edinburgh-born Kenneth Grahame (1859–1932), who authored the children's classic *The Wind in the Willows* in 1908. The book has influenced children's literature ever since.[16] Sir Winston Churchill (1874–1965), of remote Scottish ancestry through his American mother, won the Nobel Prize for literature in 1953. He was the author of *The Second World War* and *A History of the English-Speaking Peoples.*[17]

Virginia Woolf (1882–1941) pioneered the stream of consciousness novel and was a founder of the Bloomsbury Group and the Hogarth Press. She was the daughter of Sir Leslie Stephen, the first editor of the *Dictionary of National Biography* whose family's roots were in Aberdeen.[18] Another member of the Bloomsbury Group was Lytton Strachey (1880–1932), who wrote biography as art. Strachey's mother was a Grant of Rothiemurchus, and the artist Duncan Grant was his cousin.[19] Evelyn Waugh (1903–1966), the satirist and author of *Brideshead Revisited* and many other novels, was Scottish on both sides of his ancestry.[20] George Orwell (1903–1950), who has been called "the greatest satirist in the English language since Swift"[21] is famous for two books, *Nineteen Eighty-Four* and *Animal Farm*. He was born in Bengal of Scottish ancestry as Eric Arthur Blair.[22] Gilbert Keith Chesterton (1874–1936), the author of the Father Brown series, as well as a journalist, essayist, poet, and playwright, was descended from the Earl Marischal Keiths, of Scotland.[23]

Although he spoke only Gaelic until he was eight, Alastair Maclean (1922–1987) learned English well enough to become one of the bestselling British authors ever. Such books as *The Guns of Navarone* have sold two hundred million copies.[24] Sir Angus Wilson (1913–1991) made observations on the English middle class, which distinguished him as one of Britain's best authors in the late twentieth century.[25] Muriel Spark of Edinburgh, the author of *The Prime of Miss Jean Brodie*, is of Jewish and English ancestry.[26] Lewis Grassic Gibbon (1901–1935) was the author of *A Scots Quair: A Trilogy*, which was made into a popular television series.

Ian Fleming (1908–1964), the creator of James Bond, prepared for his literary career by being Moscow correspondent for the *Sunday Times* of London, and in World War II was assistant to Britain's director of naval intelligence. He was the son of Maj. Valentine Fleming, a partner in the banking house of Robert Fleming and Company, and who was born in Fife.[27]

Another bestselling author, Barbara Cartland, is a descendant of the noble Hamiltons of Scotland.[28] P. L. Travers (1899–1996), born in Australia of Scottish and Irish ancestry as Helen Lyndon Goff, was the creator of Mary Poppins. Hammond Innes, author and traveler, and Dame Iris Murdoch, the novelist and philosopher, are also prominent contemporary British writers of Scottish descent.[29] Graham Greene (1904–1991), whose novels sold over twenty million copies in twenty-seven languages, was one-fourth Scottish and the grand nephew of Robert Louis Stevenson.[30] John Innes Macintosh Stewart (1906–1994) was one of Britain's most popular mystery writers. An Oxford don, he wrote under the name of Michael Innes.[31] Ian McEwen, author of *The Cement Garden*, was born in England to a Scottish father and an English mother, and has been called by *The Times* of London, "the best young writer in Great Britain."[32] Also currently writing are Scottish authors Sara Maitland, James Campbell, Irvine Welsh, Candia McWilliam, and Elspeth Davie.[33] Alasdair Gray, author of *Poor Things*, is one of the most popular young writers in Britain. James Kelman shocked the English-speaking world in 1994 with the coarse Glaswegian of *How Late It Was, How Late*, but won the Booker Prize anyway.[34]

American Authors

Hugh Henry Brackenridge was a largely self-taught Scottish immigrant farm boy who managed to go from the Pennsylvania backwoods to Princeton and in 1770 wrote, with Philip Freneau, *Father Bombo's Pilgrimage to Mecca*, the first novel ever written in America. Publication was somewhat delayed, but it was finally published by Princeton University in 1975, 205 years after it was written.[35] Brackenridge later took a leading part in the Whiskey Rebellion[36] and was a principal founder of the University of Pittsburgh.[37]

The first American author to be widely read was Washington Irving (1783–1859), the son of an Orcadian fisherman.[38] Such classics as *Rip Van Winkle* and *The Legend of Sleepy Hollow* convinced the Old World that Americans were more than rough frontiersmen.[39] Irving, a member of Saint Andrew's Society of the State of New York, is recognized as America's first great man of letters, as the "inventor" of the short story,[40] and as the man who gave New York its nicknames Gotham and Knickerbocker.[41]

Edgar Allan Poe (1809–1849) had Scots on both sides of his ancestry. One of America's greatest authors, Poe "invented" the detective story by publishing "The Murders in the Rue Morgue" in

1841. He also wrote "The Pit and the Pendulum," "Cask of Amontillado," "The Fall of the House of Usher," "Tell-Tale Heart," and many others.[42]

The ancestors of Herman Melville (1819–1891) came from Fife. His father, Allan Melville, thought of himself as Scottish and even visited his Scottish relatives at the original Melville seat. Allan Melville married well but his fortunes fell, forcing his son Herman to ship out in order to support himself. This experience enabled Melville to produce his marvelous tales of the sea. In 1851 he published one of America's great classics, *Moby-Dick*.[43]

Harriet Beecher Stowe (1811–1896), the author of *Uncle Tom's Cabin*, was an antislavery advocate of partly Scottish ancestry whose work played an important role in causing the Civil War. When she met President Lincoln he said, "So you're the little woman who wrote the book that started this great war!"[44] Mark Twain (1835–1910), the author of the American masterpieces *Tom Sawyer* and *Huckleberry Finn*, was the great-grandson of Jane Montgomery who, because of her surname and those of her neighbors on the frontier, Knox, Logan, Hays, Duncan, and so forth, is presumed to have been of Scottish ancestry.[45] Joel Chandler Harris (1848–1908), the author of *Uncle Remus* and *The Tar Baby*, was of Scotch-Irish extraction.[46]

The James brothers, Henry (1843–1916) and William (1842–1910), were two of America's greatest men of letters and were largely of Scotch-Irish Presbyterian ancestry. The novels of Henry James bridged the cultures of Britain and the United States with such works as *The Europeans*. His masterpiece is *Portrait of a Lady*.[47] William James, the father of American psychology, authored the definitive *Principles of Psychology* in 1890. He also opened the first laboratory in psychology in the world and conferred the first Ph.D. in psychology in the United States. In addition he was a philosopher and leader of the movement called pragmatism. His version of this idea, that truth is tested by its effect, later taken up by Henri Bergson and others, became the first American philosophical movement to have international consequences.[48]

As the twentieth century came into being a Scottish-American, Lew Wallace, wrote the famous *Ben Hur*.[49] The century produced many Americans of Scottish ancestry among the most prominent of novelists. Among several who did not have Scottish surnames is Thomas Wolfe, remembered for *Look Homeward Angel* and *You Can't Go Home Again*. Wolfe was of mostly Scotch-Irish ancestry.[50] F. Scott Fitzgerald, born Francis Scott Key Fitzgerald and named after and descended from the author of "The Star-Spangled Banner," was the depictor of the Roaring Twenties. His best work was *The Great Gatsby.*[51]

J. D. Salinger, the reclusive author of the adolescent classic *The Catcher in the Rye*, was born to a Jewish father and a Scottish mother.[52] John Steinbeck, the Nobel Prize–winning author of *The Grapes of Wrath*, was of partly Scotch-Irish ancestry, having descended from Samuel Hamilton of Ulster.[53] John Hersey (1914–1993) was born in China of partly Scottish ancestry. He was noted for his novel *A Bell for Adano* and the nonfiction *Hiroshima*, which showed the horrors of atomic war.[54] William Cuthbert Faulkner (1897–1962), creator of Mississippi's Snopes family, won a Nobel Prize and was of partly Scottish ancestry.[55] Another Scottish-American, Marjorie Kinnan Rawlings, won the Pulitzer Prize in 1939 for *The Yearling.*[56]

Next to the Bible, *Gone With the Wind* has sold more copies than any other book. It is the work of Margaret Mitchell, who wrote it in a basement flat in Atlanta that is now being preserved. The Mitchells came to North Carolina from Scotland.[57]

The late twentieth century has also featured Walter B. Gibson, a prolific novelist of Scotch-Irish descent who, using the pen name Maxwell Grant, created Lamont Cranston, the "Shadow."[58] A. B. Guthrie (1901–1991), America's premier western historical novelist and the author of the motion picture *Shane*, was also Scottish.[59] Louis Auchincloss is a Scottish-American lawyer who writes tightly structured novels about the American, and particularly the New York, upper class.[60] Heywood Broun was the son of a Scottish immigrant.[61]

Helen MacInnes, born in Glasgow and the queen of international spy fiction, was a winner of the Wallace Award of the American-Scottish Foundation. Her viewpoint, in novels such as *Above Suspicion* and *Assignment in Brittany*, was against authoritarian governments, and led to sales of more than twenty million copies in the United States alone.[62]

Two bearers of the Caldwell name have been prominent. Taylor Caldwell, a prolific writer, claimed descent from Mary Queen of Scots.[63] Erskine Caldwell was the author of *Tobacco Road* and *God's Little Acre*, which introduced the poor white southerner to the world. Caldwell was the son of a Presbyterian minister and said that he was "of Scottish and Scotch-Irish descent with a touch of English to make the whole thing authentic."[64]

The Crichtons have produced Michael Crichton, who has sold over one hundred million books, including *The Andromeda Strain*,

Rising Sun, and *Jurassic Park*, and Robert Crichton (1925–1993), who wrote *The Secret of Santa Vittoria*.[65] The Clan Donald has come through with noted American authors in the twentieth century. Dwight MacDonald was an intellectual of the highest distinction. John D. MacDonald, a mystery writer and one of the world's bestselling authors, was the creator of Travis McGee.[66] A review in the *New York Times* called Ross Macdonald's books "the finest series of detective novels ever written by an American." Ross Macdonald's bestselling Lew Archer books were written by Kenneth Millar, who was born in California to Scottish-Canadian parents. He first chose the nom de plume John Macdonald only to discover that a real John MacDonald (above) was already writing books under that name.[67]

American Scots are also amply represented in nonfiction. Dale Carnegie's 1936 book *How to Win Friends and Influence People* has sold over fifteen million copies.[68] William F. Buckley, Jr., essayist, novelist, and television personality, is of largely Irish but partly Scottish ancestry.[69] John McPhee writes often for the *New Yorker* and is admired by many Scottish-Americans for his insight in *The Island of the Crofter and the Laird*, a look at his ancestral island of Colonsay.

David McCullough is the author of some of the best nonfiction books of the century, including *The Great Bridge*, about the building of the Brooklyn Bridge; and *The Path Between the Seas*, the story of the construction of the Panama Canal. He has also written *The Johnstown Flood*, *Truman*, and *Mornings on Horseback*, a biography of Theodore Roosevelt. Mr. McCullough was born in Pittsburgh of Scotch-Irish ancestry.[70]

John Kenneth Galbraith, the author of *The Affluent Society*, *The New Industrial State*, and *Economics and the Public Purpose*, was born in Ontario of Scottish parents.[71]

Gerry Spence, the Wyoming advocate and rancher, is an un-paralleled success as "the best trial lawyer in America." His 1982 book *Gunning for Justice* details a career of forty-one years, during which he has never lost a criminal trial.[72] Annie Dillard, born in Pittsburgh of partly Scotch-Irish descent, won a Pulitzer Prize for her 1974 work *Pilgrim at Tinker Creek*.[73] James MacGregor Burns, the noted political scientist and historian, is also of Scotch-Irish descent.[74] Prof. Catherine A. MacKinnon, the author of *Sexual Harassment of Working Women*, is the most prominent feminist legal theorist in the United States.[75]

Canadian Authors

Hugh MacLennan, the author of *The Watch That Ends the Night*, was of three-quarters Scottish ancestry.[76] Marshall McLuhan, who linked the mind and the medium, was of partly Scottish ancestry. "The medium is the message" is his famous pronouncement.[77] Alice Munro has been called "Canada's master storyteller" by the *New York Times*. Her ancestors came from near Melrose.[78] Scottish-descended Farley Mowat, whose books have sold fourteen million copies in fifty-two languages, is Canada's most widely read author.[79]

South African Authors

Thomas Pringle, a native of Scotland, founded South African prose and poetry in the nineteenth century.[80] Alan Paton, author of *Cry, the Beloved Country*, a book which has sold more than fifteen million copies in twenty languages, was a champion of racial reconciliation in South Africa. His father was from Glasgow.[81]

Poets

BRITISH POETS

Poetry in Scotland goes back to prehistoric times, but the first poet we can recognize as significant is the thirteenth-century bard Thomas the Rhymer (Thomas Learmonth), famous for his "Sir Tristrem."[82] John Barbour (1325?–1395) wrote the first substantial Scottish poem, "The Bruce," in 1376. A patriotic history of the Scottish War of Independence against England, the poem covers the period from 1286 to 1332 and was the first to glorify the life of King Robert I, the Bruce.[83]

In the minds of Scots the summit of Scottish poetry was reached only by Robert Burns (1759–1796), the national poet. Burns's birthday, January 25, is celebrated at hundreds of Burns dinners throughout the world.[84] Even in China every poet knows his work, and there Robert Burns is, "as close to a household name as any foreign writer has become." In 1984, Burns Nicht at the Beijing Central Drama Academy drew over eight hundred people.[85]

It is strange that James Beattie (1735–1803), a contemporary of Burns well-known then, should be so little known now. The son of a Scottish farmer, he published "The Minstrel" in 1771 and it heralded the Romantic revival, influencing Burns, Scott, Byron, and Tennyson. Beattie was welcomed into Dr. Johnson's circle in London and was even awarded a life pension by King George III.[86]

Even more influential was James Macpherson (1736–1796), one of the most controversial figures in the history of letters. In the 1760s he published works that he claimed were translations from third-century Gaelic poems by Ossian, an ancient bard. These epics played an important role in bringing about the romantic movement in European literature.[87] One poem, "Fingal," enchanted the great minds of Europe for half a century. Goethe admired it and Napoleon took an illustrated Italian copy with him on all of his campaigns.[88] Among others influenced were Schiller, Coleridge, Scott, Byron, Diderot, Massenet, Schubert, and Mendlesohn.[89] Thomas Jefferson was so moved that he attempted to learn Gaelic, and said, "I am not ashamed to own that I think this rude bard of the north the greatest Poet that has ever existed."[90] Ossian became the most popular English-language poet in Europe during the eighteenth century and, with the exception of Byron, in the nineteenth century as well.[91]

But a controversy raged for over a century as to whether Macpherson had really found and translated these poems or simply made them up. Some, particularly in Scotland, believed the poems to be genuine while others, often Englishmen, debunked them. The dispute still continues. Ian Grimble simply calls the poems a hoax.[92] Lord Clark said "it was a kind of fake put together out of scraps of evidence."[93] But whatever one thinks, someone, either Macpherson, Ossian, or some combination, demonstrated a talent sufficient to change world literature.

Sir Walter Scott (1771–1832) began his literary career as a poet and wrote some of the best lines in the English language. His "The Lay of the Last Minstrel" (1805) and "The Lady of the Lake" (1810), to name just two, were enormously successful. Works such as these brought the romance of Scotland to the notice of the literate world and made Scott the most popular poet in Britain. However, his fame was soon eclipsed by a half Scot, George Gordon Byron (1788–1824), who burst onto the literary scene in 1812 with "Childe Harold's Pilgrimage." Lord Byron soon became the most popular poet in the world and the most famous Briton of his time, forcing Scott to quit poetry and become, instead, the best British novelist of the day. Even today, many Europeans consider Byron to have been England's greatest poet, Shakespeare included:[94]

Robert Louis (Balfour) Stevenson (1850–1894), already mentioned for his prose, was one of the best-loved of literary men, particularly in the United States, where he lived for a year. His *A Child's Garden of Verses* has been a classic for a century and led to a new approach in the education of children. In 1894 the sickly Stevenson, in search of better health, died at forty-four in Samoa and left this "Requiem" as an epitaph:

> Under the wide and starry sky,
> Dig the grave and let me lie.
> Glad did I live and gladly die,
> And I lay me down with a will.
> This be the verse you grave for me:
> "Here lies he where he longed to be;
> Home is the sailor, home from the sea,
> And the hunter home from the hill."[95]

The maternal grandmother of Robert Browning (1812–1889), the English poet, was born in Scotland of German and, perhaps, some Scottish ancestry.[96] Rudyard Kipling (1865–1936), previously cited for his prose, was also the poet of British India, producing such immortal works as "Danny Deever," "Mandalay," and "Gunga Din." Edwin Muir (1887–1959), born in Scotland, was a major twentieth-century poet.[97] Alexander Alan Milne (1882–1956), known to millions of children as A. A. Milne, the creator of Winnie-the-Pooh and real-life father of Christopher Robin, was born in England to a Scottish father. His books have been translated into twenty languages and still sell more than one hundred thousand copies annually.[98]

AMERICAN POETS

Edgar Allan Poe (1809–1849), previously mentioned for his prose, was America's first important poet and was recognized as such by Beaudelaire and others. He was capable of expressing a wide variety of sentiment, from the tenderness of "To Helen" and "Annabel Lee" to the more unsettled thoughts of "The Raven" and "The Bells."[99]

Oliver Wendell Holmes (1809–1894) was a humorist, essayist, and novelist, as well as a poet. He was descended from David Hume, one of several hundred Scottish prisoners sent to America by Cromwell. Somehow the name was changed to Holmes.[100]

In the twentieth century there were many more Scottish-American poets. Vachel Lindsay (1879–1931) was noted for his "General William Booth Enters Into Heaven."[101] Robinson Jeffers (1887–1962) was of Scotch-Irish descent and became famous in 1924 on the publication of *Tamar and Other Poems*.[102] Marianne Craig Moore (1887–1972) was one of the most original and durable poets of the century. She was a staunch member of a Presbyterian church in Brooklyn and her brother served as a minister of the same denomination. She was also a baseball enthusiast and in 1968 threw out the first ball at Yankee Stadium at age eighty-one.[103]

Among many honors, Archibald MacLeish (1892–1982) was commissioned to write a poem which appeared on the front page of the *New York Times* on the occasion of the first moon landing, in 1969. Some of MacLeish's words are carved in granite in a long corridor at Harvard University: "How shall freedom be defended? By arms when it is attacked by arms; by truth when it is attacked by lies, by democratic faith when it is attacked by authoritarian dogma. Always, and in the final act, by determination and faith." Benigno S. Aquino, Jr., the exiled Philippine political leader, intended to speak these phrases on his return to the Philippines in 1983 but was murdered before he could do so.[104]

Robert Frost (1874–1963) was called "America's foremost poet, its emblem poet" by the *New York Times*.[105] In 1960 he was honored to recite his poem "The Gift Outright" at the inauguration of President John F. Kennedy. Frost's widowed mother, Isabelle Moody, was born in Scotland and her intense Scottish loyalties greatly influenced his work, which combines practicality with mysticism.[106]

e. e. cummings (1894–1962) spelled his name in a distinctive way and came from a family which claimed descent from the Red Comyn.[107] As this is written Jesse Stuart is known as a sort of American Robert Burns and "poet laureate" of Kentucky. He says, "My father's family was Scotch."[108]

AUSTRALIAN AND CANADIAN POETS

Robert W. Service, the Scottish-Canadian "bard of the Yukon" and creator of Dangerous Dan McGrew, Sam McGee, and the lady known as Lou, was born in England of Scottish parents and educated in Glasgow. He is probably the most widely-read poet of the twentieth century, his works selling in the millions.[109] Dame Mary Gilmore is known as one of Australia's most distinguished poets.[110] Adam Lindsay Gordon (1833–1870) became Australia's beloved laureate and, as one of the first to write in the Australian idiom, is called the father of Australian poetry.[111]

POETS IN OTHER LANDS

Peter Dass (1647–1708), a Norwegian poet, was the son of Peter Don Dass (Dundas) of Scotland.[112] Denmark's Latin poet of the same era was Henrik Hamilton (1588–1648), who was also of Scottish extraction.[113] Brazil's outstanding writer of the twentieth century is the poet Carlos Drummond de Andrade, who descends from a Scottish nobleman who went to Madeira in the fifteenth century.[114] Mikhail Yurevich Lermontov (1814–1841), the foremost Russian romantic poet, was descended from the seventeenth-century Scottish adventurer George Learmonth.[115] Therefore Lermontov was of the same family that produced in thirteenth-century Scotland Thomas Learmonth (Thomas the Rhymer), with whom we began this section![116]

Newspapers

In previous chapters a Scottish proclivity for founding newspapers has been observed in diverse places. In Scotland itself the *Herald* of Glasgow, founded in 1783, is the oldest national daily newspaper in the English-speaking world.[117]

In New York, Alexander Hamilton began the *New York Post* in 1801 and it is still being published today. The *Herald Tribune*, no longer a New York daily but surviving internationally, was founded as two separate papers by two different Scottish-Americans. Horace Greeley, the founder of the *New York Tribune* in 1841, was descended from Scotch-Irish settlers to Londonderry, New Hampshire.[118] His *Tribune*'s antislavery stance proved influential and was actually a contributing cause of the Civil War. In 1854, Greeley was also a founder of the Republican party, but later broke with it and ran, unsuccessfully, for president as a Democrat in 1872.[119]

The *New York Herald*, one of the most influential papers in American history, was first published in 1835 by James Gordon Bennett (1795–1872), born in Scotland near Keith, Banffshire. Bennett, who is sometimes called the founder of modern American journalism,[120] started the *Herald* with five hundred dollars. The paper was the first to print a Wall Street financial article, the first to employ European correspondents on a regular basis, and had the first society page. It pioneered the use of telegraphy in news transmission, the use of illustrations, and was the first paper to publish the story of a sexual scandal.[121] Bennett's son, James Gordon

Bennett, Jr., financed the famous African journey of Henry Morton Stanley in 1871, which relieved the great Scottish explorer with the understated, "Dr. Livingstone, I presume."[122]

In 1877 James Gordon Bennett, Jr., began what is now the *International Herald Tribune*, in Paris. This journal was the first truly international publication. It introduced the linotype to Europe and was the first paper in Europe to use wireless telegraphy for news dispatches. Today the paper has a circulation of 170,000. It is printed in nine countries and distributed in 164 others.[123] An elaborate monument commemorates the two Bennetts in Herald Square, in New York City.

The *Cincinnati Enquirer* was begun by Washington McLean.[124] The Scripps-Howard chain of American newspapers was first published by E. W. Scripps, memorialized in the Scottish-American Hall of Fame. Roy W. Howard, also of Scottish ancestry, became president of United Press International, then Scripps's partner.[125] The *Washington Post*, owned by the Graham family, is one of America's most influential papers. Donald E. Graham is now the publisher.[126]

Joseph Medill, born in Canada to a Scotch-Irish father from Belfast, bought the *Chicago Tribune* in 1855 and made it into a powerful newspaper. Its antislavery views helped to elect Abraham Lincoln president. Medill was elected mayor of Chicago one month after the great fire of 1871 and ran the rebuilding program of the city under emergency powers. He was also the founder of the Chicago Public Library and was the ancestor of three newspaper magnates.[127] Robert Rutherford McCormick, Medill's grandson, built the *Tribune* into the largest circulation of any standard-size newspaper in the United States and it led the world in advertising volume.[128] Two other grandchildren of Joseph Medill ran major newspapers: In 1939 Eleanor Medill Patterson bought and merged the *Washington Times* and the *Washington Herald* into the *Washington Times-Herald*, and Joseph M. Patterson was publisher of the *New York Daily News*, started in 1919, which had, for most of the twentieth century, the largest circulation of any daily paper in America.[129]

Among twentieth-century American editors, Benjamin McKelway, his father a Presbyterian minister of Scottish descent, served as editor of the *Washington Star* and president of the Associated Press.[130]

Iain Calder, a native Scot, is president and editor of the sensational *National Enquirer*, which he built into what is claimed as the largest circulation of any paper in America. Calder moved the *National Enquirer* from New York to Lantana, Florida.[131] Soon many sun-starved Scots followed him, creating an entire sensational tabloid industry, in Palm Beach County run largely by expatriate Britons.[132]

Among journalists, Dr. Robert Shelton MacKenzie became the first salaried European correspondent of the American press when he accepted the beat for the *New York Evening Star* in 1834.[133] William Howard Russell was the world's first war correspondent when the *Times* of London sent him to cover the Crimean War. He wrote back the famous story of "the thin red line" of the Ninety-third Sutherland Highlanders, who withstood the Russian advance at Balaklava.[134] Nellie Bly, born in 1867 near Pittsburgh as Elizabeth Cochrane, was a descendant of Admiral Cochrane. In 1889, representing the *New York World*, she attained worldwide celebrity by going around the world in seventy-two days, at that time a record.[135]

In the twentieth century Dame Rebecca West, of Scottish-Irish ancestry, was called "the greatest woman journalist of our time," "the Grand Duchess of English intellectuals," and "indisputably the world's number one woman writer."[136] Will Rogers, the American humorist, was of Scottish, Irish, and Cherokee ancestry, and wrote a nationally syndicated column in the 1920s.[137] Alan McCrae Moorehead, the distinguished World War II correspondent, was born in Melbourne and educated at the Scotch College there. He is also the author of such books as *Gallipoli* and *Darwin and the Beagle*.

Alastair Hetherington was editor of the *Guardian* (1956–1975). James Cameron was chosen as Britain's Journalist of the Year and Foreign Correspondent of the Decade in 1965.[138] Henry J. Taylor was long a syndicated columnist in American papers and a winner of the Wallace Award of the American Scottish Foundation. Clydebank-born James "Scotty" Reston, also a Wallace awardee, became the premier journalist of the *New York Times*. President Eisenhower once complained, "Who the hell does Scotty Reston think he is, telling me how to run the country!"

The two journalists who did the most to refine the taste of Americans for fine food both have Scottish antecedents. James Beard wrote extensively on food and wine and found among his Scottish ancestors "cutthroats and horse thieves." Beard's house in New York City is now a culinary museum and school.[139]

Craig Claiborne, long associated with the *New York Times*, is credited with pioneering serious restaurant criticism in American newspapers. His Craig ancestors came from Aberdeen. On his seventieth birthday he was honored at a gala dinner in Monte Carlo by an unprecedented turnout of sixty famous chefs, including ten with three stars in the *Guide Michelin*.[140]

One of the outstanding political cartoonists of all time, Sir David Alexander Cecil Low, was born in New Zealand to Scottish and Irish parents.[141]

Two Scottish-Canadians and a Scottish-Australian have been among the very greatest newspaper barons. William Maxwell Aitken (Lord Beaverbrook; 1879–1964) was the son of a Presbyterian minister who had immigrated from Scotland to New Brunswick. Aitken became a millionaire stockbroker in Montreal at age twenty-nine and moved to England, where he was elected to Parliament. In 1916 he bought control of the *London Daily Express* and two years later founded the *Sunday Express*. He bought the *Evening Standard* in 1923. Aitken greatly increased the circulation of his papers and made another fortune. He held the rank of British cabinet minister in both world wars.[142]

Roy Thomson (Lord Thomson of Fleet) was born in Toronto, the son of a Scottish barber, and ended up owning some 150 news-papers, more than anyone else in the world. His son Kenneth now presides over an empire that includes oil and gas properties and the Hudson's Bay Company.[143]

Keith Rupert Murdoch is probably the greatest of all of the newspaper barons. He created the first national Australian daily in 1964 and acquired twenty-six other Australian papers. He has owned Britain's largest daily, the *Sun*; its largest weekly, *News of the World*; its most prestigious daily, the *Times*; and its most prestigious weekly, the *Sunday Times*. In the United States he has owned the *Star*, the *Boston Herald*, the *New York Post*, the *Chicago Sun-Times*, *New York* magazine, and many other publications.

In 1985 Murdoch purchased the 20th Century–Fox Film Corpora-tion and also six major American television stations which were valued at more than two billion dollars. Since that time Mr. Murdoch has acquired one-half ownership of British Sky Broadcasting, the largest satellite service in Europe, and has paid 525 million dollars to purchase Hong Kong-based Star TV. As a result he has the potential of reaching two-thirds of the world's population and creating the first truly global TV network. Rupert Murdoch's father, Sir Keith Murdoch, was a famous Australian editor whose father, a Scottish immigrant, served as moderator of the Presbyterian church in Australia.[144]

Magazines

Almost two centuries ago Scotland was at the top of the periodical world. The *Edinburgh Review* was founded by Francis Jeffrey in 1802 and lasted until 1929. In its time it was the most important critical journal in the English-speaking world. Scott, Macaulay, and Carlyle were contributors. In America, Thomas Jefferson, James Madison, and Samuel Adams were among those who read it.[145] In England, the *Economist* was founded in 1843 by James Wilson, of Hawick. In recent years Alistair Burnet has been the magazine's award-winning editor.[146]

The *Canadian Monthly and National Review*, a powerful intellectual influence in Canada, was founded by Graeme Mercer Adam, a Scot.[147] Canada's national magazine, *Maclean's*, was founded by John B. Maclean in 1907. The present corporation is the largest communications company in Canada.[148]

Six of America's most popular magazines have had Scottish beginnings. The National Geographic Society, the world's largest nonprofit scientific and educational institution, was founded by the father-in-law of the inventor Alexander Graham Bell. The organization nearly failed, having only one thousand members and two thousand dollars in debts when Bell rescued it, taking over as the second president in 1898. Today the society, with its ten million members and world-renowned magazine, are presided over by Bell's great-grandson, Gilbert M. Grosvenor.[149]

Forbes magazine was founded in New York in 1917 by B. C. Forbes, who had worked previously at the *Rand Daily Mail* in Johannesburg. Forbes's son Malcolm, a member of Saint Andrew's Society of the State of New York, built his inheritance into one of the nation's leading business periodicals. He was also a noted balloonist, owned the sultan's palace in Tangier, a chateau in France, and a 1699 Christopher Wren house in London. After his death in 1990, Mr. Forbes was succeeded by his four sons, Malcolm S., Jr., Timothy, Christopher, and Robert, who have enhanced the image of *Forbes*, started foreign-language editions, and brought out new magazines.[150]

Forbes magazine's principal rival, *Business Week*, was founded in 1929 by Malcolm Muir, whose ancestors came to America from Kelso. Muir also headed the boards of *Newsweek* and McGraw-Hill.[151] Harold Wallace Ross, the son of an Ulster mining engineer, elevated the standards of journalism significantly when he founded the esteemed *New Yorker* in 1925.[152] Earle MacAusland began *Gourmet* magazine, by far the largest-circulation food periodical in the world, in 1941.[153]

Reader's Digest, the world's most widely read magazine, was founded by a Scottish-American couple who committed 1,800 dollars to the venture in 1921. DeWitt Wallace was the son of a Presbyterian minister, and his wife, Lila Acheson Wallace, was a descendant of Ulster Scots who were, in turn, descended from Sir Archibald Acheson, who owned the landmark house still standing on Edinburgh's Royal Mile. Mr. Wallace began the magazine by reading and condensing articles in the periodical room of the New York Public Library. The Reader's Digest Association, Inc., became one of the world's largest private companies and was owned entirely by the Wallaces, who died in the 1980s. When it went public in 1990 the company was valued at over two billion dollars, and the *Reader's Digest* magazine is presently read by over one hundred million readers in seventeen languages in every country of the world.[154]

Diana Vreeland, "the Empress of Fashion," ruled American couture for over three decades, first as fashion editor of *Harper's Bazaar* and then as editor of *Vogue*. Ms. Vreeland, a Wallace awardee, was born in Paris, the daughter of Scottish stockbroker Frederick Dalziel.[155]

Publishing

John Murray, the publishers of Byron and one of Britain's oldest and largest publishing firms, was founded in the eighteenth century by John MacMurray of Edinburgh. The firm is currently being run by John Murray VII.[156] William Collins, Ltd., the largest publishing house in Great Britain, was founded in Glasgow in 1819. In 1988 it was sold to Rupert Murdoch for 717 million dollars.[157] In 1990 George Craig, the son of a Glasgow steelworker, merged Harper and Row of New York, also owned by Murdoch, with Collins to form Harper-Collins, a British-American publishing house with 1.5 billion dollars in revenues. Mr. Craig became chief executive of the new company.[158]

Macmillan and Co., the publishers of Tennyson and Kipling and one of the most important publishers in the world, was founded in England in 1843 by Daniel and Alexander Macmillan, who were born in Scotland. A scion of the family was Prime Minister Sir Harold Macmillan.[159]

Grosset and Dunlap are major publishers who still use the thistle emblem. The firm of Hamish Hamilton was founded in 1931 by "Jamie" Hamilton, who was born in Indianapolis, raised in Scotland, and died in 1988. Hamilton's authors included John and Robert Kennedy, Jean-Paul Sartre, and Albert Camus.[160] McGraw-Hill, Inc., the giant American publisher, began in the late nineteenth century under the direction of James H. McGraw, of Scotch-Irish ancestry. In 1993 his great-grandson, Harold W. McGraw III, was elected president of the company.[161]

Ballantine Books, Penguin USA, and Bantam Books led the paperback revolution in the United States. All three were founded by Ian Ballantine (1916–1995) and his wife Betty. Ballantine, born in New York City to a Scottish father and a Russian-Jewish mother, "helped make the genres of science fiction, fantasy, western, and mystery."[162]

Reference Works

Samuel Johnson's prejudice against the Scots is well known. His landmark *Dictionary* defines "oats" thus: "A grain, which in England is generally given to horses, but in Scotland supports the people." Nevertheless, when Dr. Johnson began the monumental task of compiling this great work, five of the six amanuenses he employed were Scots: two MacBeans, a Shiels, a Stewart, and a Maitland.[163] Likewise, the editor in chief of the massive *Oxford English Dictionary*, himself the author of almost half its pages, was James A. H. Murray (1837–1915), the oldest child of a poor tailor from Roxburgh. The dictionary, which some call the most prestigious book ever published, was completed by another Scot, William Craigie.[164]

The *Encyclopaedia Britannica* was first published by a "Society of Gentlemen in Scotland" in 1768. The world's greatest reference source, still displaying its thistle emblem, was originally produced by William Smellie, printer and scholar; Colin Macfarquhar, printer; and Andrew Bell, engraver.[165] *Chambers Encyclopaedia* was founded by William and Robert Chambers, of Peebles.[166] The *Australian Encyclopaedia* was largely the work of its chief editor, Alexander Chisholm.[167]

Britain's premier biographical source, the *Dictionary of National Biography*, was founded and owned by Elgin-born George Smith (1824–1901) in 1882.[168] The first editor was Sir Leslie Stephen, of Scottish lineage and the father of the author Virginia Woolf.[169]

John Bartholomew and Son, Ltd., of Edinburgh, are undoubtedly the premier cartographers of Great Britain. John George Bartholomew (1860–1920) created the innovation of showing relief by gradations of color—dark blue to lighter blue for water, green to tan for land—all of which is now standard. He also named Antarctica. Alexander Keith Johnston set up another premium map-making firm in Edinburgh in 1826 and produced the first physical globe.[170] On the other side of the ocean, the premier map makers are Rand, McNally and Company, a founder of which, Andrew McNally, was of Scotch-Irish ancestry.[171]

The *Guinness Book of World Records* was founded in London by the twin brothers Norris Dewar McWhirter and Alan Ross McWhirter, who were sometimes pictured wearing the kilt. Ross McWhirter, who raised money to help combat IRA terrorists, was killed by an IRA gunman in 1975.[172]

Libraries

John Durie, a native of Edinburgh, wrote *The Reformed Librarie-Keeper* in London in 1650. It was the first British treatise on library management.[173] The first circulating library in Britain was set up in Scotland by the poet Allan Ramsay before 1728.[174] The Mitchell Library in Glasgow is today the largest civic-owned reference library in Europe.[175] Although it belongs to one of the smallest of countries, the National Library of Scotland became one of the dozen biggest in the world.[176] The London Library, perhaps the greatest private lending library in the world, began under the auspices of Thomas Carlyle in 1841.[177] The awesome New York Public Library was founded in 1895 by the donated collections of three men, one of whom was James Lenox, whose father, Robert Lenox, had started New York's Presbyterian Hospital and had been a president of Saint Andrew's Society of the State of New York.[178]

9

Science

Apart from their extravagant contributions to the Industrial Revolution through the medium of the practical science of invention discussed in chapter 5, the Scots have made an enormous mark on the more pure sciences of the world as well. The Scottish excellence in science began early and continues up to the present, manifesting itself in all parts of the world.

Anthropology and Archaeology

Sir Alexander Cunningham (1814–1893) was the "father" of Indian archaeology and made many contributions to the chronology of Buddhism.[1] Sir James George Frazer (1854–1941) was the author of *The Golden Bough*, published in 1890. The book compares a greater range of religious practices all over the world than any other anthropological work.[2] In the early twentieth century A. E. Douglas, an American, became the originator of dendrochronology, or tree-ring dating, which has become so important in establishing dates for events in former periods.[3] A Canadian Scot, Davidson Black, made the discovery of the Peking Man in the late 1920s.[4] The surname Leakey, which appears to be a variant of the Scottish Leckie, has become synonymous with the study of human origins. Mary Leakey, born Mary Douglas Nicol, is of definite Scottish origin and therefore so is her son Richard. The Leakey's work in Africa has greatly advanced the knowledge of our beginnings and, in a modern sense, their work has marked the beginnings of paleoanthropology.[5] Joseph Campbell (1904–1987) was one of the world's foremost experts on mythology and folklore. A prolific author, he became famous just after his death when the Public Broadcasting System aired six programs featuring discussions with him that had been taped before he died. Joseph Campbell was an American of Scottish and Irish ancestry.[6]

Astronomy

It was a Scot, James Gregory (1638–1675), who invented the Gregorian reflecting telescope. His name should have been Macgregor and he was actually related to the notorious Rob Roy. But when the Macgregors were outlawed his family was forced to chose another name.[7] The most celebrated telescope maker of the eighteenth century was a Scottish carpenter's son, James Short (1710–1768). Working in Edinburgh, he became the first person to accurately determine the difference in longitude between Greenwich and Paris, and was also the first person to deduce the solar parallax.[8] Thomas Henderson (1798–1844) was born in Dundee and became the first person to measure the distance between the earth and a star, in this case Alpha Centauri.[9] Also from Dundee, Williamina Paton Fleming (1857–1911) discovered two hundred variable stars and ten novae after moving to America. A failed marriage forced her to work as a domestic, but fortunately her master was the director of Harvard College Observatory, who encouraged her to become an astronomer.[10] Another Scottish-American woman astronomer, Maria Mitchell, was the first woman elected to the Academy of Sciences.[11] In Germany, Johann von Lamont, born John Lamont, the son of a Braemar forester, discovered the satellites of Uranus in 1837.[12] While serving as governor of New South Wales, Sir Thomas Makdougall Brisbane built an observatory and discovered over seven thousand stars beneath the Southern Cross.[13]

Biology

A little-remembered Englishman of Scottish descent discovered and was recognized immediately as the codiscoverer, with Charles Darwin, of the theories of evolution, natural selection, and the origin of species. While writing down his own ideas, Darwin received a paper containing the same theories from his friend Alfred Russel Wallace (1823–1913), who was working at the time in the distant Moluccas and had composed his paper while recovering from an attack of malaria. In his work Wallace had actually written the phrase "survival of the fittest," entering those words into the English language. Darwin immediately acknowledged that the ideas were the same as his own and magnanimously proposed that Wallace's paper be published without any reference to his own work, which was not yet complete. Even though it was clear that Wallace had the first finished work, Sir Charles Lyell and Sir James Hooker decided to read Wallace's paper and Darwin's abstract as a joint paper at the Linnean Society on July 1, 1858, and to have "both naturalists appearing as equally great and independent discoverers of the origin of species."[14]

A Glasgow University scientist, Dr. Graham Cairns-Smith, originated the "clay life" hypothesis in the 1960s, proposing that life originated in clay rather than in the sea. Discoveries by scientists in California in 1985 proved that clay has the capacity to store and transfer energy, lending support to the theory.[15]

In 1933, Thomas Hunt Morgan, an American of partly Scottish ancestry, was awarded a Nobel Prize for physiology or medicine for discovering the functions of chromosomes in heredity.[16] In 1983 Dr. Barbara McClintock (b. 1902) of New York became the first woman to win an unshared Nobel Prize in physiology or medicine, awarded for her discovery of "jumping genes" along streaks of chromosomes.[17]

In February 1944 a paper which changed the course of world history was published at Rockefeller University in New York City. In sum, the paper proved that genes are comprised of a substance called deoxyribonucleic acid, or DNA. Two of the three authors of the paper had Scottish backgrounds. Dr. Maclyn McCarty is of Scotch-Irish ancestry. Dr. Colin Munro MacLeod was the son of a Nova Scotian Presbyterian minister.[18]

In 1957 Alick Isaacs, born in Glasgow to Jewish parents, discovered and named interferon, an entirely new defense mechanism against viruses.

Many believe that the century's most important advance in medical science was working out the structure of DNA. The double helix was codiscovered by a Scottish-American, Dr. James D. Watson, for which he shared the 1962 Nobel Prize for physiology or medicine with two English fellow-scientists. In 1988 Dr. Watson, also a Wallace Award winner, became the first director of human genome research at the National Institute of Health. As head of the genome project, which will identify and map all human genes, he had assumed the leadership of the largest biological research project ever undertaken.[19]

Botany

Robert Morrison (1620–1683) of Scotland was the first botanist to propose the concept of family, genus, and species.[20] The Forsythia is named for William Forsyth (1737–1804), who was superintendent of the Royal Gardens of St. James and Kensington.[21]

David Douglas (1798–1834) was born at Scone and went to the American West Coast in 1823, where he discovered over one hundred plants and fifty trees, one of which, the Douglas fir, is named after him.[22] Asa Gray (1810–1888) is perhaps America's greatest botanist, and his book *Manual of Botany* is still the outstanding work in the field. Gray was born in New York of Scotch-Irish descent.[23] John McLaren (1846–1943) was the creator of one of the world's most magnificent botanical gardens, Golden Gate Park, in San Francisco. McLaren was born in Bannockburn and became San Francisco's parks superintendent in 1887. Throughout the years he transformed the park's 1,017 acres, which had been given to him as a barren sand dune, into its present beauty.[24]

In Australia, Montrose-born Robert Brown (1773–1858) is remembered as the "father" of that country's botany as a result of his work there in the early nineteenth century. He was the leading botanist of his time, discovering the cell nucleus and the haphazard "Brownian movement."[25] Francis Masson (1741–1805), born in Aberdeen, was the pioneer of botanical science in South Africa and introduced the gladiolus and iris to Britain.[26]

The Bagatelle Garden in the Bois de Boulogne, in Paris, includes what is now perhaps the most beautiful rose garden in the world. It was begun in the eighteenth century by Thomas Blaikie, a Scot. Blaikie worked with a great deal of imagination and the money of the Comte d'Artois, brother-in-law of Marie Antoinette.[27] John Fraser (1750–1811), born in Inverness, was botanical collector to the czar of Russia.[28] Sir Patrick Geddes (1854–1932), a native of Aberdeenshire, discovered chlorophyll in 1879. He became a world pioneer of town and urban planning. A protégé was the American Lewis Mumford. The Scottish-born American Ian McHarg (b. 1920), the premier landscape architect of his time, turned his field into a philosophy of environmental and ecological planning. Sir George Taylor, born in Edinburgh, was director of the Royal Botanic Gardens at Kew in the middle of this century.[29] The eminent botanist professor Sir Ghillean T. Prance, is the present director. Prance, who served previously as president for science at the New York Botanical Garden, was born on the isle of Skye.[30]

Chemistry

Joseph Black (1728–1799) became the founder of modern chemistry in 1754 when he presented, as a thesis for his doctoral degree at Edinburgh University, an experiment in which he rediscovered carbon dioxide and proved that it existed distinct from common air. In 1756 he proved that carbon dioxide existed in calcium carbonate (chalk). These revolutionary ideas, that air was composed of more than one gas and that a gas could exist in a solid, were soon taken up enthusiastically by others, including Lavoisier, and produced a radical change in the direction of science. Black, whose father was in the wine trade, was born in Bordeaux to parents of Scottish ancestry from Belfast.[31] James Watt, the inventor of the practical steam engine, was a friend and colleague of Black and was obviously influenced by him. Watt is sometimes given credit for the discovery that water, instead of being an element, is actually composed of two gasses.[32] Another Scot, who happened to be an uncle of Sir Walter Scott, was Daniel Rutherford (1749–1819), who discovered nitrogen at age twenty-one.[33]

Thomas Charles Hope is said to have discovered strontium in 1792.[34] Others say the discoverer's name was William Cruickshank, or a Mr. Crawford,[35] but all agree that the discovery was made at Strontian, Argyll. In 1798 the chemist Charles Tennant (1768–1838), of Ayr, helped the Scottish and world textile industry tremendously when he made the first cheap bleach from a chloride of lime.[36] Sir George Stewart Mackenzie identified carbon with diamond in 1800.[37] John Stewart MacArthur (1856–1920) did about as much as any man to make South Africa a rich nation. In 1887 the Glasgow-born MacArthur was the codiscoverer of the cyanide process for extracting gold from its ore, making possible the exploitation of low-grade ore. Initially he received royalties, but a court annulled his patents and he died poor.[38]

Thomas Thomson (1773–1852) was the first professor of chemistry at Glasgow University and wrote the first systematic book on the subject, using letters to symbolize the elements.[39] Peter Guthrie Tait (1831–1901) laid the foundation of the kinetic theory of gasses. Archibald Scott Couper (1831–1892), born in Kirkintilloch, was the first to propose the tetravalence of carbon atoms and that they could link together to form long chains.[40] Sir William Ramsay (1852–1916), born in Glasgow, made a discovery unique in the history of chemistry when he uncovered, one by one, the whole family of noble gasses: helium, argon, neon, krypton, xenon, and radon. He was awarded the Nobel Prize for chemistry in 1904.[41]

Ernest Rutherford (Baron Rutherford; 1871–1937) won the 1908 Nobel Prize for chemistry and is considered by many to have been New Zealand's greatest son. Rutherford confirmed the principles of radioactivity, discovered and named alpha and beta rays, and established the structure of matter and the nuclear structure of the atom. In short, his work was absolutely basic to all subsequent developments in nuclear physics. His father emigrated from Perth to New Zealand in 1841.[42]

An American, Irving Langmuir (1881–1957), previously mentioned for his contributions to the development of electric lighting, won the 1932 Nobel Prize for chemistry for his investigations of the fundamental properties of absorbed films and surface chemistry.[43] Another Scottish-American, Edwin Mattison McMillan (1907–1991), won a Nobel Prize for chemistry in 1951 for his work in the field of transuranium elements and his codiscovery of neptunium and plutonium.[44] Still another American of Scottish descent, Linus Carl Pauling (1901–1994) won the Nobel Prize for chemistry in 1954 for his studies of molecular structure, especially the nature of the bonding of atoms in molecules. In 1990 Dr. Pauling received the Wallace Award from the American-Scottish Foundation.[45]

In England, a Briton of Scottish ancestry, Sir Cyril Norman Hinshelwood (1897–1967), won the 1956 Nobel Prize for chemistry for his work on chemical kinetics.[46] The very next year the same award went to a native Scot, Alexander Robertus Todd (Baron Todd of Trumpington) (b. 1907) for his work on coenzymes. Todd also synthesized Vitamin B1 and Vitamin E, and elucidated the structure of Vitamin B12. His work on DNA and RNA cleared the path for the later discoveries, previously mentioned, of the structure of DNA, by James D. Watson and his two colleagues.[47] John C. Kendrew (b. 1917), an Englishman with ancestors from the Orkneys, shared the Nobel Prize in chemistry in 1962 for discovering the molecular structure of hemoglobin and myoglobin.[48]

Two Scottish-Americans were awarded Nobel Prizes for chemistry in the 1960s. Robert B. Woodward (b. 1917) won in 1965 for his synthesis of sterols, chlorophyll, and other substances once thought to be produced only by living things.[49] The next year Robert S.

Mulliken (1896–1986) received the prize for his fundamental work on the chemical bond that holds atoms together in a molecule. Dr. Mulliken, an American of Scottish ancestry known as Mr. Molecule, helped propel chemistry into the atomic era. Some say that he did more to lay the foundation of molecular science than anyone else. He is also known as the father of modern theories of structural chemistry and the creator of the molecular orbital theory.[50]

In 1987 another Scottish American, Donald J. Cram (b. 1919) won the Nobel Prize for chemistry for his discovery that crown ether molecules could be made three dimensional—a hole rather than a loop with which to grab other components. In 1989 Dr. Cram was the leader of the team at UCLA that succeeded in imprisoning molecules within other molecules, and has thereby created a new state of matter.[51]

Conservation

America's great naturalist, John Muir (1838–1914), was born in Dunbar, the son of a religious fanatic, and before Muir left for America he could recite most of the Bible from memory. John Muir is recognized as the "father" of the American conservation movement and is thought of as the country's preeminent nature lover and conservationist. His writings led to the establishment of Sequoia and Yosemite National parks. In 1892 he bacme the founder and first president of the Sierra Club, today one of the world's most influential environmental organizations. There are more places in California named for John Muir than for any other person.[52]

In the present century James "Scotty" Philip, born in Dallas, Scotland, is recognized as the savior of the American buffalo. Philip bought what few creatures he could find and bred them. In 1906 an act of Congress provided Philip with 3,500 acres at nominal rent, the first time the government of the United States moved to save a species from extinction. The herds of buffalo in the American national parks today are the descendants of the breed of Scotty Philip.[53]

George Adamson (1906–1989), born in India of Scottish ancestry, protected animals, particularly lions and their environment, in Africa. He and his wife Joy created the legend of Elsa, a lion cub they raised, and which became famous in the book and film *Born Free*.[54]

Rachel Carson launched the environmental movement in the United States with her far-reaching 1962 book *The Silent Spring*.[55]

Geology

Geology has been called the Scottish science. The work of the following men revolutionized the way people thought about the formation of the earth.

James Hutton (1726–1797) of Edinburgh was the founder of modern geology. In 1785 he published *Theory of the Earth* describing his ideas about the formation of the earth's crust. His "gradualist" theory, which claimed that the slow processes which had created and shaped the earth were still continuing, was the first general theory of the earth's development.[56] After Hutton's death his friend John Playfair (1748–1819) continued his work, transcribing his notes into the work *Illustrations of the Huttonian Theory of the Earth*.[57] Another Scot, Sir James Hall (1761–1832), is considered to have been the founder of experimental geology.[58] Sir Charles Lyell (1797–1875), also Scottish, expanded on Hutton's theories of a continuously developing earth and convinced Darwin to pursue his evolutionary ideas. Lyell was also the author of *Elements of Geology*, the standard work on stratigraphical and paleontological geology.[59] Roderick Murchison (1792–1871) identified and named the Silurian, Devonian, and Permian systems and made a geological survey of Russia (1840–1845) at the request of the tsar.[60]

In 1838 Thomas Dick, a native of Angus, wrote *Celestial Scenery* which for the first time described the movements of the earth's surface that we now call continental drift and plate tectonics. Dick suggested such things as that the bulge of Brazil had once fit into the west coast of Africa and proposed the then revolutionary idea that the continents had once been joined.[61] Sir Archibald Geikie (1835–1924) is called, simply, "the prince of geologists." Geikie was director general of the Geological Survey of the U.K. and president of the Geological Society. He was decorated by France, Italy, and the United States, and was elected president of the Royal Society in 1908.[62]

James Forbes invented the seismometer in 1842,[63] and John Milne is considered to have been the founder of the modern science of seismology.[64] James Croll of Scotland was the first geologist to present the idea that variations in the earth's orbit control long-term climatic change.[65] William Maclure (1763–1840), born in Ayr, was the father of American geology and completed the first American geological survey, probably the first in the world, in 1809.[66] In 1967 Campbell Bridges, a Scottish geologist working in Tanzania, discovered Tsavorite, a green gemstone more brilliant and durable than emerald.

Mathematics

The first great mathematician produced by Scotland was John Napier (1550–1617), who opened up an epoch in science with his invention of logarithms in 1614. He also invented the slide rule and was the first to use the decimal point to separate the fractional from the integral part of a number.[67]

Sir Isaac Newton (1642–1727), an Englishman who proudly boasted of his Scottish ancestry, was arguably the greatest scientist of all time. His 1687 book *Principia* began the development of modern science and is the most influential scientific book ever published. In mathematics he is credited with the development of the binomial theorem and, in 1666, the development of calculus, the most important single advance in mathematics since the time of the ancient Greeks.[68] About the same time, James Gregory of Scotland (previously cited under astronomy) developed calculus independently while studying in Padua, so he and Newton are sometimes recognized as coinventors.[69]

James Stirling (1692–1770), a Scot and a good friend of Newton, helped develop the differential calculus. He published papers on Newtonian mathematics in 1717 and on the differential calculus in 1730.[70] Colin Maclaurin (1698–1746) was the only British mathematician after Newton who could be ranked equally with the continental mathematicians of his day.[71] In 1717 Maclaurin, aged nineteen, became at Marischal College, Aberdeen, the youngest full professor in the history of education.[72]

In 1986 Simon Donaldson won the Fields Medal, the closest award mathematics has to the Nobel Prize, while working on four-dimensional space at Oxford. Dr. Donaldson is of Scottish ancestry on both sides of his family. In 1994 Dr. Donaldson was awarded Sweden's Crafoord Prize for his work in differential geometry.[73]

Medicine

"May no English nobleman venture out of the world
without a Scottish physician, as I am sure there is none
who ventures in."

—*William Hunter (1718–1783)*[74]

Medicine was in an advanced state in the early history of Scotland. The Beaton (Macbeth) family were an Irish clan who brought to thirteenth-century Scotland knowledge from ancient Greece and the Arab world that was not then current in the rest of Europe. The Beatons stayed in Scotland and amassed a huge library that was lost in the 1700s.[75] In 1673 Sir Thomas Burnet (1632–1715) wrote what was then the most celebrated medical textbook in Europe.[76] John Brown (1735–1788) wrote *Elementa Medicinae* in 1780. This work effectively discredited the widespread practice of bloodletting, thus creating a medical watershed.[77]

DISEASE

Although William Jenner, an Englishman, is usually credited as the discoverer of vaccination against smallpox in 1796, it appears that this distinction belongs to Charles Maitland, a Scottish physician who successfully vaccinated no fewer than eighty-five Londoners between 1721 and 1723, including the future Prince of Wales, Frederick of Hanover.[78]

Alexander Patrick Stewart (1813–1883) was the Scottish physician who distinguished typhus from typhoid. Another Scot, William Leishman (1865–1926), perfected the typhoid vaccine in 1913.[79] Sir David Bruce (1855–1931) was an Australian of Scottish descent who discovered the causes of sleeping sickness and Malta fever. When he isolated the bacteria of Malta fever it was renamed brucellosis after him, and the genus of bacteria causing it, Brucella.[80]

Sir Patrick Manson (1844–1922) theorized that biting insects were the cause of parasitic diseases.[81] Manson's work inspired Sir Ronald Ross (1857–1932), who confirmed Manson's theories by investigating the life history of the malaria parasite and discovering the complex sequence of circumstances by which the disease is spread.[82] Born in Nepal, Ross was the son of a Scottish general and a descendant of the mother of the Bride of Lammermoor.[83] He was the author of *Prevention of Malaria* and received the Nobel Prize for physiology or medicine in 1902. After Sir Alexander Fleming, he probably saved more human lives than any other man.[84]

The control of diabetes was made possible in 1921 by a team of Canadians headed by J. J. R. Macleod, a native of Scotland. The team included Frederick Grant Banting, a Canadian of partly Scottish descent. Formerly a "hopeless" disease that killed people within a year or two, their discovery of insulin has restored millions to health. Macleod and Banting were awarded the 1923 Nobel Prize for physiology or medicine.[85]

The 1928 discovery of penicillin by Sir Alexander Fleming (1881–1955) proves Pasteur's axiom that "chance favors the prepared mind." Fleming, born in Ayrshire, observed that a mold, which later proved to be *penicillium notatum*, had developed on a staphylococcus plate and created a bacteria-free circle around itself. He named the substance discharged by the mold penicillin, and found that it prevented the growth of staphylococci even when diluted eight hundred times.[86] For his discovery Fleming was awarded a share of the 1945 Nobel Prize for physiology or medicine. At his funeral ten years later it was said that "by his work he has saved more lives and relieved more suffering than any other living man, perhaps more than any man who has ever lived."[87]

HYPNOSIS

The question of who was first to use hypnotism in medicine is controversial and both claimants are Scottish. James Braid, a Scottish surgeon practicing in Manchester, England, wrote a paper on his work in 1843 using the word *hypnosis* for the first time.[88] However, another Scottish physician, James Esdaile, claimed to have used hypnotism in 1829 while practicing in India. In 1847 an investigating unit confirmed this.[89]

MILITARY MEDICINE

The founder of modern military medicine was Sir John Pringle (1707–1782), born in Scotland. In 1744 he was appointed physician general to the British forces in the Low Countries, where he improved camp sanitation and made rules for the prevention of dysentery. In 1752 he demonstrated a relation between putrification and disease, his methods greatly reducing the number of military deaths. Eventually he became physician to King George III and was elected president of the Royal Society.[90] Sir James McGrigor (1771–1868) served under Wellington in the Peninsular Army, treated ninety five thousand cases in ten months, and is known as the father of the British Army Medical Corps.[91]

Dr. James Craik was surgeon general of the American revolutionary army. With another Scot, Dr. Gustavus Brown, he was summoned to attend Washington as he died of a throat illness.[92]

THE NERVOUS SYSTEM

Robert Whytt (1714–1766), born in Scotland, discovered the sympathetic nervous system.[93] Sir Charles Bell (1774–1842) was the first great investigator of the central nervous system. Bell discovered motor, sensory, and motor-sensory nerves, the most important discoveries in physiology since Harvey's circulation of the blood. He was also the first to describe the disease we now call Bell's palsy.[94] Edgar Douglas Adrian (first baron Adrian of Cambridge) an Englishman of Scottish descent, won the 1932 Nobel Prize for physiology or medicine for his studies on the physiology of the nervous system, especially the functions of neurons.[95]

OBSTETRICS AND GYNECOLOGY

William Smellie (1697–1753), born in Lanark, was known as the master of British midwifery. Smellie ended the female monopoly and brought physicians into the practice. He also invented the "long" obstetric forceps.[96]

William Hunter (1718–1783) is considered to have been the founder of modern, scientific obstetrics, raising the standards of the practice of midwifery to a branch of medicine. Also born in Lanarkshire, he was physician extraordinary to Queen Charlotte.[97]

William Cruickshank (1745–1800) discovered the ovum in mammals.[98] Another Scottish physician, Matthew Baillie (1761–1823), was the first to describe dermoid cysts in the ovary and the first physician to treat pathology as a separate subject.[99] Marie Carmichael Stopes (1880–1958) was the Scottish-born pioneer of birth control and opened the United Kingdom's first birth control clinic in 1921.[100] Alexander J. C. Skene (1837–1900), born in Aberdeen, is probably America's most famous gynecologist. Skene was a founder of the American Gynecological Society and its president from 1886 to 1887.[101]

THE PHARMACOPOEIA

William Cullen (1710–1790) was the foremost medical teacher of his time, and at Glasgow University became Britain's first chemistry professor. But he is best remembered for his *Edinburgh Pharmacopoeia*, the first modern pharmacopoeia, published in 1776.[102] A Scottish-American, Dr. William Brown, compiled and wrote the first pharmacopoeia in America, published around 1790.[103] Sir Robert Christison (1797–1882), born in Edinburgh and physician to Queen Victoria, acted as chairman of the committee that prepared the first *Pharmacopoeia of Great Britain and Ireland*, in 1864.[104]

PSYCHIATRY

Benjamin Rush (1745–1813), "the Hippocrates of Pennsylvania" was the father of American psychiatry. Rush, of remote Scottish ancestry, was educated at Edinburgh and became a major figure in early American medicine.[105] In the twentieth century R. D. Laing, a Scottish psychoanalyst, rebelled against tradition and sought new treatment for mental patients. He became famous for suggesting that insanity may be a sane reaction to an insane world.[106] William James, who was discussed in the previous chapter, opened the first psychology laboratory in the world and in 1878 conferred the first Ph.D. in psychology in the United States.[107]

SURGERY

John Hunter (1728–1793) was the founder of scientific surgery.[108] He was the younger brother of William Hunter, the founder of scientific obstetrics. John Hunter is the man who stripped surgery away from the barber's grasp and made it a science by basing the discipline on sound biological principles. His vast achievements earned him appointment as physician extraordinary to King George III.[109] The esteem in which John Hunter was held by his contemporary Britons led one English writer to become rapturous discussing him: "As a physiologist, he was equalled, or perhaps excelled, by Aristotle; but as a pathologist he stands alone."[110]

The use of anesthesia was developed principally by Scots. One of the codiscoverers of chloroform, in 1831, was an American Scot, Samuel Guthrie.[111] Crawford Williamson Long, an American of Ulster-Scottish ancestry, was the first to use an anesthetic in surgery. On March 30, 1842, in Jefferson, Georgia, Long painlessly removed a tumor from a patient. William Thomas Green Morton (1819–1868), another Scottish-American, made the first public demonstration of the use of ether as an anesthetic, in Boston, in 1846.[112] The next year in Scotland, Sir James Young Simpson (1811–1870) became the first to use chloroform in surgery. Simpson was also the first to use anesthesia in childbirth, one of his first patients in this regard being Queen Victoria.[113]

Sir William Macewen (1848–1924) made many contributions to the development of surgery. He was an associate of Joseph Lister, an Englishman who practiced in Scotland, and together they developed antiseptic surgery. Macewen experimented with the sterilization of instruments and dressings, and the preparation of catgut for surgical use. He also conducted the first bone graft, the first excision of a lung, devised the first systematic training course for nurses, and in 1879 was the first to remove a brain tumor.[114]

One of the most remarkable events in the history of medicine occurred on the Kentucky frontier in 1809. In that year and in that unlikely place, Dr. Ephraim McDowell (1771–1830) performed the world's first ovariotomy, an operation then considered to be impossible. All of the participants in this amazing feat were Scotch-Irish-Americans. McDowell had studied at Edinburgh University and on the frontier with Dr. Alexander Humphries. The patient, Jane (Jenny) Todd Crawford, had ridden sixty miles on horseback to the operation. She had been married by the Rev. Samuel Houston, a close relative of the Texas hero. The result of the operation, performed without anesthesia, was that Dr. McDowell removed a twenty-pound tumor and Mrs. Crawford survived thirty years, to age seventy-nine. Frontiersman McDowell had become the world's first surgeon to demonstrate the feasibility of elective abdominal surgery.

Two more Scotch-Irish Presbyterians who were to become presidents of the United States came in contact with McDowell. Andrew Jackson, who became the seventh president, assisted McDowell in an operation and swore he would rather fight Indians than assist in another. McDowell also removed gallstones from the bladder of seventeen-year-old James Knox Polk, who became the eleventh president.[115]

NUTRITION

The work of two Scottish physicians caused all Englishmen to be referred to around the world as limeys. James Lind (1716–1794) was the founder of naval hygiene in England. Among his many reforms were strict delousing procedures and the use of hospital ships. In 1747 Lind conducted what is claimed as the world's first controlled clinical experiment when he studied the effects of citrus additions to the diet of sailors and proved that the practice would eliminate scurvy. He was able to convince Captain Cook, who successfully used citrus on his own crews, but not the admiralty, which remained skeptical despite his evidence. Another Scot, Sir Gilbert Blane (1749–1834), used Lind's technique on sailors in the West Indies and in 1795 finally convinced the government to mandate the use of lime juice throughout the navy.[116] Still another Scot, John Bennett (1812–1875), discovered the medicinal use of cod liver oil as a source of vitamins A and D.[117]

A Scottish-American scientist, Elmer Verner McCollum (1879–1967), first used the term *vitamin*. This pioneer nutritionist, who began life as a Kansas farm boy, was responsible for the discovery of Vitamin A in 1913, Vitamin B in 1916, and Vitamin D in 1922.[118]

MISCELLANEOUS MEDICINE

James Currie (1756–1805), the first physician to use the thermometer in clinical medicine, was born in Dumfriesshire.[119] In 1903 Alexander Graham Bell, the inventor of the telephone, was the first to publish the idea of treating deep-seated cancers with radium.[120] J. Norman Collie (1859–1942), born in England of Scottish parentage, took the first X-ray photograph ever used for medical diagnosis.[121] In 1922 Sir Archibald Vivian Hill, an Englishman with Scottish ancestry, won the Nobel Prize for physiology or medicine for his discoveries relating to the heat produced by muscular activity.[122] Sir MacFarlane Burnet, an Australian of Scottish ancestry, won the 1960 Nobel Prize for physiology or medicine for the discovery of acquired immunological tolerance to tissue transplants.[123]

In recent years two men of the Scottish nation have developed important medical machinery. In Scotland Ian Donald (1910–1987) made the first practical ultrasonic scanner and initiated and developed the techniques of pregnancy scanning now in use everywhere.[124] Allan MacLeod Cormack (b. 1924), an American born in South Africa to Scottish immigrant parents,[125] won a share of the 1979 Nobel Prize for physiology or medicine for his work in developing computed axial tomography, commonly known as the CAT or CT scan. At present this complicated machine gives physicians their best look inside the human body.

The 1988 Nobel Prize for physiology or medicine was awarded to three people, two of whom are Scottish. An American, George Hitchings (b. 1905), descended from Scottish-Canadians, has shaped drug development for more than forty years. He is the codiscoverer of drugs used against leukemia, gout, malaria, auto-immune disorders, and AIDS.[126] The other winner in 1988 was Sir James Whyte

Black, born in Scotland in 1924, who has been described as "probably the greatest and most important living pharmacologist." Sir James, who works in England, was the discoverer of beta blockers, a milestone in the treatment of high blood pressure and heart disease. He is also the discoverer of H-2 receptor-antagonists used in the treatment of ulcers.[127]

A simple test developed by Scottish-American Dr. Robert Guthrie has saved thirty thousand people from mental retardation and will continue to save many more. The test for PKU is given to all newborn infants and costs about three cents. If positive, the infants are placed on a strict diet which prevents retardation and lifetime costs of one million dollars per patient. Dr. Guthrie died in 1995, having refused all royalties on his test.[128]

Ornithology

In America, the first person to study the native birds was Alexander Wilson (1766–1813), whose *American Ornithology*, published in 1808, inspired Audubon and is still a standard work in the field. Before he left Scotland for the newly created United States, Wilson had been a poet whose work may have sold one hundred thousand copies and which is said to have been praised by Burns.[129] Another influence on Audubon was William MacGillivray (1796–1852), publisher of *A History of British Birds* and the "father" of British ornithology.[130] Allan D. Cruickshank, a New Yorker born in the Virgin Islands to a Scottish father, for many years worked as the official photographer of the National Audubon Society. A noted ornithologist, he died in the 1970s, known as the modern Audubon with a camera.[131]

Physics

Sir Isaac Newton (1642–1727) was one of the greatest men in history and made enormous contributions to astronomy and optics, as well as mathematics, for which he has been mentioned previously. It is, however, as a physicist that he is most remembered, especially for his laws of gravity and motion. His work marks the beginning of modern science. Newton claimed Scottish ancestry and is even quoted as having said that he had his Scottish relatives stay with him. In a discussion with James Gregory, previously noted as a coinventor of calculus, he said, "Gregory, I believe you don't know that I am a Scotchman?"[132]

Joseph Black (1728–1799), already cited for his work in chemistry, was also the discoverer of the principle of latent heat, which led to the achievements of James Watt and others.[133] Also contributing to physics from eighteenth-century Scotland were Thomas Melvil, who discovered the basis of spectrum analysis in 1752 and John Robinson, who, in 1769, proved the inverse square law in mechanics.[134]

In the next century David Brewster discovered the polarization of light, and in 1816 invented the kaleidoscope.[135] William John Macquorn Rankine (1820–1872) was one of the founders of thermodynamics, and the Rankine cycle of that science is named after him. Rankine was also a molecular physicist and evolved the scientific term *energy*.[136]

James Clerk Maxwell (1831–1879), born in Edinburgh, was one of the giants of science. He gave the world the theory and name of electromagnetism, and is considered to have been the father of electronics. Maxwell discovered that electricity travels at the speed of light and that electricity and magnetism are aspects of a single entity, electromagnetism. Maxwell's equations, unifying electricity and magnetism, led to the discovery that light was an electromagnetic phenomenon, and predicted the existence of radio waves. These equations have inspired later theoreticians to construct similar models.[137]

Maxwell's achievements paved the way for radio, television, and electronics. Albert Einstein described Clerk Maxwell's work as "a change in the conception of reality" that was "the most fruitful that physics has experienced since the time of Newton."[138] Einstein kept a picture of Maxwell on his wall and credited him with "putting him on the road" to his own discoveries.[139] Physicist Richard Feynman says: "From the long view of the history of mankind—seen from, say, ten thousand years from now—there can be little doubt that the most significant event of the nineteenth century will be judged as Maxwell's discovery of the laws of electrodynamics."[140]

Maxwell also gave the first demonstration of color photography, taking a picture of a tartan ribbon. In addition, he proved that the rings of Saturn were clouds of dust.[141] He was the first professor of experimental physics at Cambridge University and directly supervised the erection of the famous Cavendish Laboratory there. His *Treatise on Electricity and Magnetism* has been called by the *Encyclopaedia Britannica* "one of the most splendid monuments ever raised by the genius" of one man.[142]

Joseph Henry (1797–1878) has been called "the Nestor of American science," and was the grandson of two Scottish immigrants, William Hendrie and Hugh Alexander. Henry discovered the principle of electromagnetic induction two years before Faraday and rang a bell at the end of a mile of wire ten years before Morse, but he refused to file patents, and thus his discoveries were claimed by others. He appears to have been the first to discover the action of radio waves. Henry was also the organizer of the Smithsonian Institution, the National Academy of Science, and of the precursor of the U.S. Weather Bureau.[143]

Sir James Dewar (1842–1923), born in Scotland, invented the vacuum, or Dewar flask. Sir James did not capitalize on his invention commercially, but thermos bottles, as they are now called, appear in lunch buckets and picnic baskets almost everywhere. Sir James also studied low temperature phenomena and became the first to liquify oxygen, nitrogen, and finally hydrogen in 1898.[144]

Lord Kelvin (William Thomson; 1824–1907) who has been called the architect of nineteenth-century physics, was born in Belfast of Scottish ancestry and spent most of his life in Glasgow. Although he is previously mentioned twice in the section on inventions, Kelvin's most important work consisted of his discovery of the second law of thermodynamics. He also introduced the term *kinetic energy* to science. Kelvin holds an interesting world distinction in education. According to the *Guinness Book of World Records*, when he entered Glasgow University in 1834 at age ten, he was the youngest undergraduate in history.[145]

The Swiss physicist John Stewart Bell (1928–1990), was also born in Belfast, the son of working-class parents. He published Bell's theorem in 1964. Subsequent experiments have proved the theorem, solving one of the most basic questions in physics relating to communications between distant particles.[146] Stephen W. Hawking, the British physicist who is perhaps the world's most famous scientist since Einstein, is the author of the bestselling *A Brief History of Time*. His mother is the daughter of a Glaswegian doctor.[147]

The astronomer Erwin Findlay Freundlich (1885–1964), born in Germany of a Scottish mother, became a colleague of Einstein and was the first to prove his general theory of relativity by experiment. Freundlich left Germany at the time of Hitler and ended his career at St. Andrews.[148]

The Nobel Prize was first awarded in 1901, and people of the Scottish nation quickly became awardees out of all proportion to their small numbers.[149] The 1906 Nobel Prize for physics was received by Sir Joseph J. Thomson (1856–1940) for his investigations on how gasses conduct electricity. Sir Joseph, born in England of Scottish ancestry, discovered electrons and has been called the father of modern physics. He also trained nine Nobel Prize winners, thirty-two fellows of Britain's Royal Society, and eighty-three professors of physics.[150]

In 1908 the Nobel Prize for chemistry was granted to Lord Rutherford (1871–1937), as mentioned in the section on chemistry. As a physicist, Rutherford was called the father of atomic power,[151] and in 1919 discovered and named the proton and the atom-smashing theory. By theory and experiment, he was the first to establish that an atom consists of a loose structure of electrons surrounding a heavy central core, the nucleus. Nuclear physics was born at England's Cavendish Laboratory under Rutherford, who trained eleven future Nobel Prize winners.[152] The 1909 prize for physics was given to Marchese Guglielmo Marconi (1874–1937) for his discovery of radiotelegraphy. His mother was of Scottish ancestry, as observed in the section on inventions.

An American Scot, Robert Andrews Millikan (1868–1953), won the 1923 Nobel Prize for physics for his study of the elementary electrical charge and the photoelectric effect.[153] A Scottish farmer's son, Charles Thomson Rees Wilson (1869–1959) won the physics prize in 1927 for his discovery of the cloud chamber method of tracking paths of electrically charged particles.[154] Sir George P. Thomson (1892–1975), the son of Joseph J. Thomson, won the prize for physics in 1937 for his work on the diffraction of electrons in crystals. Walter H. Brattain (1902–1987), an American of Scottish ancestry,[155] won a share of the 1956 Nobel Prize for physics as the senior member of the team at Bell Laboratories that produced the transistor,[156] which some have said was the most important invention since James Watt produced the practical steam engine. In recent years, the greatly innovative president of Bell Labs was Ian M. Ross, also a Scottish-American. Mr. Ross was also chairman of the National Advisory Committee on Semiconductors.[157]

Another American Scot, Kenneth Geddes Wilson (b. 1936) won the Nobel Prize for physics in 1982 for developing an equation to explain the critical point at which matter changes from one phase to another, such as the moment when water boils. One of the youngest Nobelists ever, Wilson is used to doing things at an early age. He could calculate cube roots in his head at age eight and was studying at

Oxford at fifteen. He was admitted to Harvard at age sixteen, where he won a varsity letter in track for the mile run.[158]

In 1989 Norman F. Ramsey (b. 1915), descended from Scottish Covenanters, who came to America through Ireland, won the Nobel Prize for physics for his work in developing the atomic clock.[159] In 1990 the Nobel Prize for physics was shared by three men, two of whom were of Scottish ancestry. Dr. Richard E. Taylor, a Canadian, and Dr. Henry W. Kendall, an American, received their awards for their work in confirming the realty of quarks.[160]

10

Art, Architecture, Music, and Entertainment

Art

Compared to their towering achievements in science, what the Scots have accomplished in the arts may suffer in comparison. Nevertheless, for a people so small it is a substantial contribution and still far out of proportion to what would be expected of a minor nation.

BRITISH ARTISTS

The first important Scottish painter was Allan Ramsay (1713–1784) the son of Allan Ramsay, the Scottish poet previously mentioned as the creator of the first lending library. Allan Ramsay, the painter, was in great demand and painted kings and nobles by the dozen. His work is as much admired now as it was then. Scotland's premier artist was Sir Henry Raeburn (1756–1823), who resisted repeated calls to move to London and spent his life painting the portraits of important Scots instead. Perhaps his most famous work is that of the great Highland fiddler Neil Gow. Sir David Wilkie (1785–1841), born in Fife, became famous for his scenic portrayals of rural Britain. He was made painter-in-ordinary to King George IV.[1]

In the twentieth century Duncan Grant (1885–1978) and Graham Sutherland stand out. Grant, classified with the best French post-impressionists, was one of the stalwarts of the Bloomsbury Group. This influential coterie, which met in London during the first third of the century to discuss art and philosophy, included many members of Scottish-descent among them Virginia Woolf, her brother Adrian Stephen, her sister Vanessa Bell (who was Grant's lover), and the author Lytton Strachey, Grant's cousin.[2] One of Britain's best painters was Graham Sutherland (1903–1980), whose ancesctors came to England from Scotland two generations ago.[3]

AMERICAN ARTISTS

Gilbert Stuart (1755–1828), a descendant of immigrants from Perth, became America's first important painter. He is most famous for his portrait of George Washington.[4] America's greatest woman painter, and America's greatest painter of either sex according to some, was Mary Cassatt (1844–1926). She was born in Pittsburgh of Scottish ancestry and lived most of her life in France, where she became one of the noted impressionists and a close friend of Degas.[5] Thomas Eakins (1844–1916), of Philadelphia, famous for his boating scenes, was also of Scottish ancestry. Eakins was one of America's best artists and was also influential in the development of the photography of motion.[6] Another American artist with Scottish ancestry was James Abbott McNeill Whistler (1834–1903), famous for the portrait of his mother, which hangs in the Louvre. He spent much of his life in Europe and, like Mary Cassatt, was a good friend of Degas.[7]

In this century, Anna Mary Robertson Moses (Grandma Moses), Scottish on both sides of her ancestry, became famous for her paintings of rural country scenes.[8] Jackson Pollock (1912–1956), a founder of abstract expressionism, was perhaps America's most influential modern artist. His 1955 *Search* was purchased in 1988 for 4.8 million dollars, a record for any post–World War II artwork. Both of Pollock's parents were of Scotch-Irish Presbyterian descent.[9] Robert Motherwell (1915–1991), a winner of the Wallace Award and a founder of the abstract expressionist movement, was considered America's foremost painter at his death.[10]

SOUTH AFRICAN ARTISTS

Gerhardus "Hardy" Botha, one of the most imaginative of Afrikaner artists, calls himself Hardy in favor of his mother's Scottish ancestry.[11]

SCULPTORS

Three generations of the Calder family have had distinguished careers as American sculptors. The first, Alexander Milne Calder, was born in Aberdeen and immigrated to Philadelphia, where he created the statue of William Penn atop the city's famous city hall in 1894. Standing some five hundred feet above the city's streets, the statue is thirty-seven-feet high, weighs twenty-six tons, and is the largest on a building anywhere.[12] His son Alexander Stirling Calder designed the Logan Square fountain in Philadelphia.[13] His son, the third Alexander Calder (1898–1976), has been described as "the outstanding creative mind of the twentieth century" and "the most acclaimed American artist." As the originator of the mobile, Alexander Calder was the only artist in this century to create and practice his own art form.[14]

Frederick W. MacMonnies (1863–1937) was an outstanding American sculptor who made the monumental groups which adorn the Soldier's and Sailor's Memorial Arch at Grand Army Plaza in Brooklyn, where he was born. His statue of Pan is at the New York Metropolitan Museum. Dr. R. Tait McKenzie (1867–1938) was Canada's outstanding sculptor and leaves among his legacies the Scottish-American War Memorial in Edinburgh and the statue of young Franklin arriving in Philadelphia, which graces the campus of the University of Pennsylvania. McKenzie also served a term as president of the St. Andrew's Society of Philadelphia.[15]

Isamu Noguchi (1904–1988) was a Japanese-American artist of great versatility. His art, particularly his stone gardens, bridged East and West. In 1978 Hilton Kramer of the *New York Times* called Noguchi "at once the purest of living sculptors." Isamu Noguchi was born in Los Angeles, the grandson of Andrew Gilmour, a native of Scotland.[16]

MUSEUMS OF ART

The British Museum was founded with the government's 1753 purchase of the collection of Sir Hans Sloane (1660–1753), who was born in the north of Ireland of Scottish parents.[17] The basis of the museum's manuscript collection is the collection of Sir Robert Bruce Cotton, an Englishman who often boasted of his Scottish ancestry and his descent from King Robert I, the Bruce.[18] In the early years of the nineteenth century Thomas Bruce, seventh earl of Elgin, presented the museum with what are now considered to be its jewels, the Elgin Marbles, which he brought from Greece at great personal expense.[19] Not as well-known, Lord Elgin kept some of the marbles at his home near Dunfermline, where they remain to this day. In the 1980s Neil MacGregor, a forty-year-old art historian who had never worked a day in a museum, was appointed director of Britain's National Gallery and brought new life to the staid institution.[20]

In Montreal the David M. Stewart Museum and the Chateau Dufresne are two museums founded by David Macdonald Stewart. In the same city, the Chateau Ramezay museum is in the 1705 manor house built by Claude de Ramezay, the Scottish-descended governor of Montreal and New France.[21]

America's National Gallery of Art in Washington, D.C., was founded by Andrew Mellon, the Scotch-Irish-American financier. John Taylor Johnston, president of Saint Andrew's Society of the State of New York (1867–1869), was the principal founder and first president of New York's vast Metropolitan Museum of Art.[22] The famed Gardner Museum in Boston was founded by Isabella Stewart Gardner.[23]

Architecture

BRITISH ARCHITECTS

Without a doubt, the greatest Scottish architect ever was Robert Adam (1728–1792). His father, William Adam (1689–1748), was also a famous architect and thoroughly trained his son. Robert Adam's influence on architecture and interior design was felt from Russia to the United States. He designed many stately British homes and public buildings, such as the Register House in Edinburgh and the Adelphi Terrace in London. He is thought of as Britain's best neoclassic architect and is honored as one of those select Britons who are buried in Westminster Abbey.[24]

Around the same time Charles Cameron (1740–1812) was designing, in spectacular fashion, the Great Palace of Pavlosk and the interior of the Summer Palace in Russia for Catherine the Great. Some of Cameron's genius survived the ravages of World War II.[25] Nor was Cameron the first Scottish architect to achieve in Russia. In the seventeenth century Christopher Galloway had been the architect of the Kremlin's Troitski Gate, in Moscow.[26]

In the early years of the twentieth century Charles Rennie Mackintosh (1868–1928) was Scotland's best architect. As the designer of the Glasgow School of Art, and many other projects, he was one of the most important figures in the beginning of modern architecture.

In 1981 James Fraser Stirling, born in Glasgow, was awarded a Pritzker Architecture Prize worth one hundred thousand dollars, given annually since 1979 to one of the world's greatest architects. Stirling also won another one hundred thousand dollars in 1990, the second architect in the world to win the Praemium Imperiale Medal of the Japan Art Association.[27]

AMERICAN ARCHITECTS

Before the revolution a Scot had made an important architectural contribution in America. James Gibbs (1682–1754), born in Aberdeen, created the temple porticoes and pilastered spires that so characterize the beautiful Congregationalist churches of New England.[28] Robert Mills (1781–1855), an American of Scottish ancestry, was the first strictly professional architect born in the United States. He was the designer of many of the most important buildings in the capital city, including the U.S. Treasury and the Washington Monument, at 555 feet the tallest building in the world upon its completion in 1884.[29] The distinction of designing the world's tallest office building belonged, in 1974, to Bruce J. Graham, an American of Scottish ancestry and the architect of the 1,454-foot Sears Tower in Chicago.[30]

Robert Smith, a member of the St. Andrew's Society of Philadelphia in colonial times, became the architect of historic Carpenter's Hall in that city.[31] John McArthur (1823–1890), a native of Scotland, designed Philadelphia's city hall.[32] Henry Hobson Richardson (1838–1886), of Scottish descent, pioneered the American Style, which can still be seen in his Pittsburgh courthouse and jail.[33]

In New York, the city of skyscrapers, Scottish architects have always been prominent. St. Paul's Chapel, where Washington worshiped, is today the city's oldest. It was built from 1764 to 1766 by Thomas MacBean.[34] New York's city hall was designed by John McComb, Jr., and was completed in 1812.[35] St. Patrick's Cathedral was designed by the Scottish-American architect James Renwick. He was also the architect of the Smithsonian Institution in Washington, D.C., which was built by Gilbert Cameron, a native of Scotland. The ruins of Renwick's Smallpox Hospital on Roosevelt Island in New York City are permanently floodlit as part of the skyline.[36]

Washington Arch on Fifth Avenue was the work of three Scottish Americans. The arch itself was designed by Stanford White (see next page). The two statues of Washington on the arch, the one depicting him as commander in chief and the other as statesman, were sculpted, respectively, by Hermon A. MacNeil and Alexander Stirling Calder. MacNeil became the first president of the Clan MacNeil Association in 1921.[37]

The Statue of Liberty was constructed in France, but its pedestal was built by Alexander McGaw.[38] The granite used in the pedestal's construction was supplied by a Connecticut quarry owned by John Beattie, a native of Edinburgh, who also supplied the stone for the gigantic abutments of the Brooklyn Bridge.[39] John Duncan designed Grant's Tomb and the Soldiers and Sailors Memorial Arch at Grand Army Plaza in Brooklyn.[40]

New York's McKim, Mead, and White was probably the most influential architectural firm in American history. All of its three founding partners, Charles Follen McKim, William Rutherford Mead, and Stanford White, were of Scottish descent.[41] The firm was responsible for the original Madison Square Garden, Columbia University Library, Pennsylvania Station, the Morgan Library, and much more. Ironically, White, perhaps America's most famous architect, was shot to death in his own Madison Square Garden by Harry K. Thaw, who was jealous over White's affair with Evelyn Nesbitt. Thaw and Nesbitt are also Scottish surnames.

Ralph T. Walker, an American of purely Scottish ancestry, was the designer of the Irving Trust Company's skyscraper at 1 Wall Street. Frank Lloyd Wright called Walker "the only other architect in America." In 1957 the American Institute of Architects named Walker "architect of the century."[42]

CANADIAN ARCHITECTS

Canada's most distinguished architects in the twentieth century were the brothers Edward and William Sutherland Maxwell, who designed such treasures as the Winnipeg train station, the legislative buildings in Regina, and the Chateau Frontenac Hotel in Quebec. William Sutherland Maxwell's daughter is now Ruhiyyih Rabbani, spiritual leader of the Bahai Faith.[43]

Design

Robert Adam, mentioned above as the foremost Scottish architect, was also the creator of the Adam, or neoclassic, style of furniture, universally recognized as Britain's best. Robert Adam, with his three brothers John, James, and William, began this movement. It is not well-known, but the more famous Englishmen, Chippendale, Hepplewhite, and Sheraton, were all influenced by the Adamses and copied their designs. Chippendale and Hepplewhite were actually employed by the Adam brothers. Sheraton, as far as is known, never made a piece of furniture. Thus, what is acclaimed as an English legacy in furniture is actually Scottish.[44]

In America the exponent of the Adam style was Duncan Phyfe (c. 1786–1854), born in Inverness as Duncan Fife. Phyfe was probably America's greatest cabinetmaker and made a fortune in New York City, employing as many as a hundred artisans.[45]

Charles Rennie Mackintosh (1868–1928) was an artist as well as one of the most important architects in establishing modern architecture, but it is his work as a designer that has recently brought him a renewed fame. Mackintosh was the leader of the Glasgow Four, the group of artists who had a pronounced influence on modern art and architecture, which created what is known as Scottish art nouveau. The group included Herbert MacNair and the Macdonald sisters, Margaret and Frances, who married, respectively, Mackintosh and MacNair. Mies van der Rohe and the Bauhaus artists in Germany acknowledged their debt in modern art and architecture to the Glasgow Four. Today Charles Rennie Mackintosh's pieces command the highest auction prices of any twentieth-century furniture.[46]

Music

CLASSICAL MUSIC

Composers   It has been suggested that the Italian composer Gaetano Donizetti (1797–1848) was of Scottish descent from the tiny Izett (or Izat, Izatt, or Isett) family of Scotland.[47] While this claim has yet to be proven, it is interesting to note that the composer's most famous opera, *Lucia di Lammermoor*, is based on a Scottish book, Sir Walter Scott's *The Bride of Lammermuir*.

There is no doubt, however, of the Scottish ancestry of Norway's greatest composer Edvard Grieg (1843–1907), descended from Alexander Greig, a British consul general stationed at Bergen who settled there in 1779. Grieg's mother also had Scottish ancestry, being descended from one Andrew Christie.[48] Artur Rubinstein, the pianist, said that Rachmaninoff had told him that Grieg's *Concerto in A Minor* was the best concerto ever written "without exception."[49] The concerto has been called "perhaps Norway's most successful export," and not far behind are his *Holberg Suite* and *Peer Gynt*.[50]

Edward Alexander MacDowell (1861–1908) has been called America's foremost composer. MacDowell was born in New York City of Scottish ancestry and was known for his piano pieces. His widow founded the MacDowell colony in New Hampshire as a summer residence for composers and authors.[51] William Grant Still, (1895–1978) the first notable African-American composer, was partly of Scottish ancestry and the first black to conduct a professional symphony in the United States.[52] Virgil Thomson (1896–1989), probably America's premier composer in the twilight of the twentieth century, was of Scottish ancestry. He was best known for his opera *Four Saints in Three Acts* (1934), written to Gertrude Stein's libretto.[53]

Currently, James MacMillan, a native of Scotland, is being referred to as the best composer of his time.

Conductors   In this century several noted conductors have had a connection to Scotland. Leopold Stokowski was at least one-fourth Scottish. Stokowski is credited with having created an entirely new orchestral sound. He directed his strings differently from other conductors to create the sustained, silky-smooth "Philadelphia sound."[54] Sir Ernest Campbell MacMillan, the "Statesman of Canadian Music," directed and conducted the Toronto Symphony Orchestra from 1931 to 1956 and was the first person in the British Commonwealth outside Britain to be knighted for service to music.[55] New Yorker William Christie, whose roots go back to Fife and Edinburgh, is the Paris-based champion of French Baroque. As director and harpsichordist of Les Arts Florissants, which he founded in 1979, he has brought attention to works long neglected and has endeared himself to the French.[56] The much-acclaimed Sir Alexander Gibson (1926–1995), born in Scotland, conducted the Scottish National Orchestra, the Royal Philharmonic, the Saddlers Wells Opera, and founded Scottish Opera. Donald Cameron Runnicles, born in Edinburgh in 1954, conducts opera in Europe and the United States. Sir Alan Charles MacLaurin Mackerras is an Australian-born conductor of international repute as this century ends.[57]

Singers   Jenny Lind (1820–1887), the "Swedish Nightingale," according to one source, was by descent and name Scottish.[58] Another soprano, Madame Melba (Dame Nellie Melba; 1861–1931) was born in Australia as Helen Mitchell, the daughter of David Mitchell, a Scot. She was the star of many European opera houses, particularly as Violetta in *La Traviata*, and sang most often at Covent Garden and the

Metropolitan Opera. Joseph Hislop (1884–1977) was born in Edinburgh and became one of the world's best tenors, often singing with Melba.[59] Still another soprano, Mary Garden (1874–1967), was born in Scotland and made her reputation in French operatic roles. Two operas were written especially for her: *Der Rosenkavalier*, by Richard Strauss, and *Pelléas et Mélisande*, which Debussy composed after having proposed marriage to her. Mary Garden died in her native Aberdeen.[60]

James McCracken (1926–1988), a winner of the Wallace Award, was one of the greatest operatic tenors ever produced by the United States. Known as the Pillar of the Met, he was a former steel worker from Gary, Indiana, whose ancestors were Scotch-Irish.[61] Cornell McNeil has represented Scottish America as one of the best singers at the Met. Bill McCue, OBE, Scotland's most versatile singer, has sung everything around the world, from grand opera to Scottish folk songs. According to some, "the voice of the century" is possessed by Dame Joan Sutherland, who was born in Australia of almost entirely Scottish ancestry.[62]

Classical Music, Miscellany   Reginald Stewart (1900–1984), born in Edinburgh, had a diverse career as pianist, founder of the Toronto Philharmonic, head of the Peabody Conservatory, and conductor of the Baltimore Symphony.[63] William Primrose (1904–1982) was born in Glasgow and was considered to have been the greatest violist of his time, and perhaps any time.[64] On February 12, 1981, Scottish Opera claimed the record of the largest indoor opera audience in all of Europe, as 2,919 people filled the Playhouse Theatre in Edinburgh.[65]

John Broadwood (1732–1812) migrated from Edinburgh to London, then married the daughter of the harpsichord manufacturer to whom he was apprenticed. Broadwood (originally Braidwood) invented the piano and forte pedals, founded his own firm in 1827, and built the first six-octave grand piano in the world. The firm, which once led the world in the manufacture of pianos, still continues today, operated by his descendants.[66]

POPULAR MUSIC

Scottish music and dance have had an enormous effect on the music of the world. The entire development of Western popular music, and even some classical music, has been influenced by Scottish themes, traditions, composers, and performers. The reel, so popular in

American folk dance, and one of the underpinnings of American popular music, traces its origins to sixteenth-century Scotland.[67] The *écossaise*, or *schottische*, a 2/4 dance, was an inspiration for Chopin, Schubert, and Beethoven.[68] Mendelssohn collected Scottish songs on a trip to Scotland in 1829 and composed the *Hebrides Overture*.[69] Beethoven and Haydn wrote and arranged numerous Scottish songs.[70] The songs used by Sir Walter Scott to punctuate *The Lady of the Lake* inspired Franz Schubert to write seven songs based on them. One of these is the world famous "Ave Maria."[71]

From this evidence we can see that Scottish folk music and dance were sophisticated and pleasing long ago, even to Continental geniuses. Today the residue of this tradition survives in a polished form as the delicate and colorful Scottish country dancing, performed all over the world. It is no longer folk music and dancing, but rather the ballroom music and dancing of Scotland. As of 1988 there were 144 branches of the Royal Scottish Country Dance Society in places as unexpected as Hong Kong, Tokyo, Saudi Arabia, Indonesia, and the Fiji Islands. There were also 412 smaller affiliated groups.[72]

As early as 1763 American interest in Scottish music was apparent when Benjamin Franklin, thanking a friend in Scotland for sending some music, wrote that "our People here are quite charmed, and conceive the Scottish Tunes to be the finest in the World."[73] Indeed, some of the oldest and most enduring popular songs are Scottish, as "Annie Laurie," "Loch Lomond," "Comin' Through the Rye," and "Auld Lang Syne" continue to be world standards.

America's first commercial songwriter, and perhaps the world's, was Stephen Foster (1826–1864), born in Pittsburgh of solidly Scotch-Irish ancestry.[74] His first hit, "Oh! Susanna," was published in 1848 and struck a sensitive chord with the Americans moving westward to the California gold rush a year later. Many of his songs are still performed today, including "My Old Kentucky Home" and "Swanee River," which has sold more sheet music copies than any song ever published.[75]

American popular music, which has swept the world in the twentieth century, is based to a large extent on Scottish sources. Of the British ballads that survive in oral tradition and that laid the foundation for pop music, an estimated 40 to 50 percent are Scottish in origin.[76] Bluegrass music, now the basis of a gigantic industry, is the contemporary commercial descendant of this old form and was founded in 1938 by Bill Monroe, a Scottish-American and a descendant of America's fifth president, James Monroe.[77] Another descendant of this early music is the global phenomenon known as rock, traceable to two Scottish-Americans, Woody Guthrie and Burl Ives, who were the vital links between the twentieth century and "the unknown, uncharted music" of the nineteenth.[78]

A steady stream of artists has gradually developed American popular music from these beginnings, and many are Scottish. Woody Guthrie's son Arlo Guthrie is one. The group known as The Weavers is another.[79] Joan Baez, of Mexican and Scottish heritage,[80] has been very influential, as has James Taylor.[81] Bonnie Raitt is the daughter of John Raitt (see below) and a blues-rock singer whose records sell in the millions. Glen Campbell is proud of his ancestry and has occasionally appeared on television in the kilt. Johnny Cash, descended from a Scottish seaman, William Cash,[82] has spoken of Scotland as "my ancestral home" on television.[83]

In Scotland itself folk singing is still popular, and some think that Jean Redpath is the twentieth century's best. She has packed halls all over the world with her pure, dusky mezzo-soprano, which has been called "unmatched by any other contemporary folk singer." In 1988 Jean Redpath became the first folk singer to perform at New York's Mostly Mozart Festival, singing Haydn's Scottish songs.[84] People such as Aly Bain, Dougie MacLean (the Scottish James Taylor) and Phil and Johnny Cunningham have been among those featured in brilliant Celtic groups, such as the Tannahill Weavers, Boys of the Lough, Capercaille, Battlefield Band, Silly Wizard, and Runrig.[85] Ewan MacColl, also essentially a Scottish folk singer, bridged the gap to pop music when his song "The First Time Ever I Saw Your Face" became a hit in 1972.[86]

In the early part of this century the most famous Scottish popular singer and composer by far was Sir Harry Lauder, who set attendance records at halls and stadiums all over the world. Winston Churchill called him "the greatest minstrel the world has ever seen."[87]

In the 1930s and 1940s a new kind of popular music evolved into something which was much more sophisticated than the old music hall songs of Britain or the vaudeville tunes of America. Judy Garland, a singer of partly Scottish ancestry,[88] was one of the best exponents of this "standard" music. So too was Dick Haymes, born in Buenos Aires of Scottish lineage and the successor to Frank Sinatra in the Harry James and Jimmy Dorsey bands.[89] Gordon MacRae (1921–1986), who wore the kilt on *The Ed Sullivan Show*, was the star of the film versions of *Oklahoma!* and *Carousel*. His father was a toolmaker from Scotland.[90] From Canada came Giselle MacKenzie, a singer of French and Scottish ancestry, and later another Scottish-Canadian, Anne Murray.[91]

Hoagy Carmichael, an American of Scottish descent, was one of the most original of the standard composers with "Stardust" and "Georgia on My Mind," among many others to his credit.[92] Johnny Mercer, a descendant of Gen. Hugh Mercer,[93] previously mentioned, is celebrated as one of America's best lyricists. Mercer was the author of "Moon River," "Blues in the Night," "That Old Black Magic," "Laura," and "Autumn Leaves."[94] Noel Coward, the British author of "I'll See You Again" and many more songs, was Scottish on his mother's side.[95]

In the 1950s Elvis Presley (1935–1977) changed popular music forever. He descended from Andrew Presley, who had come to America from Scotland two centuries before.[96] Presley reached back to the old traditional music of the American South, but he imbued it with an energy that it had not had before and became the country's most popular singer ever.

As popular music continues to evolve, singers of Scottish background continue to appear. Leslie Uggams, of African, Scottish and American-Indian ancestry is an example.[97] Galt McDermott, the author of the precedent-setting musical *Hair*, is also of partly Scottish descent.[98] Donovan was one of the early pop successes in Scotland. In 1968 the tartan-clad Bay City Rollers were founded in Edinburgh by Alan and Derek Longmuir. David Byrne founded Talking Heads. They were followed by Jesse Rae, and the groups Ossian, Jethro Tull, Simple Minds, The Incredible String Band, The Average White Band, and Cocteau Twins. Scotland has also produced Sheena Easton, and Rod Stewart holds forth from England. Annie Lennox, pop/soul diva and a winner of multiple Grammy Awards, is a native of Scotland. From Australia came the Bee Gees and their brother Andy Gibb, born to a Scottish father.[99] The Bee Gees, composers and performers on the soundtrack of the film "Saturday Night Fever," at one point in the 1970s had four of the top five singles records in sales.[100] Another group, the Sex Pistols, the epitome of punk, were discovered, groomed, and managed by Malcolm McLaren, who was as responsible as any one for the eruption of punk rock in the mid-1970s.[101] McLaren, also an artist and fashion designer, has been called the Andy Warhol of Britain.[102]

Radio and Television

Radio broadcasting began in the early 1920s and in Britain was largely the work of a native Scot, J. C. W. Reith (Baron Reith of Stonehaven; 1889–1971), the "father" of the British Broadcasting Company. Reith became the first general manager of the BBC in 1922 and director general from 1927 to 1938. He created and developed broadcasting throughout the British Isles, inaugurated shortwave service and in 1936 the first regular high-definition television service in the world.[103]

In recent times people all over the world have watched the high quality programs of the BBC. One of the most brilliant series was *Civilisation*, a 1970s survey of Western art by Kenneth (Mackenzie) Clark (Lord Clark; 1903–1983), a Briton of entirely Scottish ancestry. Lord Clark, who was called "the most naturally gifted art historian of his generation," was, by his erudition and enthusiasm, able to enlist an enormous audience to learn of the artistic achievements of the West, in what was the most successful TV series of its kind ever made.[104]

Another gift from the BBC was *Upstairs Downstairs*, which starred two Scottish actors in the two leading male roles—playing Englishmen! David Langton (d. 1994) played the role of Lord Bellamy and Gordon Jackson (1923–1990) that of Hudson, the butler.[105] Another Scottish television star in both Britain and the United States is Lu Lu, who was born as Mary Lawrie.[106]

Amos and Andy, one of the earliest and longest-running programs in American radio, costarred Charles Correll, who was of Scotch-Irish ancestry.[107] One of the early important stars on American television was Dave Garroway (David Cunningham Garroway), the first host of the *Today* show. He was born in the Scottish district of Schenectady, New York.[108] One of the foremost American newsmen was Chet Huntley, who was of Scottish descent.[109] Perhaps the most famous anchorman was Walter Cronkite, who has Scottish, Dutch, and German roots.[110]

Perhaps the most recognizable American is Hugh (Malcolm) Downs, the American television personality who is a Wallace awardee. Mr. Downs is also a member of Saint Andrew's Society of the State of New York and addressed its annual dinner wearing his kilt. Raymond Burr, better known to millions as Perry Mason, was an American with Grant and Wallace ancestors. David McCallum, born in Glasgow, starred in *The Man From U.N.C.L.E.* Ian

Richardson, an Edinburgh native, has been seen often on television and in the theater.[111] Johnny Carson, longtime host of the *Tonight* show, is almost certainly of Scotch-Irish descent.[112] His successor as *Tonight*'s host is Jay Leno (James Douglas Muir Leno), whose mother was born in Scotland.[113] One of America's most enduring comediennes is the Scottish-American Phyllis Diller.

The pioneer of American educational television and founding president of the Public Broadcasting Service (PBS) was Hartford N. Gunn, Jr., a New Yorker of Scottish descent.[114] The standard for quality in children's educational television has been set by Mr. Rogers (Fred Rogers) of Pittsburgh, who is of Scotch-Irish ancestry and an ordained Presbyterian minister.[115] The most famous television chef and exponent of French cooking is Julia Child, born of Scottish ancestry as Julia McWilliams, in California. Her programs on public television have brought the cuisine of France to the American masses.[116]

Public broadcasting's most famous newsman is Robert MacNeil, born in Canada and a Wallace awardee. The creator of *The Prairie Home Companion*, the most popular program in the history of American public radio and of its mythical town, Lake Wobegon, is the Scottish-American Garrison Keillor.[117] *The Thistle and Shamrock*, a weekly radio program of Celtic music, is produced in Scotland by Fiona Ritchie and is heard in over two hundred American cities. It is American public radio's fourth most popular program.[118]

In Canada, television personalities of Scottish ancestry include Joyce Davidson, Ross MacLean, and the late Gordon Sinclair.[119] Sinclair was known in particular for his advocacy of harmonious relations between the United States and Canada.

Dance

The beginnings of modern dance are credited, in large measure, to Isadora Duncan (1878–1927), a Scottish-American from San Fransisco. Ms. Duncan liberated dancing by her revolutionary methods and it was said of her, "she invented herself as an icon and gained immortality."[120] In recent years other Scottish-Americans have been influential in the dance. Teena McConnell has been a prime soloist with the New York City Ballet.[121] Maria Tallchief, of American-Indian and Scotch-Irish heritage, preceded her there.[122] A successor in the New York company was Gelsey Kirkland, who later switched to the American Ballet Company and started a spectacular partnership with Mikhail Baryshnikov. Ms. Kirkland, the daughter of writer-producer Jack Kirkland, may have been the greatest Giselle ever. Sir Kenneth MacMillan (1929–1992), born in Dunfermline, was famous as a choreographer, particularly for his *Romeo and Juliet*. He had been director of the Royal Ballet and an artistic associate of the American Ballet Theater.[123]

The foremost modern dancer in America was Martha Graham (1894–1991), born in Pittsburgh of Scottish descent,[124] who was still working in her nineties. As a child she danced up the aisle of the local Presbyterian church. In 1987 Nureyev and Baryshnikov danced her *Appalachian Spring* together in New York, and later, a glittering audience watched a film of Miss Graham dancing, a half century before. Her influence on modern dance and on the choreography of the Broadway musical is incalculable.[125]

The Theatre

Every August the city of Edinburgh produces what has become the world's largest cultural extravaganza, the Edinburgh Festival. The official show features theater and music from all over the world, and the overflowing Fringe alone had nine hundred shows in 1985.[126]

Scots have long been attracted to the theater. In the nineteenth century an American, Steele MacKaye (1842–1894), became its "Renaissance man." He was a playwright, the founder of the American Academy of Dramatic Art, and the first American to play Hamlet in London. MacKaye held one hundred patents, including the one for folding theater seats, and founded the Lyceum and St. James theaters in New York. In 1893 he built the world's biggest theater in Chicago.[127]

As this is written the most successful theatrical producer in London and New York is Cameron Mackintosh, who has brought to the stage *Cats*, *Les Miserables*, and *The Phantom of the Opera*. Despite his ethnic name, he is only one-fourth Scottish, the rest being English, French, and Italian.[128] A decade or so ago the theater critics of both leading New York newspapers were Scottish, Douglas Watt of the *Daily News* and Walter Kerr of the *Times*. In 1990 a gala party was held to honor Kerr on the occasion of renaming a theater after him the Walter Kerr Theatre. Ivor Brown (1891–1974) and William Archer (1856–1924) were two of the most influential critics in the history of the British theater. Archer was also the translator of Ibsen.[129]

Leading playwrights of four different nations have claimed Scottish ancestry. Molière (1622–1673), often referred to as the greatest of French writers, professed Scottish roots.[130] Norway's foremost playwright and one of the greatest dramatists of all time was Henrik Ibsen, who had Scottish ancestors.[131] Britain's great modern dramatist, George Bernard Shaw (1856–1950), was an Irishman of Scottish ancestry, descended from a Scottish soldier who fought at the Battle of the Boyne and founded the Shaws of Ireland. George Bernard Shaw is said to have joined the Clan MacPherson Association.[132] Noel Coward (1899–1973), whom the *New Statesman* called "a national treasure" and "demonstrably the greatest living English playwright," was the author of some of this century's best plays, including *Blythe Spirit* and *Private Lives*. His mother was a member of the Scottish Veitch family.[133]

One of the most important figures in the history of the theater was Laurence Kerr Olivier (Lord Olivier; 1907–1989). He was one of the great classical actors, a motion picture star of the first magnitude, a director of prominence, and the founder of the National Theatre of Britain. As a boy Olivier wore a Kerr tartan kilt as a customary Sunday outfit, but neither he nor his father, who bore the same name, could precisely trace their Scottish connection.[134]

Bea Lillie (1894–1989) was known as "the funniest woman in the world." Although her career was spent mostly in the West End and on Broadway, she was actually born in Canada of Ulster ancestry, and was related to George Bernard Shaw.[135] Recently Scotland has sent Jamie Ross, a cousin of the movie star Sean Connery, to Broadway to play the male lead in *Woman of the Year*.[136] Another Scottish native, Lindsay Duncan, starred in *Les Liasons Dangereuses* in both London and New York.[137] Scottish-born Nicol Williamson has starred on the Broadway and West End stages.[138]

Walter Huston (1884–1950), a legendary American Broadway performer, father of director John Huston and grandfather of movie star Anjelica Huston, was born in Canada of Scottish and Scotch-Irish parents.[139] Also from Canada came the magician Doug Henning, creator of *The Magic Show* on Broadway. Henning is related to Sir Walter Scott.[140]

Bil Baird (d. 1987) the puppeteer who broke several box-office records on Broadway, was of Scottish ancestry. Baird enchanted millions on television with his "little ones" and trained a generation of puppeteers, including Jim Henson, creator of the Muppets.[141]

John Raitt, one of the greatest singers in Broadway history, created the roles of Billy Bigelow in *Carousel* (1945) and Sid Sorokin in *The*

Pajama Game (1954). He is descended from a Scottish Presbyterian minister.[142] Ethel Merman (1908?–1984), "Queen of the Musicals" on Broadway, was born Ethel Zimmerman to German and Scottish parents. Her hit shows included Cole Porter's *Anything Goes* and Irving Berlin's *Annie Get Your Gun*, as well as *Gypsy*, with music by Jule Styne and Stephen Sondheim. Over the years she introduced many songs of these composers which have since become standards. Her fame was assured at age twenty-one, when she stopped the show *Girl Crazy*, in 1930, by belting out George Gershwin's "I Got Rhythm."[143]

Cinema

One of the most influential of all Americans was Walt Disney (1901–1966) the creator of Mickey Mouse, Donald Duck, and so much more. His 1938 film *Snow White* was the first feature-length animated cartoon, and it immediately made him a major figure in entertainment. Disney, of partly Scottish ancestry, won an incredible twenty Academy Awards, more than any other person.[144] James MacDonald (1906–1991), born in Dundee, did sound effects and voice-overs for Disney for forty years, including the speeded-up track of the chipmunks. Near the end he was the voice of the world's most famous cartoon character, Mickey Mouse.[145] Every day an estimated five hundred million people in eighty countries around the world watch Tom and Jerry, Huckleberry Hound, the Flintstones, and other cartoon creations of the Scottish-American Bill Hanna and his Italian-American partner Joseph Barbera. Hanna-Barbera has produced almost thirty movies and more than one hundred cartoon series.[146]

One of America's most revered filmmakers was John Huston (1906–1987), the director of *Treasure of the Sierra Madre* and *The Maltese Falcon*. Huston won an Academy Award as director of *Sierra Madre* and directed his father, Walter Huston, mentioned in the section on the theater, to another Oscar in the same film. Near the end of his long career he directed his daughter, Anjelica Huston, to an Academy Award in *Prizzi's Honor*.[147] Mel Gibson, born in New York and raised in Australia, won an Academy Award in 1996 as best director for his Scottish epic *Braveheart*, depicting the life of Sir William Wallace. Gibson accepted the award wearing a vest in his family's Buchanan tartan.

James Cameron, born in Canada, was the director of *The Terminator* (1984), *Aliens* (1986), and *Terminator 2: Judgment Day* (1991), which together grossed over three hundred million dollars. In 1992 Cameron signed a unique five-hundred-million-dollar contract with 20th Century Fox.[148]

Born in Kilmarnock and founder of the Canadian National Film Board, John Grierson (1898–1972) became the father of documentary films. Grierson was the leader of the documentary movement and actually coined the word *documentary* himself.[149] He was joined almost immediately by another Scottish filmmaker, Norman McLaren, who helped make the National Film Board into an institution as much a part of Canada as hockey or the mounties.[150]

Alexander Mackendrick (1912–1993) was born in Boston to Scottish parents and educated in Glasgow. He was the director of *Sweet Smell of Success, The Man in the White Suit, The Ladykillers,* and *Whisky Galore,* known in America as *Tight Little Island.*[151] Bill Forsyth, the "one man Scottish movie industry," is the writer and director of *Gregory's Girl, Local Hero,* and *Housekeeping.* Charles Crichton, a Briton with roots in Ayr and Dundee, is best known as the director of *The Lavender Hill Mob* in 1951. In 1989 he was nominated for two Academy Awards as director and coauthor of *A Fish Called Wanda* at age seventy-eight.[152]

The Scottish nation has produced a host of movie stars, many from Britain. Ronald Colman (1891–1958) was born in England of Scottish ancestry. Colman won the Academy Award as best actor in 1947 for his role in *A Double Life.*[153] David Niven (James David Graham Niven; 1910–1983) was born in Kirriemuir and buried in Switzerland by a Scottish minister. He is best remembered for his role in *Around the World in Eighty Days,* and in 1958 won the Academy Award for best actor in *Separate Tables.*[154] Michael Rennie (1909–1971) was born in England to a Scottish father.[155] Alastair Sim (1900–1976) became perhaps the greatest *Christmas Carol* Scrooge. Born in Edinburgh, he is best remembered for his comedy in *The Lavender Hill Mob, The Green Man,* and *The Bells of St. Trinian's.* He was also successful as a Shakespearean actor.[156]

Sir Alec Guinness (b. 1914) won the Academy Award in 1957 for his performance in *Bridge on the River Kwai.* He is thought of as one of the best actors of his time. He is believed to be the son of Andrew Geddes, a Scottish banker.[157] Peter O'Toole (b. 1932), who starred as *Lawrence of Arabia,* was born in Ireland to an Irish father and a

Scottish mother.[158] Gordon Jackson, born in Glasgow and already mentioned as a television star, was more often seen in such Scottish films as *Whisky Galore* and *Tunes of Glory*.

The creator of the film version of James Bond is Sean Connery, born in Edinburgh in 1930 of Scottish and Irish ancestry. Connery won the Academy Award for best supporting actor in 1987 for his role in *The Untouchables*.[159] Ian Charleson (1950–1990), a native of Edinburgh, played the Scottish hero Eric Liddell in *Chariots of Fire* in 1981.[160] Deborah Kerr (b. 1921) who created the motion picture version of Anna in *The King and I* was born in Helensburgh.[161] Moira Shearer (b. 1926) of Dunfermline was the ballerina who played the lead in *The Red Shoes*, a film that has not lost its popularity since it was made in 1948.[162] British actor Hugh Grant is a Grant of Rothiemurchas.[163] Tom Conti, born in Scotland of partly Italian ancestry, has starred in film as well as in the theaters of New York and London.

In the United States, the invention of the telephone by Graham Bell was portrayed in 1941 by Don Ameche (1908–1993), of partly Scotch-Irish ancestry, and made him famous.[164] Forty-four years later Ameche received an Oscar as best supporting actor in *Cocoon*. Gene Autry (b. 1907), the cowboy star, is also partly Scottish.[165] Perhaps the greatest western hero was John Wayne (1907–1979), born of Scottish ancestry as Marion Michael Morrison.[166] Wayne received an Academy Award as best actor in 1969 for his performance in *True Grit*. Clint Eastwood (b. 1930), also Scottish, continues as an exponent of the Old West.[167] Montgomery Clift (1920–1966) was another American actor of Scottish Presbyterian ancestry.[168]

James (Maitland) Stewart (b. 1908) the son of a Scottish hardware store owner in Indiana, Pennsylvania, has had a long and extremely successful career in Hollywood.[169] He won the Academy Award as best actor in 1940 in *The Philadelphia Story*, but is better known for *It's a Wonderful Life* and *Rear Window*. Stewart Granger (1913–1993), born in London of Scottish ancestry, was also christened James Stewart, but found his name preempted in Hollywood by the other James Stewart.[170]

Tough guys Alan Ladd (1913–1964) and Robert Mitchum (b. 1917) are also Scottish-Americans.[171] The folk singer Burl Ives (b. 1909) mentioned previously in this chapter, won an Oscar as best supporting actor in *The Big Country* in 1958. Mickey Rooney (b. 1920), who has had a half-century as a star, was born in Brooklyn of Scottish ancestry as Joe Yule, Jr.[172] Rod Steiger (b. 1925) of Scottish, French, and German ancestry, won the 1967 Academy Award for best actor in *In the Heat of the Night*.[173]

George C. (for Campbell) Scott (b. 1927) has been called America's most versatile actor and is of Scottish descent.[174] He was awarded the 1970 Academy Award for best actor in *Patton* but refused it. Charlton Heston, who often wears his grandfather's kilt, won the 1959 Oscar for best actor in *Ben Hur*. Cliff Robertson (b. 1925) has stated publicly that winning the Wallace Award meant more to him than the Academy Award he won in 1968 for his role in *Charly*.[175] Warren Beatty (b. 1937) better known as an actor, won the 1985 Academy Award as best director for *Reds*. His mother is a MacLean and his sister is Shirley MacLaine.[176] Bruce Dern (b. 1936) is, through his mother, a member of the MacLeish family that founded the Carson Pirie Scott department store chain in Chicago and is the great-nephew of the poet Archibald MacLeish.[177] Tom Selleck (b. 1945) also has Scottish ancestry[178] as does Robert Redford (b. 1937).

The success of Scottish-American women in the movies has been as pronounced as that of Scottish-American men. Lillian Gish (1893–1993), her mother a McConnell, was the preeminent actress of the silent film era.[179] Greer Garson (1908–1996) a Wallace awardee, received the Academy Award for best actress in 1942 for *Mrs. Miniver*. Barbara Stanwyck (1907–1990) was born in Brooklyn as Ruby Stevens, of Scotch-Irish descent. Her most famous film was *Stella Dallas* (1937), and although she was nominated as best actress four times she never won. Instead she took another distinction, as the nation's highest-paid woman in 1944.[180] Singer-actress Jeanette MacDonald (1903–1965) was of Scottish Presbyterian stock.[181]

Several of the most famous movie "goddesses" have had Scottish roots. Marilyn Monroe (1926–1962) was Scottish on her mother's side and claimed descent from President Monroe. Her probable real father was likely Scottish also, as his name was Gifford.[182] Jane Russell (b. 1921) is Scottish on both sides of her ancestry. The Russells came from Inverness.[183] The *femme fatale* Ava Gardner (1922–1990) was Scottish on her mother's side.[184] Elizabeth Taylor (b. 1932) is of partly Scotch-Irish descent and won Academy Awards as best actress in both *Butterfield 8* (1960) and *Who's Afraid of Virginia Woolf?* (1966).[185]

Shirley MacLaine (Shirley Beaty; b. 1934), the sister of Warren Beatty, won an Oscar in 1983 as best actress for her role in *Terms of Endearment*. Another Scottish-American actress, Faye Dunaway (b.

1941) won the award for best actress in 1976 for her performance in *Network*.[186] Ali MacGraw (b. 1938), the star of *Love Story*, is also Scottish.[187]

The only performer to win four Academy Awards as best actor or actress is Katharine Hepburn (b. 1907) who was cited for *Morning Glory* (1932–1933), *Guess Who's Coming to Dinner* (1967), *The Lion in Winter* (1968), and *On Golden Pond* (1981).[188] Audrey Hepburn (1929–1993), who won an Oscar for best actress for her role in *Roman Holiday* (1953), was born in Holland to a father who was descended from James Hepburn, fourth earl of Bothwell, one of the husbands of Mary, Queen of Scots.[189]

Among the recent winners is the half-Scottish[190] Dianne Wiest, who was best supporting actress in *Hannah and Her Sisters* (1986). Anjelica Huston, daughter of John Huston and granddaughter of Walter Huston, was best supporting actress in *Prizzi's Honor* (1985).

11

Sports

The Scots have always been interested in sports and have invented or developed several of the most important games played throughout the world today. But the Scottish race is not as exceptionally good at playing games as it is in some of the other pursuits which have been shown here. In Victorian America, for instance, dozens of Caledonian Games, a combination of Scottish athletic events and American summer festival, were held in all parts of the country. The games were so successful that they can be said to have been virtually the first mass spectator sporting events in the United States. However, almost from the beginning, Irishmen, blacks, and other non-Scots competed and did most of the winning.[1] Nevertheless, the mark of the Scots in sports is significant.

ARCHERY

The oldest archery club in Britain, probably the oldest sporting club in Europe, is the Kilwinning Archers, which has been in existence for half a millenium.[2]

AUTOMOBILE RACING

The Scots have made an unusually distinguished contribution to automobile racing. The summit of this achievement were the years between 1963 and 1973, when two Scots, Jim Clark and Jackie Stewart, won almost half of the world Grand Prix championships. Jim Clark (1936–1968), the son of a Fifeshire farmer, is thought by many to have been the greatest driver in history and won twenty-five Grand Prix races. Clark won the world Grand Prix championship in 1963, capturing seven of ten races. In 1965 he repeated as Grand Prix champion and won the Indianapolis 500 as well. He was killed in an accident in 1968.[3]

Jackie Stewart, born in Dumbartonshire in 1939, retired as world champion in 1973. He won the Grand Prix championship in 1969, 1971, and 1973, and overall won an astonishing twenty-seven Grand Prix races in ninety-nine starts, beating the previous record established by his countryman, Jim Clark.[4]

Scottish achievement in this sport is long-standing and continues to the present. Sir Malcolm Campbell (1885–1948) and his son Donald Malcolm Campbell (1921–1967) set land records for speed from 146 miles per hour in 1924 to 403 miles per hour in 1964. In addition, they set water speed records from 129 miles per hour in 1937 to 260 miles per hour in 1959.[5] Ron Flockhart (1924–1962) was a native of Edinburgh and won at Le Mans in 1956 and 1957.[6] In 1959 Bruce Leslie McLaren (1937–1970) of New Zealand became, at age twenty-two, the youngest Grand Prix winner ever.[7]

Johnny Rutherford (John Sherman Rutherford III) an American of Scottish descent,[8] won the Indianapolis 500 in 1974, 1976, and 1980. Jim Crawford of Scotland raced in the 1988 Indianapolis 500 despite the pain of six screws that held his ankle together, one of which came loose and almost pierced his skin. He finished sixth but was in second place with only six laps to go when a tire blew out.[9]

BALLOONING

Malcolm S. Forbes, previously mentioned as publisher of *Forbes* magazine, became the first person ever to cross the North American continent in a hot air balloon when he went from Coos Bay, Oregon, on October 4, 1973, to the Chesapeake Bay near Gwynn Island, Virginia, landing on November 6 of the same year.[10]

BASEBALL

Americans of Scottish descent are extremely well represented in America's national game. According to the National Baseball Hall of Fame the two greatest percentage hitters in history, Ty Cobb (.367) and Rogers Hornsby (.358), as well as the three winningest pitchers, Cy Young (509), Walter Johnson (413), and Grover Alexander (374), were all of partly Scottish ancestry.[11] Altogether, 37 of the 174 players inducted into the Hall of Fame through 1989, or about 21 percent, had some Scottish ancestry.[12] Since Scottish-Americans are only about 4.4 percent of the total U.S. population, they are thus overrepresented by almost five times.

However, things are not quite as good as they once were. Only seven of the Scottish-American inductees played primarily after 1950, albeit they played with distinction. Pitcher Don Drysdale (Donald Scott Drysdale; 1936–1993) was the workhorse of the Brooklyn and Los Angeles Dodger staffs in the 1950s and 1960s.[13] Catfish Hunter (James Augustus Hunter; b. 1946), elected to the Hall of Fame in 1987, was a leader of the free-agent movement and the first player to sign a multi-million-dollar contract.[14]

Despite a career shortened by war and injuries and usually playing for hopeless teams, Ralph (McPherran) Kiner (b. 1922) became the second-best home run hitter in history in home runs per times at bat, after Babe Ruth, and won seven straight National League home run championships (1946–1952) with the then lowly Pittsburgh Pirates. Kiner is of Pennsylvania Dutch and Scotch-Irish ancestry.[15] Harmon Killebrew ranks just after Kiner and Ruth in career home runs per times at bat. Duke Snider was one of New York City's three great center fielders during that city's glorious 1950s. Early Wynn and Bob Lemon were mainstays of the awesome Cleveland pitching staff in the same decade.[16]

Though not yet in the Hall of Fame, Keith Hernandez is considered by many to be the best fielding first baseman of recent times and was also one of the game's most consistent hitters. Hernandez, of Spanish and Scottish ancestry, won the Most Valuable Player Award in 1979.[17] What is considered by many to have been baseball's most historic hit was delivered by Bobby Thomson (Robert Brown Thomson; b. 1923). On October 3, 1951, Thomson's three-run homer for the New York Giants in their last turn at bat bested the Brooklyn Dodgers for the National League pennant by one run. He is one of only nine players born in Scotland.[18]

BASKETBALL

The inventor of basketball was Dr. James Naismith (1861–1939), a Scottish-Canadian who was educated as a Presbyterian minister. Naismith devised the game as a winter sport in 1891 while working at a college in Springfield, Massachusetts, as a physical education instructor.[19] Another Scottish-Canadian-American, the sculptor Tait McKenzie, helped perfect the game.[20] Steve Kerr, of the record-breaking Chicago Bulls, is the career leader in three-point field-goal percentage (48 percent).

BICYCLE RACING

Greg LeMond, an American of largely Scotch-Irish ancestry, won the Tour de France for the third time in 1990.[21] Robert Millar, a Scot with the Peugeot team, was fourth overall in the 1984 Tour de France.[22]

BOXING

The sport of boxing is governed by a set of rules written under the direction of an enthusiast, the marquess of Queensberry, John Sholto Douglas (1844–1900), of the old Scottish family.[23] In 1950 an Associated Press poll rated heavyweight Jack Dempsey (1895–1983), whose twenty-one first-round knockouts were the most ever, as the "greatest fighter of the half century." Dempsey was an American of Irish, Scotch-Irish, and Cherokee ancestry.[24] Max Baer, heavyweight champion of the world from 1934 to 1935, wore the Star of David on his trunks to win Jewish fans but was actually of German and Scottish parentage.[25]

Benny Lynch (1913–1946) won Scotland's first world boxing title, holding the flyweight championship from 1935 to 1938. Jacky Paterson (1920–1966) of Ayrshire won the world flyweight championship in 1943. Paterson also holds the record for the world's quickest knockout, eight seconds into a championship match.[26] Ken Buchanan, the Scot who fought in trunks made in the beautiful tartan of his clan, was lightweight champion of the world in 1970.[27] Jim Watt, who insisted on fighting in his native Glasgow, followed Buchanan as lightweight champion in 1979.[28]

CANOEING

The pioneer of canoeing as a sport was John MacGregor (1825–1892), born in England to Scottish parents, who paddled in many lands and wrote and lectured extensively on his travels. On one of his journeys MacGregor was captured by hostile Arabs while canoeing on the River Jordan. His canoe, the *Rob Roy*, is on exhibit in Tel Aviv, Israel.[29]

CURLING

Curling, a sort of bowling on ice, was organized, if not invented, in Scotland and is played mainly indoors in Scotland, Canada, and the northern United States.[30]

FOOTBALL (SOCCER)

The enthusiasm for association football (soccer) in Scotland borders on religious fervor and can be demonstrated by the following joke about a man standing on a bridge in Glasgow, about to jump in a suicide attempt. A bystander pleads, "Stop, for the sake of yer family!" But the man replies, "I have nae family." The bystander then entreats, "Then stop for the sake of the Rangers!" But the reply is meekly, "I dinnae support the Rangers." The onlooker magnanimously states, "Well, I'm no prejudiced, stop for the sake of Celtic!" But the depressed man can only reply, "I dinnae support Celtic either." Finally exasperated, the bystander shrugs, "Och weel then, joomp, ye bluidy atheist!"[31]

Despite the claims of golf and curling, "fitba" is the real national sport of Scotland. In fact, from 1910 to 1950 Hampden Park, in Glasgow, capacity 149,000, was the largest football stadium in the world.[32] Although similar games have been played for millennia, the structure of the world's favorite game as it is played today was shaped to a considerable degree in Scotland. Indeed, the first clear pictorial representation of soccer is a print from Edinburgh dated 1672–1673.[33] In the 1870s, during the sport's formal beginnings, the Scottish Football Association's cup attracted more teams than did that of the English Football Association. And the famous Queen's Park team of Glasgow dominated the sport for the first fourteen years of play. In fact, the "father of the league" was William McGregor who, in 1888, wrote to the strongest clubs suggesting that the league be formed. The suggestion was accepted and twelve clubs made up the original football league for the 1888–1889 season.[34] The modern passing game also developed in Scotland.[35]

Although Scotland is one of the smallest countries in today's international soccer scene, it still finds the resources to compete, especially against its *auld enemy,* England. The 0–0 draw between the two countries on St. Andrew's Day 1872 was the sport's first international match.[36] Through 1980 Scotland had played England a total of ninety-three times, and despite a ten-to-one population disadvantage had won an amazing thirty-seven times to England's thirty-four.[37]

In a team sport such as football it is difficult for individuals to stand out and even harder to make comparisons. Yet several must be mentioned as Scottish stars. Dave MacKay and Gordon Strachan are certainly two of the greatest footballers. Others are Billy Bremner,

John Greig, Billy McNeill, Alan Morton, George Young, Jimmy Johnston, and Graeme Souness.[38] Manchester United paid the equivalent of 850,000 dollars, a record at the time, as a transfer fee to obtain the services of Gordon McQueen in 1978.[39] Alex James (1902–1953) was a star of the Arsenal and Scottish international teams.[40] Ted McDougal scored nine goals during the 1971 F.A. Cup, breaking a record set in 1928.[41] Dennis Law at one time held the record for most caps by a Scottish player, and Jim Baxter was a great wing-half for the Glasgow Rangers.[42]

In 1967 the legendary manager Jock Stein (1922–1985) directed Celtic to become the first British side ever to take the European Cup.[43] Kenny Dalglish, a native of Glasgow, has won more caps than any player in Scottish history and was voted the best player in England in three different years. His 1986 Liverpool team, for which he both played and managed, won the third "double" of the twentieth century, winning both the championship of the First Division and the F.A. Cup, the final match after lengthy playoffs.[44]

FOOTBALL (AMERICAN)

There is no evidence that Scottish-Americans have made a significant contribution to the development of football. Nevertheless, Otto Graham, of German and Scotch-Irish ancestry,[45] was arguably the best football player who ever played. As a passer, Graham ranks first among all quarterbacks, with 8.98 yards gained per attempt.[46] For ten successive years (1946–1955), his entire professional career, Graham steered the Cleveland Browns to the final game of the season, winning seven championships.[47]

GOLF

Although the origins of golf are obscure, it seems likely that it evolved from a variety of European club games.[48] Many think that Scotland imported something like golf from the Low Countries with the large Flemish immigration of the Middle Ages. There is a Dutch word, *kolf*, meaning a club, which is often mentioned in support of this position. But there is also a Scottish word, *gouff*, meaning "to strike or hit."[49] Whatever the case, certainly golf as we know it began in Scotland and was already popular with the people of St. Andrews by 1411, when the university was founded there.[50]

Alistair Cooke, the journalist and broadcaster, himself a golfer, takes us through the early development and philosophy of golf and

Scotland: "In the fifteenth century it (golf) posed a major threat to the national defense, causing ordinary citizens who should have been off at archery practice to spend all their spare time trying to hit the damn thing straight. James II of Scotland was sufficiently alarmed at the neglect of archery to put out, in 1457, a decree commanding 'golfe to be utterly cryed down and not to be used!' It was too late. James did not recognize what every other Scot knew in his bones: that golf was just what the Scottish character had been searching for for centuries. Namely, a method of self-torture disguised as a game, which would entrap irreligious youths into the principles of what was to become known first as Calvinism and then... golf. The main tenets of this faith are that life is grim and uncomfortable and that human vanity cannot prevail."[51]

Things took a turn for the better when the more enlightened King James IV bought his own equipment in 1502,[52] and the game really got going in 1603 when James VI became James I of England and moved south, taking along his sticks.[53] By 1608 Scottish noblemen had already laid out a course near Blackheath in the land of the Saxons.[54]

Of course, golf, has prospered greatly since those early days and has become an international sport. The oldest permanent golf club in North America was the Royal Montreal Golf Club, established in 1873.[55] Who has the oldest golf course and club in the United States is in dispute, but certainly a course was laid out in 1886 in the Scottish community of Sarasota, Florida, by J. Hamilton Gillespie.[56] The St. Andrew's Golf Club at Hastings-on-Hudson, New York, claims to be the oldest golf club in the United States. It was founded by John Reid, a native of Dunfermline, with the backing of another immigrant from Dunfermline, Andrew Carnegie, in 1888.[57] At any rate, from small beginnings, millions now play the old Scottish game over eleven thousand North American courses covering more than a million acres.

Scots dominated play throughout the nineteenth century, and the names of Tom Morris (Senior and Junior), Allan Robertson, Willie Park, Jamie Anderson, Robert Ferguson, and James Braid stand out. In this century, first Englishmen and then Americans have dominated the game, and the influence of Scottish players has waned. The last native Scot to win the British Open was Tommy Armour, in 1931. Today champions come from countries as diverse as Spain and South Africa, Germany, and Australia. Many of the more famous players still have Scottish names at least, and recent years have featured such as Bean, Pate, Graham, Irwin, Reid, McCumber, and Stewart. But the greatest golfers usually bear names indicative of other origins. Even Tom Watson, one of the best ever, cannot be claimed as Scottish despite his name, as his ancestry is not certain.[58]

Still, there are some of the Scottish nation who continue to excel. Arnold Palmer, the first golfer to win a million dollars and the player whose charging style made golf a big money game, is of Scotch-Irish ancestry.[59] Peter Thomson, an Australian golfer of Scottish descent,[60] won the British Open five times and was second three times. Sandy Lyle, an English-born Briton of Scottish parentage, stood as the best golfer in the world after having won the Masters in 1988. Lyle insists on being referred to as a Scot and impressed a vast television audience by participating in the 1989 Masters coat-exchanging ceremony wearing a kilt.[61]

Colin Montgomerie is a native Scot who finished tied for the U.S. Open Championship in 1994, but lost a three-way playoff the next day. In 1995 Montgomerie birdied the last three holes to tie for the PGA championship, but again, he lost the playoff.[62] Pamela Wright, a native of Scotland, was rookie-of-the-year in 1989 on the LPGA tour.[63] Alan Shepard, the Scottish-American astronaut, hit the first golf shot on the moon, a one-handed six iron that traveled over two hundred yards.[64]

HOCKEY

An increasingly important sport around the world, Canada's national game was brought to North America from the Scottish Highlands where shinty, or shinnie, *camanachd* in Gaelic, is the most popular Celtic-originated pastime. Shinty, a field game using sticks and a wooden ball, was played on ice in Canada before the word *hockey* was used.[65]

The overwhelming majority of professional hockey players are Canadians by birth, and Scottish-Canadians are well represented as players in the National Hockey League, which has teams in both Canada and the United States. A random glance at the surnames of 275 players in two seasons shows that about 13 percent of the players have Scottish surnames, versus the approximately 10 percent representation of Scottish family names in Canada's general population.[66]

Two Scottish Canadians stand out in hockey. Clarence Sutherland Campbell (1905–1984) was a Rhodes scholar who wore the kilt on occasion and served as a prosecutor of Nazis at Nuremburg. Campbell was president of the National Hockey League from 1946 to 1977, the longest reign in any professional sport. During his tenure he supervised the league's expansion from six to eighteen teams.[67]

Bobby Orr (Robert Gordon Orr) whose ancestors came to Canada from Ballymena, Ulster,[68] was arguably the greatest player in the history of hockey. There is no doubt that he was the greatest defenseman, as his rushing style completely redefined the position, turning it into a partly offensive one. Before Orr no defenseman had ever scored more than twenty goals in a season. But Bobby Orr led the league in scoring twice, the only defenseman ever to do so, led in assists four times, was judged most valuable player three times, and best defenseman eight consecutive years. His career was cut short by injuries in 1978, at age thirty.[69]

HOPSCOTCH

The children's street game, played far and wide, is called "peevers" in Scotland.

HORSE RACING

The origins of modern horse racing are, to some extent, to be found in Scotland, where the sport's oldest event, the Lanark Silver Bell, instituted by King William the Lion in the twelfth century, is still being run annually.[70] By the sixteenth century the sport had become popular and continued to enjoy royal patronage. King James IV was a royal patron and Queen Mary began the races at Haddington and Lamington.[71] Then, when James VI of Scots became James I of England, he brought his love of the turf with him, along with his golf clubs, and during his reign the races began at Croyden, Enfield, Newmarket, and Epsom. James's grandson, Charles II, was an avid breeder and is known as "the father of the British turf" from which all modern racing follows.[72]

In America certain Scots have left a mark on racing. In 1944 James Donn, Sr., an immigrant florist from Lanark, bought Gulfstream Park racetrack in Florida and made it a huge success with many innovations. John W. Galbreath (1897–1988) was a noted American breeder and distinguished himself as the only owner to win both the Epsom and Kentucky Derbys.[73]

Donald John MacBeth was the twelfth-best earning jockey in American racing history and would have ranked much higher had he not died prematurely in 1987 at age thirty-seven. In a sport known for its shady characters, MacBeth was noted for his integrity and class. He once gave a handful of grass to a dying horse because, as he said, "I knew it was the last thing the horse would ever see and I wanted it to be an act of kindness." He was widely mourned and was buried with a Presbyterian service in his hometown in Canada.[74]

Barbara Jo Rubin, of Jewish, Scottish, and other mixed ancestry, was the first female professional jockey to ride a winning horse.[75] John Campbell, a native of Ailsa Craig, Ontario, is the only American harness racing driver to win more than one hundred million dollars in purse money.[76]

ICE SKATING

The earliest ice skating club in the world was the Edinburgh Skating Club, founded in 1742.[77]

LAWN BOWLING, OR BOWLING-ON-THE-GREEN, OR LAWN BOWLS

Although the game is both English and Scottish in origin, it was in Scotland that a code of laws was developed in the mid-nineteenth century, rescuing the sport from near extinction. The Scots perfected the lush, level green and their enthusiasm for the game revived it. Scottish emigrants then made the game international, taking it with them wherever they went.[78]

MOUNTAINEERING

In addition to the Scottish effort on Mount Everest mentioned on page 16, Francis, Lord Douglas (1847–1865), was one of the party which first conquered the summit of the Matterhorn in 1865. He died in a four-thousand-foot plunge during the descent.[79]

ROWING

The first mention of rowing as a sport is the description of the Scottish king Edgar (1097–1107) being rowed by tributary kings on the River Dee with the king himself as coxswain.[80] Steve Fairbairn (1862–1928) of Australia revolutionized the stroke while at Cambridge University in the 1880s.[81] S. A. Mackenzie of Australia won the single sculls championship at Henley six consecutive years (1957–1962).[82]

RUGBY

This English game, played in Scotland by enthusiastic amateurs, is very popular, especially in the Lowlands. Through 1990 Scotland had won 40 of 106 matches with England, with 17 drawn. In the uniquely important 1990 match Scotland won the Calcutta Cup, the Grand Slam, the Triple Crown, and the Five Nations Championship, all in one match, 13 to 7. Andy Irvine was the first player to score 300 points in international rugby.[83]

SWIMMING

Murray Rose, an Australian of Scottish parentage, set the world 880-yard freestyle record in 1964.[84] R. B. McGregor of Britain set a world record for the 110-yard freestyle in 1966.[85] David Wilkie of Scotland won the gold medal in the 200-meter breaststroke at the 1976 Olympics.[86] The eight Olympic medals won by Dawn Fraser of Australia are the most ever won by any female swimmer.[87] In 1950 William Barnie (1896–1983), a native of Edinburgh, at age fifty-four became the oldest man to swim the English Channel.[88]

TENNIS

Don Budge (b. 1915) is, according to many experts, second only to Bill Tilden as the best tennis player ever. He was the first to gain the Grand Slam when he won in Australia, France, Wimbledon, and Forest Hills, in 1938. His father, Jack Budge, was a soccer star of the famous Glasgow Rangers who moved to California for his health and married the Scottish-American Pearl Kincaid.[89] In 1951 Ken McGregor of Australia became, with Frank Sedgman, half of the only men's doubles team to win the Grand Slam.[90]

Billie Jean (Moffat) King was arguably the greatest women's tennis player of all time. At her retirement, she had been female athlete of the year twice and played in over one hundred Wimbledon singles matches, a record. She was the only woman to rank in the top ten in the United States in seventeen different seasons, winning four United States and six Wimbledon titles, and becoming the first woman athlete to earn over one hundred thousand dollars in a single year. In 1982 she reached the semifinals at Wimbledon for the thirteenth time, an event without parallel, and at age thirty-eight was the oldest women's semifinalist in sixty-two years.[91]

TRACK AND FIELD

The hammer throw and the shot put, standard events in track and field today, were developed at the Scottish Highland Games.[92] Eric Liddell (1902–1945) was a legendary Scottish runner and a devout Presbyterian missionary who refused to run his specialty, the 100 meters, in the 1924 Olympics because the event was held partly on a Sunday. He ran instead in the 400 meters, an event for which he had not trained, yet won the gold medal, setting the then Olympic record of 47.6 seconds. He was the subject of the film *Chariots of Fire.*[93]

Alan Wells of Scotland won the 100-meters championship at the 1980 Olympics.[94] For a half century the most important figure and "guardian" of the Boston Marathon, the "granddaddy" of American athletic events, was a Scot, John Duncan "Jock" Semple.[95] The first international marathon ever held in Vietnam was won by Scottish lawyer, Tim Soutar, in 1992.[96] In 1994 Ffyona Campbell completed an eleven-year, twenty thousand-mile walk, starting and finishing in Scotland, becoming the first woman to walk around the world.[97]

Angus MacAskill (1825–1863) was the world's tallest nonpathological giant ever, at seven feet, nine inches. He was born in Scotland and died in Nova Scotia, and was known everywhere as the Cape Breton Giant. It is said that he could lift one hundred pounds with two fingers and hold this weight for ten minutes at arms length.[98] Donald Dinnie (1837–1916) was another Scottish giant who won eleven thousand medals and much money all over the world. Dinnie once carried two stones weighing a total of 785 pounds over a Scottish bridge, and despite many attempts to carry them back across they are still where he left them in 1860. In his vaudeville act he held fifty-six pounds at arms length for five minutes.[99]

YACHTING

When Scottish-descended skipper Russell Coutts brought home yachting's premier trophy, the America's Cup, to New Zealand in 1995, a third of the country's three million people tuned in to watch the victory party.[100]

American Colonial and Revolutionary Governors of Scottish Birth or Descent

The following is a list of Scottish governors of the American colonies before and during the American Revolution, including their years of service. The sources for the information are noted on the right. The names of governors incumbent during the revolution (1775–1781) are italicized. It should be noted that the years of service cannot be precise, as the various authorities are in some disagreement with each other.

Connecticut
Jonathan Trumbull   (1769–1784)   Raimo

Delaware
John MacKinley   (1775–1777)   Hanna, vol. 1; Black, *Scotland's Mark on America* (hereafter cited as *Mark*)

Georgia
Patrick Graham   (1752–1754)
John Huston   (1774; 1778)   Hanna, vol. 1; Black, *Mark*

William Irwin   (1775)   Hanna, vol. 1
Archibald Bulloch   (1776–1777)   Hanna, vol. 1; Raimo

Florida
George Johnstone   (1763)   Hanna, vol. 1; Black, *Mark, Encyclopaedia Brittanica* (hereafter cited as *EB*)

New Hampshire
William Burnet   (1728–1729)   Raimo
Matthew Thornton   (1775–1776)   Raimo

New Jersey
Robert Barclay   (1682)   Hanna, vol. 1; Ross

Gawen Lawrie	(1684)	Raimo
John Skene	(1685; 1688–1690)	Hanna, vol. 1; Raimo
Lord Neil Campbell	(1686–1687)	Hanna, vol. 1; Raimo; Ross
Andrew Hamilton	(1687–1688; 1691–1698; 1699–1700; 1703)	Hanna, vol. 1; Raimo; Ross
John Hamilton	(1701; 1736–1738; 1746–1747)	Hanna, vol. 1; Raimo
Robert Hunter	(1710–1719)	Raimo
William Burnet	(1720–1728)	Raimo
John Montgomerie	(1728–1731)	Raimo; Black, *Mark*
John Anderson	(1736)	Raimo
William Livingston	(1776–1790)	Hanna, vol. 1; Raimo; Black, *Mark*

New York

Robert Hunter	(1710–1719)	Hanna, vol. 1; Raimo; Black, *Mark*; Ross
William Burnet	(1720–1728)	Hanna, vol. 1; Raimo; Black, *Mark*; Ross
John Montgomerie	(1728–1731)	Hanna, vol. 1; Raimo; Black, *Mark*; Ross
John Hamilton	(1736)	Hanna, vol. 1; Black, *Mark*
Cadwallader Colden	(1760–1765; 1769–1770; 1774–1775)	Hanna, vol. 1; Raimo; Black, *Mark*; Ross
John Murray, earl of Dunmore	(1770–1771)	Hanna, vol. 1; Raimo; Black, *Mark*; Haws
James Robertson	(1780)	Hanna, vol. 1; Black, *Mark*; Ross
Andrew Elliot	(1781–1783)	Raimo; Black, *Mark*

North Carolina

William Drummond	(1663–1667)	Hanna, vol. 1; Raimo, Black, *Mark*
Thomas Pollock	(1712–1714; 1722)	Raimo
Gabriel Johnston	(1734–1752)	Hanna, vol. 1; Raimo; Black, *Mark*; Ross
Matthew Rowan	(1753–1754)	Hanna, vol. 1; Raimo; Black, *Mark*

Arthur Dobbs	(1754–1765)	Raimo
Richard Caswell	(1777–1780)	Raimo
Alexander Martin	(1781–1785)	Hanna, vol. 1; Raimo; Black, *Mark*

Pennsylvania

Andrew Hamilton	(1701–1703)	Hanna, vol. 1; Raimo; Black, *Mark*
Sir William Keith	(1717–1726)	Hanna, vol. 1; Raimo; Black, *Mark*; Ross
Patrick Gordon	(1726–1736)	Hanna, vol. 1; Raimo; Black, *Mark*
James Logan	(1736–1738)	Hanna, vol. 1; Raimo
James Hamilton	(1748–1754; 1759–1763; 1771; 1773)	Hanna, vol. 1; Raimo; Black, *Mark*
Robert Hunter Morris	(1754–1756)	Raimo; Black, *Mark*; Taylor
Joseph Reed	(1778–1781)	Hanna, vol. 1; Black, *Mark*

Rhode Island

| John Cranston | (1678–1680) | Raimo; Taylor |
| Samuel Cranston | (1698–1727) | Taylor |

South Carolina

Joseph Morton	(1682)	Hanna, vol. 1
Richard Kirk	(1684)	Hanna, vol. 1; Black, *Mark*
James Moore	(1719)	Hanna, vol. 1
James Glen	(1743–1756)	Raimo; Black, *Mark*
Lord William Campbell	(1775)	Raimo; Ross
John Rutledge	(1776–1782)	Raimo; Black, *Mark*

Virginia

George Hamilton, earl of Orkney	(1705)	Haws
Robert Hunter	(1707)	Black, *Mark*; Ross; Haws
Alexander Spottswood	(1710–1722)	Hanna, vol. 1; Raimo; EB
Hugh Drysdale	(1722–1726)	

William Gooch	(1727–1749)	Hanna, vol. 1; *EB*
James Blair	(1740–1741)	Raimo; Haws
Robert Dinwiddie	(1751–1758)	Hanna, vol. 1; Raimo; *EB*; Haws
John Campbell, earl of Loudon	(1756–1758)	Hanna, vol. 1; Black, *Mark*; Haws
John Blair	(1758–1768)	Hanna, vol. 1; Raimo; Black, *Mark*; Haws
William Nelson	(1770)	Hanna, vol. 1
John Murray, earl of Dunmore	(1771–1776)	Hanna, vol. 1; Raimo; *EB*; Haws
Patrick Henry	(1776–1779)	Hanna, vol. 1; Raimo; Black, *Mark*
Thomas Jefferson	(1779–1781)	United States Information Service; *EB*
Thomas Nelson	(1781)	Hanna, vol. 1
William Fleming	(1781)	Raimo; Black, *Mark*
David Jameson	(1781)	

Appendix B

Signers of the Declaration of Independence

At least twenty-one of the fifty-six men who risked their lives, fortunes, and sacred honor in signing the Declaration of Independence were of Scottish ancestry, including two native Scots, John Witherspoon and James Wilson. This is a score of about 38 percent, versus the 6.7 percent representation of Scots in the general colonial population in 1790. The primary source for this information is William B. Scott's article in the *Scottish Genealogist* (vol. 20, no. 1), in which he uses two other sources. Signers Clark and Morris have been added to Scott's nineteen names on the respective authorities of Hanna (vol. 1, p. 31) and the St. Andrew's Society (p. 16).

Delaware
George Read
Thomas McKean

Georgia
George Walton

New Hampshire
Josiah Bartlett
Matthew Thornton

New Jersey
Abraham Clark
John Hart
John Witherspoon

New York
Philip Livingston
Lewis Morris

North Carolina
Joseph Hewes
William Hooper

Pennsylvania
George Ross
James Smith
George Taylor
James Wilson

Rhode Island
Stephen Hopkins

South Carolina
Edward Rutledge

Virginia
Benjamin Harrison
Thomas Jefferson
Thomas Nelson, Jr.

Appendix C

American Government Leaders of Scottish Ancestry

There are, of course, thousands of Scottish-Americans who have made significant contributions to the government of the United States and its various state and local administrations. Hundreds of these, if not thousands, are documented in Black, Hanna, Ross, and Taylor, some of whom claim extremely high percentages of American government leaders as Scottish. Here we can only present a few highlights:

In Congress, one of the most distinguished Americans was Sam Rayburn (1882–1961) of Texas, who was elected to the House of Representatives twenty-five consecutive times and served forty-eight years and eight months, both records. He was also Speaker of the House for seventeen of those years, exceeding the previous mark of Henry Clay by a wide margin. Rayburn's ancestry was mostly Scottish.[1]

Jeanette Rankin (1880–1973) congresswoman from Montana, was the granddaughter of Scottish immigrants. In 1917 she became the first woman ever elected to Congress and had the distinction, in both 1917 and 1941, of being the only member to vote against a declaration of war. In the latter year, with the vote against her 388 to 1, she explained, "As a woman I can't go to war and I refuse to send anyone else."[2]

Henry B. Gonzalez (b. 1916) whose mother was Scotch-Irish and Presbyterian, has the distinction of being the first Mexican-American from Texas to be seated in the House of Representatives.[3]

Two of the most revered American senators, one a Yankee and the other a Southerner intent on preserving the Union, were Daniel Webster (1782–1852) and John Caldwell Calhoun (1782–1850), both of whom had Scottish ancestry. They were great orators and debaters, and often opposed each other on the Senate floor.[4]

Among cabinet members, James "Tama Jim" Wilson (1835–1920) stands out as the most influential secretary of agriculture in American history. Wilson, who served for sixteen years, was born in Ayrshire and was the father of scientific agriculture in the United States. In 1897 he took over a small and disorganized U.S. Department of Agriculture, added scientists for conservation and reforestation, and in 1913 left the department a major American institution.[5] Melvin Laird (b. 1922) secretary of defense in 1969, was instrumental as a White House advisor, in naming Gerald Ford as president and Nelson Rockefeller as vice president during the Watergate crisis in 1974, a feat without political precedent.[6]

There have been more than a few Scottish-Americans on the U.S. Supreme Court, including, in recent times, Hugo L. Black (1937–1971),[7] Potter Stewart (1958–1981), a winner of the Wallace Award of the American-Scottish Foundation, and William O. Douglas (1939–1975), the son of a Presbyterian minister. Douglas served for thirty-six years, the longest of any justice.[8] By common consent, the two greatest Supreme Court justices were John Marshall (1801–1835) and Oliver Wendell Holmes (1902–1932), both of whom had Scottish ancestry. Holmes was the son of Oliver Wendell Holmes, the American poet.

Rosa Parks defied the law of Montgomery, Alabama, and was arrested when she refused to yield a seat on a bus to a white person one day in 1955, provoking the world-famous Montgomery bus boycott led by the then unknown Rev. Martin Luther King, Jr., who soon became the most prominent civil rights advocate in the United States. Rosa Parks's great-grandfather was a Scotch-Irish indentured servant imported to Charleston, South Carolina.[9]

Among American diplomats, David Kirkpatrick Este Bruce (1898–1977) had no peers. He was the only man ever to serve as ambassador to all three leading western European nations, serving in Paris, Bonn, and London, and holding the British position for a record eight years. Bruce opened the U.S. liaison office in Peking in 1973 and headed the American delegation to the Paris peace talks on the Vietnam War. In all, he served under six presidents, one of whom, Eisenhower, called him "the best ambassador the United States ever had."[10]

Dean Acheson, of Scottish descent,[11] served as secretary of state from 1949 to 1953, and has been called by James Reston "the key man" of the postwar era. Acheson understood that the United Nations could not contain Russia. While President Truman was disarming America, Acheson was creating the sound programs which would keep the peace but bear other's names: the Marshall Plan and the Truman Doctrine.[12] Writing in the *New York Times Book Review*, Evan Thomas called Acheson, "perhaps the greatest secretary of state ever: coauthor of the Marshall Plan, architect of the Western Alliance—'present at the creation,' as he immodestly entitled his memoirs."[13]

For more information on Scottish figures in politics and government, see appendixes B and D, and chapter 3, "The Creation of the United States of America."

Appendix D

The Presidents of the United States of America

Of the forty-one men who have served as president an astonishing thirty-one have had at least some documented Scottish ancestry. This is a score of more than 75 percent, and when compared with the less than 4.4 percent of the American people in general who are of Scottish descent[1] amounts to an overrepresentation of more than 17 times. Some of these, including Washington, John Quincy Adams, and George Bush, are only remotely descended from Scotland. On the other hand, there have been only three first-generation American presidents and all three, Arthur, Buchanan, and Jackson were Scotch-Irish.[2]

In addition, other presidents not counted as Scottish, such as Lincoln, may very well be so. For example, Lincoln's mother was illegitimate and her ancestry is not known, but she came from a heavily Scotch-Irish district on the frontier. Also, biographer Webb Garrison has suggested that the President's father, Thomas Lincoln, was sterile and that Abraham Lincoln's real father may have been the Scotch-Irish statesman John C. Calhoun.[3]

The following table lists the presidents with the names of those of proven Scottish ancestry italicized. One source for each president's Scottishness is included.

George Washington	Washington
John Adams	
Thomas Jefferson	USIS, p. 7.
James Madison	Hanna, vol. 1, p. 32.
James Monroe	*EB*, vol. 15, p. 756.
John Quincy Adams	I. C. Harris, *Scottish-American*, Sep/Oct 1988.
Andrew Jackson	Remini, Robert. *Andrew Jackson.*
Martin Van Buren	
William Henry Harrison	*American Presidential Families*, 1993, p. 318.
John Tyler	
James Knox Polk	J. Thomson, *Highlander*, Sep 1980.

Zachary Taylor	Leyburn, James: *The Scotch-Irish.*
Millard Fillmore	
Franklin Pierce	
James Buchanan	*EB*, vol. 4, p. 341.
Abraham Lincoln	
Andrew Johnson	Black, *Surnames*, p. 510.
Ulysses S. Grant	Scottish Council for Development
Rutherford B. Hayes	*World Almanac*, 1960, p. 162.
James A. Garfield	
Chester Alan Arthur	Black, *Surnames*, p. 33.
Grover Cleveland	Nevins, Alan. *Grover Cleveland.*
Benjamin Harrison	Hanna, vol. 1, p. 33.
William McKinley	Black, *Surnames*, p. 530.
Theodore Roosevelt	*Scottish Historical Review*, vol. 1, 1904, p. 420.
William Howard Taft	Black, *Surnames*, p. 774.
Woodrow Wilson	*World Almanac*, 1960, p. 162.
Warren G. Harding	*EB*, vol. II, p. 93.
Calvin Coolidge	Feuss, C. M. *Calvin Colidge.*
Herbert C. Hoover	
Franklin Delano Roosevelt	*The Scotsman*, 31 Dec 1941.
Harry S Truman	*World Almanac*, 1960, p. 162.
Dwight David Eisenhower	
John F. Kennedy	
Lyndon Baines Johnson	Dugger, Ronnie, *The Politician.*
Richard M. Nixon	*Interplay*, Sept 1970, p. 23.
Gerald R. Ford	Cannon, James. *Time and Chance*, p. 2.
James Earl Carter	Glad, Betty. *Jimmy Carter.*
Ronald Wilson Reagan	Boyarsky, Bill. *Reagan.*
George Herbert Walker Bush	Steve Lohr, *New York Times*, 5 Jul 1988, p. B6.
William Jefferson Clinton	R. W. Apple, Jr., *New York Times*, 1 Dec 1995, p. A16.

Among the prominent Americans who have campaigned for the presidency unsuccessfully are Stephen A. Douglas, Henry Wallace, Adlai Stevenson, George C. Wallace, John Glenn, George McGovern, Walter Mondale, Alan MacGregor Cranston, Patrick J. Buchanan, and Malcolm S. Forbes, Jr.

Appendix E

Scots in American Religion

Scots were among the pioneers in American religious affairs, particularly on the frontier. Samuel Doak, a graduate of Princeton, was the first minister to settle in Tennessee and Hugh McAden was the first pastor to settle in North Carolina.[1] These men were Scotch-Irish and were part of a mass movement for religion and education that proceeded gradually from the circuit rider, to the log church, to the point where by the end of the eighteenth century there were hundreds of Presbyterian congregations across the Alleghenies.[2] Nor was this enthusiasm confined to the west. In 1816 Joanna Graham Bethune, a native of Scotland, organized the Female Sabbath School Union in New York and is remembered as the mother of Sabbath Schools in America.[3]

Six American denominations, with a membership of over ten million, came into existence through the work of Scots. American Presbyterianism, not surprisingly the first of these, was founded by Francis Makemie, who was born of Scottish parents in Donegal. In 1707, after suffering imprisonment, he won a landmark case establishing freedom of religion.[4]

The Episcopal church in America, as separate from the Church of England, was founded in Scotland. After the American Revolution Samuel Seabury was chosen to be the first American Episcopal bishop and was sent to England for consecration. But Seabury refused to take an oath of allegiance to the king and the English Episcopalians would not accept him. Instead he went to Scotland, where he had studied medicine, and the small but more liberal Scottish Episcopal church consecrated him on November 14, 1784. Thus Seabury became the first overseas bishop, the first American bishop, and the first Anglican bishop owing no allegiance to the crown.[5]

Joseph Smith (1805–1844), the founder of the Mormons in 1827, was of partly Scottish ancestry through an ancestor from Inverness.[6] The Disciples of Christ, also known as the Christian Church, was founded by Alexander Campbell (1788–1866) in 1832. He was born in County Antrim, the son of Thomas Campbell, a Presbyterian minister.[7]

In 1872 Charles Taze Russell (1852–1916), of entirely Scotch-Irish ancestry, founded Jehovah's Witnesses in Pittsburgh.[8] The Christian Scientists were founded by Mary Baker Eddy (1821–1910), of English and Scottish ancestry, in 1879.[9]

Today an American Scot, the Rev. Billy Graham (b. 1918), is probably the world's leading evangelist. He has preached to more people than anyone in history, with crowds as large as one million, in eighty-five countries all over the world. He is called America's Pastor, and has sworn in seven presidents.[10]

For more information on Scottish Americans in religion, see also chapter 3, "The Creation of the United States of America."

Appendix F

Scots in American Education

The Scottish beginnings of four of America's first six major colleges and all three of its first medical schools detailed in chapter 3 were not isolated events, but rather the acme of a broad interest in education manifested by Scottish-Americans. Between 1726 and 1837 Presbyterians founded at least sixty-five rudimentary academies, which were sometimes called log colleges. Many of these schools became seminaries and permanent colleges and one, as has been shown, bloomed into Princeton University. In fact, of the twenty-nine permanent colleges and universities established in the United States between 1780 and 1829 in all sections of the country, thirteen were founded by Presbyterians and sixteen by other religions.[1]

One of the most effective of all American educators was William Holmes McGuffey (1800–1873), the author of *McGuffey's Readers*, which have sold over 122 million copies and continue in use today, over a century and a half after their first publication. These books revolutionized and greatly improved the instruction in American public schools and were, next to the Bible, probably the most influential books in American history. McGuffey, who was born in Pennsylvania to Scottish grandparents and was almost entirely self-educated, began teaching on the Ohio frontier at age thirteen.[2]

Among the more important, or interesting, of Scottish influences on American education is the founding of the first school in Kentucky by the Scotch-Irish David Rice in 1761.[3] Alexander Robertson founded the school named after him in New York in 1789. The Alexander Robertson School, the first in New York to admit girls as well as boys, continues today as an adjunct to the "Old Scotch Church" (Second Presbyterian) on West Ninety-sixth Street. The founder of Dickinson College, originally one of the log colleges, was a Scot, John Dickinson. The Rev. Charles Nesbit of Montrose was Dickinson's first president.[4] George McClellan was the founder of Jefferson Medical College in Philadelphia.[5]

John Johnston, president of Saint Andrew's Society of the State of New York (1831–1832) was one of the three principal founders of New York University.[6]

Peter Cooper, of Scotch-Irish ancestry,[7] founded Cooper Union in New York in 1859. It continues today as the only private tuition-free college in the United States. Also in New York, Thomas Hunter, of Scotch-Irish extraction, founded Hunter College in 1870.[8] Franklin Buchanan, the Confederate admiral, took over the bankrupt Maryland Agricultural College after the Civil War and rebuilt it into the University of Maryland, becoming that institution's de facto founder.[9]

Appendix G

British Prime Ministers
of Scottish Ancestry

Below is a list of British prime ministers who are at least partly of Scottish descent. Sources for their ancestry are given on the right. Most of those named are solidly Scottish, but William Pitt and Winston Churchill are only remotely so. Margaret Thatcher has no proven Scottish ancestry and is not included, but it should be noted that her biographer says that her mother was a Stevenson whose people were "Irish."[1] Stevenson is not, of course, a native Irish name, and when found in Ireland or anywhere else spelled with a *v* it is usually an emblem of Scottish background. It is remarkable that in the near century between 1868 and 1964, men of Scottish ancestry were incumbent more than two-thirds of the time.

John Stuart (earl of Bute)	1762	McCulloch, p. 64; *EB*, vol. 2, p. 478.
William Pitt	1783–1801 1804–1806	Ellis
George Hamilton-Gordon (earl of Aberdeen)	1852–1855	McCulloch, p. 217; *EB*, vol. 1, p. 29.
William Ewart Gladstone	1868–1874 1880–1885 1886 1892–1894	McCulloch, p. 217; *EB*, vol. 10, p. 442.
Archibald Primrose (earl of Roseberry)	1894–1895	McCulloch, p. 217; *EB*, vol. 19, p. 624.
Arthur James Balfour (earl of Balfour)	1902–1905	McCulloch, p. 217; *EB*, vol. 3, p. 1.
Sir Henry Campbell-Bannerman	1905–1908	McCulloch, p. 217; *EB*, vol. 4, p. 716.
Andrew Bonar Law	1922–1923	McCulloch, p. 217; *EB*, vol. 13, p. 819.

Stanley Baldwin (earl Baldwin of Bewdley)	1923–1924 1924–1929 1935–1937	Middlemas, K. and J. Barnes, *Baldwin*.
James Ramsay MacDonald	1924 1929–1931 1931–1935	McCulloch, p. 217; *EB*, vol. 14, p. 503.
Sir Winston Churchill	1940–1945 1951–1955	Churchill, Randolph, *Winston S. Churchill*.
Harold Macmillan	1957–1963	*EB*, vol. 14, p. 542.
Sir Alexander Douglas-Home	1963–1964	*EB*, vol. 7, p. 611.

Appendix H

World Population of People of Scottish Ancestry Estimated by Country

The following table is an attempt to estimate the number of people throughout various countries of the world in the early 1980s who had any Scottish ancestry. For the United States the estimate is based on the projection of the census figure for 1980. For Scotland it is guessed that seven-eighths of the people are of the old national stock. In other countries the name-frequency method described in appendix Q is employed using various telephone directories. Appendix Q shows that in Scotland 7.8 percent, or about $1/13$, of the population bears twelve distinctly Scottish surnames. Therefore, if our count of these names in a telephone directory is ten thousand, we can multiply that number times thirteen (or 12.82, which is the exact reciprocal of 7.8 percent) and conclude that about 128,200 people in the directory have some Scottish ancestry. The following table is not scientific, but rather an estimate of Scots in the world.

Country	Total Population	Percent Scots	Total Scots
United States (U.S. Bur. Census, Suppl. Report PC80-S1-10, p. 12)	230,000,000	5.3%	12,190,000
Scotland (*estimate*)	5,200,000	87.5%	4,550,000
Canada (*Toronto telephone directory*)	23,940,000	15.8%	3,782,520
England and Wales (*London telephone directory*)	50,000,000	7.3%	3,650,000
Australia (*Sydney telephone directory*)	14,620,000	14.1%	2,061,420
New Zealand (European) (*Auckland telephone directory*)	2,880,000	16.5%	475,200

Northern Ireland *(Northern Ireland telephone directory)*	1,540,000	26.9%	414,260
South Africa (European) *(Cape Town and Johannesburg telephone directories)*	7,322,000	3.9%	285,558
Other countries *(estimated)*			500,000
Total World			27,908,958

Appendix I

A Miscellany of Scottish Invention

(A supplement to the discussion on pages 104–13)

Adhesive Postage Stamps   Invented in 1834 by James Chalmers of Dundee.[1]

Artificial Ice   Invented in 1810 by Sir John Leslie.[2]

Brassiere   The first patent was issued in 1914 to Mary Phelps Jacob, an American of Scotch-Irish descent.[3]

Contac   The formula for the world's largest-selling cold medicine was written by Scottish-American Dr. Marshall B. Guthrie, a first cousin of author A. B. Guthrie.[4]

Cornstarch   Corn flour was first produced by John Polson of Paisley in 1854.[5]

Electric Clock   Invented by Alexander Bain of Scotland in 1851.[6]

Gas Mask   Invented by John Stenhouse in 1860.[7]

Fountain Pen   Invented in 1849 by Robert William Thomson.[8]

Freon   A gas which revolutionized refrigeration was coinvented at the DuPont company by Robert MacFarlan Cole, presumably of Scottish ancestry.[9]

Kaleidoscope   The precursor of motion pictures was invented by Sir David Brewster of Jedburgh.[10]

Limelight   Used principally in theatrical lighting, limelight was invented in 1821 by Thomas Drummond (1797–1840) of Scotland.[11]

Nylon   Invented at the DuPont company by Wallace Hume Carothers, an inductee of the Scottish-American Hall of Fame.[12]

Postcard   Invented by J.H.A. MacDonald.[13]

Shoemaking Machines   Two American Scots, Duncan H. Campbell and Gordon MacKay, invented shoemaking machines that revolutionized the industry. MacKay invented a sole-stiching machine and Campbell a pegging and stitching machine for sewing uppers.[14]

Shorthand   The world's most taught and used shorthand system was invented in 1888 in England by John Robert Gregg, a native of Ireland, presumed to be of Scottish ancestry.[15]

Silly Putty   Invented by mistake at General Electric in 1945 by James Wright, a Scottish engineer.[16]

Watch   According to one source, King Robert I, the Bruce, possessed a watch in 1310, eighteen years before its supposed invention in Germany.[17]

Waterproof Fabric   Invented in 1819 by Charles Mackintosh, a Glasgow chemist, who gave his name to the mackintosh coat.[18]

Water Softening   Invented by Thomas Clark of Scotland in 1841.[19]

Appendix J

Scots in Steamship Companies

The first steamship company in Britain was the General Steam Navigation Company, Ltd., which was formed in Scotland in 1820 and in the same year built its first ship, the *City of Edinburgh*.[1]

The Anchor Line   Founded by the Hendersons of Glasgow.[2]

The Allan Line   Founded in Canada by Sir Hugh Allan (1810–1882), a native Scot.[3]

The British East India Steam Navigation Company   Founded by Sir William Mackinnon.[4]

The Cunard Line (see page 118, *supra*)

The Dollar Line   Founded by Robert Dollar, who was born in Falkirk. Dollar, who had just two years of education, ended up in San Francisco, where he built a fleet of sixty ships. He did more than any American to open trade with the Orient and gave away millions.[5]

The P&O Line   Founded by Arthur Anderson (1792–1868) of Lerwick, at one time, it had the world's largest passenger fleet.[6]

Appendix K

Scottish Brand Names

Armour Meats   Armour and Co. was founded in Chicago by Philip Armour (1832–1901). By 1923 the company was the largest meat packer in the world.[1]

Baxter's of Speyside   The Scottish food processing firm with a worldwide reputation was founded in 1914 by William and Ethel Baxter.[2]

Black and Decker   American tool firm founded by two men of Scottish ancestry, S. Duncan Black and Alonzo G. Decker.[3]

Bovril   James Lawson Johnston took a step towards providing the British with cheap protein when he invented his "fluid beef" in 1874.[4]

Burry Cookies   Started in Toronto in 1888 by Christina Burry, a widowed Scotswoman, whose storefront operation supported her five sons.[5]

Canada Dry   Concocted by a Scottish chemist in Toronto around 1890.[6]

Cannon Towels   Founded by James William Cannon, a Scottish-American.[7]

Dow Chemical   Founded by Herbert Henry Dow, a Scottish-American.[8]

Dunlop Tires   Founded by John Boyd Dunlop, a native of Scotland, in Belfast, Ireland.[9]

Graham Crackers   Sylvester Graham, an American of Scottish descent and the "father of public health in America," developed graham flour to combat malnutrition.[10]

Keiller's Marmalade   Janet Keiller made the first batch after her grocer husband bought a distressed cargo of Seville oranges in the harbor at Dundee. Her son founded James Keiller and Son, Ltd., in 1797, and it became the first large-scale producer of marmalade.[11]

Kellogg's Cereals   An old family tradition holds that the ancestors of Will Keith Kellogg originated in Scotland.[12] Today Kellogg's is the largest breakfast cereal company in the world.[13]

Lenox China   The company which makes America's finest china, including the White House services from presidents Wilson to Reagan, was founded in the nineteenth century by Walter Scott Lenox, of Scotch-Irish ancestry.[14]

Liggett-Rexall Drugs   Founded by Scottish-American Louis Liggett.[15]

McDonald's Hamburgers   The world's most successful restaurant company was founded by the Irish-American McDonald brothers, Richard and Maurice, whose parents came from County Kerry.[16] Most of the Irish McDonalds are ultimately descended from Scottish gallowglasses.[17]

McKesson and Robbins Drugs Founded by John McKesson.[18]

Monterey Jack Cheese An American cheese named after David Jack, a Scot who joined the California gold rush but who eventually got rich making the cheese.[19]

Old Crow Bourbon Whiskey Founded by Dr. James Crow, a Scottish physician who emigrated to Kentucky in 1822 and introduced the "sour-mash" method of fermentation to that state.[20]

Old Forrester Bourbon The pride of Brown-Forman distillers, founded by James Brown, of Scottish descent.[21]

Pierce Arrow Cars Developed by the father of Scottish singer Mary Garden.[22]

Procter and Gamble Cofounded by James Gamble, a Scotch-Irish soap maker. He and William Procter each invested $3,596.47 in what is now America's largest soap manufacturing company.[23]

Robertson's Jams Founded by James Robertson of Paisley.[24]

Rose's Lime Juice In the nineteenth century Lachlan Rose found a way to preserve lime juice without alcohol and founded the world-famous company currently owned by Schweppes.[25]

Simmons Beautyrest Mattresses Founded by Grant Simmons, an American of Scottish descent.[26]

Sinclair Electronics Clive Sinclair, an English entrepreneur of Scottish descent, built the first pocket calculator; designed the first pocket-size television set (six inches by four inches by one inch) and the first micro-computer to sell for less than two hundred dollars.[27]

Smith Brothers Cough Drops William ("trade") and Andrew ("mark") registered their trademark in 1877. Their father was from Scotland.[28]

Thom McAn Shoes Originated by the Melville Shoe Corp., whose chairman, Ward Melville, had built the business to over a billion dollars by the time of his death in 1977. Melville was also the founder of Scottish Heritage U.S.A., known as SHUSA.[29]

Uneeda Biscuit Robert Gair, a Scotsman from Brooklyn, developed the cutting and creasing die tool that made the mass production of folding cartons for the biscuits and many other products possible.[30]

For additional information, see also chapter 5, "The Industrial Revolution," and especially pages 122–24.

Appendix L

Business Miscellany

THE *FORTUNE* MAGAZINE BUSINESS HALL OF FAME

Of the original nineteen Americans chosen in January 1975, these seven are of Scottish ancestry,[1] although Washington's descent is only remote:

Andrew Carnegie   Steel baron
Thomas A. Edison   Founder of General Electric who invented "for the market."
Cyrus McCormick   Founder of International Harvester
Monroe Jackson Rathbone   Exxon chairman in the 1950s who foresaw the crises in the Middle East and developed reserves elsewhere. Rathbone was a descendant of General Stonewall Jackson.[2]
John Davison Rockefeller   Founder of Standard Oil, predecessor of Exxon and many other oil companies.
Alexander T. Stewart   "Inventor" of modern retailing
George Washington   Colonial land developer who owned sixty-four thousand acres and who developed a water route to the West.

Of the fifty-eight Americans named to the Hall of Fame between 1976 and 1982, at least these eighteen were of Scottish ancestry:

Elizabeth Arden   Cosmetics queen
William Blackie   A native Scot who made Caterpillar Inc. into a world-wide firm after World War II.[3]
Harry Blair Cunningham   By an innovation called K-Mart, he revitalized S. S. Kresge Co., increasing sales eighteen times. Of Scottish and Scotch-Irish ancestry.[4]
Walt Disney   Peerless creator of motion pictures
Donald Wills Douglas   Dominant aviation manufacturer
James J. Hill   Railroad magnate
Ian Kinloch MacGregor   Head of British Steel and British Coal
John J. McCloy   Director of Germany's postwar recovery; head of World Bank and Chase Manhattan Bank.
Malcolm P. McLean   Containerized freight pioneer
Andrew W. Mellon   Banker and industrialist

Joseph Irwin Miller   Head of Cummins Engine, who captured half of the U.S. diesel market. Of Scottish ancestry.[5]
David Mackenzie Ogilvy   Advertising wizard
John H. Patterson   Founder of National Cash Register who made the cash register universal.[6]
William Allan "Pat" Patterson   Built United Air Lines
DeWitt Wallace   Cofounder of *Reader's Digest*
Lila Acheson Wallace   Cofounder of *Reader's Digest*
Thomas J. Watson, Jr.   Builder of IBM
Charles Kemmons Wilson   Founder of Holiday Inns

MORE ABOUT SCOTTISH ACHIEVERS IN BUSINESS

Elizabeth Arden   Born Florence Graham to Scottish-Canadian parents, she built a worldwide cosmetics empire. Coco Chanel once said, "There is only one Mademoiselle in the world, and that is I; one Madame, and that is Rubinstein; and one Miss, and that is Arden." Added Miss Arden, "There is only one Elizabeth like me, and that's the Queen."[7]
Alastair Duncan Blair   Scottish-born designer whose 1986 show catapulted him into the front rank of British fashion.[8]
Caswell-Massey   Located in New York City, America's oldest pharmacy has sold its "Number 6" cologne to famous people, from George Washington to Albert Einstein. The business was founded in Newport, Rhode Island, in 1752 by William Hunter, a physician from Scotland, and moved to New York in 1856.[9]
James Christie   The founder of the great international auction house which is the oldest and largest such market in the world.[10]
James Crooks   Kilmarnock native who built the first paper mill in Canada.[11]
Thomas Dewar   The famous whisky distiller paid for the first musical commercial when he employed a piper to advertise his product at the London Brewer's Show in 1885.[12]
James Buchanan Duke   Partly Scotch-Irish tobacco king who endowed Duke University.[13]
General Electric   Giant American company founded in 1892 by Scottish-Americans Elihu Thomson and Thomas Edison.[14]
Sir George Grant   A Scot who rounded up some adventurers in London in the 1870s, went to Kansas, and left behind the first herd of Black Angus in America.[15]
Alexander Leith   Born in Scotland in 1847, he founded the Illinois Steel Co., which became one of the largest in the world. He merged it with

Andrew Carnegie's interests, forming Carnegie-Illinois Steel. In 1901 Carnegie-Illinois became the foundation of U.S. Steel.[16]

Lord Henry (Harry) McGowan Glasgow-born founder in 1926 of the world's largest chemical company, Imperial Chemical Industries.[17]

Ian Kinloch MacGregor An American of Scottish birth, the British government actually paid his firm, Lazard Frères, to obtain his services in operating the British steel and coal industries.[18]

Donald MacNaughton Chairman of Prudential, the world's largest insurer, and a former professional basketball player.[19]

Donald R. McLennan An American of Scottish ancestry who founded Marsh and McLennan in 1904, by far the largest insurance agency in the country.[20]

Hamish Maxwell Created the world's largest consumer goods company, displacing the British-Dutch Unilever, when he bought Kraft for Philip Morris in 1988 for 13.1 billion dollars.[21]

Jean Muir, C. B. E. Born in London of Scottish descent, her clothes, sold worldwide, made her a leading influence in international dressmaking. The *New York Times* called her "the doyenne of London fashion."[22]

David Mackenzie Ogilvy A failure at Oxford, he founded the amazing advertising firm of Ogilvy and Mather with six thousand dollars. It now has one hundred offices in thirty-five countries. In 1989 the firm was sold for 864 million dollars, the largest amount ever paid for an advertising agency. Mr Ogilvy remained as chairman.[23]

John H. Patterson The founder of National Cash Register was the descendant of Ulster Scots.[24]

Allan Pinkerton Before founding his detective agency, the world's largest, Pinkerton, who was born in Glasgow in 1819, managed a "depot" on the Underground Railroad in his cooper's shop in Chicago for the purpose of aiding runaway slaves to freedom.[25]

John Pitcairn A Scottish immigrant to Pittsburgh, he was the cofounder of a company that became America's two largest glass manufacturers, PPG Industries and Libbey-Owens-Ford.[26]

Presbyterian Minister's Fund Founded in Philadelphia in 1717, it is the oldest insurance company and the third oldest business in the United States.[27]

The Shore Porter's Society Founded in 1498 at Footdee (or Fittie, or Futtie) near Aberdeen, it is Britain's oldest company. It is currently engaged in furniture moving.[28]

Henry D. G. Wallace The first foreign president of a Japanese automobile company, who took over as head of Mazda in Hiroshima in 1996.

Thomas J. Watson The de facto founder of IBM, until recently the single most profitable enterprise on earth.[29]

Thomas J. Watson, Jr.   The principal builder of IBM and architect of the computer revolution who was often called the "businessman of the twentieth century." *Fortune* magazine went even farther, hailing him as "the greatest capitalist who ever lived." In 1987, at the age of seventy-two, Watson, a former U.S. ambassador to the Soviet Union, piloted his own Lear 55 around the world on the old Lend Lease route he had flown in World War II. Crowds of Red Army veterans greeted him at all the Russian stops through Siberia.[30]

For additional information on businessmen, see also the discussion in chapter 5, "The Industrial Revolution."

Appendix M

Scottish Organizations

FREEMASONRY

The worldwide fraternity of modern Freemasonry traces its origins back, perhaps, to ancient Egypt, Israel, and medieval cathedral builders, and now embraces millions of members of many races and religions. Freemasonry began, largely, in Scotland, where stone continued to be the main material for construction long after it had been replaced by brick in England and elsewhere. Thus as late as 1677[1] there was a master mason to the king of Scots and working stonemasons were still regarded as an elite craft organization, honored for their skill and the principles of good conduct taught in their lodges. Gradually non-stonemasons (speculative or nonoperative masons) were admitted to the lodges and came to dominate them, setting up the entirely speculative system we have today.[2]

Of course, England as well as Scotland was prominent during the early days of Freemasonry, but there is no doubt that the modern fraternity originated in Scotland and that the Scots can claim most of the "firsts." Freemasons built Kilwinning Abbey (c. 1140) and are credited with upholding the craft as it collapsed in the rest of Europe.[3] The Mason Word developed in Scotland about 1550,[4] and as early as 1598 cowans (masons "without the word," or nonmembers of the craft) were not allowed employment by members. Cowans do not appear in England until 1738.[5] The oldest surviving masonic minutes in the world go back to 1599, at Edinburgh Lodge No. 1.[6] The first nonoperative mason about whom there is any certainty was John Boswell, laird of Auchinleck, who attended Edinburgh Lodge in 1600.[7] About the same time King James VI was made a mason at what is now Lodge Scone and Perth.[8] Twenty-five Scottish lodges, of which twenty are still functioning, were operating prior to 1717. There is no evidence of any English lodge existing prior to this date.[9]

Masonry could not have been founded in class-conscious England. The fraternity's basic idea that men are equal, not in rank, station, or ability but in basic and moral worth, is central to Scottish philosophy. That noblemen and artisans could meet in a lodge as "brothers" is a Scottish idea.[10] In fact, while all the early Scottish lodges had real stonemasons as members, English lodges were usually only for the gentry and did not include working men.[11]

291

The structure of masonry also owes a debt to Scotland, which had the first organization of lodges in the world before 1599 under the Schaw Statutes, which describe the various lodges then under the control of the craft.[12] The Grand Lodge of England was not founded until 1717, and its most important person in its early years was a Scot, Rev. James Anderson of Aberdeen.[13] The Grand Lodge of France was cofounded by a chief of the Macleans, Sir Hector Maclean, of Duart, in 1736. The lodge gave its first *Écossais* degrees soon after.[14] The Royal Order of Scotland— to be a member is considered by some as masonry's highest honor—is said to have been founded by King David I (1124–1153) and restored by King Robert I, the Bruce. King Robert may have given it some sort of recognition on the battlefield of Bannockburn "to signalize the valour of a band of Knights Templars who fought with him there."[15]

THE YMCA

David Naismith founded the Glasgow City Mission in 1826 and the London City Mission in 1835, both of which were precursors of the YMCA founded in London in 1844.[16]

THE BOY SCOUTS

The Boys Brigade, the precursor of the Boy Scouts, was founded in Glasgow in 1883 by Sir William Alexander Smith. Lord Baden Powell wrote a handbook, *Scouting for Boys*, for Smith to use and in 1905 founded the Boy Scouts, which now has millions of members. The Boys Brigade continues, with about a quarter of a million members.[17]

THE GIRL SCOUTS

The first troop of Girl Scouts was formed in 1912 by second-generation Scottish-American Juliette Gordon Low of Savannah, Georgia, and was based on concepts already established in Britain.[18]

Appendix N

Science Miscellany

The principal founder of the Royal Society, Britain's oldest and most distinguished scientific organization, was a Scot, Sir Robert Moray (or Murray) who was elected as the society's first president in 1661. The Royal Society still holds its annual meeting on St. Andrew's Day in honor of the founder.[1]

Scots have also produced the founders, or "fathers," of many sciences, among them:[2]

American geology	William Maclure
American ornithology	Alexander Wilson
American psychiatry	Benjamin Rush
Antiseptic surgery	William Macewen
Atomic power	Lord Rutherford
Australian botany	Robert Brown
British ornithology	William MacGillivray
Colloid science	Thomas Graham
Electronics	Sir James Clerk Maxwell
Experimental geology	Sir James Hall
Fingerprinting	Henry Faulds
Mechanical engineering	Sir William Fairbairn
Medical midwifery	William Smellie
Meteorology	Alexander Buchan
Modern chemistry	Joseph Black
Modern geology	James Hutton
Modern obstetrics	William Hunter
Modern military medicine	Sir John Pringle
Modern naval hygiene	James Lind
Modern neurology	David Ferrier
Modern physics	Joseph Thomson
Oceanography	C. Wyville Thomson
Refrigeration	John Leslie, Robert Stirling
Scientific surgery	John Hunter
Seismology	John Milne
Thermodynamics	William John Macquorn Rankine
Tropical medicine	Sir Patrick Manson
Veterinary hygiene	James Clark

There are many scientific terms named for Scots, among them:

Bell's theorum	John Stewart Bell
The Brownian movement	Robert Brown
The decibel	Alexander Graham Bell
Graham's law	Thomas Graham
The Henry	Joseph Henry
The Kelvin scale	Lord Kelvin
Maclaurin's theorem	Colin Maclaurin
Maxwell's rule	James Clerk Maxwell
The Morse code	Samuel Finley Breese Morse
The Rankine cycle	William John Macquorn Rankine
The Watt	James Watt

James Watt also invented the term *horsepower* and exaggerated it by 50 percent in order to facilitate sales of his steam engine.[3]

For additional information on contributions to science, see also chapter 5, "The Industrial Revolution," especially pages 104–13, and chapter 9, "Science."

Appendix O

The Nobel Prize

In the first sixty-two years of Nobel prizes (1901–1962), 264 awards were made in the five categories of physics, chemistry, physiology or medicine, peace, and literature. People of Scottish birth or ancestry were involved in at least thirty-five of these, a score of over 13 percent. Of the 331 awardees during the same period at least thirty-six, or almost 11 percent, had Scottish blood. Since only about twenty-eight million of the world's 5.7 billion people, or about one half of one percent are even partly Scottish,[1] this amounts to an overrepresentation of between twenty-two and twenty-six times.

For the years 1963 to 1981, only three awardees have been identified as being Scottish, so the percentages for this period would show an alarming drop. However, between 1982 and 1990 the higher percentages have returned. Of the fifty-two awards during these years at least seven, or more than 13 percent, involved people of the Scottish nation. Of the seventy-eight awardees during this period at least nine were Scots, a score of more than 11 percent. Therefore we can say that between 1982 and 1990 the Scots have been overrepresented as Nobel Prize winners by at least twenty-three to twenty-six times.

Overall, from 1901 through 1990, people of Scottish ancestry were involved in 45 of the 416 Nobel Prizes awarded, almost one of every nine awards, for a score of 10.8 percent. This is an overrepresentation of almost twenty-two times. It should also be noted that there are many awardees with British names, some of them distinctively Scottish names, who have not been included in these tabulations because research has failed to prove their Scottishness. Undoubtedly, the Scottish scores should be even higher.

Geography seems to be no bar to excellence in the worldwide Scottish diaspora, as awardees have been born in at least thirteen different countries. In addition to the many born in Scotland, England, and the United States, we have the following countries of origin and awardees:

Australia	Burnet
Canada	Banting
China	Brattain
India	Kipling

Ireland	Shaw
Italy	Marconi
Nepal	Ross
New Zealand	Rutherford
South Africa	Cormack
Wales	Russell

Following is a list of all of the Nobel Prize winners born in Scotland or elsewhere who have proven Scottish ancestry. Detail is provided for awardees in peace and economic science. More information on the awardees in physics, chemistry, physiology or medicine, and literature can be found in the various citations in chapters 5, 8, 9, and 10.

PHYSICS

1906	*Joseph J. Thomson*	1956	*Walter H. Brattain*
1909	*Guglielmo Marconi*	1982	*Kenneth Geddes Wilson*
1923	*Robert A. Millikan*	1989	*Norman F. Ramsey*
1927	*Charles T. R. Wilson*	1990	*Richard E. Taylor*
1937	*George P. Thomson*	1990	*Henry W. Kendall*

CHEMISTRY

1904	*William Ramsay*	1957	*Alexander R. Todd*
1908	*Ernest Rutherford*	1962	*John C. Kendrew*
1932	*Irving Langmuir*	1965	*Robert B. Woodward*
1951	*Edwin M. McMillan*	1966	*Robert S. Mulliken*
1954	*Linus C. Pauling*	1987	*Donald J. Cram*
1956	*Cyril N. Hinshelwood*		

PHYSIOLOGY OR MEDICINE

1902	*Ronald Ross*	1960	*Macfarlane Burnet*
1922	*Archibald V. Hill*	1962	*James D. Watson*
1923	*Frederick Grant Banting*	1979	*Allan MacLeod Cormack*
1923	*John J. R. Macleod*	1983	*Barbara McClintock*
1932	*Edgar Douglas Adrian*	1988	*George H. Hitchings*
1933	*Thomas H. Morgan*	1988	*James W. Black*
1945	*Alexander Fleming*		

LITERATURE

1907	*Rudyard Kipling*	1950	*Bertrand Russell*

1925	*George Bernard Shaw*	1953	*Winston Churchill*
1949	*William Cuthbert Faulkner*	1962	*John Steinbeck*

PEACE

1906 Theodore Roosevelt President of the United States and conservationist. Roosevelt's mother was Martha Bulloch, descended from the Scottish colonial governor Archibald Bulloch.[2]

1919 Woodrow Wilson President of the United States and promoter of world peace through the League of Nations. An American of Scottish and Ulster-Scottish ancestry.[3]

1931 Nicholas Murray Butler Scottish-descended president of Columbia University (1901–1945) and a vigorous advocate of international understanding.[4]

1934 Arthur Henderson Principal architect of the modern Labour party and a strong advocate of disarmament who was born in Glasgow.[5]

1949 John Boyd Orr Ayrshire-born nutritionist whose recommendations were the basis for the British food rationing system during World War II. Was director general of the United Nations Food and Agriculture Organization from 1945 to 1948.[6]

1953 George C. Marshall The five-star general who became the author of the Marshall Plan for European recovery after World War II was born in Pennsylvania of Scottish ancestry.[7]

1962 Linus C. Pauling A Wallace awardee, he is the only person to win the Nobel Prize outright in two categories.

ECONOMIC SCIENCE

1986 James McGill Buchanan The father of the "public choice theory" is an American of Scotch-Irish descent.[8]

Appendix P

The Wallace Award

The Wallace Award of the American-Scottish Foundation, Inc., is presented annually in New York to distinguished Americans of Scottish descent. Awardees must appear in person at the ceremony in order to receive the award. Following is a list of the Wallace awardees through 1990.

Russell Barnett Aitken   Sculptor, author, and editor
Robert B. Anderson   Secretary of the treasury; secretary of the navy
J. Sinclair Armstrong   Chairman, U.S. Securities and Exchange Commission
Louis S. Auchincloss   Author and attorney
Drummond C. Bell   Chairman, National Distillers
William Blackie   Chairman, Caterpillar Inc.; member, *Fortune* magazine Business Hall of Fame
Herbert Brownell   Attorney general of the United States
Wiley T. Buchanan   Ambassador to Australia and Luxembourg
Robert J. Callander   President, Chemical Bank
C. Douglas Dillon   Managing director, Dillon Read; chairman, Metropolitan Museum of Art; ambassador to France.
Donald Wills Douglas   Founder, Douglas Aircraft; member, *Fortune* magazine Business Hall of Fame
Robert R. Douglass   Partner, Milbank Tweed Hadley and McCloy
Hugh Malcolm Downs   Journalist and television host
Philip Livingston DuVal   Marketing director, *New York Times*
John Elliot, Jr.   Chairman, Ogilvy and Mather
Chester H. Ferguson   Chairman, Lykes Brothers
James L. Ferguson   Chairman, General Foods
Dr. John Stuart Foster, Jr.   Vice president, TRW Corporation
Greer Garson   Actress, Academy Award winner
Gen. James W. Gerard   President and director of many civic organizations
Jean S. Gerard   Ambassador to UNESCO
Norma Lorre Goodrich, Ph.D.   Author and educator
J. Peter Grace   Chairman, W. R. Grace
Lt. Gen. Daniel O. Graham   Director of the Defense Intelligence Agency
Robert C. Graham, Sr.   Collector of fine art

John Murdoch Harbert III Founder, Harbert Corporation
Mrs. Alison McDaniel Harwood Chairman, Arthritis Foundation
Dr. D. Gilbert Highet Scholar; professor of Latin, Columbia University
Jack R. Howard President, Scripps-Howard
John Kenneth Jamieson Chairman, Exxon Corporation
Francis L. Kellogg Ambassador to the United Nations
David M. Kennedy Secretary of the Treasury
Dr. Grayson L. Kirk, K.B.E. President, Columbia University
Melvin Laird Secretary of defense; presidential advisor
Edward H. Levi Attorney general of the United States
John V. Lindsay Mayor of the city of New York
Robert Abercrombie Lovett Secretary of Defense
Mrs. Douglas MacArthur Civic leader
Howard W. McCall, Jr. President, Chemical Bank
Capt. Bruce McCandless Astronaut; first man to fly freely in space
Sen. John L. McClellan Senator; at age seventeen, America's youngest
  lawyer
William B. Macomber Ambassador to Jordan and Turkey; president,
  Metropolitan Museum of Art
James McCracken Tenor, Metroplitan Opera
Dr. Paul W. McCracken Chairman, Council of Economic Advisors
Nestor J. MacDonald, O.B.E. Chairman, Thomas and Betts; chairman,
  Scottish Heritage, U.S.A.; president, Grandfather Mountain High-
  land Games
Ray W. MacDonald Chairman, Burroughs Corporation
Sanford N. McDonnell President, McDonnell Douglas
Clark MacGregor Vice president, United Technologies
Sir Ian Kinloch MacGregor Chairman, Amax Corporation; chairman,
  British Steel; chairman, British Coal; member, *Fortune* magazine
  Business Hall of Fame
Miss Helen MacInnes Author
Malcolm A. MacIntyre President of Eastern Airlines; founder, Eastern
  Shuttle; chairman, Bunker Ramo
John Key McKinley Chairman, Texaco
Rev. Canon Dougald Lachlan Maclean President, Scottish Heritage, U.S.A.
Archibald MacLeish Poet, playwright, journalist, lawyer, librarian,
  statesman, and professor
John L. McLucas Secretary of the air force
Donald S. MacNaughton Chairman, Prudential Insurance
Malcolm MacNaughton Chairman, Castle and Cooke
Robert MacNeil Television news commentator and author
Robert L. McNeil, Jr. Chairman, McNeil Laboratories

Dr. Thomas H. Meikle, Jr.   Dean, Cornell University Medical College
Judge Leonard Moore   Judge, U.S. Court of Appeals
Robert Motherwell   Painter
Linus Carl Pauling, Ph.D.   Scientist, Nobel Prize winner; the only person to win Nobel Prizes in two different fields outright
William Wood Prince   President, Armour and Company
Rev. Dr. David H. C. Read, D.D.   Minister, Madison Avenue Presbyterian Church; author
James Reston   Journalist, *New York Times*
S. Dillon Ripley II   Author, zoologist, biologist, and ecologist; secretary emeritus, the Smithsonian Institution
Cliff Robertson   Actor, Academy Award winner
Ian Rolland   President, Lincoln National
George Russell   Vice chairman, General Motors
Hedrick Smith   Journalist, *New York Times*
R. Brinkley Smithers   Founder, Smithers Foundation
William I. Spencer   President, Citicorp and Citibank
Dr. Wallace Sterling   President, Stanford University
Justice Potter Stewart   Justice, U.S. Supreme Court
Col. Thomas H. Stewart III   Soldier; treasurer, American-Scottish Foundation, Inc.
Henry J. Taylor   Journalist; author; ambassador to Switzerland
Robert Brown "Bobby" Thomson   Professional baseball player born in Scotland who stroked the game's most famous hit
Malcolm Toon   Ambassador to the Soviet Union
James H. Van Alen   Sportsman and philanthropist
Mrs. Diana Dalziel Vreeland   Editor, *Harper's Bazaar* and *Vogue* magazines; called the Empress of Fashion
Sen. Malcolm Wallop   United States senator
James D. Watson, Ph.D.   Scientist, Nobel Prize winner for the codiscovery of the structure of DNA; author
Gov. Malcolm Wilson   Governor, state of New York; chairman, Manhattan Savings Bank
Arthur MacD. Wood   Chairman, Sears Roebuck

In Memoriam

Alexander Graham Bell   Inventor of the telephone
Andrew Carnegie   Founder, U.S. Steel; philanthropist; member, *Fortune* magazine Business Hall of Fame
Lord Malcolm Douglas-Hamilton   Soldier; aviator; founder, the American-Scottish Foundation, Inc.
Gen. Douglas MacArthur   Soldier

Appendix Q

The Scottish Achievement Demonstrated by Name-Frequency Technique

In 1966 Nathaniel Weyl invented an ingenious way of measuring the accomplishments of various ethnic groups in the United States.[1] He discovered that the Social Security Administration had published a document listing the first six letters of all surnames in the country that occurred in the Social Security file more than ten thousand times. In addition, the document ranked these 1,514 names, or part names, in order of frequency and also alphabetically. Weyl realized that he could use this information to calculate the achievement of an ethnic group.

For example, if he chose names like Kelly, Murphy, Ryan, or Sulliv(an), and compared the frequency of their occurrence on the Social Security list versus the frequency of their occurrence in *Who's Who in America*, he could establish what he called an Irish performance coefficient, or P.C., in *Who's Who in America*. If his names occurred in *Who's Who* one and a half times more frequently than in the general population he called that a P.C. of 150. An average score would be 100. He could also employ registers of lawyers, actors, scientists, politicians, and so forth to obtain a P.C. for the Irish in many fields, the total of which would be a general P.C. for the Irish in America.

Using the names Alexan(der), Campbe(ll), Cummin(s or gs), Cunnin(gham), Dougla(s or ss), Fergus(on), Ross, and Wallac(e or h), Weyl obtained a P.C. of 127 for the Scots, second only to Jewish-Americans, who scored 204. On the 225 registers he employed, Weyl found the Scots in first place on fifty-one, the most first-place scores of any ethnic group.

Weyl's brilliant system has provided us with a unique sociological tool, but it appears that the names he chose for the Scots, while all are common in Scotland, are less representative of them than the names selected for other groups. There is no doubt about Cox, Powell, Kelly, Cohen, Schult(z), Vander, Jensen, Leblan(c), Caruso, or Garcia, but the Scottish names are not clearly Scottish. Alexander is a name common in several countries. Campbell, while principally Scottish, is also Irish. Cummins is Irish, while Cummings and Cunningham are both English and Irish, in addition to being Scottish. Ross and Wallace are found in England and are also Jewish. Only Douglas and Ferguson, are clearly Scottish. Experts on the surnames of the British Isles—Bardsley,

MacLysaght, and Reaney—call Douglas, Ferguson, and Cunningham Scottish but do not agree on the others. All three call Alexander English.

To represent the Scots more accurately it was decided to try to find names more purely Scottish—names which were very common in Scotland, where the vast majority of people are of the old national stock—but at the same time were uncommon in the United States, where only a small percentage of people are of that ancestry. To do this the Scottish Register list of common surnames, as shown in the British birth, death, and marriage indexes for the years 1936 to 1940, was compared with the U.S. Social Security list for 1964. To no surprise, Smith ranked first on both lists and Brown, second in Scotland, ranked fourth in the United States. But Macdonald, the third name in Scotland, was 446th in the United States. Thomson, spelled the Scottish way, without the intrusive p and the fourth name in Scotland, was 1,079th in America.

Altogether, twelve surnames were found that had an American rank order greater than ten times their rank in Scotland. They are: Cameron, Fraser, Johnston, Kerr, MacDonald, MacGregor, MacKay, MacKenzie, MacLean, MacLeod, Reid, and Thomson.[2] This list has a great advantage over Weyl's in that the names are, at a glance, overwhelmingly Scottish.

The six "Mac" names, despite the partly Irish bias of MacDonald, are clearly Scottish, as are Cameron, Fraser, and Kerr. Johnston is for a place in Scotland and has nothing to do with the English Johnson. Thompson without the p and Reid with an i are both definitely Scottish spellings of common British surnames.

A further advantage of this list is that its names are borne by almost 7.8 percent of the people of Scotland, whereas Weyl's are carried by fewer than 2 percent.[3] In addition, all of the twelve new names are found among the fifty most common names of Scotland, whereas only four of Weyl's eight names are.[4] It is not surprising then, that when the new list of more purely Scottish names is used, the Scottish performance coefficient for *Who's Who in America* leaps from the 127 calculated by Weyl to 203, a gain of about 60 percent.

Research failed to disclose base lists of surnames in other countries, so a different approach was needed to demonstrate Scottish achievement in other English-speaking lands. An assumption was made that a count of the twelve surnames above would represent approximately 7.8 percent of the total Scots in *any* given population, as it did on the Scottish Register list. This assumption was substantially confirmed in the United States.[5] Using telephone directories for base lists, the following tables show the decimal incidence of the twelve Scottish surnames versus their decimal incidence in various *Who's Whos*. The resulting division gives a decimal, which, multiplied by 100, yields the performance coefficient, or P.C., for the Scottish achievement in several countries consistent with that found in the United States:

CANADA

Toronto Telephone Directory	*Who's Who in Canada*	Scottish P.C.
.011878	.025375	214

AUSTRALIA

Sydney Telephone Directory	*Who's Who in Australia*	Scottish P.C.
.010591	.019820	187

NEW ZEALAND

Auckland Telephone Directory	*Who's Who in New Zealand*	Scottish P.C.
.012364	.030921	250

SOUTH AFRICA

Cape Town and Johannesburg Telephone Directories	*Who's Who in Southern Africa*	Scottish P.C.
.002916	.008418	289

THE UNITED KINGDOM

London and Nottingham Telephone Directories	*Who's Who*	Scottish P.C.
.005210	.012575	241

In this survey there was a shocking anomaly:

NORTHERN IRELAND

Northern Ireland Telephone Directories	*Who's Who in Northern Ireland*	Scottish P.C.
.020193	.014128	70

Appendix R

Scottish Versatility

The Scots seem to place a high value on versatility, a trait that probably derives from their educational tradition which, unlike others, has encouraged a general rather than a specific course of study.[1] This policy encourages the development of talent in several areas and has the advantage of enabling a person to succeed in one field even if he has failed or found himself not well suited in another. This Scottish idea of versatility has carried beyond Scotland to the diaspora. Here are some examples:

Sir Thomas Makdougall Brisbane   While serving as governor of New South Wales, he became a distinguished astronomer.[2]

David K. E. Bruce   Perhaps America's greatest ambassador, he was also a lawyer, author, gentleman farmer, legislator, and banker.[3]

John Buchan   Canadian governor general whose novel *The Thirty-Nine Steps* was made into a Hitchcock film.[4]

Sir Sanford Fleming   The surveyor of the Canadian Pacific Railway initiated the first postage stamp in Canada (1851) and pioneered the establishment of Standard Time (1884).[5]

James Graham (marquess of Montrose)   One of Scotland's greatest soldiers, Montrose was also an accomplished poet. His most famous verse runs:

> "He either fears his fate too much,
> Or his deserts are small,
> Who dares not put it to the touch,
> To win or lose it all."[6]

Hamish Hamilton   British-American publisher who was an airplane pilot and rowed in the 1928 Olympics in Amsterdam.[7]

Joseph Henry   Scottish-American scientist who discovered electromagnetic induction, invented the telegraph, perfected the electromagnet, and theorized the transformer. He was also the first head of the Smithsonian Institution and the de facto founder of the U.S. Weather Bureau. At Princeton he taught physics and mathematics and lectured in chemistry, mineralogy, geology, astronomy, and architecture.[8]

Robert Hunter   While governor of colonial New York he published the first English play in the American colonies, *Androboros*, in 1714.[9]

Lord Kelvin (William Thomson) The "architect of nineteenth-century physics" was also a champion rower and founded the Glasgow University Music Society.[10]

Robert R. Livingston The man who bought Louisiana from France was also a member of the committee which drafted the Declaration of Independence and in 1781 was, under the Articles of Confederation, the first American secretary of foreign affairs. As the first chancellor of New York he swore in Washington as the first president of the United States, was himself president of Saint Andrew's Society of the State of New York, and the partner of Robert Fulton in launching the world's first commercial steamboat, the *Clermont*, named after the Livingston family's home.[11]

Sir Robert Bruce Lockhart As "boy" ambassador to Russia at age thirty-three, he was jailed for a month in 1918 during the revolution and threatened with execution in a plot to kill Lenin. He was also an author, rugby and soccer player of international repute, planter in Malaya, journalist, broadcaster, and banker.[12]

Thomas Babington Macaulay (Lord Macaulay) British author of the famous *History of England* who was a lawyer, member of Parliament, paymaster general, author of the Indian penal code, and secretary of war.[13]

Dr. R. Tait McKenzie Canada's great sculptor was also a physician, soldier, and athlete who helped invent and perfect the game of basketball.[14]

Archibald MacLeish American poet who was also a playwright, lawyer, Phi Beta Kappa scholar, and football player at Yale, first in his class at Harvard Law School, the editor of *Fortune* magazine, a professor at Harvard, a founder of UNESCO, an assistant secretary of state, and the librarian of Congress.[15]

Donald MacNaughton The president of the Prudential Life Insurance Company, the world's largest, was also a professional basketball player.

Sir John Malcolm In addition to being governor of Bombay, he was the author of *A History of Persia* and *A Life of Clive*.[16]

Samuel Finley Breese Morse The inventor of the practical telegraph and the Morse code was later a professor of natural history at Yale and an artist, one of whose paintings sold for over three million dollars in 1982.[17]

John Napier The inventor of logarithms and the first man to use a decimal point, he was also the inventor of several advanced weapons and a learned religious author.[18]

Mungo Park One of the principal African explorers who was also a botanist and surgeon.[19]

Sir Ronald Ross   The Nobel Prize winner who found the key to the conquest of Malaria wrote this poem five years before his discovery:

> The painful faces ask, can we not cure?
> We answer, No not yet; we seek the laws.
> O God reveal thro' all this thing obscure
> The unseen, small, but million-murdering cause.[20]

Alastair Sim   Britain's famous actor, best known for his comic roles and for his portrayal of Scrooge, was also a Shakespearean, a successful theatrical producer, an athlete, a university lecturer, and rector of Edinburgh University.[21]

Tobias Smollett   British novelist who practiced surgery in London, he popularized the French Riviera and invented the street-corner mailbox.[22]

Sir William Stephenson   The Canadian who became famous as the World War II spy Intrepid, was a college dropout who enlisted in World War I and was gassed in France. He faked his medical records and joined the Royal Flying Corps, roaring into action after only five hours of flight instruction. He was credited with downing twenty-six enemy planes and won the Distinguished Flying Cross and the croix de guerre. After the war he became the world lightweight amateur boxing champion, retiring undefeated in 1923. He also won the King's Cup air race and invented the first device for sending photos by radio, becoming a millionaire before he was thirty.[23]

William Walker   The man who "liberated" Nicaragua with a force of fifty-six men and became its president in 1856 had had previous careers as physician, lawyer, and journalist.[24]

Appendix S

The Scottish Passion for Education

Throughout the course of this book it is observed that Scots have made unusually significant contributions to education, not only in their own country, but all over the world. This attachment to education is very old and is one of the most persistent and distinctive of Scottish traits.

According to the historian Boece, the Emperor Charlemagne, "perceiving Scotland to be the most learned of nations," used Scottish teachers in his schools in the ninth century.[1] Michael Scot, a Continental scholar and the first man to use the word *progress*,[2] was largely responsible for bringing the works of Aristotle to the West through his early thirteenth-century translations from Hebrew and Arabic.[3]

Later, in the same century, John Duns Scotus, born in Duns, Berwickshire, and the foremost British medieval scholar, attributed the Immaculate Conception to Mary. Once merely called a "Scotist opinion," this is now dogma of the Roman Catholic church.[4]

Duns Scotus was one of the two great and opposing thinkers of the thirteenth century, the other being St. Thomas Aquinas. Wherever Duns taught, at Oxford, Paris, or Cologne, the Thomists opposed his ideas and later came to think of those who accepted them—the Dunses—as stupid. Because of this the word *dunce* entered into the English language. Through the Middle Ages and beyond, the Continent was full of Scottish scholars and professors. The University of Paris alone records four hundred Scottish names between 1519 and 1615.[5]

At the end of the fifteenth century, Scotland itself was one of only four countries to have three universities. These were founded at St. Andrews (1411), Glasgow (1451), and Aberdeen (1494). In this era England had only two universities.[6] At the time of its founding, Aberdeen was the first university in Britain with a foundation for teaching medicine.[7] A decade later, Edinburgh had the first medical school in Britain,[8] thirty years before Cambridge and forty years before Oxford.[9] By this time it is probable that "the freeholders of Scotland were already better educated than their equals in Europe."[10]

Not satisfied, however, in 1496 the Scottish Parliament passed the world's first compulsory education law. This unique act enjoined each baron and freeholder under penalty of twenty pounds "to send his eldest son to the grammar school at six, or at the utmost, nine years of age. Having been completely grounded in Latin, the pupils were directed to study three years in the schools of philosophy and law."[11] The king himself, James IV, was not exempt, and sent his sons to Italy to study with Erasmus.[12]

In 1560 the General Assembly of the Kirk carried the concept even further. It envisioned a grammar school in every parish, a high school or college in every town, and a university in each principal city of Scotland. The education required was to be "as liberal as possible."[13] John Knox, the leader of the Kirk, proposed that education be compulsory, comprehensive, democratic, and free to all those of ability.[14] Although the Kirk's plan was never fully implemented, it is clear that at this time Scotland had the clearest conception of the value of education of any nation and was centuries ahead of the other nations of the world.[15]

By the seventeenth century the Church of Scotland had parish schools all over the country and the "ignorant yokel," so familiar in English literature, had no place in Scotland.[16] The English historian Trevelyan believed that at the union with England in 1707 the Scots were the best educated people in Europe.[17] Even Dr. Johnson had to admit through his dislike of Scots that on his tour of the Hebrides he "never encountered a house in which he did not find books in more languages than one."[18] By the beginning of the eighteenth century, and indeed well into the nineteenth, Scotland, with only half a million people, had four universities while huge England still only had two. Moreover, while Oxford and Cambridge educated mainly the upper classes, Scotland's universities taught all who qualified.[19] Wright says, "... in Scotland, where the son of the laird mixed with the son of the tenant, and it was indeed more important to come in 'at the heid o' the tenants than at the tail o' the gentry', blacksmith's son's and minister's sons sat side by side."[20]

In addition, the Scots added the teaching of science to the classics earlier than England or any other country. Glasgow had the first university engineering faculty and the first college of applied science and technology in the world.[21] By the end of the eighteenth century there was "a universal diffusion of the rudiments of knowledge among the Scottish peasantry."[22] From England, the *Spectator* said that the Scots were the best educated and best behaved people in the world.[23] Between 1750 and 1800, 87 percent of British doctors were Scottish-trained.[24]

In the nineteenth century, St. Andrews gave Britain's first degrees to women,[25] while Edinburgh was first in the world to accept women as medical students.[26] By the 1860s, 1 in 140 of the Scottish population received a secondary education. In England it was 1 in 1,300. In 1865 Scotland had 1 in 1,000 people in a university and led the world in that regard.[27] By the time of the great emigration every Scot regarded a school as an essential element in a community and took this concept with him.[28] Even in places such as Hispanic California, where only about fifty Scots lived, they managed to educate their children, some going as far as Hawaii to find a Scottish schoolmaster.[29]

In the 1870s Scotland and England both passed education acts. The English act provided for filling in gaps in a voluntary system. The Scottish act made education universal and compulsory. The Scots, unlike the English, required professional training and certificates for teachers. The Scottish act provided for secondary education, the English act did not.[30]

In 1968, when the universities of the civilized world reeled in chaos, the Scottish universities remained calm. In part this was due to their tradition of student involvement in the government of the university, a tradition which derives from the twelfth-century papal recognition of the University of Bologna, but which now survives only in Scotland, where students still exercise power as they vote for the office of rector.[31] In part, also, the Scottish tranquillity of 1968 is the expression of a people almost religiously devoted to education.

Appendix T

The Scottish Nation

There is a common misperception that Scotland is really not one nation but two, divided into Highlanders and Lowlanders. Others think that there are Norse Scots in the north, Gaelic Scots in the west, and Germanic Scots in the south. To be sure, there are regional differences in Scotland, but they are primarily cultural. Despite the multi-ethnic origins of the Scots, who have roots in ancient Britain, Ireland, Scandinavia, the Low Countries, France, Germany, and elsewhere, the Scots are a race defined by *Webster's Dictionary* as "a family, tribe, people or nation belonging to the same stock." The proportions of these components may be different in the country's various regions, but basically, this diverse ancestry is shared by all Scots excepting those recently immigrated from other countries who have not yet "married in."

The miscegenation of the seven founding peoples started early in Scottish history, long before A.D. 843 when King Kenneth was able to unite the country because of his Pictish blood[1] and establish his fellow Gaels all over Scotland. For some time thereafter, Gaelic was spoken throughout the country. When the Germanic Angles, who had already absorbed a substantial British population, moved into southern Scotland the original Scots were not driven out[2] so even in the Lowlands the Gaelic strain persisted. There are still Gaelic place names down to the Borders: from Cairncross and Auchencrow on the east to Lochenbreck and Auchencairn on the west.

Many of the great families and clans were of thoroughly mixed blood long before the War of Independence. By that time the Frasers, Hamiltons, Murrays, and Stewarts all held both Highland and Lowland lands, and the supposedly "Norman" Cummings, Grahams, Hays, and Lindsays were all of largely Gaelic descent. The "British" Galbraiths were already married to Gaels, while Norse-originated families in the west, such as the MacLeods, McCorquodales, Macdonalds, and Mac-Dougalls, had completely integrated into the Scottish population and had Gaelicized their names. The progenitor of the Sutherlands of the far north was a Flemish noble from the Lowlands.[3]

For a while the various elements of this ethnic hodgepodge thought of themselves as different peoples, and as late as 1199 a charter is addressed "Francis et Englis et Flamingis et Scotis."[4] But during the War of Independence the Lowland hero Wallace appeared at Dundee wearing an "Ersche mantill," that is, a tartan plaid,[5] symbolizing the Gaelic inheritance of all Scotland. By 1320 the signatories to the Arbroath Declaration were all claiming to be, and no doubt were, of a common Scottish heritage despite the mute testimony of their surnames' disclosures of all the various strains of the Scottish nation—Pict and Briton, Gael and Angle, Viking, Norman, and Fleming.

The intermarriage of the founding groups of Scotland has continued up to the time of the Industrial Revolution and beyond, to the point where the Scots can be thought of as one great family. Today in modern Scotland Lowland names are seen on storefronts throughout Highland towns, while page after page of Gaelic patronymics swell the telephone directories of Edinburgh and Glasgow. Indeed, Sir Iain Moncrieffe doubted "whether even one of the gallant clansmen who fought at Culloden could ever have been born to be there at all, had King Kenneth MacAlpin been strangled in his cradle."[6]

Appendix U

The Baseball Hall of Fame

The following is a table listing the thirty-seven Scottish-American major league players who have been elected to membership in the National Baseball Hall of Fame.[1] In addition to these, Scottish-American members include nonplayers Branch Rickey, a general manager who built the St. Louis Cardinal and Brooklyn Dodger organizations into prominence in the 1930s and 1940s, and two managers, Miller Huggins and Bill McKechnie. Huggins won American League pennants with the New York Yankees in 1921, 1922, 1923, 1926, 1927, and 1928, taking the World Series three times. McKechnie won National League pennants with Pittsburgh in 1925, St. Louis in 1928, and Cincinnati in 1939 and 1940, taking the World Series twice. Pitching before the official beginning of the National League in 1876, William A. "Candy" Cummings invented the curve ball, and for this was elected to the Hall of Fame.[2]

Players of Scottish Ancestry Elected to the National Baseball Hall of Fame

FIELDERS

	Years	Batting Average	Home Runs
Averill, H. Earl	(1911–1930)	.318	238
Bottomley, James L. "Sunny Jim"	(1922–1937)	.310	219
Cobb, Tyrus R. "Ty"	(1905–1928)	.367	118
Cochrane, Gordon S. "Mickey"	(1925–1937)	.320	119
Crawford, Samuel E. "Wahoo Sam"	(1899–1917)	.309	97
Dickey, William Malcolm "Bill"	(1928–1946)	.313	202
Hamilton, William R. "Billy"	(1888–1901)	.344	40
Hornsby, Rogers "Rajah"	(1915–1937)	.358	302
Jackson, Travis C. "Stonewall"	(1922–1936)	.291	135
Jennings, Hugh "Hughie"	(1891–1918)	.311	18
Keeler, William H. "Wee Willie"	(1892–1910)	.341	34
Killebrew, Harmon	(1954–1975)	.256	573
Kiner, Ralph McPherran	(1946–1955)	.279	369
Rice, Edgar C. "Sam"	(1915–1934)	.322	34
Sewell, Joseph W. "Joe"	(1920–1933)	.312	49
Snider, Edwin D. "Duke"	(1947–1964)	.295	407

312

Thompson, Samuel L. "Sam"	(1885–1906)	.331	129
Vaughan, Joseph F. "Arky"	(1932–1948)	.318	96
Wallace, Roderick J. "Bobby"	(1894–1918)	.268	35
Waner, Lloyd J. "Little Poison"	(1927–1945)	.316	28
Waner, Paul G. "Big Poison"	(1926–1945)	.333	112
Ward, John Montgomery "Monte"	(1878–1894)	.275	25
Youngs, Ross S. "Pep"	(1917–1926)	.322	42

PITCHERS

	Years	Wins	ERA
Alexander, Grover C. "Pete"	(1911–1930)	374	2.56
Clarkson, John Gibson	(1882–1894)	327	2.81
Drysdale, Donald Scott "Don"	(1956–1969)	209	2.95
Grimes, Burleigh A.	(1916–1934)	270	3.53
Grove, Robert Moses "Lefty"	(1925–1941)	300	3.06
Hunter, James Augustus "Catfish"	(1965–1979)	224	3.26
Johnson, Walter P. "Big Train"	(1907–1927)	413	2.17
Lemon, Robert G. "Bob"	(1946–1958)	207	3.23
Lyons, Theodore A. "Ted"	(1923–1946)	260	3.67
Rixey, Eppa	(1912–1933)	266	3.15
Vance, Clarence Arthur "Dazzy"	(1915–1935)	197	3.24
Waddell, George E. "Rube"	(1897–1910)	191	2.16
Wynn, Early	(1939–1963)	300	3.54
Young, Denton T. "Cy"	(1890–1911)	509	2.63

A Proposed Scottish-American All-Time All-Star Team

Pitcher	Walter Johnson
Catcher	Bill Dickey
First Base	Jim Bottomley
Second Base	Rogers Hornsby
Third Base	Harmon Killebrew
Shortstop	Arky Vaughan
Left Field	Ralph Kiner
Center Field	Ty Cobb
Right Field	Duke Snider

Addendum

A 1996 book, *The Millionaire Next Door,* shows that the Scottish ancestry group makes up only 1.7% of American households, but these account for 9.3% of all of the millionaire households in the country. Furthermore, 20.8% of all the Scottish-ancestry households in the United States are millionaire households. The book also notes that, while many of the Scottish-American millionaire households have *less* than $100,000 income, they are better than most Americans at saving and investing. Also, Scottish-Americans, "Have been able to instill their values of thrift, discipline, economic achievement, and financial independence in successive generations."[1]

Scottish-born James A. Mirrlees, of Cambridge University, shared the 1996 Nobel Prize in Economic Science for his "fundamental contributions to the economic theory of incentives."[2]

A Scottish-American, Robert C. Richardson, shared the 1996 Nobel Prize in Physics when his team at Cornell discovered a phenomenon called superfluidity in a rare form of Helium.[3]

William Spiers Bruce (1867–1921) led the Scottish National Antarctic Expedition (1902–1904), which discovered Coats Land and established the oldest Antarctic base. The expedition, financed entirely in Scotland, employed only Scottish scientists.[4]

Carlos J. Finlay (1833–1915), born in Cuba to a French mother and a Scottish father, was the first to report a theory that yellow fever might be transmitted by a mosquito. His theory was later proven true. There is a statue of Dr. Finlay in Finlay Square, Havana.[5] In 1908, the French government made Finlay an officer of the Legion d'Honneur, its highest award for a foreigner. There is a rue du Docteur Finlay in Paris.[6]

The world's first professional body of accountants, The Society of Accountants in Edinburgh (SAE), was founded in 1853. At the end of the nineteenth century about sixty members immigrated to the United States where they had a great influence on the infant American accounting profession. Two of these founded major firms:

Young founded the firm of the same name, and J. B. Niven founded Touche, Niven.[7] Scots also founded the international firms presently named KPMG, and Coopers and Lybrand.

Don McLean, the singer of "American Pie," is an American of Scottish and Italian ancestry.[8]

Thomas Blake Gover (see page 168) built Japan's first tennis court, paved Japan's first road and founded the new world famous Kirin Brewing Company, "Whose name apparently came from a couple of statues depicting him as a mustachioed kirin, a mythical Asian animal.[9]

In 1997 James Cameron (see page 249) wrote, directed, and produced *Titanic*, which won eleven Academy Awards in 1998, and is the highest-grossing film of all time.

In the 1997 elections in Great Britain, Labour swept to victory with a government dominated by people born in Scotland or of Scottish ancestry:[10]

Prime Minister	Tony Blair
Lord Chancellor	Lord Irvine of Lairg
Foreign Secretary	Robin Cook
Chancellor of the Eschequer	Gordon Brown
Secretary of State for Defence	George Robertson
Secretary of State for Scotland	Donald Dewar
Chief Secretary of the Treasury	Alistair Darling
Minister of Transport	Gavin Strang

The new government's offer of Scottland's first parliament in three centuries was enthusiastically accepted by Scots in the referendum held on September 11, 1997, the seven hundredth anniversary of William Wallace's victory over the English Army at Stirling Bridge.

Notes and References

Author to Reader, pp. xiii–xvi

1. Reid, p. 22.
2. See appendix T.
3. See chapter 5.
4. Donaldson, preface.

5. See Weyl, Nathaniel. *The Creative Elite in America* (1966); or for a summary relevant to this book, see appendix Q.

Chapter 1: The Mark of the Scots, pp. 3–7

1. See appendix H.
2. See appendix O.
3. Scottish Development Agency pamphlets.
4. *New York Times*, 27 May 1973.
5. *The Public Interest* (1970).
6. See appendix D.
7. Taylor, p. 15.

8. See appendix Q.
9. U.S. Bureau of Census. "Ancestry and Language in the United States." Current population reports, series P-23, no. 116. Washington, D.C., 1982.
10. See appendix G.
11. Weyl and Possony, p. 28
12. Ellis, pp. 20, 21, and 56; Weyl, p. 83.

Chapter 2: The Exploring Scots, pp. 8–17

1. Rand McNally.
2. Geddes; Barth Healy, *New York Times*, 5 Feb 1989, p. 54.
3. *Encyclopaedia Britannica* (hereafter cited as *EB*), vol. 20, p. 196.
4. Ibid., p. 558.
5. Pohl, p. 10.
6. Ibid., pp. 21, 42.
7. Ibid., p. 63.
8. Ibid., pp. 77–78.
9. Ibid., p. 98; Sinclair, pp. 129–31, says the Zenos were brothers.
10. Ibid., p. 108.
11. Ibid., p. 130; Sinclair, p. 137, makes an interesting case for Louisburg, Cape Breton, as the landing place based on finding a late fourteenth-century Venetian cannon there.
12. Pohl, p. 164.
13. Ibid., p. 115.
14. Ibid., p. 103.

15. Brochure available at Roslin Chapel.
16. Andrew Sinclair, *New York Times*, 22 Sep 1991, Travel section, pp. 14, 16; *EB*, vol. 20, pp. 558–59.
17. *The Scottish Tradition in Canada* (hereafter cited as *Scottish Tradition*), p. ix.
18. Villiers, p. 7; Beaglehole, p. 2.
19. *EB*, vol. 6, pp. 442–43.
20. *New York Times*, 18 Jan 1978; Rand McNally, p. 215.
21. *Scottish World*, p. 250.
22. *National Geographic*, Aug 1987, p. 218; *EB*, vol. 14, p. 532; *The World Almanac and Book of Facts*, 1982 (hereafter cited as *WA*), p. 497.
23. W. N. McDonald, III, *Highlander*, Nov/Dec 1980, p. 44.
24. Reid, p. 42.
25. United States Information Service. "Scottish Contributions to the Making of America," 1950. (hereafter cited as USIS), p. 7.

26. *EB*, vol. 3, p. 441.

27. *EB*, vol. 4, p. 297.

28. *EB*, vol. 17, p. 368.

29. *Highlander*, Nov/Dec 1984, p. 62.

30. *EB*, vol. 13, p. 605.

31. *Collins Encyclopaedia of Scotland* (hereafter cited as *CES*), p. 51; Macgregor, F., p. 101.

32. *EB*, vol. 5, p. 261; *Information Please Almanac* (1977), p. 291.

33. *CES*, p. 131.

34. Donaldson, p. 182; *EB*, vol. 20, p. 1193; *CES*, p. 486.

35. *EB*, vol. 4, p. 701; Gibb, *Scottish Empire* (hereafter cited as *Empire*), p. 124.

36. Roger Watts, *Scottish World* (magazine), Mar 1990, p. 41; R. Glendenning, *Highlander*, Jul/Aug 1994, p. 39.

37. Rand McNally, p. 215.

38. Jane Perlez, *New York Times*, 2 Mar 1990, p. A4.

39. *New York Times*, 12 May 1973; *New York Times*, 29 Jan 1989, p. E22, letter from Barry Kosmin; Bill Keller, *New York Times*, 1 Jun 1993, p. A6; Donatella Lorch, *New York Times*, 10 Feb. 1994, p. A4.

40. Macgregor, F., p. 105.

41. Gordon Bryan, *Highlander*, Jul/Aug 1993, p. 19; *EB*, vol. 16, p. 639.

42. Campbell, p. 86.

43. Macgregor, F., p. 105.

44. Allen, Everett S., *Arctic Odyssey*, 1962.

45. Pound, Reginald, *Scott of Antarctica*, 1966; *EB*, vol. 20, p. 80; John Mackay, *Highlander*, Sep/Oct 1988, p. 49.

46. *National Geographic* map, Antarctica, 1957.

47. National Geographic, May 1989, p. 584; Letter dated Oct 16, 1989, from Jeff MacInnis.

48. *Scottish American*, Oct/Nov 1989, p. 1.

49. See appendix D.

50. *Scots Kith and Kin*, Edinburgh, p. 38.

51. *Scotia News*, 1969.

52. *Life*, 24 Mar 1972.

53. Undated letter from Gordon Cooper; letter dated May 4, 1983, from John Glenn; July 16, 1996 conversation with Mrs. Walter Schirra; conversation with Alan Shepard; letter dated July 23, 1996, from Malcolm Scott Carpenter.

54. Letter dated April 8, 1983, from James B. Irwin; letter (1983) from David R. Scott; *WA*, p. 146.

55. *Highlander*, Apr 1974.

56. *Scottish American*, Oct 1991, p. 10.

57. *Highlander*, Jul/Aug 1992, p. 34.

58. Tom Ferrell, review of *The First Continental Flight*, by Eileen F. Lebow, *New York Times Book Review*, 31 Dec 1989, p. 6

59. *EB*, vol. 20, p. 696.

60. *New York Times*, 30 Mar 1990, p. D17; Undated letter from Eileen Maitland Knoop.

61. Lindbergh, Charles A., *Autobiography of Values* (1976).

62. Geddes.

63. Moncreiffe, p. 51; Walker, pp. 195–200.

64. J. Wickwire, review of *First on Everest* (1987), by T. Holzel and A. Salkeld, *New York Times Book Review*, 1 Feb 1987, p. 21; Carr, Herbert, *The Irvine Draries* (1979).

65. *New York Times*, 7 Nov 1973.

66. *New York Times*, 31 Jul 1978.

67. Undated letter (1986) from Alastair Boyd.

68. *New York Times*, 30 Aug 1982; Undated letter (1982) from Mrs. Bill Dunlop.

69. *New York Times*, 14 Jul 1990, p. 23; *New York Post*, 14 Jul 1990, p. 5; *New York Daily News*, 14 Jul 1990, p. 7.

Chapter 3: The Creation of the United States of America, pp. 18–58

1. USIS, p. 16.

2. Taylor, pp. 7–8.

3. See appendix A.

4. Taylor, p. 7.

5. *EB*, vol. 18, p. 312.

6. Ross, p. 23; Reid, p. 24.

7. W. N. McDonald, III, *Highlander*, Sep/Oct 1984, p. 30.

8. Ross, p. 48.

9. *Scottish Tradition*, p. 181.

10. Insh, p. 186.

11. Ibid., p. 185; Hewitson, p. 18.

12. See chapter 6.

13. Roy, p. 10.

14. Gibb, *Empire*, p. 24.

15. *New York Times*, 18 Sep 1973; Guin-

ness 87, p. 413; Lindblad's Special Expeditions, Costa Rica and Panama, p. 4, 1993.

16. Prebble, pp. 281–85; Gibb, *Empire*, p. 28.

17. Ross, p. 321.

18. *Harvard Encyclopaedia*, p. 899.

19. Black, *Scotland's Mark on America* (hereafter cited as *Mark*), p. 31.

20. Price, Jacob M., in the *William and Mary Quarterly*, April 1954; Haws, passim.

21. Haws, passim; Soltow, p. 83ff; Joyce Somerville, *Highlander*, May/Jun 1993, p. 12.

22. Haws, p. 118.

23. See chapters 6 and 7.

24. D. Dobson, *Scottish-American*, Nov/Dec 1986, p. 5.

25. Graham, p. 142.

26. Hook, p. 48.

27. Hanna, vol. 2, p. 18.

28. Donaldson, p. 35.

29. Hook, p. 49, quoting *Scots* magazine, vol. 38 (1776), p. 366.

30. Hook, p. 55; also see appendix A.

31. Hook, p. 52; Shepperson, p. 9.

32. Hook, p. 58.

33. Haws, passim.

34. Ross, p. 104; Kenneth A. MacIver, *Highlander*, Mar/Apr 1992, p. 33.

35. Begley, p. 202.

36. See appendix A.

37. *EB*, vol. 21, p. 57.

38. Black, *The Surgames of Scotland* (hereafter cited as *Surnames*), p. 742.

39. *EB*, vol. 7, p. 458.

40. Shaw, p. 165.

41. Hanna, vol. 2, p. 189.

42. Taylor, pp. 8–9.

43. Ross, p. 81.

44. Ibid., p. 91.

45. See appendices F and S.

46. Ross, p. 246; Black, *Mark*, p. 108.

47. Black, *Mark*, p. 109; *EB*, vol. 16, p. 385.

48. Black, *Mark*, p. 109.

49. *EB*, vol. 16, p. 386.

50. Black, *Mark*, p. 108.

51. Ibid. p. 111.

52. Ibid. p. 111.

53. Ross, p. 246.

54. Black, *Surnames*, p. 339.

55. Ibid., p. 11.

56. USIS, p. 8.

57. Hook, p. 34; *EB*, vol. 3, p. 754.

58. See appendix F.

59. Woodburn, p. 381.

60. Wertenbaker, p. 18.

61. Hook, p. 33.

62. Lehmann, p. 110.

63. M. Meyers, *Pennsylvania Gazette*, Dec 1986, p. 15.

64. *Pennsylvania Gazette*, Oct 1986, p. 61.

65. Lehmann, p. 75.

66. Saint Andrew's Society, pp. 140, 145, 149.

67. Hook, p. 44.

68. Pryde, p. 36.

69. See appendix F.

70. Hook, p. 29.

71. Ford, p. 449; *WA*, p. 704.

72. Pryde, pp. 5–6.

73. Esmond Wright, *Pennsylvania Gazette*, Feb/Mar 1990, p. 49.

74. Pryde, p. 12.

75. *Scottish Genealogist*, 1974, p. 21.

76. Hook, p. 11; Bailyn, Bernard. *Voyagers to the West*, pp. 25–26.

77. Johnson, p. 20; Wertenbaker, pp. 20–21.

78. Black, *Mark*, p. 36.

79. McCosh, p. 79.

80. Ibid., p. 79.

81. J. Thomson, *Highlander*, Sep/Oct 1984, p. 34.

82. *EB*, vol. 11, p. 380.

83. Ibid., p. 380.

84. *WA*, p. 289; The Randolphs, including Jefferson through his mother Jane Randolph, claimed descent from a blood nephew of King Robert I, the Bruce, Thomas Randolph, Earl of Moray; See USIA, p. 11.

85. Hoyt, pp. 28–29; Graham, G. W., passim.

86. Klett, p. 15.

87. Grimble, p. 224.

88. *Highlander*; Black, *Surnames*, p. 664.

89. Black, *Mark*, p. 37.

90. Haws, p. 4.

91. Donaldson, pp. 50, 109.

92. Ibid., p. 109.

93. Black, *Mark*, p. 5.

94. Wertenbaker, p. 24.

95. *New York Times*, 28 Jul 1975.

96. USIS, p. 11.

97. Ross, pp. 111–13; USIS, p. 11.

98. Johnson, pp. 46–49.

99. Reid, p. 40.

100. John F. Dunn, *New York Times*, 28 Jul 1985; *EB*, vol. 13, p. 433.

101. W. N. McDonald, III, *Highlander*, Mar/Apr 1984, pp. 1, 34, 35; *EB*, vol. 13, pp. 72–73.

102. Washington; Nigel Tranter, *Scottish Banner*, Dec 1994, p. 7.

103. Nolan, p. 19; Ross, p. 305.

104. Black, *Mark*, p. 4.

105. Hanna, vol. 2, p. 186; USIS, p. 11.

106. Klett, p. 37; *EB*, vol. 6, p. 419.

107. Black, *Mark*, p. 109.

108. Green, p. 24.

109. Black, *Surnames*, p. 548.

110. Moncreiffe, p. 156; telephone conversation with Mr. Kingsley of Betsy Ross House, Philadelphia, Jul 24, 1974.

111. See appendix B.

112. See appendix A.

113. U.S. Census Bureau, *A Century of Population Growth* (1909).

114. *EB*, vol. 11, p. 28.

115. Lorant, p. 14.

116. *WA*, p. 475; Lorant, p. 14.

117. Lorant, p. 15.

118. Ibid., p. 16.

119. Wills, *Explaining America* (hereafter cited as *Explaining*), p. 7

120. Hanna, vol. 1, p. 32.

121. Lorant, p. 14.

122. *EB*, vol. 11, p. 380.

123. *National Geographic*, Sep 1987, p. 365.

124. Wills, *Explaining*, passim, and p. ix, 169; Sheila Keenan, Scottish Heritage Files; Reid, p. 45.

125. M. Ledger, *Pennsylvania Gazette*, Oct 1986, p. 34.

126. Esmond Wright, *Pennsylvania Gazette*, Feb/Mar 1990, p. 45.

127. Wills, *Inventing America* (hereafter cited as *Inventing*), p. 175.

128. See chapter 5.

129. See chapter 9.

130. Hook, p. 176.

131. *EB*, vol. 6, p. 167.

132. *Scotia*, p. 10.

133. Lehmann, p. 162.

134. Wills, *Inventing*, p. 229.

135. Ibid., p. 181.

136. Edwards, p. 10.

137. Soma Golden, *New York Times*, 9 Mar 1976.

138. Smith, Adam. *An Inquiry Into the Nature and Causes of the Wealth of Nations* (1776), Random House edition (1937), pp. 576–82.

139. McCosh, pp. 187–88.

140. Wills, *Explaining*, p. 37.

141. Ibid., p. 18; Johnson, p. 37

142. Lehmann, p. 139.

143. McCosh, pp. 187–88.

144. Esmond Wright, *Pennsylvania Gazette*, Feb/March 1990, p. 46.

145. Parks, p. 31; Wills, *Inventing*, pp. 176–77.

146. Hook, p. 22; Haws, p. 110.

147. Garry Wills, *New York Times*, travel section, 9 Jan 1983, p. 39.

148. Nolan, pp. 60, 201.

149. Esmond Wright, *Pennsylvania Gazette*, Feb/Mar 1990, p. 44.

150. Hook, p. 175.

151. Wills, *Inventing*, p. 175.

152. Black, *Mark*, p. 77.

153. Lehmann, p. 110.

154. Haws, p. 57.

155. *National Geographic*, Sep 1987, p. 345; Wills, *Explaining*, pp. 14, 23.

156. *Highlander*, Jan 1980, p. 28.

157. McCosh, p. 187.

158. Cox, p. 11.

159. Chitwood, p. 6; Haws, p. 19.

160. Wills, *Explaining*, p. 63.

161. Gerson, p. 10.

162. *EB*, vol. 7, p. 162.

163. Prebble, p. 242.

164. Ibid., p. 242.

165. The Arbroath Declaration was written in Latin. The translation used here is from National Manuscripts of Scotland, Part 2, 1870. It is not known which translations might have been used in 1776. It is likely that some of the American founding fathers could have read the original Latin. Nevertheless, the translations of some of the words used here for comparison are obvious: *libertatem*, liberty; *vita*, life; *consensus*, consent; *princeps*, prince; *barbaracis*, barbarous, etc.

166. Johnson, p. 50.

167. Hanna, vol. 1, p. 32; Hanna, vol. 2, p. 186.

168. Reid, p. 50.

169. James Reston, *New York Times*, 12 Dec 1971.

170. Saint Andrew's Society, pp. 158–59.

171. Lehmann, p. 174.

172. John Douglas Gillespie, *Scottish Genealogist* 10, no. 4, p. 10.

173. Black, *Surnames*, p. 779. Trent's father, also William Trent, for whom New Jersey's state capital is named, was born in Inverness. His 1719 house is now a Trenton city museum.

174. Commager, pp. 19–20.

175. Geddes.

176. Ross, p. 112.

177. Commager, pp. 18–24; *EB*, vol. 4, p. 56.

178. Ellis, p. 272.

179. Ross, p. 29; Commager, p. 31.

180. David L. Peet, *Highlander*, Jul 1976, pp. 1–4.

181. Commager, p. 44.

182. Saint Andrew's Society, p. 17.

183. *EB*, vol. 23, pp. 479–80.

184. Black, *Mark*, p. 31.

185. Collection of R. T. Aitchison exhibited at Wichita State University (hereafter cited as WSU exhibit).

186. Letter dated May 3, 1991, from Lynne Tolley, a descendant of Jack Daniel.

187. *Forbes*, 15 May 1973, p. 104.

188. *EB*, vol. 23, p. 479.

189. Black, *Mark*, p. 103; Black, *Surnames*, p. 188.

190. Black, *Mark*, p. 31; William Lindsay, proceedings of the Scotch-Irish Society, third congress (1891), p. 193.

191. Hanna, vol. 1, p. 30.

192. *EB*, vol. 5, p. 870.

193. Jim Buchanan, *Highlander*, Mar/Apr 1988, pp. 42–43; Lydia Chavez, *New York Times*, 11 Sep 1988, p. XX 10.

194. *EB*, vol. 5, p. 870.

195. Interview with Amb. Henry J. Taylor, 1973.

196. Hanna, vol. 1, p. 137.

197. *Highlander*, Nov/Dec 1985, p. 26; *EB*, vol. 5, p. 909.

198. R. F. Berkhofer, *New York Times Book Review*, 16 Sep 1984, p. 22.

199. *Highlander*, Mar/Apr 1981, p. 43.

200. WSU exhibit; Black, *Mark*, p. 109.

201. WSU exhibit.

202. WSU exhibit.

203. F. S. Buchanan, "Scots Among the Mormons," *Utah Historical Quarterly* 36, no. 4 (1968), p. 346.

204. *New York Times*, 25 Nov 1976.

205. Black, *Mark*, p. 99.

206. *Highlander*, Mar 1979, p. 33; *EB*, vol. 3, p. 946.

207. USIS, p. 13; *EB*, vol. 4, p. 32.

208. Johnson, p. 15; *EB*, vol., 4 p. 968.

209. Hanna, vol. 1, p. 50; *EB*, vol. 6, p. 787.

210. Ross, pp. 1, 20.

211. *Scottish-American*, Nov/Dec 1986, p. 2.

212. Hewitson, p. 171.

213. Ross, p. 18.

214. Sue Kerr Wood, *Scottish Genealogist*, no. 4; *Scottish-American*, Oct 1991, p. 10.

215. Bernardo, pp. 14–17.

216. Todd S. Purdom, *New York Times*, 7 Jan 1994, p. A22.

217. USIS, p. 13; *EB*, vol. 14, p. 358; *WA*, p. 704.

218. *EB*, vol. 16, p. 369; Hanley, p. 60; see pp. 114–15.

219. *EB*, vol. 9, p. 471.

220. Ibid., p. 471.

221. *EB*, vol. 18, pp. 174–75.

222. *Highlander*, Sep 1979, p. 10.

223. J. Thomson, *Highlander*, Mar 1979, p. 33.

224. Texas International Gathering brochure.

225. W. N. McDonald, III, *Highlander*, Mar 1980.

226. *Highlander*, Jan/Feb 1983, p. 46.

227. *National Geographic*, Jan 1988, p. 36; Scottish Heritage U.S.A.

228. *EB*, vol. 19, p. 1007; Rogers, Fred B. *Montgomery and the Portsmouth*, (1958).

229. USIS, p. 12.

230. Stephen W. Sears, review of *So Far From God* (1989), by John S. D. Eisenhower, *New York Times Book Review*, 2 Apr 1989, p. 13.

231. Jim Buchanan, *Highlander*, Nov/Dec 1991, p. 64.

232. *EB*, vol. 18, pp. 174–75; Nevins, Allan, *Polk* (1952), p. 404; Sellers, Charles, *James K. Polk* (1966), pp. 484–87.

233. Klett, p. 25.

234. *EB*, vol. 15, p. 537.

235. Carter, Harvey L. *Zebulon Montgomery Pike*, 1956.

236. Warren Hinckle, III, and Frederick Hobbs, *Highlander*, Nov/Dec 1981, p. 32.

237. Lake, Stuart N. *Wyatt Earp*, p. 1.

238. Bernardo, p. 162.

239. *Scottish Heritage U.S.A.* magazine, Jun 1981, p. 3.

240. Jackson, pp. 301, 305, 316.

241. Bell, Brian, ed., *Insight Guides— Scotland* (1990), p. 48.

242. Hewitson, p. 51.

243. *Scottish Tradition*, p. 45.

244. K. Bartholomew, *Highlander*, Jul/Aug 1983, p. 28; *EB*, vol. 21, p. 48.

245. T. Hunter, *Highlander*, May/Jun 1987, p. 36.

246. Dan McPherson, *Highlander*, Jul/Aug 1989, pp. 10–20.

247. Martha Voight, *Scottish Historical Review*, vol. 52, pp. 141, 144, 148.

248. *Ibid.*, p. 140; Nicholson, A. *American Houses in History*, 1965, pp. 240-42; Robert G. Douglass, *Highlander*, Sep/Oct 1992, pp. 24–28.

249. Martha Voight, *Scottish Historical Review*, vol. 52, pp. 138–42.

250. J. Thomson, *Highlander*, Sep 1980, p. 45.

251. Black, *Mark*, p. 97.

252. *EB*, vol. 7, p. 103.

253. W. N. McDonald, III, *Highlander*, May/Jun 1984, pp. 40–41.

254. Brown, p. 52; Walker, Lewis. *Speak for Yourself, Daniel* (1969), p. 1.

255. *Highlander*, Mar/Apr 1982, p. 43.

256. Day, A. Grove. *History Makers of Hawaii*.

257. *New York Times*, 15 Feb 1987, p. 36.

258. Day, op. cit.

259. *EB*, vol. 16, p. 388.

260. *EB*, vol. 11, p. 178.

261. USIS, p. 14.

262. Black, *Mark*, p. 100.

263. U.S. Census Supplementary report 1990 CP-S-1-2, P. III-4.

264. U.S. Census Bureau. *A Century of Population Growth* (1909).

265. See appendix D.

266. *EB*, vol. 22, p. 267; Harold Farber, *New York Times*, 12 Jan 1989, p. 36.

Chapter 4: The Construction of the British Empire, pp. 59–101

1. See pp. 19–20.

2. Donaldson, p. 206.

3. Fraser, pp. 183–87.

4. *Highlander*, Mar/Apr 1984, p. 39.

5. Adam, Frank. *The Clans, Septs and Regiments of the Scottish Highlands* (1908), p. 572.

6. Will, p. 34.

7. *WA*, p. 401.

8. Roy, p. 19.

9. Caledonian Society of London, p. 37.

10. Will, p. 46; Royal Scottish Corporation Pamphlet; *Pibroch*, Saint Andrew's Society of the State of New York, June 1990.

11. McCulloch, p. 69.

12. Hook, p. 55.

13. Murray, William (Lord Mansfield). *The Thistle the Scotch* (London, 1746), p. 25.

14. Will, p. 36.

15. Roy, p. 19.

16. John Clive, and Bernard Bailyn: *England's Cultural Provinces: Scotland and America*, p. 212; Hook, p. 63.

17. Will, p. 38.

18. See appendix H.

19. See appendix G.

20. Gilmour, p. 45.

21. Churchill, Randolph. *Winston S. Churchill* (1966), p. 15.

22. *New York Daily News*, 13 Dec 1977.

23. *EB*, vol. 14, p. 806; *EB*, vol. 4, p. 715; *EB*, vol. 5, p. 997.

24. E. McIntyre, *Highlander*, Nov/Dec 1988, p. 24.

25. *CES*, pp. 103, 358, 371, 401, 969.

26. Kellas, p. 139.

27. Grimble, p. 15.

28. Martin: *The Woman He Loved*

29. Letter received from assistant to Neil Gordon Kinnock.

30. John Newhouse, *The New Yorker*, 21 May 1984, p. 48.

31. *New York Times*, 16 Jan 1987.

32. Craig, R. Whitney, *New York Times*, 19 Jul 1992, p. 3., Richard W. Stevenson, *New York Times*, 13 May 1994, p. A11.

33. Richard W. Stevenson, *New York Times*, 22 Jul 1994, p. A2.

34. *EB*, vol. 16, p. 1187.

35. *CES*, p. 986.
36. Wills, E. p. 25.
37. MacKenzie, p. 133.
38. *EB*, vol. 4, p. 281.
39. *New York Times Book Review*, 27 Mar 1977.
40. *New York Times*, 25 Sept 1973.
41. Black, *Surnames*, p. 762.
42. *EB*, vol. 7, p. 100.
43. Black, *Surnames*, p. 415.
44. *New York Times*, 26 Mar 1980, p. A3.
45. Letter dated Nov 9, 1982, from Basil Cardinal Hume.
46. *EB*, vol. 6, p. 677; Gilmour, p. 61.
47. McCulloch, p. 146.
48. Geddes.
49. Will, p. 38.
50. Geddes; *EB*, vol. 2, p. 476.
51. *EB*, vol. 14, p. 490.
52. McCulloch, p. 146.
53. Geddes.
54. P. Horvitz, *New York Times*, 6 Oct 1987, p. C1; S. Lohr, *New York Times*, 17 Nov 1987, p. D6.
55. See pp. 225–226.
56. Moncreiffe, p. 52.
57. John Gross, *New York Times*, 31 Jan 1985, p. C21.
58. Woodburn, title page.
59. Donald Whyte, *Scottish Genealogist* 21, no. 4, p. 119.
60. Gibb, *Empire*, p. 12.
61. Hill, passim; *EB*, vol. 16, pp. 964–6; Beckett, p. 45.
62. Gibb, *Empire*, p. 8.
63. Black, *Mark*, p. 14.
64. *Scottish Studies*, vol. 8 (1964), p. 236.
65. Woodburn, p. 403.
66. *EB*, vol. 6, p. 692.
67. *EB*, vol. 12, p. 568; *EB*, vol. 20, pp. 56–7.
68. MacGregor, G. p. 151, quoting from *Blackwood's* magazine, Sept 1829.
69. Census of Canada, Bulletin 7. 1–6, pp. 6–21.
70. See appendix H.
71. *Scottish Tradition*, p. ix.
72. Ibid., p. ix.
73. Black, *Surnames*, p. 319.
74. Ross, p. 66.
75. *EB*, vol. 16, p. 639.
76. *New York Times* 22 Sep 69.
77. *Scottish Tradition*, pp. 16–17; Campbell, p. 134; *Scottish Genealogist* 21, no.4, p. 117.
78. Black, *Surnames*, p. 750.
79. *Scottish Tradition*, p. 144.
80. Ibid., pp. 18–19; Roy, p. 61.
81. Ibid., p. 197.
82. Campbell, p. 39.
83. Gibbon, p. 82.
84. WSU exhibit.
85. *New York Times*, 26 Sep 1979.
86. *Scottish Tradition*, p. 281.
87. Ibid., p. 199.
88. Ibid., p. 27.
89. Gibb, *Empire*, p. 308; Sc. Trad., p. 32.
90. *Scottish Tradition*, p. 30.
91. Gibb, *Empire*, p. 40.
92. *Scottish Tradition*, p. 185.
93. Ibid., p. 36.
94. Campbell, p. 51.
95. *Scottish Tradition*, p. 39.
96. P. Hutchinson, *Scottish Genealogist* 29, no. 2, p. 36.
97. *National Geographic*, Aug 1987, p. 194.
98. *Scottish Tradition*, p. 42.
99. *EB*, vol. 21, p. 301.
100. *National Geographic*, Aug 1987, p. 210.
101. Ibid, p. 194.
102. *Scottish Tradition*, p. 142.
103. Campbell, p. 110.
104. Rattray, p. 224.
105. *Scottish Tradition*, p. 129.
106. Rattray, p. 290.
107. *Scottish Tradition*, p. 53.
108. Ibid., p. 279.
109. Rattray, p. 469.
110. Moncreiffe, p. 212; *EB*, vol. 14, p. 534.
111. *Scottish Tradition*, p. 96; W. N. McDonald, III, *Highlander*, May/June 1988, p.47.
112. Rattray, p. 564; *New York Times*, 11 Jan 1985, p. A18.
113. *EB*, vol. 14, p. 505.
114. Campbell, p. 123.
115. Gibbon, p. 60.
116. Campbell, p. 124.
117. *Scottish Tradition*, p. 192.
118. Ibid., p. 195.
119. Rothney, p. 7; Campbell, p. 250.
120. See p. 19.
121. Rattray, p. 288.
122. Rothney, p. 20.
123. Ibid. p. 25.
124. Campbell, p. 115; *EB*, vol. 18, p. 536.

125. Campbell, pp. 115, 122.
126. Ibid., p. 117.
127. *Scottish Tradition*, p. 59.
128. *EB*, vol. 4, p. 233.
129. Gibbon.
130. K. M. Bartholomew, *Highlander*, Jul/Aug 1983, p. 28.
131. Gibb, *Empire*, p. 60.
132. Rattray, p. 1107.
133. W. N. McDonald, III, *Highlander*, Jul/Aug 1991, p. 54.
134. *Highlander*, May/Jun 1986, p. 26; Geraldine Hearsey, *Scottish Banner*, Mar 1995, p. 25.
135. *Scottish Tradition*, p. 79.
136. *EB*, vol. 4, p. 233.
137. *Scottish Tradition*, p. 87.
138. Morton.
139. W. N. McDonald, III, *Highlander*, Jul/Aug, 1980, p. 34.
140. *EB*, vol. 20, p. 196.
141. *EB*, vol. 14, p. 792.
142. *Scottish Tradition*, pp. 60–61.
143. W. N. McDonald, III, *Highlander*, Jul/Aug 1991, p. 54.
144. *Scottish Tradition*, p. 78.
145. Ibid., p. 79.
146. Morton, p. 172.
147. *Scottish Tradition*, p. 86.
148. Ibid., p. 86.
149. Ibid., p. 78.
150. Bryce, p. 312.
151. *CES*, p. 891.
152. Rattray, p. 956.
153. *Scottish Tradition*, p. 77.
154. Ibid., p. 80.
155. Ibid., pp. 85–86.
156. Ibid., p. 81.
157. Ibid., p. 82.
158. Ibid., p. 87.
159. *EB*, vol. 19, p. 1081; *New York Times*, 25 Feb 1986.
160. Gibb, *Empire*, p. 42
161. Conversation with Burt Udall, Edmonton Telephone Historical Center, Oct 11, 1995.
162. *New York Times*, 9 Apr 1979.
163. *Scottish Tradition*, p. 87.
164. Ibid., p. 43; Bryce, p. 75; Gibbon, p. 147.
165. Gibbon, p. 145; *Scottish Tradition*, p. 80.
166. Gibbon, p. 143.
167. Campbell, p. 249.
168. Ibid., p. 250. Also see p. 76.
169. Ibid., p. 250. Also see p. 70.
170. Gibb, *Empire*, p. 65.
171. Campbell.
172. Gibb, *Empire*, p. 67.
173. Rattray, vol. 2, p. 495.
174. Campbell.
175. Ibid.
176. Gibb, *Empire*, p. 79.
177. Campbell.
178. Ibid.
179. Moncrieffe, p. 116.
180. Campbell.
181. *EB*, vol. 15, p. 558.
182. *Scottish Historical Review* 10, p. 1.
183. *EB*, vol. 8, p. 280; *EB*, vol. 4, p. 737.
184. Roy, p. 102.
185. Rattray, vol. 2, p. 633.
186. *Scottish Tradition*, pp. 289–91.
187. W. N. McDonald, III, *Highlander*, Jan 1978, p. 2.
188. *Scottish Tradition*, pp. 289–90.
189. *EB*, vol. 14, pp. 504, 532
190. W. N. McDonald, III, *Highlander*, Jan 1978, p. 1–2; W. N. McDonald, III, *Highlander*, Nov/Dec 1981, p. 36; *EB*, vol. 21, p. 301; *EB*, vol. 9, p. 437; Gibb, *Empire*, p. 99; *Scottish Tradition*, p. 293.
191. *EB*, vol. 14, p. 504.
192. Ibid., p. 532.
193. Donaldson, Gordon. *Eighteen Men, the Prime Ministers of Canada* (1985), p. 52.
194. *EB*, vol. 3, p. 953.
195. Donaldson, op. cit., p. 101.
196. *Scottish Tradition*, p. 296.
197. Ibid., p. 297.
198. *New York Times*, Oct 19, 1970.
199. Letter dated Sep 29, 1993, from K. A. MacNeil, special assistant to the Rt. Hon. Kim Campbell.
200. *Highlander*, Oct 1977, p. 31.
201. *Scottish Tradition*, p. 297.
202. Campbell, p. 297.
203. Ibid., p. 296.
204. *Scottish Tradition*, p. 252.
205. *New York Times*, 10 Sep 1979.
206. Roy, p. 112.
207. Campbell, p. 293.
208. *Scottish Tradition*, p. 106.
209. *EB*, vol. 21, p. 301.
210. Roy, p. 112.
211. McGill: John Neil (Sc. Trad., p. 129);

McMaster: Rev. J. H. Fyfe (Sc. Trad. p. 131); Queen's: Dr. James Liddell (Roy, p. 112); Dalhousie: Rev. Thomas McCulloch (Sc. Trad., p. 106); Toronto: John Strachan (Campbell, p. 271).

212. Irving, p. 49; Telephone conversation with Ms. D. Lemieux at Ogilvy's, Aug 22, 1990.

213. Roy, p. 111.

214. Munro, p. 39; *EB*, vol. 15, p. 134; Gibb, *Empire*, p. 190.

215. Ernest McIntyre, *Highlander*, Jan/Feb 1993, p. 37.

216. Gibb, *Empire*, p. 185.

217. Ibid., p. 185; *CES*, p. 259.

218. Donaldson, p. 202.

219. *EB*, vol. 12, p. 147.

220. Gibb, *Empire*, p. 205.

221. Mason, pp. 75–95.

222. *EB*, vol. 15, p. 1174.

223. Grimble, p. 236; Gibb, *Empire* pp. 218–26; *EB*, vol. 7, pp. 5–6.

224. Grimble, p. 44.

225. Woodburn, p. 385; Gibb, *Empire*, p. 233; *EB*, vol. 12, p. 112A; *EB*, vol. 13, pp. 827–28; McCulloch, p. 278; *Highlander*, Sep/Oct 1987, p. 46; Macgregor, F., p. 41.

226. Munro, p. 163; *EB*, vol. 21, p. 301.

227. *EB*, vol. 8, p. 280; Woodburn, p. 385.

228. *EB*, vol. 12, p. 150; Gilmour, p. 38.

229. Macgregor, F., p. 173.

230. Ibid. p. 76; Geddes.

231. *CES*, p. 713.

232. Gibb, *Empire*, p. 245.

233. Gibb,*Empire*, p. 190.

234. *CES*, p. 985.

235. *Dictionary of National Biography* (hereafter cited as *DNB*); *CES*, p. 984.

236. Gilmour, p. 18.

237. Geddes; *EB*, vol. 21, p. 738; *CES*, p. 363.

238. Gibb, *Empire*, p. 252.

239. *EB*, vol. 2, p. 785.

240. Black, *Surnames*, p. 757.

241. Gibb, *Empire*.

242. *EB*, vol. 2, p. 786.

243. Ibid., p. 786; Gibb, *Empire*, p. 268.

244. *EB*, vol. 2, p. 787; Gibb, *Empire*, p. 268.

245. Munro, p. 127.

246. Rand McNally, p. 215; Chisholm, p. 116.

247. *DNB*, vol. 19, p. 136.

248. *EB*, vol. 2, pp. 786–87.

249. Rand McNally, p. 215; Gibb, *Empire*, p. 268; Macgregor, F., p. 108.

250. Gibb, *Empire*, p. 257.

251. Alexander Smart, *Scots Magazine*, Oct 1940.

252. Grimble, p. 134.

253. Gibb, *Empire*, p. 257; Donaldson, p. 154; Grimble, p. 134.

254. Grimble, p. 134.

255. Chisholm, p. 109.

256. George R. Bard, *Highlander*, Jul/Aug 1995, p. 6.

257. Wills, E. p. 82.

258. Gibb, *Empire*; Grimble, p. 134.

259. W. N. McDonald, III, *Highlander*, Jul/Aug 1983, p. 1.

260. Gibb, *Empire*; Munro, p. 139.

261. W. N. McDonald, III, *Highlander*, Jul/Aug 1983, pp. 36–37; Grimble, p. 204; Chisholm, p. 108.

262. *EB*, vol. 2, p. 788.

263. Gibb, *Empire*; *EB*, vol. 4, p. 217; Chisholm, p. 108.

264. MacMillan, p. 151.

265. Gibb, *Empire*; *EB*, vol. 23, p. 425; Chisholm, p. 116.

266. Black, *Surnames*, p. 24.

267. MacMillan, p. 111.

268. Alexander Smart, *Scots Magazine*, Oct 1940, p. 47.

269. *New York Times*, travel section, 7 Jun 1992, p. 12, letter from Tamara Pristin.

270. Donaldson, pp. 162–63.

271. Gibb, *Empire*.

272. Geddes.

273. Taylor, p. 15; Munro, pp. 153, 167.

274. *New York Times*, 26 Mar 1991, p. B8.

275. Chisholm, p. 112.

276. *EB*, vol. 9, p. 361.

277. Edwards, Cecil. *Bruce of Melbourne*, p. 8.

278. *New York Times*, 16 May 1978.

279. *New York Times*, 12 Dec 1977.

280. *Highlander*, Jul 1979, p. 4.

281. Walker, pp. 116, 124.

282. *New York Times*, 16 May 1978.

283. *Scotland's Magazine* Jan 1968, p. 46.

284. MacMillan, p. 109.

285. Nicholson, G. Harvey. *First 100 Years*, 1952.

286. Chisholm, p. 111; Wills, E. p. 82; Duncan-Hughes, J. G. *The Scots Invasion of*

Australia; CES, p. 656.

287. Gibb, *Empire* p. 286.

288. Bill Kinnaird, *Highlander*, Jan/Feb 1991, p. 36.

289. *EB*, vol. 16, p. 407; Chisholm, p. 110.

290. Chisholm, p. 110.

291. Pearce; *EB*, vol. 16, p. 453.

292. Pearce, p. 35.

293. M. F. Lloyd Prichard, *Scottich Genealogist* 25, no. 3, p. 81.

294. Pearce, p. 50.

295. Ibid., p. 41.

296. M. F. Lloyd Prichard, *Scottish Genealogist* 25, no. 3, p. 82; *EB*, vol. 2, p. 741.

297. Gibb, *Empire*; Donaldson.

298. Pearce, p. 50.

299. McKenzie, N.R. *The Gael Fares Forth* (Wellington, 1942); Macdonald, Gordon. *The Highlanders of Waipu* (Dunedin, 1928).

300. Pearce, p. 141.

301. Whyte, p. 124.

302. Geddes; *WA*, p. 447.

303. M. F. Lloyd Prichard, *Scottish Genealogist* 25, no. 3, p. 82.

304. Pearce, p. 110.

305. Moncreiffe, p. 100.

306. Pearce, p. 103; Gibb, *Empire*, p. 303.

307. Pearce, p. 122.

308. Donaldson, p. 178.

309. *New York Times*.

310. Donaldson, p. 179.

311. *WA*, p. 564.

312. *New York Times*, 17 May 1973.

313. Gibb, *Empire*, p. 106.

314. Ibid., p. 107; Campbell, C. T.

315. Bond.

316. Hockly, p. 12.

317. Bond, p. 30.

318. Ibid., pp. 49, 111.

319. Hockly, p. 143.

320. Alistair Campbell of Airds, *Scottish World* magazine, Mar/Apr 1992, p. 45.

321. C.D.I.G. Forrester, *Scottish Genealogist* 30, no. 3, p. 91.

322. Bond, p. 139; donaldson, p. 189.

323. Hockly, p. 119; Bond, p. 129.

324. Hattersley, p. 290.

325. Bond, p. 118.

326. Ibid. p. 126.

327. *Scottish Genealogist* 14, no. 2, p. 39.

328. Taylor, p. 14.

329. *EB*, vol. 19, p. 277.

330. *EB*, vol. 12, p. 866; *CES*, p. 557.

331. *New York Times*, 4 Mar 1978.

332. Gibb, *Empire*, p. 142.

333. *CES*, p. 583.

334. A. G. Macdonnell, *Geographic*, vol. 7, (1938), pp. 19–30.

335. Gibb, *Empire*, p. 138.

336. *EB*, vol. 14, p. 494.

337. *EB*, vol. 13, p. 605; *EB*, vol. 2, p. 1046; Gibb, *Empire*, p. 178.

338. Gibb, *Empire* p. 179; Keary, M. R. *Great Scotswomen* (London, 1933).

339. *New York Times*, 10 Nov 1971.

340. Bryant S. Mason, *New York Times*, 30 Oct 1994, p. XX 7.

341. Grimble, p. 76.

342. Moncrieffe, p. 188; *EB*, vol. 4, pp. 917–18; Harlow, V. T. *A History of Barbados* (London, 1926).

343. Ross, p. 89; Geddes.

344. *Scottish Genealogist* 15, no. 3, p. 61.

345. Bulloch, J. M. *The Making of the West Indies* (1915).

346. Moncreiffe, p. 210.

347. *New York Times*, 31 Oct 1980, p. 1.

348. *Scotsman*, 23 Oct 1961.

349. *Edinburgh Evening News*, 6 Nov 1961.

350. *Highlander*, Nov 1978, quoting the *Manchester Guardian Weekly; New York Times*, 14 Aug 1977; *New York Times*, 7 Apr 1984.

351. Gibb, *Empire*, p. 291.

352. Ibid.

353. *EB*, vol. 16, pp. 344–45; MacLean and Dunnett, p. 119; Gibb, *Empire*, p. 284.

354. *Scots Magazine* 35, no. 5, pp. 386–91.

355. McCulloch, p. 276; Gibb, *Empire*, p. 212.

356. Gibb, *Empire*, p. 193.

357. Bill Kinnaird, *Highlander*, Nov/Dec 1990, pp. 54–55.

358. *Scottish Genealogist* 29, no. 3, p. 73, quoting H. E. Richardson, *Scottish Genealogist* 29, no. 3, p. 73; Geddes; *EB*, vol. 21, p. 1110G; *CES*, p. 88.

359. Rattray, p. 631.

360. *EB*, vol. 10, p. 580; *Scottish Tradition* p. 12; Waller, John H. *Gordon of Khartoum*, 1988, p. 15.

361. Hanna, vol. 1, p. 138.

362. *Fortune*, Nov 1971; *New York Times*, 25 Nov. 1980; N. D. Kristof, *New York Times*, 1 Dec 1986, p. D1; N. D. Kristof, *New York Times*, 21 Jun 1987, p. 8F; *New York Times*, 9 Nov 1987, p. A10; *CES*, p. 558.

363. Edward A. Gargan, *New York Times*, 21 Aug 1994, sec. 3, p. 1; *Brief History* furnished by the Hong Kong and Shanghai Banking Corporation, Ltd.
364. *CES*, p. 635.
365. Hanna, vol. 1, p. 143.
366. *New York Times*, 14 May 1982.
367. *New York Times*, 27 Sep. 1987.
368. *CES*, p. 679.
369. *EB*, vol. 15, p. 862; Geddes.

370. *New York Times*, 20 Nov 1987, p. C3; CES, p. 562.
371. M. A. Uhlilg, *New York Times*, 27 Nov 1987, p. B27.
372. F. M. Hechinger, *New York Times*, 9 Sep 1986, p. C9, quoting Robert MacNeil, *The Story of English* (1986).
373. R. F. Shepard, *New York Times*, 11 Sep 1986, p. C21.
374. Wills, E. p. 9.

Chapter 5: The Industrial Revolution, pp. 102–130

1. Reid, J. M. *Scotland's Progress*, Eyre and Spottswood.
2. Clark, p. 258–59.
3. Soma Golden, *New York Times*, 9 Mar 1976, p. 55. Quotation comparing Smith and Newton is from the economist Paul Samuelson in the same article.
4. Wills, E., p. 80.
5. *New York Times*, 19 Jul 1987.
6. Prebble, p. 312; Fischer, S. *Uptown, Downtown* (1976), p. 248; Craig Whitney, *New York Times*, 20 May 1990, p. xx 36; Donaldson, p. 86.
7. *Scottish Tradition*, p. 198.
8. For more Scottish inventions, see appendix I.
9. Donaldson and Morpeth, p. 212.
10. MacLean and Dunnett, p. 168.
11. *New York Times*, 1 Jun 1975.
12. Kellas, p. 159; Wills, E., p. 36; *EB*, vol. 3, p. 766.
13. MacKenzie, p. 47; Geddes; *CES*, p. 729.
14. Robertson, "Secular Changes in Scottish Genius," (hereafter cited as "Secular Changes")
15. McCulloch, p. 168; MacGregor, G., p. 231; Margaret Henderson, *Highlander*, Sep/Oct 1984, pp. 20–21.
16. *EB*, vol. 17, p. 938.
17. *Highlander*, Jul/Aug 1987, p. 30.
18. Robertson, "Secular Changes"; *CES*, p. 727.
19. Brenda Maddox, review of *The Calculating Passion of Ada Byron*, by Joan Baum, *New York Times Book Review*, 5 Oct 1986, p. 44; letter to the *New York Times*, 19 Mar 1989, p. E26.

20. Rodgers, William. *THINK* (1969).
21. Belden, T. and M. *The Lengthening Shadow* (1962).
22. Bowes.
23. Jeremy Bernstein, *New York Times Magazine*, 15 Feb 1976, p. 35.
24. See p. 149.
25. *WA*, p. 816.
26. Letter dated Jun 4, 1982, from Grace Murray Hopper; J. Cushman, *New York Times*, 14 Aug 1986, p. B6; John Markoff, *New York Times*, 3 Jan 1992, p. A17.
27. Letter dated Jun 4, 1982, from Clive Sinclair; Barnaby Feder, *New York Times Magazine*, 19 May 1985, p. 101.
28. Letter dated Jan 11, 1973, from Walter Brattain; Leroy Pope, *Pittsburgh Press*, 26 Dec 1972, p. 29; Susan Heller Anderson, *New York Times*, 14 Oct 1987, p. B12.
29. *New York Times*, 22 Oct 1985, p. C1.
30. MacKenzie, p. 108, quoting *Encyclopaedia Britannica*, Diss. VI, 8th ed., p. 963.
31. *EB*, vol. 11, p. 379.
32. *WA*, p. 818; Woodbury, D. O. *Beloved Scientist*.
33. Black, *Surnames*, p. 620; *EB*, vol. 15, p. 1006.
34. McCulloch, pp. 179–80; *DNB*, vol. 24, p. 518.
35. Hanna, vol. 1, p. 52.
36. *EB*, vol. 14, p. 4; *WA*, p. 817.
37. *Fortune*, Jan 1975.
38. *WA*, p. 818; Bernardo, p. 388.
39. *WA*, p. 817
40. *EB*, vol. 15, p. 898
41. *NBC Nightly News*, 16 Feb 1983.
42. *Scottish Tradition*, p. 171.

43. Wills, E., p. 81.

44. McCulloch, p. 247.

45. *EB*, vol. 9, p. 91; Robertson, "Secular Changes."

46. MacKenzie, p. 34.

47. *Scottish Tradition*, p. 171; McCulloch, p. 249.

48. Black, *Mark*, p. 96.

49. MacKenzie, p. 38.

50. Ross, p. 194.

51. *EB*, vol. 15, p. 863; USIS, p. 14.

52. MacKenzie, p. 31.

53. *Highlander*, Jan/Feb 1993, p. 64.

54. *New York Times*, 20 Jun 1989, p. A22.

55. *EB*, vol. 3, p. 439; *EB*, vol. 21, p. 775.

56. *New York Times*, 19 Dec 1982; *EB*, vol. 14, p. 856.

57. Macgregor, F., p. 156; *New York Times*, 7 Dec 1973.

58. Wills, E. p. 62.

59. *EB*, vol. 2, p. 1050; *New York Times*, 9 Jun 1989, p. A30, letter from Donald Flamm, former owner of New York station WMCA who tried to bring Baird to America to produce commercial television.

60. Bowes.

61. *Guinness Book of World Records* (1987), (hereafter cited as *Guinness* [1987]), p. 227; Bowes, quoted in the Watertown, Connecticut *Times*, 16 Jun 1983, p. 2.

62. J. Thomson, *Highlander*, May/Jun 1983, p. 36.

63. MacKenzie, p. 58; McCulloch, p. 166.

64. *CES*, p. 800.

65. *CES*, p. 896.

66. Black, *Surnames*, p. 747; *EB*, vol. 18, p. 1106; *EB*, vol. 21, p. 213; *WA*, p. 817.

67. Hanna, vol. 1, p. 135; *EB*, vol. 6, p. 450.

68. *CES*, p. 309.

69. Ross, p. 196; *National Geographic*, Jun 1987, p. 737; *New York Times*, 16 Oct 1987.

70. McCulloch, p. 171; MacGregor, F., p. 146.

71. McCulloch, p. 171; *Guinness Book of World Records* (1979), (hereafter cited as *Guinness* [1979]), p. 286. The country of Robert Fulton's birth is disputed.

72. Cynthia Philip, *New York Times*, 17 Nov 1987, p. A34.

73. *EB*, vol. 9, p. 999.

74. *EB*, vol. 3, p. 440–41; *New York Scottish-American*, 4 Sep 1912.

75. MacGregor, G., p. 231; Wills, E. pp. 42, 46.

76. British Information Service, 1974.

77. *EB*, vol. 13, p. 275.

78. MacGregor, G., p. 231; Robertson, "Secular Changes"; *WA*, p. 817 credits an American named Stevens in 1804 and the Scoto-Swedish-American John Ericsson in 1837; Hanna, vol. 1, p. 135.

79. McCulloch, p. 178.

80. *EB*, vol. 3, p. 594.

81. Irving, p. 36.

82. Wills, E., p. 45.

83. John Mackay, *Highlander*, Mar/Apr 1990, p. 26.

84. Geddes.

85. *EB*, vol. 5, p. 904.

86. *EB*, vol. 7, p. 396.

87. Taylor, p. 18; Robert N. Stormont, *Highlander*, Nov/Dec 1993, pp. 66–68.

88. *EB*, vol. 22, p. 13; Robertson, "Secular Changes."

89. McCulloch, p. 179.

90. Wills, E., p. 54.

91. J. Thomson, *Highlander*, Jul 1978, p. 28; Tom Ferrell, review of *Wilbur and Orville* (1987), by Fred Howard, *New York Times Book Review*, 19 Jul 1987, p.8.

92. Stevenson, O. J. *The Talking Wire* (1947), p. 186.

93. David Patten, *Highlander*, Jul /Aug 1984, pp. 46–52, reprinted from *History Today*.

94. *EB*, vol. 20, p. 669; Macgregor, F., p. 146.

95. Black, *Mark*, p. 97.

96. *EB*, vol. 3, p. 193.

97. Gilmour, p. 31; *EB*, vol. 20, p. 674.

98. Bernardo, p. 162.

99. *New York Times*, 20 Jan 1985.

100. Hanna, vol. 1, p. 135.

101. Moncreiffe, p. 196.

102. *WA*, p. 818.

103. *EB*, vol. 3, p. 97; Gordon Irving, *Highlander*, Nov 1978, p. 10.

104. See p. 20.

105. Fleming, *Huguenot Influence in Scotland*, p. 57; Train, John. *Famous Financial Fiascos* (1985); *EB*, vol. 3, p. 93; *EB*, vol. 13, p. 820.

106. *EB*, vol. 11, pp. 29–30.

107. Ross, p. 230.

108. *New York Times*, 6 May 1995, p. 18, letter from Julian Kane.

109. Black, *Mark*, p. 113.

110. Ibid. p. 101.

111. Ross, p. 256.

112. Pittsburgh Chamber of Commerce pamphlet.

113. Black, *Mark*, p. 105; Telephone interview with Agnes Mattis, librarian of Brown Brothers Harriman and Company, March 14, 1990.

114. *New York Times*, 10 Feb 1972.

115. Letter dated Nov 20, 1972, from R. Fleming, London; Letter dated Feb 3, 1983, from G. F. Miles, archivist at Barclays Bank, London; *New York Times*, 30 Aug 1989, p. D4.

116. Geddes; *New York Times*, 19 Aug 1978; Kennedy, Ian M. *Some Scottish Banking Families*.

117. Checkland, S. G. *Scottish Banking: a History*, quoted by Tyson, R. E. in *Scottish Historical Review* 40, p. 201.

118. James Gracie, *Highlander*, Nov/Dec 1991, p. 41.

119. *World Almanac* (1973), p. 121.

120. *Highlander*, Jul/Aug 1982, p. 36.

121. B. J. Feder, *New York Times*, 2 Sep 1985, p. 29.

122. S. Tully, *Fortune*, 31 Aug 1987, pp. 58–60.

123. Wills, E., p. 103.

124. Calder, p. 121.

125. *CES*, p. 814.

126. Calder, pp. 119–23; *CES*, p. 869.

127. *Guinness* (1979), p. 286.

128. *EB*, vol. 13, p. 605; *Guinness* (1979), pp. 286–87.

129. Geddes; lecture by Jack Webster, Oct 19 1995, New York.

130. *EB*, vol. 5, p. 930.

131. J. Buchanan, *Highlander*, Nov/Dec 1983, p. 30; *EB*, vol. 14, p. 531; L. M. Fischer, *New York Times*, 13 Dec 1989, p. C2.

132. Bill Kinnaird, *Highlander*, Nov/Dec 1990, p. 56; *EB*, vol. 21, p. 738.

133. *EB*, vol. 5, p. 931; Wills, E., p. 46.

134. See appendix J.

135. MacKenzie, p. 70; McCulloch, p. 175; Calder, p. 116; *Scottish World* magazine, Jun 1990, pp. 26–27.

136. Geddes.

137. *Highlander*, Nov/Dec 1982, p. 46.

138. *CES*, p. 636.

139. *New York Times*, 17 Jul 1982, p. 7.

140. *New York Times*, 3 Feb 1981, p. B14; *New York Times*, 1 Dec 1985, p. 30.

141. *New York Times*, 23 Aug 1980.

142. Ross, p. 266.

143. *Harvard Encyclopaedia*, p. 905.

144. Ibid., p. 905; *New York Times*, 4 Mar 1979.

145. Hewitson, p. 78.

146. Saint Andrew's Society, p. 199.

147. *New York Times*, 7 Aug 1972, pp. 1, 30.

148. D. O'Donnell, *Highlander*, Nov/Dec 1987, pp. 32–33.

149. *Scottish Tradition*, p. 197; Letter dated Mar 24, 1986, from Judith McErvel, archivist, Eaton's of Canada, Ltd.

150. *New York Times*, 12 Jan 1972; ibid., 8 Mar 1974; Ibid., 8 Dec 1976.

151. *New York Times*, 3 Dec 1985; ibid., 9 April 1986.

152. *EB*, vol. 1, p. 81.

153. Gilmour, p. 38.

154. USIS, p. 15

155. Ibid., p. 15.

156. *New York Times*, 5 Mar 1982.

157. *New York Times*, 21 May 1983, p. 12; *NBC Nightly News*, May 13, 1983.

158. Peter T. Kilborn, *New York Times Magazine*, 21 Jun 1992, p. 26.

159. Letter dated Sep 28, 1982, from Lane Kirkland; Eric Breindel, *New York Post*, 15 Jun 1995.

160. See appendix K.

161. Letter dated April 1, 1982, from Neil A. McConnell.

162. Bernardo, p. 407.

163. D. P. Levin, *New York Times*, 9 Dec 1988, p. A22.

164. Bowes.

165. *New York Times*.

166. *Garden*, Jan/Feb 1987, pp. 6–7.

167. Document from Campbell Soup Co., Apr 1983.

168. *Fortune*, Mar 1982, p. 105.

169. Waugh, Alec. *The Lipton Story* (1950).

170. Bernardo, p. 412.

171. *New York Times*, 14 Apr 1982.

172. Letter dated Jul 8, 1985, from

Richard Beaumont, chairman, James Purdey and Sons, Ltd.

173. Drew Middleton, *New York Times Magazine*, Nov 19, 1995, p. 98.

174. *DNB* (1901–1911), p. 226.

175. Letter dated Jan 29, 1973 from William L. McKnight; *Times*, 9 Mar 1975.

176. Woodbury, D. O. *Beloved Scientist* (1944); *EB*, vol. 21, p. 1069; Document from Thomson, Paris 1987; *New York Times*, 10 Mar 1990, p. L31.

177. *Fortune*, May 1968, p. 156.

178. Letter dated Mar 14, 1989 from Bruce R. McCaw; *USA Today*, 11 Oct 1988, pp. 4B, 5B, quoting *Forbes* magazine; Edmund L. Andrews, *New York Times*, 17 Aug 1993, p. D1.

179. *New York Times*, 11 Jun 1994, p. 28; Letter dated Jul 15, 1994, from William H. Gates.

180. R. J. Brown, *Highlander*, Jan/Feb 1988, p. 76.

181. Ross, p. 243.

182. Ibid., p. 236; Casson, p. 609; Saint Andrew's Society, p. 160.

183. *New York Times*, 1 Jun 1983.

184. *New York Times*, 10 Mar 1983, p. 33; Coon, Horace. *American Tel and Tel*, (1939), p. 33.

185. *New York Times*, 8 Nov 1985; Patricia Brown, *New York Times*, 30 May 1987, p. 56; Suzy, *New York Post*, 22 May 1987, p. 8; W. Norwich, *New York Daily News*, 29 May 1987, p. 44; Alan Riding, *New York Times*, 21 Aug 1989, p. A4.

186. *New York Times*, 5 Oct 1987, p. B1; Trump, Donald J. and Tony Schwartz. *The Art of the Deal*, 1987.

187. *EB*, vol. 11, p. 64; Leyburn, James G. *The Scotch-Irish* (1962).

188. Letter dated Nov 15, 1983, from John W. Galbreath.

189. Meeting with Jane Mathes Kelton and Andrew Kelton, New York, c. 1985.

190. Gross, Ken. *Ross Perot* (1993), p. 4.

191. *History of Humble Oil and Refining Company*; *New York Times*.

192. *New York Times*, 1969.

193. Letter dated Oct 30, 1986, from W. A. Moncrief, Jr.; *New York Times*, 24 May 1986, p. 28.

194. Hewins, Ralph. *The Richest American*

195. *New York Times*, 24 Sep 1974; *New York Times*, 9 May 1982; *Guinness* (1987), p. 483.

196. Black, *Mark*, p. 27.

197. Genealogical data supplied by the Irvine Company, 1972; *New York Times*, Nov 1971; *New York Times*, 16 Apr 1983; *Fortune*, Mar 1982.

198. WSU exhibit.

199. Letter, 1981 from Malcolm McLean; *New York Times*, 8 May 1974; *Fortune*, Mar 1982.

200. Arrington, Leonard J. *David Eccles* (1975).

201. *New York Times*, 3 Jun 1973; *New York Times*, 11 Jan 1974; *New York Times*, 23 Jan 1977; *New York Times*, 7 Jan 1978.

202. *Fortune*, May 1968.

203. Preliminary prospectus, Goldman Sachs and Co., Dec 19, 1989; also see chapter 8.

204. J. Thomson, *Highlander*, May 1979 and May/Jun 1987; *New York Times*, 2 Aug 1984; *New York Times*, 30 Mar 1986; *New York Times*, 14 Dec 1991; *New York Times*, 8 Nov 1994, p. B7.

205. Letter dated Dec 8, 1987, from John M. Templeton; Carole Gould, *New York Times*, 1 Aug 1992, p. L39; Kathleen Teltsch, *New York Times*, 1 Feb 1992, p. 10; *New York Times*, 18 Nov 1990, p. F17.

206. Telephone conversation with Mr. Irving's biographer, Ralph Costello, 26 Mar 1990.

207. *New York Post*, 26 Aug 1988, p. 8, quoting *Fortune* magazine.

208. *Fortune*, Jan 1975, 1976, 1977, 1978; 21 Apr 1980; 23 Mar 1981; 22 Mar 1982. For details on the *Fortune* Magazine Hall of Fame and other miscellaneous information on Scots in business, see appendix L.

209. *New York Times*, Sep 1992, p. D14; *New York Times*, 2 Nov 1993, p. B1; *New York Times*, 29 Oct 1993, p. B11.

Chapter 6: Scottish Soldiers and Sailors, pp. 131–163

1. Churchill, pp. 40–41; Dickinson, pp. 23–29; Prebble, p. 12; Taylor, p. 3; *EB*, vol. 10, p. 1105; Maclean, p. 10; *Highlander*, Sep/Oct 1980, p. 1, 20, from *Scots* magazine.

2. McCulloch, p. 263; *Webster's New Biographical Dictionary* (1983), p. 305.

3. John T. Kerr, *Highlander*, Jul 1979, p. 27.

4. C. Bancroft, *Highlander*, May/Jun 1987, p. 48.

5. Geddes; Grimble, pp. 75–76.

6. *EB*, vol. 7, p. 757.

7. *EB*, vol. 1, p. 28.

8. *EB*, vol. 13, p. 270.

9. Geddes.

10. *EB*, vol. 15, p. 818; *EB*, vol. 17, p. 555.

11. *EB*, vol. 14, p. 479.

12. Norman H. MacDonald, *Highlander*, Mar 1980, p. 18; Grimble, p. 147.

13. McCulloch, p. 274; Gilmour, p. 30; *Scottish Banner*, Aug 1994, p. 13.

14. Daniel E. Harmon, *Highlander*, May/Jun 1986, p. 39.

15. Moncreiffe, p. 244; *DNB*.

16. *Highlander*, Sep/Oct 1980.

17. McCulloch, p. 276.

18. Gilmour, p. 31.

19. *Scottish Tradition*, p. 12; *EB*, vol. 10, pp. 581–82.

20. Macgregor, F., p. 42; W. N. McDonald, III, *Highlander*, Nov/Dec 1988, p. 40.

21. Erica Trent, *Scots*, vol. 34, no. 1, 1940, p. 33.

22. Geddes.

23. Scottish Heritage Publications of America (Phoenix, 1980).

24. Geddes; *Scottish World* (magazine), Sep 1990, p. 21. McCrae was a lieutenant colonel and surgeon who saved many lives during the war. His shelter in Flanders is currently being restored as a memorial to him. McCrae was born in Canada of Scottish ancestry.

25. Bonham-Carter, Victor. *Soldier True*, 1963; *EB*, vol. 19, p. 387.

26. *EB*, vol. 10, p. 1115.

27. Geddes.

28. Moncreiffe, p. 208.

29. *EB*, vol. 13, pp. 829–30; Aldington, Richard. *Lawrence of Arabia*, 1969; Wilson, Jeremy. *Lawrence of Arabia* (1990), p. 31.

30. *DNB*; *EB*, vol. 12, p. 993; Applin, Arthur. *Jellicoe*.

31. Aspinall-Oglander, Cecil. *Roger Keyes* (1951); *EB*, vol. 13, p. 320.

32. Munro, p. 191; *DNB*.

33. Caledonian Society of London, 1930, vol. 3.

34. Windrow and Mason, p. 171; Cassel.

Memoirs of Captain Liddell-Hart, 1965.

35. Black, *Surnames*, p. 697.

36. Green, p. 30; *Highlander*, Jan/Feb 1982, p. 42.

37. Hanna, vol. 1, p. 50.

38. Key, Hobart, Jr. *By My Strong Hand* (1965). (Note that this title refers to the Clan MacKay motto, *Manu Forti*); Armstrong, Zella. *Notable Southern Families* (1918).

39. *EB*, vol. 23, p. 224.

40. Black, *Surnames*, p. 746.

41. Hook, pp. 145, 170.

42. *EB*, vol. 7, pp. 103–104.

43. Easterby, J. H. *History of the St. Andrew's Society of Charleston, South Carolina* (1929), p. 111.

44. *EB*, vol. 1, p. 731.

45. Ibid., p. 734; *EB*, vol. 14, p. 499; *Highlander*, Nov/Dec 1981, p. 8.

46. Black, *Mark*, p. 63.

47. J. Thomson, *Highlander*, Jul/Aug 1981, p. 35.

48. USIS, p. 12; *EB*, vol. 4, p. 405; *EB*, vol. 12, p. 832.

49. Hart, A. B. *Salmon Portland Chase* (1899).

50. *EB*, vol. 5, pp. 340–41.

51. USIS, p. 12.

52. F. Thompson, *Scottish American*, Jan/Feb 1987, p. 12.

53. *EB*, vol. 14, p. 493.

54. *Highlander*, May 1980, p. 41.

55. J. Buchanan, *Highlander*, May/Jun 1982, p. 39.

56. USIS, p. 12.

57. *EB*, vol. 9, pp. 101–102.

58. Saint Andrew's Society, p. 93.

59. *EB*, vol. 22, pp. 386–87.

60. Brown, p. 52.

61. *EB*, vol. 1, p. 738; *EB*, vol. 10, p. 684.

62. Peter McCabe, *New York Times*, 13 Oct 1984, p. 27.

63. C. M. Robinson, III, *Highlander*, Nov/Dec 1986, pp. 38–40.

64. Letter dated Mar 15, 1983, from Col. George Armstrong Custer, III, Ret., referring to Merrington, Marguerete, *The Custer Story* (1950).

65. *Highlander*, Oct 1975, p. 8.

66. *Highlander*, Jan/Feb 1982, p. 42.

67. *EB*, vol. 20, p. 555; Morison, E. E. *Admiral Sims* (1942), p. 6.

68. Alfonso A. Narvaez, *New York Times*, 17 Oct 1990, p. D24; letter dated from

Douglas Campbell, Jr., Feb 18, 1991.

69. J. Thomson, *Highlander*, Mar/Apr 1986, pp. 41–43.

70. Gilmour, p. 29.

71. *Time*, 30 Nov 1992, p. 58.

72. Geddes.

73. *DNB, EB*, vol. 7, p. 438.

74. Geddes.

75. Geddes.

76. *EB*, vol. 14, p. 80.

77. *EB*, vol. 14, p. 325.

78. *New York Times*, 7 Dec 1973.

79. Geddes.

80. *EB*, vol. 7, p. 615.

81. Walker, pp. 73, 77.

82. Moncreiffe, p. 61.

83. Brickhill, Paul. *Reach for the Sky* (1954), p. 10.

84. Grimble, p. 76.

85. *New York Times*, 25 Mar 1981, p. B10; Windrow and Mason; Connell, John. *Auchinleck* (1959), p. 3.

86. Connell. *Wavell* (1964); *EB*, vol. 23, p. 313.

87. *EB*, vol. 21, p. 754.

88. Windrow and Mason, p. 8.

89. Moncreiffe, p. 63; *EB*, vol. 1, p. 580.

90. Hamilton, Nigel. *Monty* (1981), p. 12; *New York Times*, 25 Mar 1976; *New York Times*, 26 Oct 1984, p. A2.

91. *DNB*.

92. Moncreiffe, p. 146; *Scotia News*, Jan 1980, p. 4; *Scottish Banner*, May 1993, p. 23; Anne King, *Scottish Banner*, May 1995, p. 6.

93. *New York Times*, 16 Dec 1988, p. D16.

94. Drummond, p. 232.

95. Kahn, E. J., Jr. *McNair* (1945), pp. 1, 50; *EB*, vol. 14, p. 543.

96. *EB*, vol. 17, p. 468; Drew Middleton, *New York Times Magazine*, 16 Dec 1984, p. 118; Whiting, Charles. *Patton* (1970), p. 12; D'Este, Carlo. *Patton, A Genius for War* (1994), pp. 9, 10.

97. *Scotia News*, Aug/Sep 1966, p. 1.

98. *Highlander*, Jan/Feb 1983, pp. 31–32; Grant, Roderick. *The 51st Highland Division at War*, p. 160.

99. Saint Andrew's Society, p. 309; *EB*, vol. 11, p. 21.

100. Taylor, p. 16.

101. *Rocky Mountain News*, 27 Aug 1978.

102. *New York Times*, 13 Feb 1981; *EB*, vol. 6, p. 900; *EB*, vol. 9, p. 811–12.

103. Wolfgang Saxon, *New York Times*, 24 Dec 1993, p. B7; Alastair Campbell of Airds, *Scottish World* magazine, Mar/Apr 1994, p. 47.

104. *EB*, vol. 14, p. 493.

105. Geddes.

106. Geddes.

107. Michael H. Kelly, *Highlander*, Mar/Apr 1995, pp. 44–45.

108. *EB*, vol. 23, p. 633.

109. *Scottish Tradition*, p. 309.

110. Geddes.

111. *DNB; Simon and Schuster Encyclopedia of World War II*, p. 333.

112. Moncreiffe, p. 77; McLynn, Frank. *Fitzroy Maclean*, p. 74.

113. Windrow and Mason, p. 280.

114. *EB*, vol. 23, p. 768.

115. *New York Times*, 21 May 1983.

116. *New York Times*, 8 Sep 1979.

117. *EB*, vol. 14, pp. 958–59; Letter dated Mar 30, 1973, from Forrest C. Pogue, executive director of the George C. Marshall Foundation.

118. John le Carre, review of *The Secret War* (1976), by William Stevenson, *New York Times Book Review*, 29 Feb 1976, p. 1.

119. Brown, Anthony L. *Bodyguard of Lies* (1975).

120. *New York Times*, 6 Dec 1977.

121. Benson D. Adams in the *Pennsylvania Gazette*, Feb 1983; Garlinski, Józef. *Intercept* (1979), p. 45.

122. *New York Times*, 26 Nov 1987, p. C15.

123. Brown, op. cit.

124. *New York Times*, 11 Sep 1975.

125. William J. Broad, *New York Times*, 1 Dec 1992, pp. C1, C11.

126. Berg, p. 12.

127. Fischer, *The Scots in Germany* (hereafter cited as *Germany*), p. 75.

128. Fischer, *The Scots in Sweden* (hereafter cited as *Sweden*), p. 20.

129. Donner, p. 12.

130. Ibid., p. 9.

131. Ibid., p. 25.

132. Ibid., p. 12.

133. *Highlander*, Sep/Oct 1988, p. 29.

134. Gayre of Gayre, p. 12.

135. *EB*, vol. 10, p. 984.

136. Moncreiffe, p. 231.

137. Dunlop, p. 6; Pratt, p. 38; Maclean, p. 53.

138. de Comminges, p. 6.

139. Pratt, p. 39.

140. Dunlop, p. 5.

141. Ibid., p. 5.

142. Pratt, p. 41.

143. Ibid., pp. 44–46.

144. Churchill, pp. 304–305.

145. Dunlop, p. 6; Moncreiffe, p. 240; *EB*, vol. 11, p. 848; Black, *Surnames*, p. 668; Wills, E., p. 86; de Comminges, p. 10.

146. Moncreiffe, p. 216.

147. Fischer, *Germany*, pp. 87–89.

148. Washington, G.S.H.L. *Napoleon and the Masque de Fer*, in *The Stewarts*, Aberdeen, The Stewart Society, vol. XVI, no. 4, 1983, p. 208.

149. Moncreiffe, p. 30; *EB*, vol. 14, p. 503.

150. John Mackay, *Highlander*, May/Jun 1991, pp. 54–55.

151. *EB*, vol. 13, p. 270.

152. Black, *Surnames*, p. 159; Gilmour, p. 29; *CES*, p. 594.

153. Fischer, *Germany*, p. 70.

154. Fischer, *Germany*, p. 72.

155. Grimble, p. 116; Munro, p. 69.

156. Fischer, *Germany*, pp. 113–16; Ross Mackenzie, *Highlander*, Mar/Apr 1990, pp. 18–20.

157. Fischer, *Germany*, pp. 130–32; *EB*, vol. 13, p. 808.

158. Bond, p. 23; *New York Times*, 3 May 1985, p. 30; V. R. Berghahn, review of *Letters to Freya*, by Helmuth James von Moltke, *New York Times Book Review*, 1 Jul 1990, p. 10.

159. Cunningham, p. 58; Mackay, pp. 7–8; Drummond, p. 78; D. Dobson, *Scottish American*, Nov/Dec 1986, p. 5.

160. *Jerusalem Post*, 8 Apr 1994.

161. Moncreiffe, p. 78.

162. Black, *Surnames*, p. 615.

163. Gibb, *Empire*, p. 204.

164. Fischer, *Germany*, p. 69.

165. Geddes; *Chambers Scottish Biographical Dictionary*.

166. Steuart, *Scottish Influences on Russian History* (hereafter cited as *Influence*), p. 39.

167. Ibid., pp. 47–57, 62–63; Burton, vol. 2, p. 204; *EB*, vol. 10, pp. 582–83.

168. Steuart, *Influence*, p. 73.

169. Ibid., pp. 75, 96, 97, 103; Margaret Henderson, *Highlander*, May/Jun 1990, p. 46.

170. Steuart, *Influence*, pp. 107, 111, 112; Fischer, *Germany*, pp. 125–26.

171. Steuart, *Influence*, p. 85; Geddes.

172. Steuart, *Influence*, pp. 124–29; Burton, vol. 2, p. 216; Margaret Henderson, *Highlander*, May/Jun 1990, p. 46.

173. *EB*, vol. 13, p. 73.

174. *Highlander*, May/Jun 1982, p. 22; *EB*, vol. 3, p. 157.

175. Geddes; Moncreiffe, p. 159; D. MacPherson, *Scottish Historical Review* 9, p. 449.

176. Grimble, p. 53; *EB*, vol. 7, p. 760; Alastair Campbell of Airds, *Scottish World*, magazine May/Jun 1994, p. 45.

177. Fischer, *Germany*, p. 74.

178. Berg, p. 13.

179. Dow, p. 1.

180. Mitchell, Thomas. *Scottish Expedition to Norway* (1886).

181. George A. Sinclair, *Scottish Historical Review* 9, p. 37; Drummond, p. 60; Fischer, *Germany*, p. 73.

182. Fischer, *Germany*, p. 75; Drummond, p. 60; Sinclair, op. cit., p. 47.

183. Berg, p. 7; Fischer, *Germany*, pp. 282–83.

184. Fischer, *Germany*, p. 282; George A. Sinclair, *Scottish Historical Review* 21, pp. 182–83; Black, *Surnames*, p. 153.

185. Moncreiffe, p. 176; Fischer, *Germany*, p. 80.

186. Peter Philip, *Scottish Genealogist* 15, no. 3 (1968), p. 59.

187. Rattray, vol. 1, p. 218; Burton, vol. 2, p. 225.

188. George A. Sinclair, *Scottish Historical Review* 21, p. 190.

189. Telephone conversation, Apr 10, 1989, with librarian of the Swedish consulate, New York; *Highlander*, May/Jun 1988, p. 46; Berg, p. 48.

190. Fischer, *Germany*, pp. 75–87; Berg, p. 7; *Sruth*, 16 Oct 1969, p. 8.

191. *EB*, vol. 21, p. 1056.

192. George A. Sinclair, *Scottish Historical Review* 9, p. 37.

193. Maclean, p. 119.

194. Alastair Campbell of Airds, *Scottish World* (magazine) Mar/Apr 1992, p. 45.

195. Windrow and Mason.

196. J. Buchanan, *Highlander*, Mar/Apr 1987, p. 56; *WA*, p. 333.

197. Geddes.

198. Morris, Roger. *Haig* (1982), p. 4.

199. W. N. McDonald, III, *Highlander,* Jan 1980.

200. Moncreiffe, p. 109.

201. *National Geographic,* Jul 1985, p. 76; Letter dated Jul 27, 1985, from Adm. W. L. McDonald.

202. Powell, Colin. *My American Journey* (1995), p. 8.

203. Eric Schmitt, *New York Times,* 12 Feb 1991, p. A13; Eric Schmitt, *New York Times,* 8 Dec 1992, p. A18.

204. Eric Schmitt, *New York Times,* 29 Jun 1992, p. A1.

Chapter 7: Civilian Scots Abroad, pp. 164–191

1. *Heritage Scotland,* vol. 1, no. 6, p. 9.

2. John Malcolm Bulloch, *Scots,* vol. 20, p. 102.

3. T. C. Smout, *Scottish Historical Review* 39, p. 122.

4. *EB,* vol. 13, p. 1025.

5. Irving, p. 30.

6. *New York Times,* 24 Jun 1979.

7. David Dobson, *Scottish American,* Jul/Aug 1988, p. 7.

8. D. MacPherson, *Scottish Historical Review* 9, p. 449.

9. Black, *Surnames,* p. 422.

10. Black, *Surnames,* p. 715.

11. From the Gunn Salute, as quoted by the *Family Tree,* Jun/Jul, 1995.

12. James Dow, *Scottish Historical Review* 44, pp. 36–43.

13. Fischer, *Sweden,* p. 5.

14. G. A. F. Simpson, *Scottish Genealogist* 27, no. 4, p. 129; Thorkild Christiansen, *Scottish Historical Review* 49, p. 126.

15. Christiansen, ibid., p. 129; Dunlop, p. 16; Black, *Surnames,* p. 202.

16. Christiansen, ibid., p. 131.

17. Ibid., pp. 132, 137.

18. Ibid., p. 136; David Dobson, *Scottish American,* Mar/Apr 1987, p. 18.

19. Christiansen, ibid., pp. 131, 144.

20. Ibid., p. 144; Black, *Surnames,* p. 400.

21. Black, *Surnames,* p. 603.

22. Bulloch, John Malcolm. *The Making of the West Indies* (1915), p. 40.

23. *New York Times,* 26 Mar 1984, p. 2.

24. *New York Times,* 29 Jun 1978.

25. *New York Times,* 15 Jul 1990, p. XX 19.

26. Jim Buchanan, *Highlander,* May/Jun 1982, p. 40; *EB,* vol. 17, p. 643; *Highlander,* Jan/Feb 1982, p. 42.

27. *EB,* vol. 8, p. 280.

28. Hanna, vol. 1, p. 138; *Chambers Scottish Biographical Dictionary.*

29. *CES,* pp. 276, 277; *CES,* p. 355.

30. Vivienne Forrest, *Highlander,* May/Jun 1992, pp. 48–52.

31. *New York Times,* 22 Oct 1988, p. 13; Letter dated March 2, 1989, from Elizabeth Gray Vining; Historical Catalogue of the St. Andrew's Society of Philadelphia, vol. 3, pp. xiv, 61, 127.

32. Donner, p. 24; Berg, p. 48.

33. Donner, pp. 40, 42.

34. Burton, vol. 1, p. 2.

35. Moncreiffe, Thomas. *Memoirs of Alliance Between Scotland and France* (1751), p. 1.

36. de Comminges, p. 1.

37. *EB,* vol. 14, p. 339.

38. *CES,* p. 46.

39. Fenwick.

40. *EB,* vol. 12, p. 859B.

41. Maclean, p. 91.

42. Maclean, p. 93.

43. Nigel Tranter, *Scottish American,* Mar 1984, p. 5.

44. Moncreiffe, Thomas, op. cit.

45. Fleming, *The Medieval Scots Scholar in France* (hereafter cited as *Medieval*), p. 50.

46. Nigel Tranter, *Scottish American,* Mar 1984, p. 5.

47. Burton, vol. 1, p. 78.

48. Moncreiffe, p. 49.

49. Burton, vol. 1, p. 104.

50. Will, p. 26; Fleming, *Medieval,* p. 49.

51. Letter dated 25 Jul 1995, from Prof. André Crépin.

52. Fleming, *Medieval,* p. 81, quoting Sir John Sinclair's *Statistical Account of Universities,* which also claims Scottish origins for other continental universities. "It can hardly be questioned that the University of Paris...was founded by Scotsmen..."

53. Fischer, *Germany,* p. 216.

54. *EB,* vol. 7, p. 605.

55. Dunlop. p. 16.

56. Black, *Surnames,* p. 805.

57. John Durkan, "John Rutherford and

Montaigne," in *Bibliotheque d'Humanisme et Renaissance*, vol. 41 (1979); Geddes.

58. Drummond, p. 36.

59. Robertson, "Secular Changes," p. 25.

60. Moncreiffe, p. 121.

61. *EB*, vol. 6, pp. 39–40; Burton, vol. 1, p. 93.

62. Olivier Bernard, review of *Marie Antoinette*, by Joan Haslip (1988), *New York Times Book Review*, 9 Oct 1988, p. 17; *EB*, vol. 9, p. 203.

63. Nigel Tranter, *Scottish American*, Nov/Dec 1986, p. 11.

64. Letter dated Sep 27 1990, from M. Nath. L. Johnston.

65. *EB*, vol. 6, p. 167.

66. Gordon Mott, *New York Times*, 26 Jul 1987, p. xx 21, Black, *Surnames*, p. 407.

67. *New York Times*, 2 Nov 1980; Nan Gillespie, *New York Times*, 20 May 1973.

68. Willan, Anne. *French Regional Cooking* (1981), p. 289. *EB*, vol. 4, pp. 280, 784.

69. Drummond, p. 232.

70. *New York Post*, 20 Oct 1987, p. 62; *Times*, 3 Jan 1988, p. xx 12.

71. Crozier, Bryan. *De Gaulle* (1973), p. 18.

72. Fischer, *Germany*, pp. 139–42; *CES*, p. 391.

73. Dilworth, p. 11.

74. Fischer, *Germany*, pp. 144–61.

75. Ibid., p. 217; *EB*, vol. 7, p. 766.

76. Fischer, *Germany*, pp. 3–4.

77. Ibid., pp. 3, 18, 19.

78. Fischer, *The Scots in Eastern and Western Prussia* (hereafter cited as *Prussia*), pp. 6, 153, 232.

79. James Dow, *Scottish Historical Review*, vol. 44, p. 42.

80. Fischer, *Prussia*, p. 18.

81. Ibid., pp. 19–30, 68, 118.

82. Ibid., pp. 3, 29, 30, 112.

83. Dunlop, p. 16.

84. Fischer, *Germany*, p. 233.

85. Ibid., p. 231, 232.

86. Black, *Surnames*, p. 413; *EB*, vol. 13, p. 626; Geddes; *CES*, p. 96.

87. *Scots* (magazine), vol. 30, no. 2, 1938, p. 101.

88. Moncreiffe, p. 164.

89. *New York Times*, 12 Mar 1989, p. 44.

90. *New York Times*, 19 Apr 1974; *EB*, vol.

4, p. 511.

91. Alexander Boyle, *Scottish Historical Review* 60, no. 1, p. 160.

92. Donaldson and Morpeth.

93. Hayes-McCoy, Gerard A. *Scottish Mercenary Forces in Ireland*, (1937), pp. 9, 15.

94. *EB*, vol. 14, pp. 505–506.

95. Lyons, F. S. L. *Parnell* (1977), p. 22; *EB*, vol. 17, p. 396; Hanna, vol. 1, p. 50.

96. Letter dated Feb 23 1984 from Frank Aiken; *New York Times*, 19 May 1983.

97. Eban, Abba. *Heritage*, pp. 256–57.

98. *New York Times*, 29 Nov 1985; Letter dated May 13, 1986, from Ruhiyyih Rabbani.

99. Helga Abraham, *Jerusalem Post*, 10 April 1993, p. 14.

100. Wills, E., p. 79.

101. Gayre of Gayre; *CES*, p. 639.

102. *New York Times*, 3 Dec 1985, p. C1.

103. Janet Fyfe, *Scottish Historical Review* 57, p. 168.

104. Drummond, p. 176.

105. Marlise Simons, *New York Times*, 13 Dec 1989, p. A4.

106. Black, *Surnames*, p. 81; Katie Crooks, *Scottish American*, Mar/Apr 1988, p. 5, quoting G. R. G. Conway, *A Scotsman in America*.

107. *Highlander*, May 1979, p. 16, quoting the *Glasgow Herald*.

108. Grimble, p. 161.

109. Janet Hole, *Scottish World* magazine, Feb 1990, p. 50.

110. Dodds, pp. 2, 54, 136, 265; Ted Morgan, review of *In Patagonia*, by Bruce Chatwin, *New York Times Book Review*, 16 July 1978; Neil A. R. MacKay, *Highlander*, Apr 1976, p. 28; Nathaniel C. Nash, *New York Times*, 19 Mar 1994, p. 1.

111. Charles McCarry, *National Geographic*, Apr 1982, p. 511.

112. *EB*, vol. 23, pp. 163–64; James W. McClain, *Highlander*, Mar/Apr 1988, p. 38; Carr, Albert Z. *The World of William Walker* (1963).

113. J. Douglas Porteus, *Geographical Review*, vol. 68 (1978).

114. Richardson, Don. *Eternity in Their Hearts* (1981), p. 28; *National Geographic*, letter to the editor, Sept 1982.

115. Conversation (c. 1980) with Leopoldo Henriquez, a graduate of the

MacKay School.

116. *New York Times*, 16 Dec 1984, pp. 1, 22; *New York Times*, 19 Nov 1992, p. A7.

117. *Highlander*, May/Jun 1986, p. 78; Nathaniel C. Nash, *New York Times*, 17 Jun 1992, p. A4.

118. Conversation with Emma Gibbs-Battie, a native of Colombia, March 1994.

119. Suzanne Ruta, *New York Times Book Review*, 13 Feb 1994, p. 20; letter from Robert M. Laughlin, March 1, 1994.

120. Ross, p. 204.

121. Sherry-Lehman Christmas catalogue, New York, 1988.

122. *Highlander*, Jul/Aug 1980, p. 36.

123. Black, *Surnames*, p. 389; Ernest McIntyre, *Highlander*, Nov/Dec 1987, pp. 64–67.

124. Black, *Surnames*, p. 620.

125. Geddes.

126. Janet McCall, *Highlander*, Sep/Oct 1992, p. 42; *EB*, vol. 21, pp. 366–68.

127. Daniel Yergin, *New York Times*, 13 Jan 1991, p. F11.

128. Fischer, *Germany*, p. 3.

129. Wills, E., p. 76; Drummond, pp. 80, 99; David Dobson, *Scottish-American*, Nov/Dec 1986, p. 5; James Dow, *Scottish Historical Review* 44, pp. 42–43.

130. Geddes.

131. Moncreiffe, p. 174; Ian Grimble, *Scottish American*, Mar 1984, p. 8.

132. James Dow, *Scottish Historical Review* 44, pp. 42–43.

133. Black, *Surnames*, p. 615.

134. Moncreiffe, p. 167.

135. *National Geographic*, Apr 1982, p. 419A.

136. Fischer, *Germany*, pp. 32–33; Donald Whyte, *Scottish Genealogist* 21, no. 4, p. 117; Tomaszewski, p. 3.

137. Donald Whyte, *Scottish Genealogist* 21, no. 4, p. 117.

138. Tomaszewski, p. 2.

139. Fischer, *Germany*, p. 32.

140. Tomaszewski, p. 4.

141. Seliga and Koczy, p. 4.

142. Fischer, *Germany*, pp. 58–59.

143. Tomaszewski, p. 10.

144. Fischer, *Germany*, pp. 58–59.

145. Ibid., p. 39.

146. Tomaszewski, p. 5; *Scottish-Polish Society*, no. 2 *Scots in Old Poland* (Edinburgh, 1941), p. 13.

147. Steuart, *The Scots in Poland*, p. xxxii.

148. Seliga and Koczy, p. 1.

149. Tomaszewski, p. 23.

150. Tomaszewski.

151. Fischer, *Prussia*, p. 33; Steuart, *The Scots in Poland*, p. xiv.

152. Steuart, *The Scots in Poland*, p. xxxiii.

153. Bullock, John Malcolm. *The Polish Marquises of Huntly* (1932), p. 114; Seliga and Koczy, p. 15.

154. Tomaszewski, p. 10.

155. Walesa, Lech. *A Day of Hope* (1987), p. 16.

156. *New York Times*, 23 Jan 1983.

157. Hugh Johnson, *Gourmet*, May 1971, p. 24.

158. Rob Roy Buckingham, *New York Times Magazine*, 15 May 1983, pp. 112, 116.

159. Croft-Cooke, Rupert. *Port* (1962).

160. Gilmour, p. 58.

161. Frank J. Prial, *New York Times*, 21 Mar 1990, p. C11.

162. Mackie, p. 315.

163. *EB*, vol. 19, p. 553.

164. Shaw, p. 374, quoting from *Proceedings of the Anglo-Russian Literary Society*.

165. Steuart, *Influence*, pp. 115, 123, 129.

166. Moncreiffe, p. 220; Steuart, *Influence*, p. 37.

167. *CES*, p. 108.

168. Steuart, *Influence*, p. 120.

169. Glen, William. *Journal of a Tour From Astrachan to Karass* (1823).

170. *New York Times*, 5 Sep 1987, p. 10.

171. Steuart, *Influence*, pp. 38, 42, 43.

172. Margaret Henderson, *Highlander*, May/Jun 1990, p. 46; *CES*, p. 359.

173. Steuart, *Influence*, pp. 78, 113, 114, 121, 131, 136; Margaret Henderson, *Highlander*, May/Jun 1990, p. 46; *Scottish Genealogist* 21, no. 4, p. 117.

174. *Scottish Genealogist* 15, no. 3, p. 64; *Times Literary Supplement*, review of *Muir and Mirieless*, by Harvey Pitcher, 24 Feb 1995, p. 28.

175. *Highlander*, Nov/Dec 1982, p. 58; Taylor, Maurice. *The Scots College in Spain*, 1971.

176. *Fortune*, May 1973.

177. Howard Goldberg, *New York Times*, 12 Nov 1986.

178. Speech given in New York, Nov 15, 1988, by Darrell Corti at a meeting sponsored by the Commercial Office of Spain.

179. John Malcolm Bulloch, *Scots Magazine*, new series, vol. 20, pp. 101–108.

180. G. A. F. Simpson, *Scottish Genealogist* 27, no. 4, p. 129; Fischer, *Sweden*, p. 8; G. A. Sinclair, *Scottish Historical Review* 25, p. 290; EB X, p. 596.

181. Fischer, *Sweden*, p. 10; G. A. Sinclair, *Scottish Historical Review* 25, p. 291.

182. *EB*, vol. 10, p. 596.

183. Berg, p. 60; Cormack, Alexander A. *Colin Campbell, Merchant* (1960), p. 27.

184. Wills, E., p. 38; *EB*, vol. 10, p. 596; G. A. Sinclair, *Scottish Historical Review* 25, p. 298.

185. G. A. Sinclair, *Scottish Historical Review* 25, p. 294.

186. Cormack, op. cit., p. 70.

187. Gösta Bodman. *Scottish Genealogist* 8, no. 4, pp. 26, 52; Cormack, op. cit., p. 52.

188. Berg, p. 65.

189. Fischer, *Sweden*, p. 29.

190. G. A. Sinclair, *Scottish Historical Review* 25, p. 289.

191. Fischer, *Sweden*, p. 7.

192. Gösta Bodman. *Scottish Genealogist* 8, no. 4, p. 28, *Scottish Family Names in Swedish Industry and Technics*.

193. Fischer, *Sweden*, p. 259; Bodman, Gösta. *Skotska Slaktnamn i Svensk*, (1948); Moncreiffe, p. 216; G. A. Sinclair, *Scottish Historical Review* 21, p. 186.

194. Fischer, *Sweden*, p. 120.

195. G. A. Sinclair, *Scottish Historical Review* 25, p. 293.

196. G. A. Sinclair, *Scottish Historical Review* 21, pp. 180, 191.

197. Black, *Surnames*, p. 695; G. A. Sinclair, *Scottish Historical Review* 25, p. 290.

198. G. A. Sinclair, *Scottish Historical Review* 25, p. 293.

199. *EB*, vol. 9, p. 203; D. MacPherson, *Scottish Historical Review* 9, p. 449.

200. G. A. Sinclair, *Scottish Historical Review* 25, p. 296.

201. Berg, p. 66.

202. Letter, dated Sep 13, 1992, from Carl-George Crafoord.

Chapter 8: The Printed Word, pp. 192–211

1. Grimble, p. 68.

2. *EB*, vol. 20, p. 80.

3. *Old Manhattan News*, Aug 1986, p. 15.

4. *EB*, vol. 20, p. 702.

5. *New York Times*, 25 Jul 1980.

6. Macgregor, F., pp. 245–46; *EB*, vol. 4, p. 923.

7. Grimble, p. 135; *EB*, vol. 14, p. 494.

8. David Spitz, *New York Times Book Review*, 28 Jul 1974.

9. Cox, Catherine Morris. *Genetic Study of Genius* (1926); *EB*, vol. 15, p. 460.

10. *EB*, vol. 21, pp. 240–41.

11. *EB*, vol. 19, p. 766.

12. Viljoen, Helen Gill. *Ruskin's Scottish Heritage* (1956).

13. *CES*, p. 961.

14. Baldwin, A. W. *The MacDonald Sisters*, 1960.

15. Russell, Bertrand and Patricia. *The Amberley Papers* (1937), pp. 29–30.

16. Geddes; *EB*, vol. 10, pp. 658–59.

17. Churchill, Randolph. *Winston S. Churchill* (1966), p. 15.

18. *EB*, vol. 23, pp. 668–69; Bell, Quentin. *Virginia Woolf* (1972).

19. *DNB*; *EB*, vol. 21, p. 282; Harrod, R. F. *The Life of John Maynard Keynes*, p. 83.

20. Sykes, Christopher. *Evelyn Waugh* (1975).

21. *New York Times Magazine*, 8 Oct 1972.

22. Letter dated Feb 8, 1973, from Wilfred Sheed of the *New York Times*; *EB*, vol. 16, p. 1132.

23. *Scots Magazine*, vol. 35, no. 5, p. 399.

24. *Rocky Mountain News*, 27 Aug 1978; *CES*, p. 665.

25. *Who's Who*; *New York Times*, 2 Jun 1991, p. 45.

26. Helen Bevington, *New York Times Book Review*, 16 May 1993, p. 13.

27. Fleming, Ian. *Live and Let Die* (1954).

28. Robyns, Gwen. *Barbara Cartland*, 1985, p. 20.

29. Letter dated Sep 12, 1983, from Dame Iris Murdoch; Letter dated Aug 1, 1983 from Hammond Innes.

30. V. S. Prichett, *New York Times Magazine*, 26 Feb 1978, p. 33; *New York Times*, 4 Jun 1991, p. 1.

31. *New York Times*, 16 Nov 1994, p. D25.

32. Marshall Ledger, *Pennsylvania Gazette*, Apr 1985, pp. 1, 37.

33. John Elsen, *New York Times Book Review*, 13 Mar 1994, p. 12; C. Lehman-Haupt, *New York Times*, 13 Feb 1995, p. C20; Michael Upchurch, *New York Times Book Review*, 12 Mar 1995, p. 9.

34. Sarah Lyall, *New York Times*, 29 Nov 1994, p. C15.

35. *New York Times*, 27 Sep 1975.

36. *EB*, vol. 23, p. 479; also see chapter 3.

37. Lorant, p. 52.

38. Ross, p. 357.

39. Ian T. MacAuley, *New York Times*, 22 Apr 1983.

40. *EB*, vol. 12, p. 649.

41. Ian T. Macaulay, *New York Times*, 22 Apr 1983.

42. Mankowitz, Wolf. *Mr. Poe* (1978).

43. Mumford, Lewis. *Herman Melville* (1929).

44. *EB*, vol. 21, p. 281; Bernardo, p. 367; E. L. Doctorow, review of *Harriet Beecher Stowe*, by Joan D. Hedrick, *New York Times Book Review*, 13 Feb 1994, p. 33.

45. New York Public Library, genealogical records.

46. Hanna, vol. 1, p. 51.

47. Johnson, p. 78; *EB*, vol. 12, pp. 860–62.

48. Eugene Taylor, *New York Times Book Review*, 16 Apr 1989, p. 30; *EB*, vol. 12, p. 863.

49. Black, *Mark*, p. 82.

50. Turnbull, Andrew. *Thomas Wolfe* (1967), p. 4.

51. Turnbull, Andrew. *Scott Fitzgerald* (1962), pp. 5–7.

52. French, Warren. *J. D. Salinger Revisited* (1988).

53. Letter dated Dec 8, 1972, from Tetsumaro Hayashi, editor of *Steinbeck Quarterly.*

54. Letter from Brook Hersey, Mar 1993; Richard Severo, *New York Times*, 25 Mar 1993, p. B11.

55. Letter dated Dec 5, 1972, from Murry C. Falkner.

56. Silverthorne, Elizabeth. *Marjorie Kinnan Rawlings* (1988), p. 9.

57. Edwards, Anne. *The Road to Tara* (1983), p. 15; Jerry Schwartz, *New York*

Times, 18 Dec 1994, p. 26.

58. Letter dated Mar 12, 1986, from Robert W. Gibson, M.D.

59. *New York Times*, 3 Mar 1983; Richard Severo, *New York Times*, 27 Apr 1991, p. 13; Letter received in March 1983 from A. B. Guthrie.

60. Mr. Auchincloss is a Wallace awardee.

61. O'Connor, Richard. *Heywood Broun.* (Putnam, 1975), p. 17.

62. Edwin McDowell, *New York Times*, 2 Oct 1985.

63. Stearn, Jess. *In Search of Taylor Caldwell* (1984), p. 12.

64. Letter dated Feb 14, 1983, from Erskine Caldwell; Edwin McDowell, *New York Times*, 1 Dec 1982.

65. Letter from Michael Crichton; Bernard Weinraub, *New York Times*, 5 Jan 1994, p. C11.

66. Letter, 1983, from the Office of Dwight MacDonald; letter dated May 22, 1985, from John D. MacDonald.

67. *Newsweek*, 22 Mar 1971, p. 101.

68. D. Johnson, *New York Times*, 13 Dec 1987, p. 28; Letter dated Dec 30, 1987, from Dorothy Carnegie.

69. *Life*, 18 Dec 1970, p. 36.

70. Letter dated Feb 27, 1989, from David McCullough.

71. Galbraith, John Kenneth. *The Scotch* (1964), p. 12.

72. Letter from Gerry Spence, Oct 1993; Jan Hoffman, *New York Times*, 15 Oct 1993, p. B18.

73. Dillard, Annie. *An American Childhood* (1987), p. 57.

74. Letter dated Jun 11, 1993, from James MacGregor Burns.

75. Letter from Catherine A. MacKinnon, March 1993; Fred Strebeigh, *New York Times Magazine*, 6 Oct 1991.

76. MacLennan, Hugh. *Scotchman's Return* (1960), p. 1.

77. C. Lehmann-Haupt, *New York Times*, 20 Mar 1989, p. C17; Marchand, Philip. *Marshall McLuhan* (1989), p. 3.

78. D. J. R. Bruckner, *New York Times*, 17 Apr 1990, p. C13.

79. Clyde H. Farnsworth, *New York Times*, 28 Mar 1994, p. A4; undated letter, 1994, from Farley Mowat.

80. *Scottish World*, pp. 245–46.

81. *New York Times Book Review*, 14 Dec 1980; *New York Times*, 2 Apr 1988, p. L11.

82. Macgregor, F., p. 219.

83. *EB*, vol. 3, p. 152; Macgregor, F., p. 220.

84. Grimble, p. 33.

85. Fergus M. Bordewitch, *New York Times Book Review*, 12 Feb 1984, p. 14.

86. *EB*, vol. 3, p. 335.

87. Cole, Sonia. *Counterfeit* (1955).

88. Clark, pp. 302–304.

89. *Scottish World*, pp. 254–55.

90. Hook, p. 167.

91. Smart, J. S. *James MacPherson, an Episode in Literature* (1905), p. 11, quoted by Adam Potkay, in Modern Language Association pamphlet (1992).

92. Grimble, p. 202.

93. Clark, p. 302.

94. Macgregor, F., p. 229–30; *EB*, vol. 4, pp. 509–10.

95. Macgregor, F., pp. 230–31.

96. Ellis, p. 330; *DNB*.

97. *CES*, p. 712.

98. *DNB*; *Newsweek*, 28 Sep 1987, p. 73.

99. *EB*, vol. 18, p. 88.

100. Black, *Surnames*, p. 363, quoting Finley, *The Coming of the Scot*, p. 28; *Highlander*, Nov/Dec 1985, p. 49.

101. *Highlander*, Apr 1978, p. 28.

102. Czeslaw Milosz, *New York Times Book Review*, 7 Jul 1974; *EB*, vol. 12, p. 984.

103. *New York Times*, 6 Feb 1972; *New York Times*, 13 Nov 1987.

104. *New York Times*, 22 Aug 1983.

105. William Stafford, *New York Times Magazine*, 18 Aug 1974.

106. *EB*, vol. 9, p. 962.

107. Kennedy, Richard S. *Dreams in the Mirror* (1980), p. 11.

108. *New York Times*, 19 Feb 1984.

109. Campbell, p. 296.

110. Chisholm, p. 110.

111. Grimble, p. 95; Booklet number 5, Scottish Heritage Publications of America, 1980.

112. Black, *Surnames*, p. 229; James Dow, *Scottish Historical Review* 44, pp. 42–43.

113. Black, *Surnames*, p. 340.

114. *New York Times*, 3 Oct 1986; Letter dated Aug 3, 1983, from Carlos Drummond de Andrade.

115. *EB*, vol. 13, p. 984.

116. Steuart, *Influence*, p. 134.

117. *EB*, vol. 16, p. 397; *Highlander*, Jan/Feb 1987, p. 68.

118. Black, *Mark*; *Highlander*, Jan/Feb 1982, p. 42.

119. *EB*, vol. 10, pp. 888–89.

120. Casson, p. 607.

121. *EB*, vol. 3, p. 480.

122. Ibid., p. 481.

123. *New York Times*, 4 Oct 1987, p. 55.

124. Black, *Mark*, p. 110.

125. Jack R. Howard is a winner of the Wallace Award.

126. Brochure from the *Washington Post*, 24 Oct 1995.

127. *EB*, vol. 15, p. 106.

128. *EB*, vol. 14, p. 501.

129. *EB*, vol. 15, p. 106; *Current Biography*, 1940–1948.

130. *New York Times*, 1 Sep 1976.

131. Telephone conversation, Jan 21, 1985, with Ann Bell of the *National Enquirer*.

132. J. Nordheimer, *New York Times*, 4 Feb 1988, p. A1.

133. Saint Andrew's Society.

134. Gilmour, p. 7.

135. Noble, Iris. *Nelly Bly, First Woman Reporter* (1956).

136. *New York Times Magazine*, 4 Apr 1982, p. 32; *New York Times Book Review*, 18 Oct 1987, p. 3.

137. O'Brien, P. J. *Will Rogers* (1935), p. 24.

138. *Chambers Scottish Biographical Dictionary*; Geddes.

139. Letter dated Feb 19, 1981, from Emily K. Gilder, secretary to James Beard.

140. Bryan Miller, *New York Times*, 20 May 1988, p. C20; Florence Fabricant, *New York Times*, 5 Sep 1990, p. C9; Letter dated Feb 9, 1985, from Craig Claiborne.

141. *EB*, vol. 14, p. 367.

142. *EB*, vol. 3., p. 349.

143. *New York Times*, 5 Feb 1973; Geddes.

144. *New York Times*, 9 Feb 1981; *New York Times*, 20 Nov 1976; *New York Times*, 2 Nov 1983; *EB*, vol. 16, p. 407; *New York Times*, 7 May 1985, p. 1; S. Lohr, *New York Times*, 7 Jan 1989, p. 35; Philip Shenon, *New York Times*, 23 Aug 1993, p. D1.

145. *EB*, vol. 17, p. 611; J. Thomson, *Highlander*, Sep/Oct 1982, p. 28; Alexandra Lea Levin, *Highlander*, Nov/Dec 1988, p. 26.

146. Gilmour, p. 8; Geddes.

147. *Scottish Tradition*, p. 228.

148. Chalmers, Floyd S. *A Gentleman of the Press* (1969); Martin Douglas, *New York Times*, 28 Nov 1983, p. D1.

149. *New York Times*, 24 Apr 1982; *National Geographic*, Sep 1988, p. 288.

150. Dierdre Carmody, *New York Times*, 8 Nov 1993, p. D1.

151. *New York Times*, 31 Jan 1979; Bernardo, p. 180.

152. *EB*, vol. 19, p. 633; letter dated May 18, 1982, from Polly Morrice of *The New Yorker*.

153. Conversation (c. 1972) with Elizabeth Ortiz, writer for *Gourmet*.

154. Letter dated Apr 20, 1983, from Dorothy Little, assistant to Lila Acheson Wallace; preliminary prospectus, Goldman Sachs and Co., Lazard Freres and Co., December 19, 1989; *New York Times Magazine*, 10 Jan 1993, p. 3.

155. *People*, 8 Dec 1980; *New York Times*, 14 Sep 1982.

156. *EB*, vol. 15, p. 1011; *New York Times*, 25 Jul 1993, p. 38.

157. Pearce, p. 175; Lohr, S. *New York Times*, 7 Jan 1989, p. 35.

158. Roger Cohen, *New York Times*, 11 Jun 1990, p. D1.

159. *EB*, vol. 14, p. 541.

160. E. McDowell, *New York Times*, 27 May 1988, p. D19.

161. Letter dated Apr 21, 1983, from Harold W. McGraw, Jr.; *New York Times*, 29 Jul 1993, p.21.

162. Letter of August 1995 from Betty Ballantine; Mary B. W. Tabor, *New York Times*, 10 Mar 1995, p. B7, including quote of Irwyn Applebaum.

163. McCulloch, p. 91.

164. *New York Times*, 19 Oct 1977; *Oxford English Dictionary*, p. xix; A. J. Aitken, *Scottish Studies*, vol. 8, (1964), p. 130.

165. *EB*, vol. 8, pp. 374, 376D.

166. Bell, Brian, ed., *Insight Guides— Scotland* (1990), p. 117.

167. Geddes.

168. *DNB*; *CES*, p. 886.

169. Denis Donoghue, review of *Leslie Stephen* (1984), by Noel Annan, *New York Times Book Review*, 30 Dec 1984, p. 8.

170. *EB*, vol. 3, p. 206; *CES*, p. 68; *CES*, p. 561.

171. Montgomery, p. 30.

172. *Newsweek*, 8 Dec 1975, p. 41.

173. Black, *Surnames*, p. 233.

174. *EB*, vol. 18, p. 1149.

175. *Highlander*, Mar/Apr 1983, p. 22.

176. *CBS Almanac* (1976), pp. 757–58.

177. Judith Chernaik, *New York Times Book Review*, 30 Jun 1991, p. 24.

178. Saint Andrew's Society, pp. 160–61; *EB*, vol. 13, p. 947.

Chapter 9: Science, pp. 212–231

1. *CES*, p. 208

2. *EB*, vol. 9, p. 821.

3. *New York Times*, 14 Sep 1982.

4. *EB*, vol. 3, p. 738; Hood, Dora. *Davidson Black* (1964), p. 5.

5. John Noble Wilford; *New York Times*, 30 Oct 1984, p. C1; Leakey, Mary. *Disclosing the Past* (1984).

6. *New York Times*, 2 Nov 1987, p. D15; Telephone conversation, Aug 9, 1988, with Alice Campbell Lenning.

7. Macgregor, F., p. 140.

8. *Highlander*, Jul/Aug 1985, p. 20; Macgregor, F., p. 110.

9. MacGregor, G., p. 231; Macgregor, F., p. 111.

10. Scottish Council, Development and Industry pamphlet (1976); *CES*, p. 378.

11. Black, *Mark*, p. 70.

12. Robertson, "Secular Changes"; Black, *Surnames*, p. 413.

13. Macgregor, F., p. 107.

14. Graham, T. M., p. 437; *EB*, vol. 7, p. 83; *EB*, vol. 23, pp. 164–65; Wallace, Alfred. *My Life* (1905), p. 3; *Geographical Journal*, vol. 43, p. 90.

15. *New York Times*, 3 April 1985, p. 1; *New York Times*, 5 May 1987, pp. C1, C5.

16. Allen, Garland. *Thomas Hunt Morgan*, 1978.

17. *New York Times*, 11 Oct 1983, p. 1; Biographical information from the American-Scottish Foundation.

18. Nadine Brozan, *New York Times*, 2 Feb 1994, p. B5; Letter dated May 10, 1994, from Maclyn McCarty, M.D.

19. *New York Times*, 12 Apr 1983; *New York Times*, 27 Sep 1988, H. M. Schmeck, Jr., *New York Times*, 4 Oct 1988.

20. Robertson, "Secular Changes".

21. Geddes.

22. *EB*, vol. 7, p. 608; Bryce, p. 74; Robertson, "Secular Changes."

23. Black, *Mark*, p. 67; Hanna, vol. 1 p. 52; *EB*, vol. 10, p. 728.

24. Christopher McCooey, *Highlander*, Jan/Feb 1989, pp. 43–44.

25. Chisolm, p. 110; MacGregor, G., p. 231; Robertson, "Secular Changes;" *EB*, vol. 4, p. 286.

26. Black, *Surnames*, p. 586; *CES*, p. 685.

27. *New York Times*, 25 Sep 1988, p. XX 19; Karl Meyer, *New York Times*, 5 Sep 1993, p. E10.

28. Geddes.

29. *CES*, p. 414; Robert Campbell, *New York Times Book Review*, 5 May 1996, p. 20.

30. Conversation with David Graham Black, Jr.; *Chambers Scottish Biographical Dictionary*; Paula Dietz, *New York Times*, 16 Jun 1996, p. xx 18.

31. *EB*, vol. 3, p. 739; *EB*, vol. 5, p. 391; MacGregor, G., p. 230.

32. Buckle, p. 339, quoting Muirhead, *Life of Watt*, pp. 301–70.

33. Black, *Surnames*, p. 705; Wills, E., p. 16; MacGregor, G., p. 230.

34. Robertson, "Secular Changes"; MacGregor, G., p. 230.

35. *Highlander*, Mar/Apr 1985, p. 50; *EB*, vol. 21, p. 321; *WA*, p. 816.

36. Robertson, "Secular Changes."

37. Ibid.

38. *EB*, vol. 6, p. 934; David Harvie, *Highlander*, May/Jun 1989, pp. 56, 60, 62.

39. Wills, E., p. 97.

40. MacGregor, G., p. 231; *Chambers Scottish Biographical Dictionary*.

41. *EB*, vol. 18, p. 1150.

42. *EB*, vol. 19, p. 834; Evans, Ivor B. *Man of Power*.

43. Letter dated Dec 1, 1972, from R. Ned Landon of General Electric Company; *EB*, vol. 13, p. 696.

44. Letter received Nov 1972 from Edwin M. McMillan; *EB*, vol. 14, pp. 541–42.

45. *EB*, vol. 17, p. 482.

46. Biographical memoirs of the Fellows of the Royal Society, vol. 19, p. 375; *EB*,

vol. 11, p. 515.

47. *EB*, vol. 22, p. 50; Wills, E., p. 20.

48. Letter dated Dec 26, 1972, from John C. Kendrew; *EB*, vol. 13, p. 280.

49. Letter received Dec 1972, from Robert B. Woodward.

50. Letter dated Dec 11, 1972, from Robert S. Mulliken; Wolfgang Saxon, *New York Times*, 2 Nov 1986, p. 44.

51. Schmeck, H., *New York Times*, 15 Oct 1987, p. A14; Letter received, Jan 1988, from Donald J. Cram; Malcolm E. Browne, *New York Times*, 21 Mar 1989, pp. C1, C9.

52. James Wilson, *Highlander*, Mar/Apr 1988, pp. 6, 10; Walker, p. 89; Suzie Boss, *New York Times*, 2 Jun 1991, p. xx26.

53. *Highlander*, Mar/Apr 1983, pp. 1, 32–33.

54. Jane Perlez, *New York Times*, 22 Aug 1989, p. A2; House, Adrian. *The Great Safari* (1993), p. 16.

55. Graham, Frank. *Since Silent Spring* (1970); *WA*, p. 711.

56. Donaldson and Morpeth, p. 201; Wills, E., p. 20.

57. Macgregor, F., p. 113.

58. *EB*, vol. 11, p. 6.

59. Wills, E., p. 21; *EB*, vol. 14, p. 467.

60. *CES*, p. 717.

61. John McPhee, *The New Yorker*, 14 Sep 1992, pp. 49–50.

62. Black, *Surnames*, p. 294.

63. MacGregor, G., p. 231.

64. Clement and Robertson, p. 5.

65. N. Pisias, and J. Imbrie, *Oceanus*, winter 1986/1987, p. 45.

66. Ross, p. 203; *EB*, vol. 14, p. 540.

67. *EB*, vol. 15, p. 1174–75; Grimble, p. 230; Robertson, "Secular Changes."

68. More, Louis. *Isaac Newton*, p. 459; Malcolm W. Browne, *New York Times*, 31 Mar 1987; *EB*, vol. 16, p. 418.

69. Robertson, "Secular Changes"; *EB*, vol. 10, p. 912.

70. Robertson, "Secular Changes."

71. *EB*, vol. 14, p. 539.

72. *Guinness* (1987), p. 416.

73. Letter dated Jan 22, 1988, from Dr. Simon Donaldson; James Gleick, *New York Times*, 4 Aug 1986. Nadine Brozan, *New York Times*, 18 Jan 1994, p. B5.

74. Begley, p. 123.

75. Grimble, pp. 21, 141.

76. Robertson, "Secular Changes."

77. *Scottish World*, p. 190.

78. Dr. Charles Maitland, *Highlander*, May/Jun 1986, p. 36.

79. Robertson, "Secular Changes."

80. Geddes; *New Columbia Encyclopaedia*, (1975), p. 38.

81. Macgregor, F., p. 95.

82. Ibid., pp. 95–96.

83. Megroy, R. L. *Ronald Ross*, p. 31.

84. Macgregor, F., p. 96.

85. *New York Times*, 14 Sep 1982, p. C1.

86. *EB*, vol. 9, p. 437.

87. *Scotia News*, Jan 1976.

88. *EB*, vol. 4, p. 68.

89. Pearce, p. 231; *New York Times Book Review*, 26 Nov 1978.

90. *EB*, vol. 18, pp. 539–40; MacGregor, G., p. 230; Asimov, Isaac. *The Kite That Won the Revolution* (1963), p. 99.

91. Macgregor, F., pp. 90–91.

92. Black, *Mark*, p. 73.

93. Macgregor, G., p. 230.

94. *EB*, vol. 3, pp. 440–41; Jane E. Brody, *New York Times*, 28 Jul 1993, p. C11.

95. *EB*, vol. 1, p. 169; Letter dated Jan 12, 1972, from Lord Adrian.

96. *EB*, vol. 20, p. 687.

97. *EB*, vol. 11, p. 880.

98. Macgregor, G., p. 230; Robertson, "Secular Changes."

99. *DNB*; *EB*, vol. 10, p. 1070; *Scottish World*, p. 191.

100. *EB*, vol. 21, p. 277.

101. USIS, p. 15; *Dictionary of Medical Biography* (1984), p. 685.

102. Wills, E., p. 96; Macgregor, F., p. 84; *CES*, p. 204.

103. Haws, p. 46.

104. Macgregor, F., pp. 92–93.

105. J. Thomson, *Highlander*, Sep/Oct 1982, p. 28; Lehmann, p. 75.

106. *New York Times*, 1 Dec 1970; J. T. McQuiston, *New York Times*, 24 Aug 1989, p. D21.

107. Eugene Taylor, *New York Times Book Review*, 16 Apr 1989, p. 30.

108. Robertson, "Secular Changes"; Geddes.

109. Wills, E., p. 26; *EB*, vol. 11, p. 881.

110. Buckle, p. 374.

111. Black, *Surnames*, p. 333.

112. J. Thomson, *Highlander*, Sep/Oct

1982, p. 29; *EB*, vol. 14, p. 296; Taylor, Frances Long. *Crawford, W. Long and the Discovery of Anesthesia*, 1928, p. 5; *EB*, vol. 15, p. 869.

113. MacGregor, G., p. 231; Wills, E., p. 26.

114. *EB*, vol. 14, p. 514; Wills, E., p. 29; *CES*, p. 653.

115. J. Thomson, *Highlander*, Sep/Oct 1982, p. 26; *EB*, vol. 14, p. 506; Trout, Hugh H., M.D. *Annals of Medical History* 10, pp. 71–82, 162–68; J. Thomson, *Highlander*, May/Jun 1985, p. 30.

116. *EB*, vol. 14, pp. 58–49; *EB*, vol. 3, p. 761; Wills, E., p. 25.

117. Geddes.

118. *EB*, vol. 7, p. 404; *WA*, p. 819; *Biographical Memoirs of the Fellows of the Royal Society*, vol. 15, p. 159 (London, 1969); McCollum, Elmer Verner. *From Kansas Farm Boy to Scientist* (1964).

119. Macgregor, F., p. 209.

120. *National Geographic*, Sep 1988, p. 375.

121. Ray Eagle, *Highlander*, Mar/Apr 1992, pp. 20, 22.

122. Letter dated Dec 12, 1972, from A. V. Hill.

123. Burnet, Sir MacFarlane. *Changing Patterns*.

124. Wills, E., p. 32.

125. Letter dated Nov 22, 1979, from Allan M. Cormack.

126. Lawrence K. Altman and G. Kolata, *New York Times*, 18 Oct 1988, pp. 1, C16–17; Letter dated Feb 15, 1989 from George H. Hitchings.

127. H. M. Schmeck, Jr., *New York Times*, 18 Oct 1988, pp. C16–17.

128. Letter dated Aug 21, 1995, from James P. Guthrie; Vicki Cheng, *New York Times*, 27 Jun 1995, p. D21.

129. Black, *Mark*, p. 67; *EB*, vol. 23, p. 546; Ross, p. 207.

130. *CES*, p. 654.

131. *New York Times*, 12 Oct 1974.

132. Clement and Robertson, p. 6; More, Louis. *Isaac Newton* (1934), p. 459.

133. *EB*, vol. 3, p. 739; Macgregor, F., p. 88.

134. MacGregor, G., p. 230.

135. Ibid., p. 231.

136. *EB*, vol. 18, p. 1163; Geddes.

137. Interview with Dr. James F. Goff,

McLean, Virginia, 1993.

138. Bell, Brian, ed., *Insight Guides—Scotland* (1990), p. 75.

139. Timothy Ferris, *New York Times Magazine*, 26 Sep 1982, p. 44; Gilmour, p. 35.

140. Hans Christian von Baeyer, *New York Times Book Review*, 26 Sep 1993, p. 34, quoting Richard Feynman.

141. *Highlander*, Jan/Feb 1984, p. 38.

142. *EB*, vol. 15, pp. 3–4.

143. J. Thomson, *Highlander*, Sep 1979, pp. 38–40; USIS, p. 14; *EB*, vol. 11, pp. 378–79.

144. Wills, E., p. 19; *EB*, vol. 7, p. 344.

145. *Guinness* (1987), p. 416; Wills, E., p. 44; *EB*, vol. 13, p. 275; Gilmour, p. 34.

146. Walter Sullivan, *New York Times*, 10 Oct 1990, p. B24.

147. White, Michael and John Gribbin. *Stephen Hawking* (1993), p. 6.

148. John Noble Wilford, *New York Times*, 24 Mar 1992, p. C1.

149. See appendix O.

150. *New York Times*, 11 Sep 1975; Letter dated Jan 24, 1973 from Sir George Paget Thomson; Marcia Bartusiak, review of *Discovering*, by Robert Scott Root-Bernstein, *New York Times Book Review*, 28 Jan 1990, p. 24.

151. In this chapter there are mentioned various men who were the "founder" or the "father" of certain sciences. For a summary of these and for a list of scientific terms named for Scots, see appendix N.

152. *WA*, pp. 818–19; *EB*, vol. 2, p. 716; S. Koch, *New York Times*, 8 Mar 1987; Zuckerman, Harriet. *Scientific Elite* (1977), p. 103.

153. Millikan, R. A. *Autobiography* (1950).

154. MacCallum, Thomas W. *The Nobel Prize Winners and the Nobel Foundation* (1938).

155. Letter dated Jan 11, 1973, from Walter Brattain.

156. *New York Times*, 14 Oct 1987, p. B12.

157. Andrew Pollack, *New York Times*, 21 Feb 1991, p. D2.

158. *New York Times*, 19 Oct 1982, p. C6; letter dated Dec 13, 1982, from Kenneth G. Wilson.

159. William J. Broad, *New York Times*, 13 Oct 1989, p. A10; undated letter from Norman F. Ramsey.

160. Malcolm W. Browne, *New York Times*, 18 Oct 1990, p. A20; undated letter from Dr. Henry W. Kendall; Letter dated Jan 8, 1991, from Richard E. Taylor.

Chapter 10: Art, Architecture, Music, and Entertainment, p. 232–252

1. Macgregor, F., pp. 271–74.

2. John Russell, *New York Times*, 12 May 1978, p. B2; *EB*, vol. 3, p. 811–12.

3. Buttioni, Roger. *Graham Sutherland* (1982).

4. USIS, p. 15.

5. *EB*, vol. 5, p. 18; Hale, Nancy. *Mary Cassat*, p. 5.

6. *Highlander*, Jan/Feb 1982, p. 42; *EB*, vol. 7, p. 835.

7. Hanna, vol. 1, p. 51; *EB*, vol. 23, p. 481.

8. *Highlander*, Nov/Dec 81, p. 8.

9. O'Connor, Francis and Eugene V. Thaw. *Jackson Pollock*, 1978; Rita Reif, *New York Times*, 3 May 1988, p. C16.

10. Grace Glueck, *New York Times*, 18 Jul 1991, p. A1.

11. *National Geographic*, Oct 1988, p. 584.

12. *Philadelphia Journal*, 22 Mar 1978, p. 6.

13. Ted Morgan, *New York Times Magazine*, 8 Jul 1973, p. 29.

14. John Russell, *New York Times*, 12 Nov 1976, pp. A1, D14.

15. Black, *Mark*, p. 91; David Dunlap, *New York Times*, 19 Oct 1987, p. B7; *Scottish Tradition*, p. 306.

16. Letter dated Mar 4, 1989, from Ailes Gilmour Spinden; Michael Brenson. *New York Times*, 31 Dec 1988, p. 1.

17. Black, *Surnames*, p. 732.

18. *EB*, vol. 6, p. 612.

19. *EB*, vol. 8, p. 280.

20. John Russell, *New York Times Magazine*, 22 Jul 1990, p. 22.

21. L. Sabbath, *New York Times*, 24 Jan 1988, p. XX 19.

22. Saint Andrew's Society, pp. 186–87.

23. Telephone conversation on Aug 15, 1990, with Karen Haas at the Gardner Museum.

24. Macgregor, F., p. 285; *EB*, vol. 1, pp. 118–19; Clark, p. 259.

25. Olivier Bernier, *New York Times*, 1

Oct 1989, p. XX 8; *EB*, vol. 18, p. 887; Clark, p. 260; Macgregor, F., pp. 285–86.

26. Steuart, *Influence*, p. 42.

27. *New York Times*, 25 Jun 1990, p. A47.

28. *Scottish World*, p. 219.

29. *EB*, vol. 15, p. 471; Macgregor, F., p. 286.

30. *Guinness*, (1987), p. 244; letter dated Jul 30, 1982, from Bruce J. Graham.

31. Historical Catalogue of the St. Andrew's Society of Philadelphia.

32. Black, *Mark*, p. 92.

33. Ibid., p. 92; *EB*, vol. 19, p. 307.

34. Donaldson, P. 119.

35. Ross, p. 191.

36. Black, *Mark*, p. 92; *New York Times*, 21 May 1993, p. B3.

37. Clan MacNeil newsletter, c. 1974; Nina Reyes, *New York Times*, 2 Jan 1994, p. CV5.

38. Black, *Mark*, p. 93.

39. *New York Times*, 11 Jan 1986, p. 22.

40. Wist, Ronda. *On Fifth Avenue Then and Now* (1992), p. 43.

41. Klett, p. 25; Baldwin, Charles. *Stanford White* (1931).

42. *New York Times*, 18 Jan 1973; letter dated Mar 7, 1973, from Mildred Mohr, secretary to Ralph T. Walker.

43. Letter dated May 13, 1986, from Ruhiyyih Rabbani.

44. C. Edmiston Douglas, *Scottish Field*, Aug 1972, p. 71; *EB*, vol. 5, p. 661; *EB*, vol. 11, p. 384.

45. *EB*, vol. 17, p. 1011.

46. *Scottish World*, pp. 290–91; *EB*, vol. 14, p. 538; *New York Times*, 30 Sep 1979.

47. *Opera News*, 27 Dec 1948, pp. 4–5; *Opera News*, 15 Jan 1977, p. 22.

48. Black, *Surnames*, p. 328; Jean Dunlop, review of *Grieg and His Scottish Ancestry* (1956), by J. R. Grieg, *Scottish Genealogist* 3, no. 2 (1956).

49. Interview with Artur Rubinstein on *NBC Nightly News*, 21 Dec 1982.

50. Bernard Holland, *New York Times*, 9 Jan 1993, p. 13.

51. *EB*, vol. 14, p. 506; Hanna, vol. 1, p. 51.

52. *EB*, vol. 21, p. 246.

53. *New York Times*, 1 Oct 1989, pp. 1, 42; Thomson, Virgil. *Virgil Thomson* (1967).

54. Daniel, Oliver. *A Counterpoint of*

View (1982), pp. 1, 294, 300; *New York Times*, 19 Dec 1982; Smith, William Ander. *The Mystery of Leopold Stokowski* (1990), p. 28; *Baker's Biographical Dictionary of Musicians* (1992), p. 1793.

55. *New York Times*, 8 May 1973.

56. Letter dated July 10, 1995 from William Christie; J. James, *New York Times*, 10 May 1992, p. 25; A. Kozinn, *New York Times*, 19 May 1994, p. C13.

57. *Who's Who* (1984); *Chambers Scottish Biographical Dictionary*.

58. Shaw, p. 417.

59. Chisholm, pp. 109; *EB*, vol. 15, p. 124; Daiches, David, *The New Companion to Scottish Culture*, 1993, p. 142.

60. Jim Thomson, *Highlander*, Sep/Oct 1983, p. 22; *EB*, vol. 9, p. 1139.

61. Will Crutchfield, *New York Times*, 1 May 1988, p. 46.

62. *The New Yorker*, 1 Apr 1971, p. 52; *Cue*, 27 Feb 1972.

63. *New York Times*, 11 Jul 1984.

64. *New York Times*, 4 May 1982.

65. Scottish Opera pamphlet.

66. Wills, E., p. 72; *EB*, vol. 17, p. 1040; Gilmour, p. 53; *CES*, p. 102.

67. *EB*, vol. 19, p. 35.

68. *EB*, vol. 7, p. 947.

69. *EB*, vol. 15, p. 150.

70. J. Dunning, *New York Times*, 19 Aug 1988, p. C3.

71. Louis Stott, *Highlander*, Nov/Dec 1992, p. 22.

72. Cynthia Gordon, *Highlander*, May/Jun 1988, p. 24.

73. Hook, p. 132.

74. Mornweck. *Chronicles of Stephen Foster's Family*, pp. 4–5.

75. *Guinness* (1987), p. 218.

76. Hook, p. 168, note 40.

77. Rinzler, Ralph. *Sing Out!*, vol. 13, no. 1, p. 6.

78. John Rockwell, *New York Times*, 3 Dec 1982; Klein, Joe. *Woody Guthrie*, 1980.

79. *Travel and Leisure*, Apr 1986, p. 48.

80. Barbara Goldsmith, *New York Times Book Review*, 21 Jun 1987, p. 30.

81. *New York Times*, 21 Feb 1971.

82. Zondervan. *Johnny Cash-Man in Black*, p. 25.

83. ABC television, December 9, 1981.

84. J. Dunning, *New York Times*, 19 Aug

1988, p. C3; Stephen Holden, *New York Times*, 18 Apr 1986, p. C1.

85. Stephen Holden, *New York Times*, 2 May 1995, p. C18; *Chambers Scottish Biographical Dictionary*.

86. *New York Times*, 24 Oct 1989.

87. *Highlander*, May/Jun 1984, p. 2, quoting Lee Hamilton in the *Glasgow Evening Times*.

88. Frank, Gerald. *Judy Garland*, p. 5.

89. *New York Times*, 30 Mar 1980.

90. Peter B. Flint, *New York Times*, 25 Jan 1986, p. 11.

91. *Scottish Tradition*, p. 306.

92. Letter dated Jun 27, 1973, from Georgia Carmichael.

93. Letter dated Aug 29, 1983, from Leonora Gidlund, Georgia State University.

94. *Billboard*, 10 Jul 1976.

95. Coward, Noel. *Present Indicative*, p. 4.

96. Bernardo, p. 432.

97. Ibid., p. 434.

98. Undated letter from Galt McDermott.

99. *New York Times*, 19 Mar 1978; *New York Post*, 23 Sep 1977; *Chambers Scottish Biographical Dictionary*.

100. *New York Post*, 23 Sep 1977.

101. Robert Palmer, *New York Times*, 8 Dec 1982; Jon Pareles, *New York Times*, 11 Sep 1988, sec. 2, p. 1; Bromberg, Craig. *The Wicked Ways of Malcolm McLaren* (1989).

102. Michael Kimmelman, *New York Times*, 16 Sep 1988, p. C27.

103. *EB*, vol. 19, p. 94; Geddes.

104. *New York Times*, 22 May 1983, pp. 1, 36.

105. *New York Times*, 30 Apr 1994, p. 13; *New York Times*, 16 Jan 1990, p. D26.

106. Geddes.

107. Current Biography, 1947.

108. Letter dated Apr 7, 1983, from Mrs. David C. Garroway.

109. Personal meeting with Chet Huntley.

110. *Look*, Nov 17, 1970.

111. *Highlander*, May/Jun 1987, p. 75; *Chambers Scottish Biographical Dictionary*.

112. Institute of Family Research. *Roots of Johnny Carson*, Salt Lake City. Telephone interview with Institute of Family Research, Apr 11, 1982.

113. Telephone conversation with Mr. Leno's office, Mar 1989; *New York Times*, 29 Jun 1993, p. D23.

114. Letter dated Mar 12, 1986, from Albert E. Gunn, M.D.

115. *New York Times*, 19 Jun 1983; Letter received Nov 1972, from Fred Rogers.

116. Letter dated Oct 31, 1989, from Julia Child.

117. Undated letter received in Dec 1987, from Garrison Keillor.

118. *Scottish-American*, Sep/Oct 1990, p. 19.

119. *Scottish Tradition*, p. 306.

120. *Highlander*, Apr 1978, p. 4; Lincoln Kirstein, *New York Times*, 23 Nov 1986, p. H28.

121. *New York Times*, 5 Nov 1970.

122. Bernardo, p. 438.

123. *New York Times*, 5 Jan 1985, p. 14; Jack Anderson, *New York Times*, 31 Oct 1992, p. L11; letter dated Aug 12, 1985, from Sir Kenneth MacMillan.

124. Undated letter, 1982, from Allen Wallace of Martha Graham's office.

125. Anna Kisselgoff, *New York Times*, 8 Oct 1987, p. C31; Jennifer Dunning, *New York Times* 12 Jun 1990, p. C15.

126. Michael Billington, *New York Times*, 31 Aug 1986, p. H4.

127. *EB*, vol. 14, p. 531; Mackaye, Percy. *The Life of Steele Mackaye* (1927).

128. Jeremy Gerard, *New York Times*, 7 Dec 1986, p. H8.

129. Mervyn Rothstein, *New York Times*, 6 Mar 1990, p. C16; Undated letters received in 1973, from Walter Kerr and Douglas Watt; *Chambers Scottish Biographical Dictionary*.

130. *EB*, vol. 15, p. 661; Burton, p. 93; Rattray, p. 214.

131. *EB*, vol. 11, p. 1024; Gibb, *Scotland in Eclipse*, p. 17; MacFall, Haldane. *Ibsen* (1907), p. 34.

132. Pine, L. G. *The Story of Surnames* (1969), p. 109.

133. Coward, Noel. *Present Indicative* (1947), p. 4.

134. *New York Times*, 12 July 1989, p. 1; Olivier, Laurence. *Confessions of An Actor*, (1982).

135. Albin Krebs, *New York Times*, 21 Jan 1989, p. 34; Lillie, Beatrice. *Every Inch a Lady* (1972).

136. Interview with Jamie Ross.
137. *New York Times*, 7 May 1987, p. C23.
138. Mervyn Rothstein, *New York Times*, 15 Apr 1991, p. C14.
139. Current Biography, (1949); Harris, Martha. *Anjelica Huston*, 1989, p. 21.
140. Undated letter from Doug Henning.
141. *New York Times*, 26 Jun 1983; Nan Robertson, *New York Times*, 20 Mar 1987, p. B6; undated letter, 1983, from Bil Baird.
142. Alex Witchel, *New York Times*, 2 Feb 1994, p. C1; Letter dated May 26, 1994, from John Raitt.
143. Murray Schumach, *New York Times*, 16 Feb 1984, pp. 1, D26.
144. Thomas, Bob. *Walt Disney*, p. 22; *Guinness* (1987), p. 237.
145. *CES*, p. 650.
146. Bernardo, p. 449.
147. *New York Daily News*, 29 Aug 1987, p. 1.
148. Bernard Weinraub, *New York Times*, 22 Apr 1992, p. C15; telephone call April 15, 1994 to Mr. Cameron's secretary.
149. Macgregor, F., p. 282; Wills, E., p. 99.
150. *Scottish Tradition*, p. 306; John Curtin, *New York Times*, 30 Apr 1989, p. H17.
151. William Grimes, *New York Times*, 24 Dec 1993.
152. Aljean Harmetz, *New York Times*, 20 Mar 1989, p. C1; letter dated Oct 27, 1989, from C. R. Crichton.
153. Colman, Julia Benita. *Ronald Colman*, p. 1.
154. Eric Pace, *New York Times*, 30 Jul 1983, p. 6.
155. *New York Times*, 11 Jun 1971, p. 38.
156. *New York Times*, 21 Aug 1976.
157. Guinness, Alec. *Blessings in Disguise* (1986), pp. 220–24; Taylor, John Russell. *Alec Guinness* (1984), p. 11.
158. Wapshott, Nicholas. *Peter O'Toole* (1983), p. 19; *Who's Who in America*.
159. Interview with Mr. Connery's cousin, Jamie Ross; Passingham, Kenneth. *Sean Connery*, 1983, p. 13.
160. *New York Times*, 8 Jan 1990, p. D11.
161. Celebrity Register.
162. Geddes.

163. Letter dated July 1995, from James M. Grant.
164. Bernardo, p. 443.
165. Current Biography, 1947.
166. Goldstein, Norm. *John Wayne* (1979), p. 12.
167. *Eastern Airlines Review*, February 1984, p. 39.
168. LaGuardia, Robert. *Monty* (1977), p. 7.
169. Celebrity Register.
170. Granger, Stewart. *Sparks Fly Upward* (1981), p. 11; William Grimes, *New York Times*, 18 Aug 1993, p. D18.
171. Linet, Beverly. *Ladd* (1979), p. 44; Eells, George. *Robert Mitchum*, 1984, p. 11.
172. Letter dated Apr 22, 1985, from Mark Russell.
173. Bernardo, p. 104.
174. Letter dated Oct 23, 1972 from George C. Scott; *New York Times Magazine*, 23 Jan 1977, cover.
175. Speech by Cliff Robertson at the annual banquet of St. Andrew's Society of New York, Nov 18, 1988.
176. *New York Times*, 3 Jul 1978, p. 74.
177. *New York Times*, 4 Mar 1979.
178. *Phil Donahue Show*, NBC, Mar 18, 1983.
179. Gish, Lillian. *Lillian Gish* (1969), p. 2; Albin Krebs, *New York Times*, 1 Mar 1993, p. 1.
180. Peter B. Flint, *New York Times*, 22 Jan 1990, p. D11.
181. Parish, James Robert. *The Jeanette MacDonald Story* (1976), pp. 5–6.
182. Riese, Randall and Neal Hutchins. *Marilyn* (1987), pp. 175, 337, 347.
183. Russell, Jane. *An Autobiography* (1985), p. 21.
184. Flamini, Roland. *Ava* (1983), p. 25.
185. Letter dated May 13, 1988, from Roger Wall on stationery of Elizabeth Taylor.
186. *People*, 5 Oct 1981, p. 98.
187. Direct research.
188. Bernardo, p. 445.
189. Harris, Warren G. *Audrey Hepburn* (1994), pp. 12–13.
190. L. Bennetts, *New York Times*, 18 Mar 1987, p. C16.

Chapter 11: Sports, pp. 253–264

1. Berthoff, p. 8.
2. *Highlander*, May/Jun 1984, p. 26.
3. Macgregor, F., p. 314; *New York Times*, 17 Dec 1982.
4. *New York Times*, 15 Oct 1973.
5. *EB*, vol. 4, p. 716.
6. Macgregor, F., pp. 313–14.
7. *Guinness* (1987), p. 494.
8. Undated letter, 1983, from Johnny Rutherford.
9. *New York Times*, 16 May 1988, p. C4; Greg Logan, *Newsday* 31 May 1988, p. 98.
10. *New York Times*, 7 Nov 1973.
11. Direct from Bill Deane, senior research associate of the National Baseball Hall of Fame and Museum, Inc., at Cooperstown, New York, citing the 1989 study *Ethnic Origins of Hall of Fame Members*, compiled by Christy Zajack. Statistics here and below from *The Baseball Encyclopedia* (MacMillan, 1969 and 1988).
12. See appendix U.
13. Letter dated Feb 28, 1988, from Don Drysdale.
14. Letter from Jim "Catfish" Hunter, 1987.
15. Undated letter from Ralph Kiner, 1987.
16. See appendix U.
17. George Vecsey, *New York Times*, 5 Aug 1987, p. A24.
18. From Bill Carle, baseball and computer expert. Besides Thomson, those born in Scotland are David Abercrombie, George Chalmers, John Connor, Michael Hopkins, Malcolm MacArthur, Jim McCormick, Hugh Nicol, and Tom Waddell.
19. *EB*, vol. 15, p. 1154; *Highlander*, Jul/Aug 1983, p. 47.
20. Earl C. Douglas, *Scottish Genealogist* 15, no. 3 (1968), p. 70.
21. News report on ABC television, Jul 22, 1990.
22. *New York Times*, 23 Jul 1984, p. C5.
23. *EB*, vol. 4, p. 41; *CES*, p. 94.
24. Dempsey, Jack. *Jack Dempsey*, p. 2.; *New York Times*, 1 Jun 1983.
25. *New York Times*, 6 Nov 1978, p. 61.
26. Macgregor, F., pp. 316–17.
27. *WA*, p. 863.

28. Ibid.
29. Macgregor, F., p. 311.
30. *EB*, vol. 6, p. 908.
31. Hanley, p. 45.
32. *CES*, p. 447.
33. *Guinness* (1987), p. 616.
34. *EB*, vol. 9, p. 587A.
35. *CES*, p. 381.
36. Ibid., p. 382.
37. Gilmour, p. 63.
38. Geddes; Walker, p. 174; *CES*, p. 383.
39. *New York Times*, 10 Feb 1978.
40. Macgregor, F., p. 302.
41. *Scottish World* magazine, winter 1992, p. 11.
42. Telephone conversation with Sonny McEwen, barman at the Scottish-American Club, Kearney, New Jersey, Jan 19, 1988.
43. *CES*, p. 895.
44. *New York Times*, 11 May 1986, p. 10S; Sonny McEwen.
45. Letter dated Jul 20, 1984, from Otto Graham.
46. *New York Times*, 24 Sep 1989, p. 2 S.
47. Ray Corio, *New York Times*, 22 Jan 1990, p. C6.
48. *Golf Digest*, Feb 1982.
49. Warrack, Alexander. *Scots Dictionary* (1965), p. 222.
50. *Golf Digest*, Feb 1982.
51. Alistair Cooke, *New York Times Magazine*, 30 Sep 1973.
52. *Golf Digest*, Feb 1982.
53. Maclean, p. 189.
54. *Golf Digest*, Feb 1982.
55. *EB*, vol. 10, p. 551.
56. *Highlander*, Sep/Oct 1983, p. 42.
57. J. Thomson, *Highlander*, Jan/Feb 1982, p. 18; Donaldson, p. 127.
58. Letter dated Aug 18, 1982, from Tom Watson.
59. McCormick, Mark H. *Arnie* (1967), p. 29.
60. Undated letter from Peter Thomson.
61. Gordon S. White, Jr., *New York Times*, 11 Apr 1989, p. D31.
62. *New York Times*, 14 Aug 1995, p. C8.
63. Alex Yannis, *New York Times*, 17 Jun 1990, p. 4S.
64. *New York Times*, 20 Jul 1974.

65. *Scottish Tradition*, p. 246.

66. Census of Canada, Bulletin, 7.1–6, pp. 6–21.

67. *New York Times*, 25 Jun 1984, p. D13.

68. Telephone conversation with Bobby Orr, Pittsburgh, Dec 1972.

69. *New York Times*, 9 Nov 1978; Thomas Rodgers, *New York Times*, 5 Oct 1981, p. C2.

70. *Guinness* (1979), p. 600.

71. Dougald L. Maclean, Scottish Heritage, U.S.A. newsletter, Jun 1990, p. 2.

72. *EB*, vol. 11, p. 714.

73. *New York Times*, 21 Jul 1988, p. D22.

74. *New York Times*, 4 Mar 1987; *New York Daily News*, 3 Mar 1987; *New York Post*, 3 Mar 1987.

75. Bernardo, p. 273.

76. Ira Berkow, *New York Times*, 26 Aug 1993, p. B11.

77. *Guinness* (1979), p. 605.

78. Pearce, p. 170; *EB*, vol 4, p. 37.

79. Macgregor, F., p. 308.

80. *EB*, vol. 19, p. 666.

81. Macgregor, F., p. 311.

82. *EB*, vol 21, p. 57H.

83. *CES*, p. 829; *Chambers Scottish Biographical Dictionary.*

84. *EB*, vol. 21, p. 57K.

85. Ibid.

86. *WA*, p. 827; Gilmour, p. 63.

87. *Guinness* (1987), p. 630.

88. Macgregor, F., p. 317.

89. H. W. Wind, *The New Yorker*, 15 Feb 1988, pp. 75–76.

90. *Guinness* (1987), p. 637.

91. Bernardo, p. 15; *New York Times*, 16 Jan 1974; *New York Times*, 1 Jul 1982.

92. R. Smith, *Highlander*, May/Jun 1987, p. 52.

93. Macgregor, F., p. 306.

94. *New York Times*, 23 Jan 1984, p. C16.

95. Boston Athletic Association 100th anniversary commemorative program (1988), pp. 9, 13.

96. Barbara Basler, *New York Times*, 17 Feb 1992, p. C4.

97. *People*, 14 Nov 1994.

98. *CES*, p. 644.

99. *Highlander*, May/Jun 1989, pp. 66, 68.

100. Letter dated Sep 11, 1995, from Jane Smith, Mr. Coutt's aunt; Barbara Lloyd, *New York Times*, 28 Jun 1995, p. B15.

Appendix C: American Government Leaders of Scottish Ancestry, pp. 270–271

1. *EB*, vol. 18, p. 1192.

2. Susan Brownmiller, review of *Jeanette Rankin*, by Hannah Josephson, *New York Times Book Review*, 3 Nov 1974, p. 6.

3. Bernardo, p. 456.

4. *EB*, vol. 4, p. 629; *EB*, vol. 23, p. 358; Brown, p. 52.

5. J. Thomson, *Highlander*, Mar 1980, pp. 33–35.

6. Rowland Evans and Robert Novak in *New York* magazine, c. 1975.

7. Bernardo, p. 461.

8. *New York Times Book Review*, 14 Apr 1974; *New York Times*, 20 Jan 1980; *New York Times*, 21 Jul 1990, p. A7.

9. Jack Greenberg, review of *My Own Story*, by Rosa Parks with Jim Haskins, *New York Times Book Review*, 2 Feb 1992, p. 30.

10. *New York Times*, 6 Dec 1977.

11. McLellan. *D.A.*

12. R. W. Apple, Jr., *New York Times*, 5 Nov 1989, p. 34.

13. Evan Thomas, *New York Times*, 8 Nov 1992, p. 7.

Appendix D: The Presidents of the United States of America, pp. 272–273

1. U.S. Census, Supplementary Report, 1990 CP-S-1-2, p. III-4.

2. Montgomery, p. 3; McBride, George. *American Presidents of Ulster Descent* (1969).

3. Garrison, Webb. *The Lincoln No One Knows* (1993), pp. 9–10.

Appendix E: Scots in American Religion, pp. 274–275

1. Ford, pp. 401, 450.
2. Wertenbaker, p. 22.
3. Bernardo, p. 378.
4. Black, *Surnames*, p. 525; *Highlander*, Jul/Aug 1983, p. 47.
5. Hart, p. 22; *EB*, vol. 20, p. 120.
6. Hill, Donna. *Joseph Smith, the First Mormon* (1977), p. 25; Bernardo, p. 253.

7. *EB*, vol. 4, p. 714; J. Thomson, *Highlander*, Nov 1979, p. 30.
8. Bernardo, p. 255.
9. Silburger, Julius, Jr. *Mary Baker Eddy* (1980), p. 14.
10. Bernardo, p. 256; Peter Steinfels, *New York Times*, 3 Nov 1993, p. A14.

Appendix F: Scots in American Education, pp. 276–277

1. Lehman, pp. 111, 120; Klett, p. 42.
2. *EB*, vol. 14, p. 515; *New York Times* 18 Jun 1975; Lehmann, p. 109; George Roussos, *Scottish-American*, Nov/Dec 1990, p. 4.
3. Ford, p. 450.
4. Black, *Mark*, p. 30; Hook, p. 73; USIS, p. 8.
5. Black, *Mark*, p. 74.

6. Old Scotch Church, New York City, pamphlet.
7. Hanna, vol. 1, p. 135.
8. *The Autobiography of Dr. Thomas Hunter* (1931).
9. J. Buchanan, *Highlander*, May/Jun 1982, p. 41.

Appendix G: British Prime Ministers of Scottish Ancestry, pp. 278–279

1. Mayer, Allan J. *Margaret Thatcher* (1979), pp. 27–28.

Appendix I: A Miscellany of Scottish Invention, pp. 282–283

1. MacGregor, G., p. 231.
2. McCulloch, p. 178.
3. Bernardo, p. 387.
4. Letter dated Sep 12, 1990, from Louise C. Guthrie; *New York Times*, 27 Dec 1989, p. D18.
5. Wills, E., p. 74.
6. Geddes.
7. MacGregor, G., p. 232.
8. Ibid., p. 231.
9. *New York Times*, 23 Jan 1986.
10. James A. Troup, *Highlander*, Sep/Oct

1982, p. 36; MacGregor, G., p. 231.
11. Robertson, "Secular Changes."
12. *EB*, vol. 4, p. 945.
13. Files of Scottish Heritage, U.S.A.
14. Ross, p. 212; Casson, p. 609; Hewitson, p. 83.
15. *EB*, vol. 20, p. 447; Bernardo, p. 385.
16. Bernardo, p. 261.
17. MacKenzie, p. 107.
18. Irving, p. 28.
19. Robertson, "Secular Changes."

Appendix J: Scots in Steamship Companies, p. 284

1. *New York Evening Sun*, 17 Sep 1912.
2. MacKenzie, p. 70.
3. Ibid.
4. *EB*, vol. 4, p. 238; Gilmour, p. 15.

5. Gilmour, p. 15; J. Thomson, *Highlander*, Mar/Apr 1988, pp. 17–20.
6. Geddes.

Appendix K: Scottish Brand Names, pp. 285–286

1. Black, *Mark*, p. 103; *EB*, vol. 2, p. 431.
2. Walker, p. 143.
3. Bernardo, p. 419.
4. Wills, E., p. 71.
5. Bernardo, p. 297.
6. Geddes.
7. Bernardo, p. 417.
8. Letter dated Jun 2, 1982, from Herbert H. Dow.
9. McCulloch, p. 179.
10. Bernardo, p. 326.
11. Paula Dietz, *New York Times*, 10 Feb 1985, sec. 10, p. 55.
12. Powell, Horace B. *W. K. Kellogg* (1956), p. 4.
13. *New York Times*, 16 Apr 1985.
14. Lenox Archives, letter dated Feb 23 1989, from Ellen Paul Denker.

15. Bernardo, p. 318.
16. Letter dated Oct 17, 1973, from Richard J. McDonald.
17. See pp. 67, 177.
18. Black, *Mark*, p. 102.
19. *Highlander*, Jul/Aug 1985, p. 8.
20. Bernardo, p. 313.
21. Ibid., p. 314.
22. *CES*, p. 412.
23. Bernardo, p. 417.
24. Geddes.
25. Wills, E., p. 73.
26. American-Scottish Foundation, Inc.
27. Letter dated Jun 4, 1982, from Clive Sinclair; *New York Times*, 12 Apr 1981.
28. *New York Times*, 13 Jan 1972.
29. Scottish Heritage, U.S.A.
30. Bernardo, p. 372.

Appendix L: Business Miscellany, pp. 287–290

1. Sources throughout this appendix are not given if already included elsewhere.
2. *New York Times*, 4 May 1975.
3. Blackie won the Wallace Award from the American-Scottish Foundation, Inc.
4. Letter dated 1983, from H. B. Cunningham.
5. Letter dated Nov 1963, from J. I. Miller.
6. Crowther, Samuel. *John H. Patterson* (1923), p. 23.
7. Lewis, Alfred and Constance Woodworth. *Miss Elizabeth Arden* (1972), p. 28.
8. Bernadine Morris, *New York Times*, 18 Mar 1986, p. A24.
9. Glenn Collins, *New York Times*, 8 Nov 1994, p. B7.
10. Letter dated Feb 4, 1983, from John S. Herbert of Christie's.
11. Ross, p. 14.
12. Dewar's advertisement.
13. Jenkins, John Wilber. *James B. Duke, Master Builder* (1927), p. 12.
14. *American Heritage Dictionary*, 3rd ed. (1992), p. 1866.

15. *Travel and Leisure*, Apr/May 1973, p. 39.
16. *CES*, p. 614.
17. Gilmore, p. 37; *Guinness* (1979), p. 342.
18. *New York Times* 8 Feb 1983.
19. *New York Times*, 9 Jan 1972.
20. *New York Times*, 22 Jun 1983; direct research.
21. *New York Times*, 6 Nov 1988, p. F12.
22. *New York Times Magazine*, 27 Jan 1985, p. 43; Letter dated Aug 18, 1985, from Carole Finch, assistant to Jean Muir.
23. Randall Rothenberg, *New York Times*, 16 May 1989, p. D1.
24. Crowther, Samuel. *John H. Patterson* (1923), p. 23.
25. *National Geographic*, Jul 1984, p. 13.
26. *Forbes*, 1 Oct 1984.
27. *New York Times*, 20 Apr 1974.
28. Bell, Brian, ed., *Insight Guides—Scotland* (1990), p. 224.
29. American-Scottish Foundation, Inc.
30. B. Garamekian, *New York Times*, 21 Jul 1987, p. A16; Steve Lohr, *New York Times*, 1 Jan 1994, p. 1.

Appendix M: Scottish Organizations, pp. 291–292

1. Stevenson, David. *The Origins of Freemasonry*, p. 115.
2. Draffen, George. *Masons and Masonry*, pp. 124–27.
3. MacKenzie, p. 100.
4. *EB*, vol. 9, p. 842.
5. Britannia Lodge No. 1166, New York, notice of Oct 13, 1989, quoting Fred Pick and Norman Knight. *The Pocket Book of Freemasonry*.
6. *Scots Magazine*, vol. 25, no. 3; Harvey, William. *King and Craft* (1936).
7. *EB*, vol. 9, p. 842.
8. Moncreiffe, p. 21.

9. Stevenson, op. cit., p. 216.
10. Duncan A. Bruce, *Empire State Mason*, winter 1992, p. 4.
11. Stevenson, op. cit., p. 216.
12. Draffen, op. cit., p. 125.
13. *Scots Magazine*, op. cit., p. 200.
14. Moncreiffe, p. 78.
15. *Scots Magazine*, op. cit., p. 201.
16. *EB*, vol. 19, p. 195; MacKenzie, p. 102.
17. Saint Andrew's Society of New York, *Pibroch*, Oct 1982, p. 19; *EB*, vol. 4, pp. 47–48.
18. *Highlander*, Jan/Feb 1982, p. 42; *EB*, vol. 10, p. 434.

Appendix N: Science Miscellany, pp. 293–294

1. McCulloch, p. 47; *EB*, vol. 19, p. 674; *CES*, p. 707.
2. Mainly Robertson, "The Output of Scientists in Scotland."
3. Scottish Heritage, U.S.A. newsletter, Mar 1981.

Appendix O: The Nobel Prize, pp. 295–297

1. See appendix H.
2. USIS, p. 7; *EB*, vol. 19, p. 606.
3. World Almanac (1960), p. 162; USIS, p. 11; *EB*, vol. 23, p. 550.
4. Butler, Nicholas Murray. *Across the Busy Years* (1935), p. 22.

5. *EB*, vol. 11, p. 354.
6. *EB*, vol. 4, p. 46.
7. See p. 147.
8. Undated letter from Snow Simpson, assistant to Dr. Buchanan.

Appendix Q: The Scottish Achievement Demonstrated by Name-Frequency Technique, pp. 302–304

1. See Weyl, Nathaniel. *The Creative Elite in America* (1966).
2. In the instances of the names bearing the Gaelic patronymic prefix *Mac* and *Mc*, the latter being an abbreviation, they are considered to be equivalent. For example, MacKenzie and McKenzie are treated here as the same name and their instances in all calculations are totalled together. Where the *Mac* form does not appear in sufficient frequency for inclusion in the Social Security list, it is interpolated as being 25 percent of the total name as this is the approximate relationship of those *Mac* names which do occur in sufficient frequency.

3. Scottish Register list, 1936–40.
4. Dorward, David. *Scottish Surnames*, p. 64, from the Registrar General (1976).
5. In the 1976 Social Security list 885,369 people out of 239,927,977 bore the twelve selected surnames, including the *Mac* interpolations. Since the 1980 census shows that 5.3 percent of Americans had Scottish ancestry, about 12,716,182 on the 1976 Social Security list would have been Scottish (239,927,977 X .053). It could then be expected that 991,862 would bear the twelve surnames (12,716,182 X .078), and 991,862 is reasonably close to 885,369.

Appendix R: Scottish Versatility, pp. 305–307

1. Maclean and Dunett, p. 156.
2. See p. 213.
3. *New York Times*, 6 Dec 1977.
4. *National Geographic*, vol. 112, no. 4, p. 461.
5. *Scottish Tradition*, pp. 80, 172.
6. A. McKerracher, *Highlander*, May/Jun 1988, p. 42.
7. E. McDowell, *New York Times*, 27 May 1988, p. D19.
8. *EB*, vol. 11, p. 379.
9. *Old Manhattan News*, 6 Aug 1986, p. 8.
10. Wills, E., p. 44.
11. *EB*, vol. 14, p. 154.
12. *New York Times*, 28 Feb 1970.
13. Geddes, *EB*, vol. 14, pp. 494–96.
14. Earl C. Douglas, *Scottish Genealogist* 15, No. 3 p. 70.
15. *EB*, vol. 14, p. 540; *New York Times*, 21 Apr 1982; *New York Times Book Review*, 2 Jan 1983.
16. Mason.
17. *New York Times*, 30 Jul 1982; *EB*, vol. 21, p. 765.
18. *EB*, vol. 15, pp. 1174–75; Macgregor, F., pp. 139–40.
19. Janet Rowan Cramond, *Highlander*, Nov/Dec 1984, p. 58.
20. *Scottish World*, pp. 248–49.
21. *New York Times*, 21 Aug 1976.
22. Geddes; *New York Times Book Review*, 28 Dec 1986, p. 31.
23. John Le Carre, review of *The Secret War*, by William Stevenson, *New York Times Book Review*, 29 Feb 1976, p. 1; Albin Krebs, *New York Times*, 3 Feb 1989, p. D17.
24. *EB*, vol. 23, pp. 163–64.

Appendix S: The Scottish Passion for Education, pp. 308–310

1. Burton, p. 2.
2. Robertson, "Secular Changes".
3. *EB*, vol. 20, p. 30.
4. *EB*, vol. 7, pp. 765–66.
5. Donaldson, p. 25.
6. *EB*, vol. 22, pp. 746–49.
7. Prebble, p. 156.
8. *EB*, vol. 15, p. 96.
9. Gilmour, p. 48.
10. Prebble, p. 152.
11. Scott, p. 337.
12. Prebble, p. 156.
13. Ross, p. 282.
14. Robert McKinnon, *Scotland Today*, p. 16.
15. Alexander Gray, *Scottish Historical Review* 9, p. 114.
16. Donaldson, p. 20.
17. *Scottish Tradition*, p. 9.
18. Brown, *Scottish Historical Review* 10, p. 130.
19. Lehmann, pp. 22–23.
20. Esmond Wright, *Pennsylvania Gazette*, Feb/Mar 1990, p. 44.
21. *Scotia Newsletter*, Dec 1985, no. 2, p. 31; *Highlander*, Nov/Dec 1987, p. 37.
22. Lehmann, pp. 22–23.
23. R. K. Webb, *Scottish Historical Review* 33, p. 100.
24. Wills, E., p. 24.
25. MacGregor, G., pp. 64, 71.
26. Gilmour, p. 57.
27. Kellas, pp. 58–59.
28. Donaldson, p. 20.
29. Martha Voight, *Scottish Historical Review* 52, p. 145.
30. *CES*, p. 348.
31. Montague, p. 22.

Appendix T: The Scottish Nation, pp. 311–312

1. Maclean, p. 21.
2. Black, *Surnames*, p. xiv.
3. Moncrieffe, passim.
4. Black, *Surnames*, p. xvii.
5. Innes of Learney. *The Tartans of the Clans and Families of Scotland*, p. 6.
6. Moncreiffe, p. 31.

Appendix U: The Baseball Hall of Fame, pp. 312–313

1. The Scottish ancestry of thirty-three of the thirty-seven players has been supplied by Bill Deane, senior research associate of the National Baseball Hall of Fame and Museum at Cooperstown, New York, citing the 1989 study *Ethnic Origins of Hall of Fame Members*, compiled by Christy Zajack. Paul Waner was added to this group because his brother Lloyd is listed in the study as being partly Scottish. Wee Willie Keeler and Rube Waddell were added because the study was not able to find any ethnic origin for either of them, and by their names they appear to be most probably Scottish. Catfish Hunter was added to the list when he confirmed his Scottish ancestry directly.

2. The sources for this and the table following are cited above, along with *The Baseball Encyclopaedia* (MacMillan, 1969 and 1988).

Addendum, pp. 314–315

1. Thomas J. Stanley and William D. Danko. *The Millionaire Next Door* (1996), pp. 17–21.

2. Peter Passell, *New York Times*, 9 Oct 1996, p. D2.

3. Letter dated 30 Dec 1996, from Robert C. Richardson; Malcolm W. Browne, *New York Times*, 10 October 1996, p. D21.

4. Letter dated 3 Feb 1997, from Moira E. Watson; *Chambers Scottish Biographical Dictionary; Scotland on Sunday*, 26 Jan 1997; EB, vol. 2, p. 13.

5. Letters dated 12 Dec 1996 and 28 Jan 1997, from F. W. Henderson, M.D.; *JAMA*, 12 December 1996, p. 189.

6. Lewis J. Amster, *Hospital Practice*, 15 May 1987, p. 244.

7. T. A. Lee and S. P. Walker, *The CPA Journal*, Dec 1996, p. 46; *Encyclopedia of New York City*, p. 59.

8. Undated letter, 1997, from Don McLean; David Browne, *New York Times*, 9 Feb 1997, p. 40H.

9. Nicholas D. Kristof, *New York Times*, 16 Feb 1997, p. XX9.

10. Letter from Karin Henriksen, Scotland International, 1 Oct 1997; telephone interview with Derek Munn, Labour Party Scottish Headquarters, 13 Oct 1997.

11. Sylvia Nasar, *A Beautiful Mind* (1998), p. 26.

Bibliography

Arbroath Declaration of Scottish Independence. Transcript and translation from National Manuscripts of Scotland, Part 2, 1870.

Beaglehole, J. C. *Life of Captain James Cook.* Stanford, 1974

Beame, Abraham D. Speech given at Scotland House, New York, October 26, 1976.

Beckett, J. C. *The Making of Modern Ireland.* London, 1966.

Begley, Eve. *Of Scottish Ways.* Minneapolis, 1977.

Berg, Jonas. *Scots in Sweden.* Edinburgh: Royal Scottish Museum, 1962.

Bernardo, Stephanie. *The Ethnic Almanac.* New York, 1981.

Berthoff, Rowland. "Under the Kilt." *Journal of American Ethnic History* 1, no. 2 (spring 1982).

Black, George F. *Scotland's Mark on America,* Scottish Section of "America's Making." New York, 1921.

_____. *The Surnames of Scotland.* New York, 1946.

Bond, John. *They Were South Africans.* London, 1956.

Bowes, Robert M., miscellaneous pamphlets, various dates.

Brown, Francis James. *One America.* New York, 1952.

Bryce, George. *The Scotsman in Canada.* Vol. 2, *Western Canada.* Toronto, 1911.

Buckle, Henry Thomas. *On Scotland and the Scotch Intellect.* Chicago, 1970.

Burton, John Hill. *The Scot Abroad.* London, 1864.

Calder, Jenni. *The Enterprising Scot.* Edinburgh: Royal Museum of Scotland, 1986.

Caledonian Society of London, Chronicles of the. Vol. 3, London, 1930.

Campbell, Colin Turing. *British South Africa.* London, 1897.

Campbell, Wilfred. *The Scotsman in Canada.* Vol. 1, *Eastern Canada.* Toronto, 1911.

Casson, Herbert N. "The Sons of Old Scotland in America." *Munsey's.* Vol. 34, 1906.

Chalmers, George. *Caledonia.* Vol. 1. London, 1807.

Chambers Scottish Biographical Dictionary, Edinburgh, 1992. Edited by Rosemary Goring.

Chisholm, Alec H. *Scots Wha Hae.* Sydney, 1950.

Chitwood, O. P. *Richard Henry Lee.* Morgantown, W.V., 1967.

Churchill, Winston S. *The Birth of Britain.* New York, 1958.

Clark, Kenneth. *Civilisation.* New York, 1969.

Clement, A. G. and Robert H. S. Robertson. *Scotland's Scientific Heritage.* Edinburgh, 1961.

Collins Encyclopaedia of Scotland (cited as CES), John Keay and Julia Keay eds., London, 1994.

Commager, Henry Steele. In *Pittsburgh, the Story of an American City,* by Stefan Lorant. New York, 1964.

Cox, Marian B. *George Mason of Gunstan Hall.* Richmond, 1954.

Cunningham, J. *Some Account of the Scotch Brigade and Strictures on Military Discipline in Holland.* London, 1774.

de Comminges, Elie. *Charles VII et les Écossais,* Extrait des Cahiers d'Archéologie et d'Histoire du Berry, no. 43 (Decembre 1975).

Dickinson, W. Croft. *Scotland From the Earliest Times to 1603.* London, 1961.

Dickinson, W. Croft revised by Archibald A. M. Duncan. *Scotland From the Earliest Times to 1603.* Oxford, 1977.

Dictionary of National Biography (cited as *DNB*). Oxford, 1917-.

Dilworth, Mark. *The Scots in Franconia.* Edinburgh, 1974.

Dodds, James. *Scottish Settlers in the River Plate.* Buenos Aires, 1897.

Donaldson, Gordon. *The Scots Overseas.* London, 1966.

Donaldson, Gordon and Robert S. Morpeth. *Who's Who in Scottish History.* Oxford, 1973.

Donner, Otto. *Scottish Families in Finland.* Helsingfors, 1884.

Dow, J. B. A., *Ruthven's Army in Sweden and Estonia.* Kungl. Vitterhets, Historie Och Antkvitets Akademien, Historiskt Arkiv 13.

Drummond, Andrew. *The Kirk and the Continent.* Edinburgh, 1956.

Dunlop, Annie I. *Scots Abroad.* Historical Association of London leaflet no. 124, 1942.

Ellis, Havelock. *A Study of British Genius.* Boston, 1926.

Encyclopaedia Britannica. 14th ed. (cited as *EB*), 1969.

Fenwick, Hubert. *The Auld Alliance.* Roundwood Press, 1971.

Fischer, T. A. *The Scots in Eastern and Western Prussia.* Edinburgh, 1903.

––––––. *The Scots in Germany.* Edinburgh, 1902.

––––––. *The Scots in Sweden.* Edinburgh, 1907.

Fleming, John Arnold. *Fleming Influence in Britain.* Glasgow, 1930.

––––––. *Huguenot Influence in Scotland.* Glasgow, 1953.

––––––. *The Medieval Scots Scholar in France.* Glasgow, 1952.

Ford, Henry Jones. *The Scotch-Irish in America.* Hamden, Conn., 1966.

Fraser, Antonia. *King James.* New York, 1975.

Gayre of Gayre, R. *The Lost Clan, Sant' Andrea Degli Scozzesi of Gurro Novarra, Italy.* Edinburgh, 1974.

Geddes, John. *Great Scots.* Ilfracombe, Devon, 1974.

Geographical Journal, 43 (1914).

Gerson, Noel [Samuel Edwards]. *Rebel—A Biography of Thomas Paine.* New York, 1974.

Gibb, Andrew Dewar. *Scottish Empire.* London, 1937.

––––––. *Scotland in Eclipse.* London, 1930.

Gibbon, John Murray. *Scots in Canada.* Toronto, 1911.

Gilmour, Weir. *Famous Scots.* Glasgow, 1979.

Gordon, Marshall. *Presbyteries and Profit.* Oxford, 1980.

Graham, George W. *The Mecklenburg Declaration of Independence.* New York, 1905.

Graham, I. C. G. *Colonists From Scotland.* Ithaca, N.Y., 1956.

Graham, Tom M. *Biology.* New York, 1982.

Green, Samuel Swett. *The Scotch-Irish in America.* Worcester, Mass., 1895.

Grimble, Ian. *Scottish Clans and Tartans.* New York, 1973.

Guinness Book of World Records, New York, 1979.

Guinness Book of World Records, New York, 1987.

Hanley, Cliff. *A Skinfull of Scotch.* London, 1965.

Hanna, Charles A. *The Scotch-Irish*. 2 vols. New York, 1902.

Hart, Hector McBean, Address given December 21, 1954. Published in *Transactions of the Hawick Archeological Society*. Hawick, 1956.

Harvard Encyclopaedia of American Ethnic Groups. Cambridge, Mass., 1980.

Hattersley, Alan F. *The British Settlement of Natal*. Cambridge, England, 1950.

Haws, Charles H. *Scots in the Old Dominion*. Edinburgh, 1980.

Hewitson, Jim. *Tam Blake and Co*. Edinburgh, 1993.

Highlander, The. Barrington, Ill., 1963–.

Hill, Rev. George. *An Historical Account of the Plantation of Ulster*. Belfast, 1877.

Hockly, H. E. *The Story of British Settlers of 1820 in South Africa*. Cape Town, 1949.

Hook, Andrew. *Scotland and America*. Glasgow, 1975.

Hoyt, William Henry. *The Mecklenburg Declaration of Independence*. New York, 1907.

Innes of Learney, Sir Thomas. *Scots Heraldry*. Edinburgh, 1934.

––––––.*The Tartans of the Clans and Families of Scotland*. Edinburgh, 1938.

Insh, George P. *Scottish Colonial Schemes*. Glasgow, 1922.

Irving, Gordon. *Brush Up Your Scotland*. 1972.

Jackson, W. Turrentine. *The Enterprising Scot*. Edinburgh, 1968.

Johnson, James E. *The Scots and Scotch-Irish in America*. Minneapolis, 1966.

Kellas, James G. *Modern Scotland*. Winchester, Mass., 1980

Klett, G. S. *The Scotch-Irish in Pennsylvania*. Pennsylvania Historical Studies no. 3. Gettysburg, Pa., 1948.

Lehmann, William C. *Scottish and Scotch-Irish Contributions to Early American Life and Culture*. Port Washington, N.Y., 1978.

Lorant, Stefan. *The Glorious Burden*. New York, 1968.

McCosh, James. *The Scottish Philosophy*. New York, 1875.

McCulloch, John Herries. *The Scot in England*. London, 1935.

Macgregor, Forbes. *Famous Scots*. Edinburgh, 1984.

MacGregor, Geddes. *Scotland Forever Home*. New York, 1980.

Mackay, George. *A Scots Brigade Flag for Amsterdam*. Stirling, 1931.

MacKenzie, Rev. Canon. *Scotland's Share in Civilizing the World*. Chicago, 1899.

Mackie, J. D. *A History of Scotland*. New York, 1964.

McKinnon, Robert. *Scotland Today*. The Scottish Office, c. 1980.

Maclean, Alistair and Alastair M. Dunnett. *Alistair Maclean Introduces Scotland*. New York, 1972.

Maclean, Fitzroy. *A Concise History of Scotland*. New York, 1970.

MacMillan, David S. *Scotland and Australia 1788–1850*. Oxford, 1967.

Mason, Philip. *The Men Who Ruled India*. London, 1985.

Moncreiffe, Sir Iain and David Hicks. *The Highland Clans*. London, 1967.

Montague, Lt. Col. Herbert P. *The Scottish University Tradition*. Scottish Ball Program: New York, 1972.

Montgomery, Eric. *The Scotch-Irish in America's History*. The Ulster-Scot Historical Society: Belfast, 1965.

Morton, W. L. *Manitoba, a History*. Toronto, 1957.

Munro, R. W. *Clansmen and Kinsmen*. London and Edinburgh, 1971.

National Covenant, The. Glasgow, 1767.

National Geographic, Washington, D.C.

New York Times, 1851–.

Nolan, J. B. *Benjamin Franklin in Scotland*. Philadelphia, 1938.

Notestein, Wallace. *The Scot in History*. Westport, Conn., 1970.

Oxford Companion to American Literature. New York, 1965.

Parks, William. "Scottish Sentimentalist Ethics in Jefferson's American." Proceedings of the conference on Scottish studies no. 1, Charles H. Haws, ed., Norfolk, Va., 1973.

Pearce, G. L. *The Scots of New Zealand*. Auckland, 1976.

Pohl, Frederick J. *Prince Henry Sinclair, His Expedition to the New World in 1398*. New York, 1974.

Pratt, Tinsley. *Scots Soldiers Under French Kings*. London, 1916.

Prebble, John. *The Lion in the North*. New York, 1971.

Pryde, George S. *The Scottish Universities in Colonial America*. New Series 1. Glasgow University Publications: Glasgow, 1957.

Raimo, John W. *Biographical Dictionary of American Colonial and Revolutionary Governors*. Westport, Conn., 1980.

Rand McNally. *New Cosmopolitan World Atlas*. Chicago, 1968.

Rattray, William J. *The Scot in British North America*. Toronto, 1881.

Reid, Whitelaw. *The Scot in America and the Ulster Scot*. London, 1912.

Robertson, Robert H. S. "The Output of Scientists in Scotland, 1600–1950." *Eugenics Review* 52, no. 2 (1960).

———. "Secular Changes in Scottish Genius." *Mankind Quarterly* (1962).

Ross, Peter. *The Scot in America*. New York, 1896.

Rothney, G. O. *Newfoundland*. Historical booklet no. 10. Canadian Historical Association: Ottawa, 1959.

Roy, James A. *The Scot and Canada*. Toronto, 1947.

Royal Scottish Corporation pamphlet. London, 1796.

St. Andrew's Society. *200th Anniversary 1756–1956 of Saint Andrew's Society of the State of New York*. New York, 1956.

Scotia; American-Canadian Journal of Scottish Studies. Norfolk, Va., 1977–.

Scotia News. New York, 1964–.

Scots Magazine. Twentieth-century ed., 1924–.

Scott, Sir Walter. *History of Scotland*. Cambridge, 1830.

Scottish-American (succeeded by the *Scottish Banner*). 1982–1992.

Scottish Banner. Lewiston, N.Y., 1992–.

Scottish Genealogist. Edinburgh, 1954–.

Scottish Historical Review. Edinburgh, 1904–.

Scottish Studies. Edinburgh, 1957–.

Scottish Tradition in Canada, The. Toronto, 1976. Citations: pp. i–14: Reid, W. Stanford; pp. 15–26: Best, Henry B. M.; pp. 27–48: Mitchell, Elaine Allan; pp. 49–75: Duncan, K. J.; pp. 76–92: Turner, Alan R.; pp. 93–117: MacLean, R.; pp. 118–36: Reid, W. Stanford; pp. 137–60: Stanley, George F. G.; pp. 161–78: McIntyre, J. A.; pp. 179–202: MacMillan, David S.; pp. 203–31: Waterston, Elizabeth; pp. 232–47: Emmerson, George S.; pp. 248–72: Masters, D.C.; pp. 273–301: Evans, Margaret MacLaren; pp. 302–10: Reid, W. Stanford; pp. 311–21, Kirkconnell, Watson.

Scottish World magazine. Oban, Argyll, 1989–.

Scottish World, The. Joanne Greenspan, ed., New York 1981.

Seliga, Stanislaw, and Leon Koczy. *Scotland and Poland.* Edinburgh, 1969.

Shaw, James. *The Scotch-Irish in History.* New York 1899.

Shepperson, George. "The American Revolution and Scotland," *Scotia.* Norfolk, Va., 1977.

Sinclair, Andrew. *The Sword and the Grail.* New York, 1992.

Soltow, J. H. "Scottish Traders in Virginia." *Economic History Review,* ser. 2 (1959–1960).

Steuart, Archibald Francis. *Scottish Influences on Russian History.* Glasgow, 1913.

————. *Papers Relating to the Scots in Poland.* Edinburgh, 1915.

Taylor, James. *The Pictorial History of Scotland.* Vol. 1. London, 1859.

Taylor, William A., "Scottish Contributions to World Civilization." An address given to the St. Andrew's Society of Philadelphia, October 31, 1946.

Tomaszewski, Wiktor, ed. *The University of Edinburgh and Poland.* Stanislaw Seliga: *The Scots and Old Poland.* Leon Koczy: *Scottish-Polish Cultural Relations.* Edinburgh, 1968.

U.S. Bureau of Census. "Ancestry and Language in the United States." Current population reports, series P-23, no. 116. Washington, D.C., 1982.

United States Information Service (cited as *USIS*). *Scottish Contributions to the Making of America.* Edinburgh, 1950.

Villiers, Alan. *Captain James Cook.* New York, 1967.

Visher, Stephen Sargent. "Geography of American Notables." *Indiana University Studies,* 15, no. 79 (1918).

Wichita State University exhibit (cited as *WSU exhibit*). Collection of R. T. Aitchison, printed by McCormick and Armstrong, 1932. Wichita, Kansas, c. 1972.

Walker, Charles T., ed. *A Legacy of Scots.* Edinburgh, 1988.

Washington, George S. H. L. *The Earliest Washingtons and Their Anglo-Scottish Connections.* Cambridge, 1964.

Wertenbaker, T. J. *Scotch Contributions to the United States.* Glasgow, 1945.

Weyl, Nathaniel. *The Creative Elite in America.* Washington, 1966.

Weyl, Nathaniel, and Stefan T. Possony. *The Geography of Intellect.* Chicago, 1963.

Whyte, Donald. "Bibliography of Scots Abroad." *Scottish Genealogist* 21, 65–86. Edinburgh, 1974.

Will, William. "Scotland in London." *Buchan Field Club Transactions.* Vol. 14. Peterhead, 1930.

Wills, Elspeth. *Scottish Firsts.* Glasgow: Scottish Development Agency, 1985.

Wills, Garry. *Inventing America.* New York, 1978.

————. *Explaining America.* New York, 1981.

Windrow, Martin, and Francis K. Mason. *A Concise Dictionary of Military Biography.* Reading, England, 1975.

Woodburn, Rev. James Barkley. *The Ulster Scot.* London.

World Almanac and Book of Facts (cited as *WA*). New York, 1982.

Selected Index